The river is within us, the sea is all about us;
The sea is the land's edge also, the granite
Into which it reaches, the beaches where it tosses
Its hints of earlier and other creation.
The starfish, the horseshoe crab, the whale's backbone;
The pools where it offers to our curiosity
The more delicate algae and the sea anemone.
It tosses up our losses, the torn seine,
The shattered lobsterpot, the broken oar
And the gear of foreign dead men.
The sea has many voices,
Many gods and many voices.

From *The Dry Salvages*, in
T. S. ELIOT: *Four Quartets*
Faber and Faber, London, 1968

STUDIES IN ECOLOGY

GENERAL EDITORS

D. J. ANDERSON BSc, PhD
Department of Botany
University of New South Wales
Sydney

P. GREIG-SMITH MA, DSc
School of Plant Biology
University College of North Wales
Bangor

and

FRANK A. PITELKA PhD
Department of Zoology
University of California, Berkeley

STUDIES IN ECOLOGY · VOLUME 8

ECOLOGY OF COASTAL WATERS

A Systems Approach

by K. H. MANN

Marine Ecology Laboratory
Bedford Institute of Oceanography
Dartmouth, Canada

BLACKWELL SCIENTIFIC PUBLICATIONS

OXFORD LONDON EDINBURGH
BOSTON MELBOURNE

First published 1982

British Library Cataloguing in Publication Data

Mann, K.H.
    Ecology of coastal waters.—(Studies in
    ecology; v. 8)
    1. Coastal ecology
    I. Title   II. Series
    574.5′2636   QH541.5.C65

ISBN 0-632-00669-2
ISBN 0–632–00953–5 (PBK)

Distributed in the United States of America by
the University of California Press
Berkeley, California

Set by Santype International Ltd., Salisbury, Wiltshire.
Printed and bound in Great Britain
by Billing and Sons Limited and Kemp Hall Bindery,
Guildford, London, Oxford, Worcester.

FOR ISABEL

CONTENTS

PREFACE

The approach used in this book differs from that used in many others, in concentrating first and foremost on ecological processes rather than on organisms or populations. In fact, when experimenting with earlier versions, I wondered whether it would be possible to make a useful contribution without naming a plant or an animal. The thought stemmed not from the idea that organismal biology is in any way inferior to process-oriented ecology, but from the conviction that someone has to focus attention on large-scale ecological processes in coastal waters which have major effects on organisms and populations, sometimes with unfortunate economic consequences. Parts of the text do indeed have the names of plants and animals scattered through them, but they are incidental to the accounts of ecological processes such as primary production, grazing, predation, secondary production, detritus formation, decomposition, energy flow, nutrient cycling, and so on. I make no apology for the omission of large areas of the literature of classical organismal marine biology.

While I hope that the book will prove useful to advanced undergraduates, graduate students and professionals involved in research or in coastal zone management, I must explain that no attempt has been made to give an exhaustive coverage of the literature. Rather, I have tried to enunciate the principles involved and give a few key references to each. For full coverage of the literature the reader should consult the reference lists of the authors I have quoted, especially those that are review articles.

New contributions to the field are being made at a remarkable rate. Several new journals appeared while the book was being written. As a result, it has been necessary to concentrate almost all attention on recent work, leaving no room to develop the history of the ideas being discussed. I therefore apologize to those who contributed to that history and whose efforts are not acknowledged. It can be most annoying, as I know from personal experience, but in a work of this scope it is difficult enough to cover the present literature, without digging very far into the past.

The book was written in several places. It was begun while on leave at the University of East Anglia, Norwich, England; was continued for a year while Professor of Biology at Dalhousie University, Halifax, Canada;

advanced considerably while I was Scholar in Residence at the Duke University Marine Laboratory, Beaufort, North Carolina, and was completed at the Bedford Institute of Oceanography, Dartmouth, Nova Scotia. To all those whose kindness, hospitality, discussions, criticism and practical help made this book possible, my warmest thanks. I am particularly grateful for critical readings of parts of the book by the following colleagues in Canada: Drs Bob Conover, Lloyd Dickie, Barry Hargrave, Brenda Harrison, Paul Harrison, Steve Kerr, John Lauzier, Trevor Platt, Alistar Robertson and Bill Silvert; Drs J. Kitching and D. S. Ranwell at the University of East Anglia, and by Dr J. Ramus at the Duke University Marine Laboratory.

K. H. Mann
Dartmouth, Canada

CHAPTER 1
THE SUBJECT AND
THE APPROACH

1.1   COASTAL WATERS

As used in this book, the term coastal waters should be taken in its most straightforward sense of waters near the coastlines of land masses. Most of the systems under discussion lie shoreward of the 200 m depth contour which marks the edge of the continental shelf, but in places where the edge of the shelf is close to shore and major upwelling systems occur, these will not be excluded from consideration. Hence, we shall discuss estuaries of various kinds, continental shelf systems in convenient subdivisions, coral reefs, and upwelling areas.

The justification for selecting these systems for attention is that they are both very productive and very vulnerable. A large proportion of the world's population is concentrated along the coastline and along the banks of rivers which drain into coastal waters. Hence, the effects of pollution are most marked in nearshore waters. At the same time, man has come to rely heavily on coastal waters for food, and for recreation. The double impact of adding pollutants while harvesting plants and animals places a great strain on coastal aquatic ecosystems. Only by exploring and understanding their modes of operation shall we be able to preserve their value as a food source and their recreational potential.

I

1.2   THE HIGH PRODUCTIVITY OF
COASTAL WATERS

Coastal waters include some of the world's most productive plant systems. Westlake (1963) reviewed plant productivity on a global scale and showed that when agricultural systems were discounted tropical rain forests appeared to be the most productive of all (5–8 kg m^{-2} organic dry weight per annum), but salt marshes, reed swamps, and submerged macrophytes were the next most productive (in the range 2·9–7·5 kg m^{-2} yr^{-1}). Surveys of phytoplankton productivity in the sea have shown that whereas the greater part of the ocean fixes less than 50 g C m^{-2} yr^{-1} (<0·1 kg m^{-2} organic dry weight) coastal waters have productivities up to 5 times this level, and upwelling areas much higher still (Koblentz-Mishke *et al.* 1970; Ryther 1969). Hence, when planktonic and macrophyte systems are taken together, the coastal waters undoubtedly have much higher primary production than the open ocean. The production is not uniformly distributed, but is concentrated in two main areas: the upwelling areas and the narrow inshore strip where attached macrophytes flourish. Let us examine some of the factors which make this high productivity possible.

1.2.1   Factors enhancing phytoplankton productivity

There are several processes occurring at the interface of land and sea that tend to enhance phytoplankton productivity. The first is wind-induced mixing. Primary production is confined to the upper, euphotic layer of water but as the phytoplankton dies and decays, or is grazed and incorporated in zooplankton faecal pellets, it sinks inexorably towards the sea floor. Here, dead plant and animal material is processed through benthic food webs and minerals are released. There is now a spatial separation between nutrient-rich water at the bottom and the euphotic zone at the surface. Any process causing the upwelling of nutrient-rich water (Fig. 1.1) will enhance phyto-plankton production. In places where the wind induces an offshore current at the surface, it is inevitable that a compensatory upwelling of nutrient-rich deeper water will occur close to land. For example, Platt *et al.* (1972) showed that when a strong wind blows for several days parallel with the coast of Nova Scotia, the Coriolis effect causes a net movement of water away from the coast, and there is a replacement of surface water by deeper water in all the inlets along the coast more or less simultaneously. This type of phen-omenon ranges in scale from the purely local and irregular to highly predict-able seasonal upwellings, such as those occurring in the eastern boundary currents of the major oceans.

A second major stimulant to phytoplankton production is river runoff. Detailed discussion of the functioning of estuaries will be given in Chapter 8,

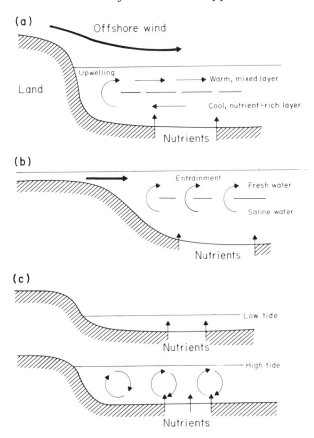

Fig. 1.1 Diagram illustrating three main mechanisms causing the upwelling of nutrient-rich water in the coastal zone. (a) Wind mixing; (b) river runoff; (c) tidal mixing.

but a common type of example is given in Fig. 1.1(b). Fresh water from the river flowing seaward at the surface gives rise to a stratified estuary. The shear forces at the junction of upper and lower layers give rise to turbulent mixing, so that salt water is progressively entrained in the freshwater outflow. The net result is that the volume leaving the estuary near the surface is much greater than the fresh water flow. For example, El Sabh (1974) calculated that the St. Lawrence River causes on average 25 times its own volume of water to move out of the estuary. All this outward movement at the surface must be compensated by an equivalent influx of nutrient-rich deep water, which rises to the surface in the estuary, and thus promotes primary production. The volume involved in the St. Lawrence system is 200 000–750 000 m^3 sec^{-1}, carrying 510–2040 tonnes of phosphate phosphorus per day.

The rise and fall of the tide in an estuary is a third major factor promoting vertical mixing of nutrient-rich water from the bottom. When the volume of tidal exchange is large compared with river input to an estuary, vertical salinity gradients may be broken down so that the estuary is of virtually the same salinity from top to bottom. The most noticeable salinity gradient is then the horizontal one, from the river mouth to the open sea. Under these conditions, nutrients regenerated at the sediment surface are carried rapidly to the water surface and used in primary production. A well documented example is Naragansett Bay, Rhode Island, USA (Kremer & Nixon 1978).

Finally, it can easily be shown that coastal waters, by virtue of their relative shallowness, are more readily mixed by the seasonal patterns of convective cooling that occur in temperate latitudes. After a period of thermal stratification, when there is a surface layer of warmer, lighter water and a lower layer of cool, nutrient-rich water, the onset of surface cooling in autumn leads to sinking of the cooler water and its replacement by deeper water. Eventually such mixing extends to the bottom. In shallow coastal waters this convective mixing is more effective in bringing up bottom waters than it is in deeper waters offshore.

1.2.2   The role of marine macrophytes

Marine macrophytes, whether flowering plants or algae, are normally attached to a solid object. This gives them an immediate advantage over planktonic forms. They are held in one place while water moves over them, driven by tides, waves or wind action. Any aquatic plant which photosynthesizes rapidly is liable to build up a gradient of carbon dioxide or nutrients in the boundary layer close to its surface. If the only method of obtaining carbon, nitrogen, etc., were by diffusion through these boundary layers, aquatic photosynthesis would be held to a very low level. Fortunately, in nature, all water is turbulent to some degree, and the turbulent diffusion supplements molecular diffusion. Attached macrophytic plants have a very great advantage over the phytoplankton in this respect. The turbulence created by tidal and wind-driven currents moving over them while they remain in one place creates an extremely effective mechanism for breaking down diffusion gradients. It is not surprising, therefore, that the productivity per unit area of large attached algae can be an order of magnitude greater than that of phytoplankton.

Macrophyte communities develop at the edge of the sea in all climatic zones and on most types of shore. On exposed, rocky shores there is no soil for rooted plants but algae have evolved the holdfast, with which they cling effectively to any solid surface. In sheltered, sedimented situations, rooted plant communities flourish. Those high in the intertidal zone are salt-marshes or mangrove swamps, while in the subtidal are found beds of seagrasses. The areas that are noticeably lacking in marine macrophytes are high energy sandy beaches and the adjacent sand flats. They appear to be too unstable for either macrophytic algae or flowering plants. Instead, they sometimes have a rich diatom flora living interstitially among the sand grains.

Salt-marshes are characteristic of temperate zones, while in the tropics and subtropics they are replaced by mangrove communities or mangals (Chapman 1975). The most common genera on salt-marshes are *Salicornia*, *Spartina*, *Arthrocnemum* and *Plantago*. In Mangals *Rhizophora*, *Avicennia*, *Acrostichum* and *Bruguiera* are all widespread. Productivity of these systems is seldom as high as in kelp beds, but has been shown to be in the range 300–2000 g C m^{-2} yr^{-1}, equivalent to dry matter production of over 4 kg m^{-2} yr^{-1} (see Chapter 2). Most of this plant material is not grazed directly, but enters detritus food webs either on the marsh itself or in nearby waters.

On rocky shores the intertidal is dominated by algal genera such as *Fucus* and *Ascophyllum* and by a great variety of small forms which provide an 'algal turf' for grazing invertebrates. In general, algal tissues are softer and less resistant to decay than those of flowering plants, so many are consumed directly by herbivores or assimilated very rapidly into detritus food webs. Subtidally, macro-algae dominate on hard surfaces, while seagrass communities are formed on soft substrates. Dense beds of algae or of seagrasses provide habitat as well as food for a rich assortment of invertebrates and their predators. As mentioned earlier, large algae have very high levels of productivity. Seagrasses, though productive, are less spectacular than the algae from this point of view. Common algal genera are *Macrocystis*, *Ecklonia*, and *Laminaria*, while *Zostera*, *Thalassia* and *Cymodocia* are among the more common seagrasses.

There are very few assessments of the relative magnitudes of production by macrophytes and by phytoplankton in particular sections of coastal waters. Mann (1972b) showed that in St. Margaret's Bay, Nova Scotia, which has an area of about 140 km^2, the macrophytic algae were contributing about 75% of the total primary production (see section 3.2.1). Peters and Schaaf (unpublished) made a much more extensive estimate. As part of a study of the food web supporting the fisheries of the eastern USA they estimated that about two-thirds of the total US commercial fish landings are taken within five miles of shore, and chose as their study area a five mile wide strip of coastal water extending from North Long Island, New York, to Southern Georgia. They concluded that macrophytes contributed 62% and the phytoplankton and benthic diatoms 38% of the total annual primary production. Details of this calculation are given in section 2.4.

1.3   SECONDARY PRODUCTION IN COASTAL WATERS

In a global view of marine productivity it is easy to disregard the contribution of waters close inshore, on the grounds that they occupy a very small area of the world's oceans. However, nearshore waters play a role out of all proportion to their global productivity. They are sheltered areas of high localized productivity, and as such they form ideal nursery areas for a wide variety of fish and shellfish including many species of commercial importance.

Korringa (1973) showed how the inlets and estuaries of the coast of Holland serve as nursery grounds for sole (*Solea*) and plaice (*Pleuronectes*). The young fish congregate there in densities up to 1 per m^2 and feed on the rich assortment of benthic organisms living in a mosaic of sediment types. McHugh (1976) recorded that of the 2925×10^6 kg per annum of fish landed in the USA, about 2025×10^6 kg were species dependent on estuaries as nursery areas. In Australia, where the life histories of many species of fish are poorly known, a recent study of ecological relationships in a seagrass bed showed that large numbers of the commercially important species *Sillaginodes punctatus* lived and grew there for the first three years of life (Robertson 1977).

The nursery function is important to crustaceans as well as fish. In Louisiana there is a shrimp fishery which in the 1960's landed over 14×10^6 kg per annum. The adults spawn at depths of 15–100 m, and the postlarvae migrate into the estuaries to feed and grow. Two species are involved, brown shrimps which migrate into the estuaries in spring, and white shrimps which do so in late summer. The brown shrimps forage among submerged macrophytes at about 1 m depth, while white shrimps concentrate in shallower water with large amounts of organic detritus (Day *et al.* 1973).

In addition to the role as a nursery for young fish and crustaceans, there is abundant evidence of highly productive populations resident in nearshore waters. Lobsters, crabs, oysters, scallops, clams and mussels are all taken close to shore, and are among the most highly priced seafoods. An example is the Canadian lobster catch which for the past half century has amounted to $13 \cdot 5$–$22 \cdot 5 \times 10^6$ kg a year, currently worth more than 100 million dollars. Almost all of it has been taken close to shore by small boat operators.

If we now shift our attention to the continental shelves, we find that the greater part of the world's marine fish catch, over 51×10^6 tonnes, is taken there. Some areas such as the North Sea and the north-east Pacific are both heavily exploited and intensively studied. Others have recently begun to be heavily fished but very little is known about them.

Finally, there are the major upwelling areas of the world such as those off

Peru, the western USA and West Africa, where the potential fish production is enormous and where intensive ecological studies have begun in the last decade. It will prove impossible in this book to give equal weight to all the major fishing grounds of the world, but every effort will be made to explore the ecological processes which they have in common.

1.4 THE SYSTEMS APPROACH

Ecology has two aspects, like the two sides of a coin. One side is labelled *organism* while the other is marked *ecological process*. They are not mutually exclusive, but complementary, yet many people tend to concentrate on one side only, paying scant attention to the other.

Historically, ecology grew out of organismal biology and for a long time an accepted definition of the subject was 'the relationships between organisms and their environments'. Fields of specialization included autecology, physiological ecology, population ecology, etc., and summaries could be found in such texts as Daubenmire's (1947) *Plants and Environment*, or Andrewartha and Birch's (1954) *The Distribution and Abundance of Animals*. As ecology advanced, sophisticated techniques were borrowed from mathematics and the physical sciences to permit the development of a high level of understanding in such areas as environmental tolerance, population regulation, or community structure. The concepts of variation, selection, and competition were integrated with population biology to give rewarding insights into the processes of evolution. In all this, the basic unit of observation was the individual organism.

More recently, attention has been directed towards the *interactions between organisms*, rather than the organisms themselves. Lindeman (1942) emphasized the flow of energy and matter through food webs as a result of feeding (or trophic) interactions. Others have emphasized the cycling of elements in natural communities beginning with uptake by plants, and proceeding by way of trophic transfers, excretion and decomposition, to the physical transports needed to bring those elements back to the site of primary production. Gradually, the idea emerged that such fluxes were occurring in recognizable patterns which could be associated with systems of interacting components, or ecosystems. It was seen that in the hierarchy of organisation that begins with molecules, and proceeds by way of cells, tissues, organs, organisms, populations and communities, there is one higher level of organization, the ecosystem. It is well recognized that at each level in a hierarchy there are emergent properties that cannot be completely explained in terms of lower levels (Fiebleman 1954). Cells have self-regulatory properties that are not the properties of their constituent molecules, and organisms have behavioural characteristics that are not to be observed in individual tissues or organs. Similarly, ecosystems have properties that can not be adequately studied at the level of organisms or populations. Many of these properties are associated with the flux of energy and materials through the system, and may be termed ecological processes.

In discussion of levels of biological organization, Odum (1971) said:

> In the long run, no one level is any more or less important or any more or less deserving of scientific study than any other level ... the findings at any one level aid in the study at another level, but never completely explain the phenomenon occurring at that level. This is an important point because persons sometimes contend that it is useless to try to work on complex populations and communities when the smaller units are not yet fully understood.

Applying these remarks to ecosystem ecology, we see that the study of organisms and populations aids the study of processes in ecosystems, but never completely explains them. Moreover, we do not need to wait for a full understanding of the organisms and populations involved before embarking on studies at the ecosystem level. In coastal marine ecology we have much more information about organisms and populations than we have about ecosystem processes. The aim of this book is to emphasise the processes, in the hope of stimulating others to help redress the balance.

1.5   WHY WORK AT THE ECOSYSTEM   LEVEL?

Studies of whole ecosystems are often difficult and expensive, so that the reasons for undertaking them must be made as explicit as possible. The question of difficulty is sometimes more apparent than real. Observing a whole ecosystem often means working on a large scale, which is logistically difficult, and measuring rates of processes, rather than numbers and biomasses, which may be technically more difficult. At the same time, shifting from the small to the large unit may mean simplication. It is easier to measure the carbon fixation of all phytoplankton in a sample than to record the changes in population density of each constituent species, and there is less variability in the total annual primary production than in the productivity of the constituent species. Similarly, it is easier to measure the energy flow through a total benthic community than to study the energetics of all constituent species. Questions of difficulty notwithstanding, the scientific reasons for working at the ecosystem level are compelling. Once we can see that ecosystem processes are occurring, and are influencing events at the level of organisms and populations, it becomes essential to our understanding of events at any of these levels to know about the system processes.

The economic question is also very real. If persons in an organization are charged with the responsibility of managing an economically important stock, such as a fish or shellfish population, it is natural for them to put most

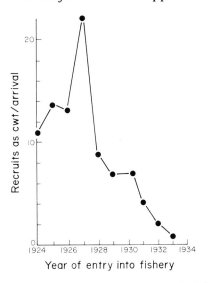

Fig. 1.2 Recruitment to the herring fishery off Plymouth, England, in the years 1924–33. Data are in relative units, cwt (1 cwt ≈ 51 kg) of fish per arrival of a vessel in port. (From Cushing 1961.)

or all of their effort into attempting to understand the dynamics of that population. Nevertheless, the history of such efforts indicates that studies at the ecosystem level would often have been more useful. Cushing (1961) re-analysed the failure of the herring fishery at Plymouth, England, in the 1930's. Catches of over 450 000 kg in 1925–26 dropped to less than one quarter that figure six years later (Fig. 1.2) and never recovered. Cushing showed that there were two competing food chains, operating at different times of year. Success of a food chain leading to young pilchards led to phosphorus in the water column being locked up in the bodies of the pilchards, and thus not available to the phytoplankton in the food chain leading to herrings. Hence, failure of the herring fishery was associated with a pattern of interactions involving young pelagic fish, zooplankton, phytoplankton, nutrients, and by implication the water movements responsible for transporting the nutrients. The underlying cause of the success of the pilchard food chain has not been made clear, but it is obvious that it would have to be couched in terms of the whole ecosystem.

A parallel example is the decline and collapse of the fishery for the Pacific sardine (*Sardinops caerulea*) off California. The catch in 1944–45 was 550 000 tonnes, but it declined over 20 years to a catch of a few hundred tonnes and since then fishing for sardine has been completely prohibited. The immediate cause of decline was a reduction in recruitment, and it was shown that heavy fishing had reduced the number of spawning adults (Murphy

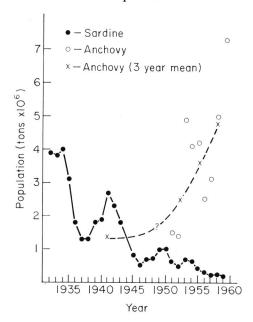

Fig. 1.3   Estimates of the population sizes of sardines and anchovy in the California fishery in the years 1932–59. (From Murphy 1966.)

1966). The situation was further complicated by changes in water temperature (Marr 1960) and by the greatly increased abundance of anchovy (*Engraulis mordax*) which, at least in the larval stage, compete with sardines for food. In a re-working of the data, Gulland (1974) showed that the survival of young sardines was proportional to the total biomass of sardines plus anchovies (Fig. 1.3), suggesting that competition with anchovies was an important factor. Once again, the underlying cause of the change is unclear, and lies in the broader aspects of the total ecosystem. In making recommendations for further work, Gulland (1974) suggested studies on factors determining the survival and growth of young fish and studies on the population dynamics of the food organisms. This would be a beginning, but a really thorough study would reveal that there were still other factors influencing the population dynamics of the food organisms so that an understanding of the whole ecosystem is required.

   One more example of an anchovy fishery serves to illustrate the need for an understanding of the total system, and the inadequacy of present knowledge. The Peruvian anchoveta fishery is found where there is an intense upwelling of nutrient-rich deep water during the winter. In this area there is intense phytoplankton production which forms the food of dense zooplankton stocks. The anchoveta feed on both zooplankton and phytoplankton, and occur in enormous numbers. Paulik (1971) reviewed the estimates of potential fish production in the upwelling area by three different scientists. The first, extrapolating from catch statistics and assuming that about half the production is taken by fishing, estimated total production at 20 million tonnes. The second obtained the same estimate by assuming a primary production of 235·7 tonnes of carbon per km^2 over an area of 479 000 km^2, and a two-link food chain with an efficiency of 10% at each step, or 1% overall. The third arrived at the same estimate as the other two but assumed an area of only 60 000 km^2 and a 1·5 step food chain with an overall efficiency of 12%. As Paulik (1971) says, such gross discrepancies are shocking and serve to remind us of the inadequacy of our knowledge of marine production processes. At the time of writing, the Peruvian anchoveta fishery is in a state of decline. A good understanding of the total ecosystem of which it is a part is badly needed.

1.6 SOME TECHNIQUES OF ECOSYSTEM RESEARCH

1.6.1 Compartmental flow diagrams

The first step in developing concepts about an ecosystem is to decide on the common units in which biomasses and fluxes are to be expressed. Early workers (e.g. Lindeman 1942; Teal 1957; Slobodkin 1959) emphasized energy flow, and tended to express everything in calories. In practice, energy of photosynthesis and respiration is usually estimated from flux of oxygen or carbon, and calorific values of biomass are often approximated by carbon content, so carbon is a good unit for expressing ecosystem properties, and can be directly compared with energy units. The major alternative unit is nitrogen. Carbon fixation and nitrogen uptake in plants are often out of phase, and conversely there is often a difference in the patterns of carbon respiration and nitrogen excretion in animals. In many cases, as will be shown later, the flux of carbon and energy through an ecosystem are limited by the availability of nitrogen. Hence, for full understanding we need to know fluxes of both carbon/energy and nitrogen. In practice, it is usual to begin with one or the other.

A technique, borrowed from systems science, which is useful for making a preliminary analysis of an ecosystem is the compartmental diagram. All the entities in the system are represented as compartments, and the fluxes between them are represented as arrows. Fig. 1.4 shows such a diagram for a salt marsh system in Louisiana. This diagram in some respects resembles a traditional food web, except that the entities in the compartments are not single species, but groups of species having the same functional relationship to the system. The diagram summarizes what is known

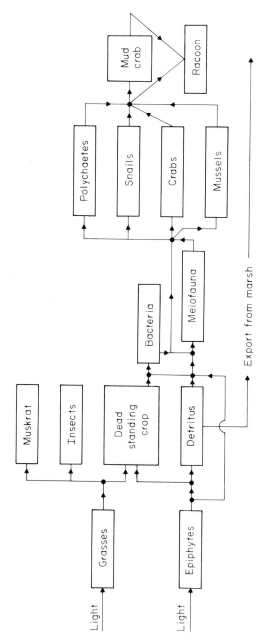

Fig. 1.4 Compartmental flow diagram of a salt marsh in Louisiana. (From data in Day *et al.* 1973.)

about trophic interactions in the system, and serves to illustrate the point that if we wish to understand the functioning of the system we must have data on both the biomasses in the compartments and the fluxes between them.

1.6.2 Estimating mean flows

As a framework for discussing fluxes of energy or carbon, it is useful to refer to the symbols proposed by Odum (1971) (Fig. 1.5). Fundamental to the flux of energy and materials in trophic transfers are the concepts of net production i.e. the amount of new biomass synthesized per unit time, and the removal of that biomass by consumers. Methods of measuring production were developed during the International Biological Programme and the techniques needed for coastal aquatic ecosystems can be found in Vollenweider (1969) (primary production), Holme and McIntyre (1971) (benthos), Edmondson and Winberg (1971) (zooplankton) and Ricker (1971) (fish). Using these techniques it is possible to estimate mean biomass values for the compartments and mean values for the fluxes, over some convenient period, such as one year. Fig. 1.6 shows the mean annual fluxes in the water column adjacent to the Louisiana marsh illustrated in Fig. 1.4. From it can be read the productivity of the commercially important species, such as oysters, shrimp, and the blue crab, and it can be seen that the fluxes through those compartments are small compared with those through the zooplankton. However, it appears that less than 10% of the zooplankton production is consumed adjacent to the marsh, the remainder is exported to coastal waters. As a description of a system for management purposes, this type of flow diagram is vastly superior to a simple set of biomass data.

In theory, it should be possible to produce an analogous model of the flux of nitrogen in an ecosystem. In practice, it proves to be much more difficult. The main features of an energy/carbon budget can be determined from measurements of ^{14}C uptake by plants, plus respiration and growth measurements on the consumers. As we have seen, nitrogen and carbon fluxes are only loosely coupled and are often out of phase, so nitrogen uptake, accumulation and loss must be measured separately. The techniques

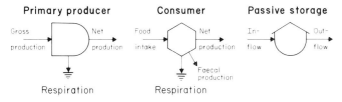

Fig. 1.5 Symbols from the energy circuit language of Odum (1971).

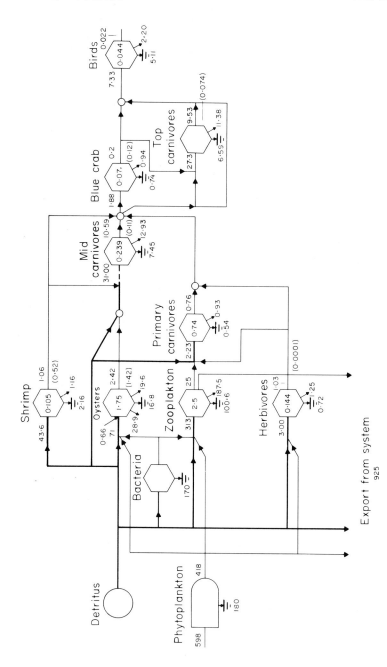

Fig. 1.6 Mean annual fluxes (in g organic matter m⁻²yr⁻¹) in the water adjacent to the Louisiana marsh referred to in Fig. 1.4. (From Day *et al.* 1973.)

are made much more difficult by the lack of radioactive isotope of nitrogen, and by the fact that the laws governing rates of nitrogen loss in excretion appear to be much more complex than the laws governing rates of carbon loss in respiration. These topics are discussed in relation to fish in Gerking (1978).

1.6.3 Process models

Compartmental flow diagrams lack any indication of the mechanism underlying the transfers between the compartments. Without them there is no way of predicting how the system will behave under perturbation. Hence, we are led to investigate the relationships between the fluxes and the variables which influence them. Such work is not, of course, unique to ecosystem studies, and many useful process models can be culled from the physiological literature. Nevertheless, a laboratory investigation designed to clarify a physiological mechanism will not necessarily yield data that can be extrapolated to field conditions. For example, there is an abundant literature on photosynthesis in named species of algae, but the most useful models for use in marine ecosystems are those developed with natural, multi-species assemblages of phytoplankton (e.g. Platt & Jassby 1976). Similarly, rates of carbon or energy flux (respiration) have been measured countless times under differing conditions of temperature, activity and feeding rate. In practice, however, feeding rate is influenced by food availability and also by the activity of the animal in seeking food. Hence, there is complex interaction of factors which tends to maximize food obtained for energy expended. Resolution of the problem of predicting what this rate will be for fish in nature is discussed in Mann (1978).

Many of the models widely used in population dynamics can be regarded as process models. These include the logistic model of population growth (Verhulst 1838) and the Lotka–Volterra equations for population growth in two competing species (Lotka 1925; Volterra 1926). These are, of course, resolvable into several interacting processes such as natality and mortality. In fact, there is a whole spectrum of process models from the simplest of single process models through to complex representations of many processes interacting. The latter form the subject of the next section.

1.6.4 Coupled process models: dynamic simulations

The results of studying process models are commonly represented as regression equations and graphically by lines or curves. When we come to study numerous processes interacting, these techniques are not adequate. A compartmental diagram such as that shown in Fig. 1.4 may serve to summarize the processes that have to be considered, and ecology has borrowed from

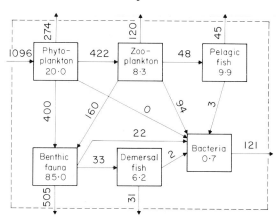

Fig. 1.7   Block diagram of energy flow for the English Channel. Standing crops are in kcal m⁻² and energy flows in kcal m⁻²yr⁻¹. (From Brylinsky 1972.)

systems science well-established techniques for simulating the time course of interactions between all the processes. Suitable initial values are assigned to the state variables (usually biomasses) in the compartments, and equations are written to represent all the transfers between compartments. The whole constitutes a computer model which can be used to calculate the effect of transfers in and out of the compartments as time progresses. Fig. 1.7 and Table 1.1 (from Brylinsky 1972) show how some quite old numerical data from the English Channel were transformed into a compartmental diagram by the addition of some literature values on calorific values and metabolic rates. Then, transfer coefficients were listed for feeding, respiration and mortality in each compartment, and the assumption was made that transfer of energy from a donor to a receiving compartment was proportional to the amount of energy contained in the donor compartment. It was then possible

Table 1.1   Summary of Harvey's data from the English Channel. (From Brylinsky 1972.)

Organism group	Standing crop (dry organic matter) (g m⁻²)	Daily production (dry organic matter) (g m⁻²)	Daily respiration (% standing crop)
Phytoplankton	4	0·4–0·5	—
Zooplankton	1·5	0·15	4
Pelagic fish	1·8	0·0016	1·25
Demersal fish	1·00–1·25	0·001	1·25
Benthic fauna	17	0·03	1·25–2·00
Bacteria	0·14	—	30

to obtain a time series for each state variable and explore the way in which the dynamics of each part of the system responded to small changes in the other parts. The assumptions used in the model were great simplifications of reality, but at least it was possible to explore the effect of numerous processes interacting. In Chapter 10 we shall discuss the contribution of simulation models to our understanding of ecosystem function.

1.6.5 The possibilities for holistic approaches

At the beginning of this chapter, attention was drawn to the need to work at various levels in ecology, including the ecosystem level. Without observations at the level above those of the organism and the population, we shall never fully understand the behaviour of ecosystems. Up to the present, dynamic simulation models have been as it were at the leading edge of ecosystems as such. Work of this kind is very much in its infancy. Productivity of a trophic level can be used as an ecosystem property, and species or populations. There is still a great lack of observations on the properties of ecosystems as such. Work of this kind is very much in its infancy. Productivity of a trophic level can be used as an ecosystem property, and species diversity of a community, if applied to a broad enough taxonomic grouping, is an ecosystem property. Questions of persistence and stability usually refer to ecosystems, although they have yet to be framed in terms of rigorously testable hypotheses. Theoretical ecologists have begun to address themselves to thermodynamic and cybernetic aspects of ecosystems (e.g. Ulanowicz 1972; Mulholland & Sims 1976) and the new ways of analysing food web structure (e.g. Sheldon *et al.* 1973; Kerr 1974; Platt & Denman 1977; Lange & Hurley 1975). All of these are attempts to develop ideas at the highest level of the ecological hierarchy. We shall never make good predictions about ecosystems unless we learn to observe ecosystems, and make testable hypotheses about them.

CHAPTER 2
SEAGRASS, MARSH GRASS AND MANGROVE SYSTEMS

2.1 SALT-MARSHES

Salt-marsh communities develop intertidally in sheltered places where silt and mud can accumulate. Two of the most common sites for salt-marshes are in estuaries where river silt is deposited, and on the sheltered sides of sand or shingle spits where longshore currents deposit coarser material on beaches but carry finer material in suspension until it reaches the quieter water behind the barrier. Colonization of relatively sheltered sites by a few plants leads to a further slowing of tidal currents and accelerating deposition of silt. Growth of plants is often able to keep pace with rising sediment levels, so that over a long period considerable accumulation of sediment and plant remains takes place. In places where the sea level is rising relative to the land, accumulations of sediment several metres deep may occur (Redfield 1972). One of the characteristics of a fully developed salt-marsh is the presence of creeks and drainage channels. These form a network over the marsh and are routes by which the tidal waters enter and leave the marsh. Since tidal height varies on a lunar cycle, there are some tides which flood the whole marsh and others which do not rise beyond the banks of the creeks. A good general account of salt-marsh formation is to be found in Chapman (1964).

The species of plants which colonize such an area vary from place to place around the world. On the Atlantic coast of North America, which has over 600 000 ha of salt-marshes, *Spartina alterniflora* dominates the area between mean sea level and mean high water. Just above this zone are found one or more species of *Juncus*, together with *Distichlis spicata*, *Spartina patens* and various species of *Salicornia*. On the European side of the North Atlantic the flora is much more diverse and heterogeneous; for example, in Britain, there are marked differences between marshes bordering the North Sea, the English Channel and the Atlantic. The North Sea marshes frequently have as co-dominants the sea pink (*Armeria*), sea lavender (*Limonium*), sea plantain (*Plantago maritima*) and species of *Spergularia* and *Triglochin*. The Atlantic marshes tend to be used for cattle and sheep grazing and are dominated by the grasses *Puccinella* and *Festuca*. On the south coast of England, *Spartina townsendii* and *S. anglica* have been spreading and replacing the more diverse flora which occurred there in times past. Teal and Kanwisher (1966) showed that *Spartina* is adapted to growing in anaerobic mud by having air spaces that are continuous from the leaves to the tips of the roots. A very full account of the vegetation of salt-marshes the world over is given in Chapman (1977).

2.1.1 Primary production

At least 90% of the work on system processes in salt-marshes has been done in North America, so it is inevitable that this section will report mainly on marshes dominated by *Spartina alterniflora*, with *S. patens* and *Distichlis spicata* on the landward side. Since these marshes extend from about the Gulf of St. Lawrence (latitude 46°) to Texas (latitude 27°) it is possible to see that average net primary production above ground varies from over 1000 g dry weight m^{-2} yr^{-1} (about 500 g C m^{-2} yr^{-1}) in the south to little more than half that figure in the north (Fig. 2.1). Ranwell (1961) reported a net productivity of 960 g dry weight m^{-2} yr^{-1} by *Spartina* in south-western England, and Jefferies (1972) gave figures of 867–1050 g dry weight m^{-2} yr^{-1} for *Spartina*, *Limonium* and *Salicornia* in eastern England. Hence, most figures for salt-marsh net productivity appear to lie in the range of 0·5–1 kg dry matter or 200–400 g C m^{-2} yr^{-1}.

There is a great deal of variation about the mean. On every marsh there is a tendency for *Spartina* to be taller and more productive along the edges of the creeks, and shorter and less productive as distance from the creek increases. Odum and Fanning (1973) documented this difference on sites subject to daily tidal irrigation (Table 2.1). These data are remarkable for the high levels of productivity recorded, as well as for the difference between sites. Most marshes also show higher productivity on the 'low marsh' (subject to daily inundation) than on the 'high marsh' (subject to infrequent inundation). Two main hypotheses have been put forward to account for

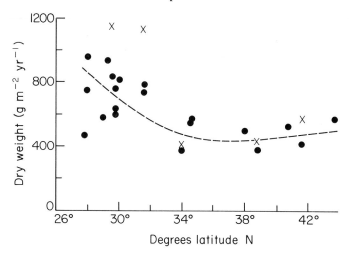

Fig. 2.1 Some plots of primary production in salt-marshes plotted against latitude. Solid circles plot the end of season biomass; crosses are plots calculated by Smalley method. (From data in Turner 1976.)

patterns of variation in productivity. Valiela and Teal (1974) reported that salt-marsh vegetation showed increasing growth in response to nitrogen fertilization but not to phosphorus addition (Fig. 2.2). *Spartina alterniflora* showed the major growth response in low marsh, while on the high marsh *Spartina patens* responded in early summer, followed by *Distichlis spicata* in late summer. These results led them to suggest that 'the great variations in height, colour and standing crop seen in marshes are related to nitrogen supplies'.

Table 2.1 Annual net productivity of *Spartina alterniflora* in optimum habitat (daily tidal irrigation) on Sapelo Island, Georgia. (From Odum & Fanning 1973.)

Marsh type	Standing crop, end of season		Export from living stems (g m^{-2})	Estimated net production	
	Living (g m^{-2})	Dead increment (g m^{-2})		(g m^{-2})	(Kcal m^{-2})
Tall *Spartina*, streamside and creek head marsh	3018	297	675	3990	16359
medium *Spartina*, low and levee marsh	2018	164	180	2362	9684
Mean, prorated by area				2883	11820

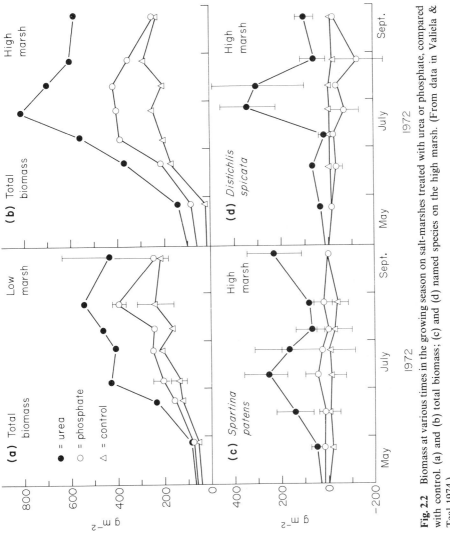

Fig. 2.2 Biomass at various times in the growing season on salt-marshes treated with urea or phosphate, compared with control. (a) and (b) total biomass; (c) and (d) named species on the high marsh. (From data in Valiela & Teal 1974.)

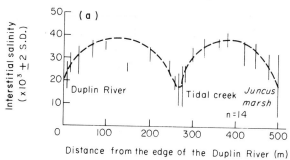

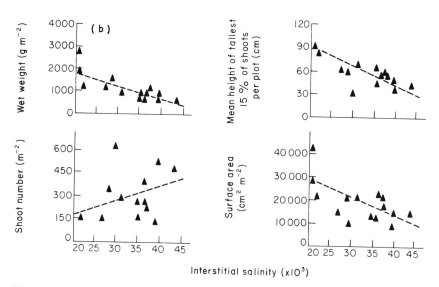

Fig. 2.3 (a) Distribution of salinity on a Georgian salt-marsh; (b) correlation between salinity and *Spartina* production. (From Nestler 1977.)

The second hypothesis put forward to account for variation in growth according to distance from creek bank emphasizes the salinity of the interstitial water. Nestler (1977) found that the interstitial water in the sediments formed salinity clines across the marsh, with lowest average values in the creek beds and increasing values with increasing distance away from them (Fig. 2.3(a)). Biomass, height and leaf area of plants were all negatively correlated with interstitial salinity (Fig. 2.3(b)). There is no doubt that high salinity is a physiological stress on the plants. Mooring *et al.* (1971) showed that seedlings grown to 100–150 cm tall under controlled salinity conditions exhibited optimum growth at 5–10×10^{-3}, and that there was no significant difference according to whether the seeds came from short, medium or tall plants. Phleger (1971) showed that *Spartina foliosa* in California, grown in nutrient solutions, made the best growth at zero salinity. On the other hand, Longstreth and Strain (1977) found that plants growing in high salinity and high illumination were able to maintain a rate of photosynthesis not very much lower than that found in plants grown at low salinity stress, by developing thick leaves and a more efficient photosynthetic mechanism. The authors doubted that salinity normally limits photosynthesis in *Spartina alterniflora*. When Nestler (1977) tried to confirm the results of his correlational analysis by irrigating high-salinity sites with either estuarine or deionized water, he could not detect a change in plant height, weight or leaf surface area. He did detect an increase in number of shoots per unit area. He conceded that variation in growth form could not be accounted for solely on the basis of interstitial salinity.

An observation which may throw light on the rival claims of nitrogen and salinity as determinants of *Spartina* productivity is that made by Steever *et al.* (1976). Working in Long Island Sound, where the tidal range changes from 0·7 m near the mouth to 2·26 m near the head of the inlet, they found that marsh productivity was correlated with tidal range, the correlation coefficient being better than 0·96. They compared two sites in the same general area, one of which had the tidal range reduced by a gate, and found that there was a 26% reduction in productivity on the gated marsh. Finally, they showed that a variety of data from Atlantic coastal marshes fitted the same trend (Fig. 2.4).

Obviously, increasing production with increasing tidal range cannot go on indefinitely. For example, the Bay of Fundy has a tidal range of up to 16 m, but the salt-marsh production is probably at the lower end of the range reported by Steever *et al.* (1976). Odum (1974) refers to tidal inundation as an energy subsidy, performing the work of mineral cycling, food transport, waste removal, and so on. He claims that 'it is clear that the energy subsidy provided by tidal flow more than compensates for the energy drain of osmoregulation required by the high salinity environment'. He also suggests that a range of about 2–2·5 m is optimum, and greater ranges incur a stress. The energy subsidy theory is an attractive one, of wide applicability in coastal ecosystems, but the evidence is mainly correlational. If the main mechanism controlling variation in *Spartina* production is interstitial salinity, the correlation with the tidal amplitude can only be explained if the rise and fall of the tide always serves to moderate salinity stress. It requires that the water flowing in and out of the creeks be of markedly less than full salinity. This may well be true in an estuarine situation, but is unlikely to be true of marshes behind barrier beaches in non-estuarine embayments. It seems worthwhile at this point to return to the question of nitrogen relations.

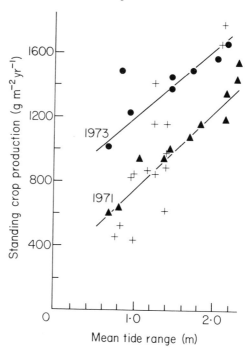

Fig. 2.4 Production of *Spartina* in relation to tidal range. Circles and triangles are authors' own data in different years, with regression lines fitted by eye. Crosses are data from the literature. (From Steeves *et al.* 1976.)

2.1.2   Nitrogen relations of salt-marshes

In the summer of 1971 Sutcliffe (reported in Mann 1975) found that there was a large export of dissolved nitrogen from an estuary containing considerable areas of *Spartina* marsh. Heinle and Flemer (1976) found net export of nitrogen with the evidence (Valiela & Teal 1974; Broome *et al.* cent to the Patuxent estuary. It is difficult to reconcile the idea of a net export of nitrogen with the evidence (Valiela and Teal 1974; Broome *et al.* 1975) that *Spartina* production is nitrogen limited, and the discrepancy leads one to examine salt-marshes for sites of N_2 fixation. On a *Puccinellia* and *Festuca* salt-marsh in north-west England, Jones (1974) showed nitrogen fixation by blue-green algae of the order of 20 g m^{-2} yr^{-1} on the mud surface, and more than twice that level in pools. Whitney *et al.* (1975) calculated the average value of nitrogen fixation, mainly by blue-green algae, over an entire marsh in Long Island. The rate was 4·6 mg N m^{-2} day^{-1}, which might tentatively be extrapolated to 0·5–1·0 g N m^{-2} yr^{-1}.

   A different, and apparently more important route of nitrogen fixation was demonstrated by Patriquin (1978) and Patriquin and McLung (1978).

Table 2.2 Acetylene reduction assays *in situ* on a salt-marsh. (From Patriquin 1978.)

Marsh type	Nitrogenase activity (μ moles C_2H_2 m^{-2} h^{-1})	
	mud surface	total under cylinders
Tall *Spartina*, creek bank	$6\cdot8 \pm 3\cdot6$	$46\cdot5 \pm 5\cdot1$
Short *Spartina*, away from creek	$27\cdot6 \pm 16\cdot5$	$95\cdot0 \pm 24\cdot8$

Incubation of whole plants on the marsh surface in cylinders with acetylene showed that there was nitrogenase activity far beyond that attributable to algae on the mud surface (Table 2.2). When plants were brought into the laboratory, rates of acetylene reduction up to 257 μ moles m^{-2} h^{-1} were observed. The greater part occurred in the subsurface vegetation, and was mostly in underground stems and their attached roots. Patriquin identified a number of types of nitrogen-fixing bacteria distributed over the surfaces of stems and roots, but also within cells of the cortical layer. Some types had a requirement for low oxygen concentrations (i.e. were microaerophilic), and were therefore ideally adapted to life at the periphery of a *Spartina* root. Oxygen reaches the root by diffusion through air spaces in the middle cortical region (Teal & Kanwisher 1966), but the root is embedded in anaerobic sediment. Hence, the gradient of oxygen is from the air spaces to the periphery of the root. It seems that the microaerophils were particularly abundant within the root tissues, while anaerobes were more abundant in the soil, close to the root surface.

In a detailed study of a Nova Scotia marsh, Patriquin (1978) showed that the total annual nitrogen accretion in the tissues of *Spartina* was 7·8 g m^{-2} above ground and 7·7 g m^{-2} below ground. His estimates of N_2 fixation were 2·2 g m^{-2} yr^{-1} on the mud surface and 9·3 g m^{-2} yr^{-1} in the rhizosphere of the plant. Hence, N_2 fixation is of almost sufficient magnitude to provide for the nitrogen requirements of the plants. Transfer of the nitrogen fixed to the growing plants has not yet been demonstrated, but there is strong presumption that it occurs.

Nitrogen fixation is known to be inhibited by the presence of other forms of combined nitrogen. For example, in the plots that Valiela and Teal (1974) fertilized with urea or sewage sludge, there was a marked reduction in nitrogen fixation in the heavily treated sites. This shows up as an inverse relationship between nitrogen fixation and concentration of ammonia nitrogen in the pore water (Fig. 2.5) (Van Raalte *et al.* 1974). One may speculate that the explanation of lower rates of nitrogen fixation among the tall *Spartina* (Table 2.2) is that there are higher concentrations of ammonia in the sediments along the creek banks, compared with the interior, or on the

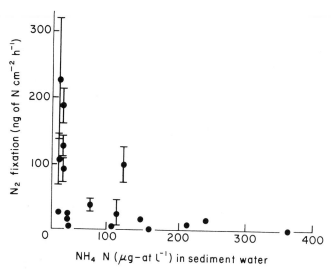

Fig. 2.5 The relationship between nitrogen fixation and ammonium content of soil water. (From Van Raalte *et al.* 1974.)

marsh at low elevation compared with the high marsh. There is some support for this idea in the data presented by Haines *et al.* (1976) from a Georgia salt-marsh. Measurements were made in each of the six months from February to July, and in four of these the values for exchangeable ammonium in the soil were higher in the low marsh than in the high marsh. The peak value in the low marsh was about 450 mg of ammonia nitrogen per m^2, compared with 300 mg m^{-2} in the high marsh. The difference might conceivably be related to the more frequent inundation of the low marsh, and could be a reflection of either the presence of dissolved nitrogen in the tidal water, or of the sedimentation and subsequent mineralization of organic matter carried in the creek water.

If we accept that nitrogen is limiting to salt-marsh productivity, we can see that nitrogen fixation by algae on the mud surface and in the rhizosphere of *Spartina* represent mechanisms by which the limiting factor can be alleviated. However, it has been estimated (Postgate 1971) that nitrogen fixing organisms require about 1 g of carbohydrate in order to fix 1 mg of N$_2$. This is a considerable drain on the photosynthetic capacity of the community, and it looks very much as if the plants subject to more frequent inundation are able to produce more biomass because they can satisfy their nitrogen needs while supporting less nitrogen fixation. In that sense, inundation by the tides can be seen as an energy subsidy because it saves the plants draining energy away in support of nitrogen fixation. In situations such as that reported by Nestler (1977) where tidal inundation also serves to alleviate salinity stress, this too can be seen as an energy subsidy to plants that otherwise have to divert energy to combatting the stress. Ubben and Hanson (1980) attempted to reconcile the influences of salinity and of nitrogen metabolism by looking for a change in amounts of nitrogen fixation with changing salinities in a Georgia salt-marsh. They found no correlation, but reported a trend towards higher levels of nitrogen fixation in areas inundated more frequently. The authors also reviewed other attempts to find a pattern of microbial activity that could be related to salinity or to frequency of inundation. In no case was a clear interpretation obtained.

Great Sippewissett Marsh, near Woods Hole, Massachusetts, has been the subject of detailed study by John Teal, Ivan Valiela and various collaborators (Valiela *et al.* 1978; Teal *et al.* 1979). They measured input of nutrients by means of groundwater, rain and tidal flooding, and the fluxes of both inorganic nutrients and organic matter in the creek which connects the marsh with the coastal waters. There was a substantial influx of nitrate and organic nitrogen to the marsh in groundwater; it was 20 times greater than the amount brought in by rain, and more than enough to provide for plant production on the marsh. Nitrogen fixation was measured in cores of sediment. It was found to be higher in vegetated than in non-vegetated areas, and highest near the surface of the sediments in the warm parts of the year. Teal *et al.* (1979) concluded that the total fixed was less than one third of that required by the vegetation. However, the work of Patriquin quoted earlier suggests that they would have obtained higher estimates if they had concentrated attention on the rhizomes and roots of the *Spartina*. In general, their work confirms the importance of nitrogen fixation, but draws attention to the possibility of massive influxes of nitrogen in ground water. Such fluxes will depend a great deal on local topography and land use patterns.

2.1.3 Ecological fate of salt-marsh production

Studies of estuaries in Georgia about 20 years ago (Teal 1962) showed that only a small proportion of the net production of *Spartina* is grazed while it is alive. More than nine-tenths die and become colonized by microorganisms to form plant detritus. Various species of invertebrates function as 'shredders' (Welsh 1975) thereby reducing particle size and increasing the surface-to-volume ratio. Odum and de la Cruz (1967) collected detritus particles in suspension from a tidal creek and sorted them into a range of size classes. They showed that with decreasing particle size there was an increasing nitrogen content, which they attributed to an increasing proportion of microbial biomass. This result has been amply confirmed (Fenchel 1971; Gessner *et al.* 1972) and it is apparent that *Spartina* tissue is relatively indigestible to invertebrates but that it is colonized and attacked by bacteria and fungi. These microorganisms are able to render the *Spartina* tissues soluble, then take up a good proportion of the dissolved organic matter and incorporate it into their own tissues. They are therefore functioning as an essential step in the process of transfer of *Spartina* production to inverte-brate and vertebrate consumers.

Gosselink and Kirby (1974) studied the efficiency with which *Spartina* tissue was converted to microbial biomass, by solving the simultaneous equations:

$$C_d = C_s + C_m$$
$$N_d \times C_d = (N_m \times C_m) + (N_s \times C_s)$$

(2.1)

where C_d, C_s and C_m are the ash-free dry weights per unit volume of total particulate detritus, *Spartina* component, and microbial components respec-tively, and N_d and N_s are the nitrogen fractions of those three sets of dry weights.

The assumption was made that the proportion of nitrogen in the *Spar-tina* component remained unchanged during incubation. One representative

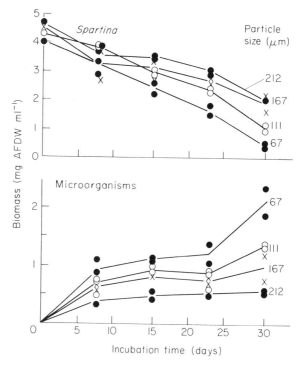

Fig. 2.6 Changes in *Spartina* biomass and microbial biomass during decomposition. (From Gosselink & Kirby 1974.)

value (13%) was used throughout for the proportion of nitrogen in the microbial component. Although these assumptions are only approximately true, it was possible to plot changes in *Spartina* and microbial biomass with time (Fig. 2.6) and to conclude that conversion efficiency ranged from 24% (212 μm fraction) to 66% (67 μm fraction). It has been shown that calculations such as these overestimate microbial biomass, because much of the increase in N on detritus is not due to living microbes but to the remains and excreta of past generations of microbes (Hobbie & Lee 1980). Robinson (1980) showed that much of the N in old detritus is resistant to bacterial attack, so that C : N ratios are poor descriptors of the nutritive value of detritus. More work is needed to obtain good data with fewer assumptions, but the Gosselink and Kirby result is an important indication that conversion of dead macrophyte tissue to microbial biomass, ready for assimilation by detritivores, can take place without the 80–90% loss which we associate with trophic transfers between higher organisms.

There is also evidence for a significant production of dissolved organic matter from living *Spartina*. Gallagher *et al.* (1976) showed that when clean *Spartina* leaves were incubated in sterile bags on the marsh, dissolved organic carbon (DOC) was released at a rate which, when integrated for the marsh, averaged 6.1 g C m^{-2} yr^{-1}. The material released appeared to be readily utilizable by microbes. A subsequent study of production of DOC from standing dead plants indicated that a further 10.2 g C m^{-2} yr^{-1} was being contributed from this source. Hence, we have abundant evidence that *Spartina* biomass is being efficiently converted to microbial biomass. It seems (Gessner *et al.* 1972; Meyers 1974) that fungi are particularly important in the early stages of decomposition, but that bacterial growths develop later, even on the fungal biomass.

The next question to arise is: How effectively is the microbial biomass incorporated into the macroscopic food chains? A question which appears to be very different, yet has a practical bearing on the solution to the first problem is: Where does consumption by detritivores take place? Is it on the marsh, in the creeks, or is there a major export of microbial biomass to adjacent waters?

One of the first suggestions on this point came from Odum and de la Cruz (1967). They measured the amounts of detritus in suspension at the mouth of a salt-marsh creek and showed that the concentrations were about twice as high on falling tides as on rising tides. Microscopic examination suggested that over 90% of the detritus originated from *Spartina* plant biomass. Hence, they concluded that there was a massive export of suspended organic detritus from Georgia salt-marshes, and thus originated the idea of an 'outwelling' (Odum 1971) of nutritive material from the marshes to the coastal waters. For almost a decade the strongest argument brought forward for the preservation of salt-marshes was that they were responsible for the production and export of large amounts of highly nutritive particulate organic matter, without which the food chains of commercial importance in adjacent coastal waters would be impoverished.

In recent years it has become clear that not all marshes export their organic production as detritus. Petpeswick Inlet, in Nova Scotia, has large areas of salt-marsh with a productivity estimated at 710 g dry weight m^{-2} yr^{-1} (Hatcher & Mann 1975), but when particulate organic carbon in suspension was measured throughout a tidal cycle on five separate occasions in the summer of 1971, there was very little export, and on some occasions there was a net import (Mann 1975). In 1973–74 Woodwell *et al.* (1977) monitored exchange at the mouth of a tidal marsh on Long Island, New York, and found that it was a net importer of particulate organic carbon throughout the year, receiving on average 61·3 g C m^{-2} yr^{-1} in particulate form, but exporting 8·4 g C m^{-2} yr^{-1} in the dissolved form. Nixon and Oviatt (1973) made an intensive study of a salt-marsh and its adjacent embayment in Rhode Island, USA, and found that virtually all the production of the emergent *Spartina* was consumed within the confines of the marsh-embayment system.

On the other hand, the study of Day *et al.* (1973) for Bartaria Bay, Louisiana, shows that an estimated 30% of the net production in the whole estuary was exported to the Gulf of Mexico. At the other end of the climatic range in a study of a *Spartina* marsh bordering the Bay of Fundy, Nova Scotia, Morantz (1976) found that almost all of the year's aboveground production was exported to coastal waters as a result of being frozen in to the undersides of ice floes. These formed over the surface of the marsh during the winter but were carried away when the ice broke up in the spring. In Massachusetts, Valiela *et al.* (1978) estimated that 40% of the net annual production of Great Sippiwissett Marsh was exported as particulate matter to coastal waters.

Haines (1979) reviewed the role of the Georgia salt-marshes as components of coastal ecosystems, and concluded that the old generalizations about 'outwelling' were no longer tenable. She, and colleagues at the Sapelo Island laboratory, arrived at this conclusion primarily as a result of studies of the stable carbon isotope ratio in various organisms. Different groups of plants have different photosynthetic pathways (C_3, C_4, etc.), and it has been found that they also have differing ratios of the stable isotopes ^{13}C and ^{12}C. The conventional way of representing this ratio is by the quantity $\delta^{13}C$, defined as

$$\delta^{13}C = \left(\frac{^{13}C/^{12}C \text{ sample}}{^{13}C/^{12}C \text{ standard}} - 1 \right) \times 1000 \qquad (2.2)$$

C_3 vascular plants have low $\delta^{13}C$ values around -24 to -34 per thousand while C_4 plants have higher values, of -6 to -19×10^{-3}. Algae tend to have intermediate values, -12 to -23×10^{-3}. On the Georgia salt-marsh it was found that the $\delta^{13}C$ value for *Spartina* was about -13×10^{-3}, for benthic diatoms it was about -17×10^{-3} and for offshore algae it was about -21×10^{-3}.

The seston in Georgia estuaries had a $\delta^{13}C$ which implied that it was part of a food chain based on algae, rather than on *Spartina* detritus. Oysters and menhaden had a carbon isotope composition similar to phytoplankton, while mullet, killifish, shrimp, and blue crabs had a ratio indicating a mixed diet of *Spartina*, benthic algae and phytoplankton. These results led to a renewed appreciation of the importance of algal production in the Georgia marshes, and the conclusion that perhaps the most important role of *Spartina* is the physical one of providing shelter and a trap for nutrient-rich sediment, both of which are components of the nursery environment for coastal organisms.

Further evidence of the importance of algae in a salt-marsh was provided by Ribelin and Collier (1979), who studied a *Juncus* marsh on the Gulf coast of Florida. They found that the vascular plant tissue was decomposed beneath a layer of benthic algae, and was not exported from the marsh. Instead, the mat of benthic algae generated a film of organic matter which floated off on each tide and broke up to form amorphous aggregates in which diatoms were entangled. These aggregates made up more than 98% of the detrital material exported from the marsh.

There will be a detailed discussion of detritus food webs in Chapter 5. For the present we may summarize by saying that salt-marshes have a net productivity of at least 200–400 g C m^{-2} yr^{-1}, often more, but that very little of that production is consumed while the plants are living. Instead, they die and are colonized by fungi and bacteria, and are converted first to soluble organic matter, then to microbial biomass with a relatively high efficiency. The subsequent fate of the mixture of plant tissue and microbes seems to vary from place to place, according to the physical structure of the area and the climate. In some cases it seems likely that the nutrients taken up by *Spartina* are recycled within the marsh and used by algae, which then are exported. In other cases, export of *Spartina* detritus undoubtedly occurs.

2.2   SEAGRASS ECOSYSTEMS

Some clarification of terminology may be needed here. Chapman (1964), referring specifically to British vegetation, stated under the heading 'Salt-Marshes' that the lowest phanerogram community is that of eel-grasses, *Zostera marina* and *Z. nana*, which occur on mud-flats that are exposed at low tide. Similarly, Beeftink (1977) included a *Zostera* community in his review of the coastal salt-marshes of western and northern Europe. What then, is the justification for treating seagrass ecosystems as distinct from salt-marshes? Basically, it is that on a world-wide scale seagrass beds frequently occur quite independently of the intertidal salt-marsh communities discussed earlier, and while they may reach into the lower intertidal zone, they normally exhibit maximum biomass under conditions of complete submergence.

According to den Hartog (1970) there are 12 genera of aquatic angiosperms which have the ability to function normally and complete the generative cycle when fully submerged in a saline medium. In temperate climates, *Zostera*, or eelgrass, is the most common genus, while in tropical climates the genus most intensively studied is *Thalassia*, or turtle-grass. This is often accompanied by *Syringodium* or *Halodule*. In the Mediterranean area *Posidonia* and *Cymodocia* are important genera. In Australia *Amphibolis* is widespread, but *Posidonia australis* is probably the most productive.

Since they are rooted plants, they need a soft bottom to begin the colonization process. Once established, they collect sediment by slowing down water movement within the beds. A characteristic of seagrasses, which marks them off from both marsh grasses and algae, is that they support large numbers of epiphytic organisms, the biomass of which may be almost as great as that of the seagrass itself. As noted earlier, they may extend into the intertidal zone. The extent to which they are able to do this depends on the climate of the area, for extremes of either heat or cold are likely to kill plants exposed to the air for any considerable time. From the edge of the water, seagrasses extend outwards and downwards for as far as conditions of substrate and penetration of light permit. Some genera are tolerant of estuarine conditions and flourish in salinities as low as 10%. They also flourish in situations in which the water temperature in winter is only a little above 0°C, but for flowering they require temperatures in the 10–20°C range. Zieman (1970) showed that for the subtropical species *Thalassia testudinum* (turtle grass) there is an interaction between salinity stress and temperature stress: the plants can withstand low salinities at low temperatures, but a combination of high temperatures and low salinities is lethal.

2.2.1   Seagrass productivity

Seagrasses, even more than salt-marsh plants, benefit from being anchored in one place while tidal currents and wave action bring nutrients and create turbulent diffusion patterns. Reviews of levels of productivity are found in Phillips (1974) and in McRoy and Helfferich (1977). Many have recorded production in the range 300–800 g organic dry matter m^{-2} yr^{-1}, which is equivalent to 120–320 g C m^{-2} yr^{-1}. Seagrass beds are often characterized by the presence of highly productive associated species, growing epiphytically and otherwise. For example, Thayer et al. (1975) showed that a *Zostera marina* bed in North Carolina produced on average 350 g C m^{-2} yr^{-1}, but that associated plants (*Holodule* and *Ectocarpus*) together contributed a further 300 g C m^{-2} yr^{-1}. Jones (1968) estimated that *Thalassia testudinum* in dense stands in Florida was producing 900 g C m^{-2} yr^{-1} while its epiphytes were contributing a further 200 g C m^{-2} yr^{-1}. However, these were rather rough estimates obtained using oxygen exchange techniques, and it is not clear that interference by respiration of consumers in the epiphytic community was eliminated. Penhale (1977) measured ^{14}C uptake by *Zostera* and epiphytes separately, and estimated that the macrophytes averaged 0·9 g C m^{-2} yr^{-1} while the epiphytes averaged 0·2 g C m^{-2} day^{-1}. She pointed out that these values are lower than many others in the literature and suggested that the coating of epiphytes depressed photosynthesis by the *Zostera*.

Some of the most favourable conditions for seagrass production are found in tropical and subtropical lagoons. Zieman (1968) found that growth of *Thalassia* leaves in Florida was 2–4 mm per day, amounting to 5 g dry weight m^{-2} day^{-1}, about 2 g C m^{-2} day^{-1}, which was maintained for eight months of the year. On the Laccadive Archipelago, in the Indian Ocean, Qasim and Bhattathiri (1971) measured diurnal changes in the water over-beds of *Thalassia* and *Cymodocia*, from which they were able to calculate a gross primary production of 11·97 g C m^{-2} day^{-1}, and an excess of production over total community respiration of 5·81 g C m^{-2} day^{-1}. They emphasised that this is probably a seasonal maximum. It is not, however, inconsistent with an annual production of the order of 1000 g C m^{-2}. Estimates of net productivity of 8, 9, 12, 16 and 18 g C m^{-2} day^{-1} have been made (McRoy & Helfferich 1977) but it is not clear for how long these might be maintained.

2.2.2   Nutrient relations

An obvious place to start consideration of nutrient relations in seagrass beds is the highly productive *Thalassia* system which flourishes in nutrient-poor tropical waters. It is well known (e.g. Ryther 1963) that tropical and subtropical seas are characteristically deficient in nutrients and have low phytoplankton productivity. This rules out the possibility that *Thalassia* obtains the nutrients to support its high growth rate by taking them directly from the water. Patriquin (1972) working in Barbados, measured the nitrogen and phosphorus content of *Thalassia* leaves and rhizomes, and of the water around the roots, and compared these with leaf tissue production. He found a very close correlation between the production and the water soluble N and P content of the rhizomes, from which he concluded that the plants draw their nutrients from the rhizomes and ultimately from the soil. When the requirements of the plants were compared with the amounts of available N and P in the root layer of soil (Table 2.3) it was found that there was enough

Table 2.3 Nitrogen and phosphorus budgets for *Thalassia testudinum*. (From data in Patriquin 1972.)

Item	NH_4-N (mg m^{-2})	PO_4-P (mg m^{-2})
Daily requirements for leaf growth (range)	21–71	0·9–3·1
Total in interstitial water in root layer	5·3	1·7
Total extractable (N) or available (P) in root layer	340	960
Number of days' supply in root layer	5–15	300–1000

phosphate for 300–1000 days of growth, but inorganic nitrogen for only 5–15 days growth. There was a good correlation between leaf production and NH_4-N in the interstitial water of the root layer, so Patriquin concluded that the supply of nitrogen limits the productivity of *Thalassia*. In a later paper (Patriquin & Knowles 1972) he showed that high rates of nitrogen fixation (acetylene reduction) were occurring in the rhizosphere of these plants, sufficient to supply their nitrogen needs. The agents of nitrogen fixation appeared to be anaerobic bacteria numbering 10^5 to 10^8 g of sediment^{-1}. Patriquin further showed that high rates of nitrogen fixation occurred in the sediments beneath the sea grasses *Diplanthera* and *Syringodium* in the West Indies, and *Zostera marina* in Canada.

McRoy *et al.* (1973) attempted to confirm the results of Patriquin and Knowles (1972), examining leaves, roots, rhizomes and sediment for evidence of nitrogen fixation. They found rates of fixation that were low or undetectable, and suggested that whereas their own experiments were carried out soon after removal from their natural environment, and were of short duration, Patriquin and Knowles' results were rendered abnormal by the delays involved in transporting their samples, and by the 3–5 day duration of their experiments. It now appears (Patriquin 1978) that in the *Spartina* root system discussed earlier there is a lag phase in nitrogenase activity that is explained by the need of the bacteria to have low-oxygen micro-sites in their vicinity. Handling of the root systems admits oxygen to the micro-sites and the lag is caused by the time required to deplete that oxygen by root and microbe respiration. It seems likely that the negative results of McRoy *et al.* (1973) were due to the short duration of their experiments, and that Patriquin's results are credible.

McRoy and co-workers (McRoy & Barsdate 1970; McRoy *et al.* 1972) made an extensive study of the phosphorus relations of *Zostera* in Alaska. They showed with ^{32}P experiments that *Zostera* may take up phosphorus either from the sediment through its roots, or from the water through its leaves. In a tidal pool dominated by eelgrass they found that the concentration of reactive phosphate in the interstitial water of the sediments was up to 75 μg-atoms g^{-1} while in the water above, it was about 2. The plants absorbed 166 mg P m^{-2} day^{-1} from the sediment, incorporated 104 mg in their tissues, and excreted 62 mg m^{-2} day^{-1} into the water. There was no direct evidence as to the source of replenishment of sediment phosphorus, but the authors suggested that part is derived from sedimented detritus and another part from chemical weathering of the black volcanic sands in the sediment. Harlin (1971) showed that ^{32}P released by the seagrasses *Zostera* and *Phyllospadix* is incorporated in the tissues of an epiphytic red algae, *Smithora naiadum*, and McRoy and Goering (1974) showed that ^{15}N supplied to the roots of *Zostera* as NH_4^+, NO_3^- or $(NH_2)_2CO$ subsequently appeared in the epiphyte community. These results help explain the rich development of epiphytes on seagrasses, even in waters that are very deficient in nutrients.

2.2.3   Consumers of seagrass production

Harrison and Mann (1975b) carried out decomposition experiments with *Zostera* analogous to those reported for *Spartina*. They soon found that *Zostera* is much more resistant to decay than *Spartina*. Starting with dried, ground plant material, they found that in the laboratory no more than 20% of organic matter was lost after incubation for 100 days at 20°C, with ample microorganisms and nutrients provided. Moreover, 82% of this loss was due to leaching, and occurred even when the experiments were run under sterile conditions. Compare this with the results of Gosselink and Kirby (1974) on *Spartina* where 30–42% of the biomass was lost in 30 days at 30°C.

There is a different kind of experiment often undertaken to determine rates of decomposition of aquatic plants. Weighed samples are placed in 'litter-bags' in the natural environment. The bags have a mesh of specified size which permit small particles to wash away after partial decomposition. Rates can be compared between experiments only if the size of mesh and the degree of wave action is the same. Odum and de la Cruz (1967) used 2·5 mm nylon mesh and gave comparative data for four species of salt-marsh plant. Zieman (1968) studied the decomposition of *Thalassia* using the same techniques, and found it to be much faster (Fig. 2.7). One of the factors influencing such results is the activity of any invertebrate 'shredders' which may gain entry to the bags and accelerate reduction of particle size. Fenchel (1970) showed that the amphipod *Parhyalella* greatly accelerated particle size reduction of *Thalassia*, and in his experiments almost doubled the rate of oxygen uptake of the detritus within four days. Since the oxygen uptake is proportional to microbial metabolism, we may take it that the amphipods almost doubled the rate of decomposition.

A mysid shrimp (*Mysis stenolepis*) lives in large numbers in *Zostera* beds

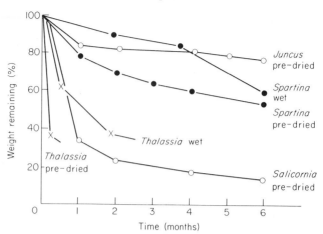

Fig. 2.7 Rates of disappearance of named marine macrophytes from litter bags of 2.5 mm mesh. (From Wood *et al.* 1967.)

on the coast of Nova Scotia throughout the eelgrass growing season (Foulds & Mann 1978) and can be observed to pick up detritus particles and eat them. To test its ability to utilize structural cellulose from the *Zostera* detritus, it was induced to feed on ^{14}C-labelled raw cellulose. Surprisingly, the ^{14}C-label appeared in the tissues of the mysids in such amounts as to indicate an assimilation efficiency of over 40% (Fig. 2.8). The assimilation efficiency was greater when the food consisted of sterile cellulose than when it consisted of cellulose that had been incubated with a culture of cellulolytic microbes from local waters. Similar results were obtained with uniformly labelled ^{14}C hay. The explanation (Wainwright & Mann in press) could be

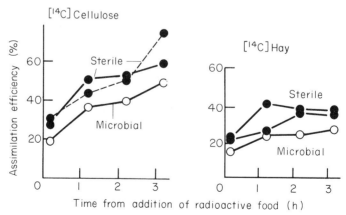

Fig. 2.8 Assimilation of radioactive carbon from labelled cellulose and from labelled hay by *Mysis stenolepis* at different times after feeding. (From Foulds & Mann 1978.)

that the mysid carries in its gut a microflora capable of digesting cellulose. When the mysids are treated with antibiotics, their ability to digest cellulose disappears, but can be restored by feeding them on fresh mysid guts. However, recent work (Frieson 1981) casts some doubt on this explanation. Search for a microflora revealed none, and the cellulose may be produced by the *Mysis* itself.

There will be more detailed discussion of microbial processes in Chapter 5 but this result is mentioned to show that while *Zostera* may be resistant to microbial degradation on the sea floor, it is susceptible to the digestive action in the guts of animals. Fong and Mann (1980) have shown that the sea urchin *Strongylocentrotus*, which browses on living and dead algae and seagrasses, does have a gut flora capable of cellulose digestion.

However, the overall picture of events in a *Zostera* bed (Harrison & Mann 1975b) is that very little of the plant tissue is consumed while alive, and that after death a high proportion of the leaves are buried almost intact in the sediments, so that a considerable bank of slowly decaying organic matter accumulates in the sediments and is used over a number of years by detritivores. This storage of reduced carbon confers year-to-year stability on the populations which make use of it, and evens out the effects of variations in annual primary productivity.

A quantitative assessment of the fate of seagrass production was made by Kirkman and Reid (1979) for a bed of *Posidonia australis* in an estuary near Sydney, Australia. They found that 37% of a year's production sank to the bottom and was utilized by benthic detritivores, 12% was exported from the bed as floating leaves, and only 3% of production was eaten by herbivores. Most remarkable of all was the finding that when plastic cylinders were placed over shoots and the ends sealed round the stems with split rubber stoppers, there was a release of dissolved organic matter (DOM) equivalent to 48% of a year's primary production. It should be noted that this included loss of DOM by dying tissues included in the cylinders. The measurements of dissolved organic loss were made on only three occasions and the data had a considerable scatter. Nevertheless, the indication of a large amount of organic carbon in solution, which is almost certain to be taken up by microorganisms, is an important clue to the functioning of this system.

A comprehensive view of the kinds and quantities of consumer organisms found in seagrass beds is given in Kikuchi and Pérès (1977). There are numerous heterotrophs such as protozoa, nematodes and other meiofauna in the epiphytic community which develops on the older leaves and stems. There are also numerous larger filter-feeding organisms (hydrozoans, actinians, bryozoans, tube-building polychaetes, and ascidians) which use the seagrasses as surfaces for attachment. Over these assemblages crawl gastropods, crustaceans and a variety of other invertebrates. Numerous kinds of free-swimming invertebrates and fishes congregate in the shelter of the

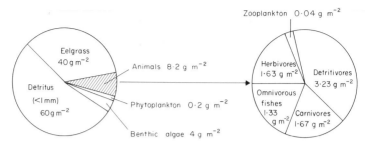

Fig. 2.9 Composition of the biomass in an eelgrass bed in California. (From Thayer *et al.* 1975.)

plants, and in the sediment around their roots is found a rich and diverse bottom fauna.

One of the few quantitative studies of consumer relations in a seagrass bed is that of the group at Beaufort, North Carolina (Thayer, Wolf & Williams 1975; Thayer, Adams & La Croix 1975). At the time of the study the biomass of eelgrass was low, and has since increased markedly, so we should avoid any idea that the values given represent steady state. Biomasses of the functional groups are shown in Fig. 2.9. Polychaetes and bivalve molluscs dominated the biomass of detritivores, gastropods were the most abundant herbivores, while decapods were the main carnivores. Respiration of each consumer species was measured, and used to calculate probable consumption and assimilation rates. The results were used to plot an energy flow diagram (Fig. 2.10). From a measured primary production of 1545 kcal m^{-2} yr^{-1} it was estimated that macrofauna consumed 841 kcal, or approximately 55%. Microbial metabolism accounted for 467 kcal m^{-2} yr^{-1}, or 30%, leaving a small surplus for export, however, there was an additional contribution of primary production by epiphytes and by benthic diatoms, which was not measured.

The average biomass of fish in the Beaufort eelgrass bed (6 kcal, or 1.33 g dry weight m^{-2}) is similar to that encountered by Robertson and Howard (1978), who studied the fish community of a *Zostera* and *Heterozostera* bed in Australia. In the latter study, interesting insights were obtained into the relationship between the fish and their food supply. The water was about 2.0 m deep over the seagrass beds at high tide, and 0.3 m deep at low tide. Samples were taken with fish nets and with towed plankton nets on rising and falling tides, by day and by night. 41 species of fish were taken, of which 11 consumed planktonic forms in large numbers. During the day, the plankton samples were dominated by copepods and decapod larvae, but at night amphipods and ostracods rose from the bottom and were taken in plankton samples. The stomach contents of the fish reflected this change. By day, the decapod larvae, especially the large *Callianassa* larvae, were selected in

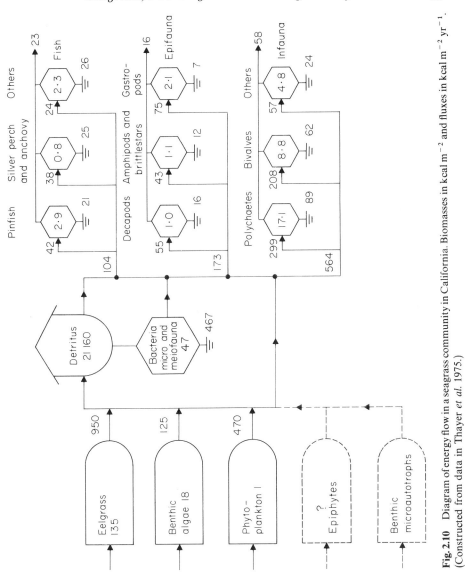

Fig. 2.10 Diagram of energy flow in a seagrass community in California. Biomasses in kcal m^{-2} and fluxes in kcal m^{-2} yr^{-1}. (Constructed from data in Thayer *et al.* 1975.)

preference over the small copepods. By night, amphipods were the prime target of planktivorous fish. Even in the relatively shallow water it was possible to detect strategies for predator avoidance among the various species. Those remaining in the water column on a 24 h basis tended to congregate near the bottom, in lower levels of illumination, during the day. They also tended to have transparent bodies. The amphipods, which moved into the water column only at night, had pigmented bodies. Almost all the amphipods in the water column were males, the females remaining in the sediment. It appeared from the data that moving into the water column increased the probability of predation, and it was suggested that the males did so in order to move about and locate females for mating. They minimized the risk by doing so only at night.

One of the fish species occurring frequently in the samples was the commercially important King George Whiting (*Sillaginodes punctatus*). The young fish inhabited the dense seagrass beds for the first five months of life and consumed mainly harpacticoid copepods, mysids and small amphipods. Older fish were taken mostly over adjacent mud flats, and preyed chiefly on the ghost prawn *Callianassa australensis*. This is a well documented case of seagrass beds functioning as nursery grounds for a commercially important fish species. A review of the role of seagrass beds in Japan (Kikuchi 1974) indicates that the fish that are permanent residents in the beds are of no commercial importance, but that the seasonal residents include young stages of several commerically important species. Records have been kept in Japan which show that in a number of bays *Zostera* beds have been reduced or eliminated by land filling or pollution. A comparison of the fauna taken in sledge net hauls in three bays, with (1) well developed *Zostera* beds, (2) reduced beds, and (3) no *Zostera*, showed that the fauna was much more abundant in the rich *Zostera*. For example, the total crustaceans taken in six hauls (excluding planktonic forms) were 2054, 391 and 435 animals at sites (1), (2) and (3) respectively. Decline of eelgrass beds is associated with declining catches of Japanese sea bass, black and red sea bream, rockfish and spinefeet.

In Moreton Bay, Australia, there is a prawn fishery yielding about 2000 tonnes per annum. There is an extensive littoral band of sediment, fringed on the landward side by mangroves and often on the seaward side by a band of seagrasses. The seagrasses form five distinct communities (Young 1978): (i) *Zostera capricorni* with *Halophila ovalis*, (ii) *Cymodocia serratula* (iii) *Syringodium isoetifolium*, (iv) *Zostera capricorni* with *Halodule uninervis*, and (v) *Halophila ovalis* with *Halophila spinulosa*. Young (1978) found that prawn postlarval stages were more abundant in seagrass beds than at stations over bare mud. Greatest abundances were associated with *Zostera capricorni*, *Halodule uninervis* and *Halophila ovalis*.

Finally in this section we come to consideration of the very large consumers in seagrass beds, namely sea-cows and turtles. Sea-cows, or Sirenia, were once represented by a diverse and widespread group which were probably descended from the same stock as the elephants. Today there are only four living species of Sirenia, three species of manatee (genus *Trichecus*) and one dugong, *Dugong dugon*. A related species, Steller's sea-cow, *Hydrodamalis gigas* was hunted to extinction within 30 years of its discovery in the Bering Sea in 1741. The manatees are on eastern and western shores of the Atlantic, while dugongs are found from East Africa round the shores of the Indian Ocean to south-east Asia and in tropical and subtropical Australia. They are 2–3 m in length and feed in seagrass beds by ploughing their way along the bottom, producing trails about 25 cm wide, 3–5 cm deep, and up to 5 m long. Each winding trail is thought to represent the feeding effort of a single dive lasting 2–8 minutes. Most of the time their guts are found to be filled with rhizomes, stems and leaves of seagrasses, but when these become scarce they will turn to *Sargassum* and other algae. Most of the digestion is carried out by bacteria in the large intestine. It has been calculated that each dugong needs the biomass from 3·5 ha of seagrass bed to support it for a year. (Heinsohn *et al.* 1977). Since dugongs in north-eastern and northern Australia can occur in herds of 100–200, it is obvious that their grazing pressure on seagrass beds can be very great indeed. Because of the potential food limitation, they cannot stay in one area for very long, but migrate along quite considerable lengths of coastline.

Green turtles (*Chelonia midas*) are competitors with dugongs for sea grass as food. They occur throughout the tropics and are much more abundant than dugongs. They come ashore on beaches to lay their eggs, and nesting colonies of 11–12 000 have been seen in the Great Barrier Reef area. However, their feeding habits are rather different from those of the dugongs. When eating seagrasses they crop and eat only the leaves, and they appear to thrive perfectly well on a diet of algae taken from rocky shores.

2.2.4 The wasting disease of eelgrass

The section on seagrasses should not be concluded without a reference to the so-called wasting disease of eelgrass. In the summer of 1931 and 1932 there was a sudden appearance, first in the USA and Canada, then in Europe, of a black-brown discolouration of the leaves of *Zostera* over enormously large areas. The leaves dropped off, the rhizomes died, and there was a greatly reduced biomass in the following years. On close examination it was found that the first symptoms were brownish-grey spots on the leaves and rhizomes, associated with growths of the fungus *Ophiobolus halimus* and the slime mould *Labyrinthula macrocystis*. The view became widespread that the *Zostera* had been 'attacked' by 'disease-causing' organisms. Later, however, it was shown (Young 1938) that *Labyrinthula* occurs in healthy

Zostera and it is entirely possible that both *Ophiobolus* and *Labyrinthula* are important in the normal process of decomposition (Rasmussen 1977).

In place of the 'wasting disease' hypothesis, Rasmussen proposed a temperature stress hypothesis. Earlier work had shown that there are ecological races of *Zostera marina* which are adapted to different temperature regimes, but each is adapted rather closely to a specific range and shows signs of stress at temperatures outside that range. Rasmussen drew attention to the fact that about this time the whole North Atlantic showed a warming trend. A quotation from Southward (1960) illustrates the point very well:

> For 1932 there is much biological data to suggest the end of an epoch. It was the last year in which many plankton 'indicator' species were abundant or appeared off Plymouth, particularly the northern or boreal forms likely to be adversely affected by warmer conditions— *Aglantha*, *Sagitta elegans* and *Meganyctiphanes* for example. To judge from the evidence obtained by Ford, there was a practically total failure of recruitment of herring in the Plymouth area in the winter of 1931–32.

Hence, Rasmussen argued, *Zostera marina* was weakened by the unaccustomed rise in temperature, and succumbed to attacks from fungus and slime mould. As a corollary to the temperature stress hypothesis he suggested that stands of *Zostera* in brackish water (less than 12–15 per thousand) were living under optimal conditions and were better able to stand temperature stress. This would explain the survival of the eelgrass in estuarine areas, when eelgrass in nearby fully saline areas succumbed to the 'wasting-disease'.

Loss of eelgrass beds seemed like an ideal opportunity to test the hypothesis that there are important food chains dependent on eelgrass production. Unfortunately, the results are confusing, and the source of the confusion seems to lie in the diversity of environments in which eelgrass is found. There is a long history of eelgrass ecology in the Baltic, but it appears that under conditions of minimal tidal flow the water and sediment in an eelgrass bed tends to become anoxic and unsuitable for many invertebrates. Destruction of eelgrass beds in these areas actually resulted in increased population densities of invertebrates. On the other hand, as has been shown above, there are many seagrass beds where populations of invertebrates and fish are much higher than on the surrounding sand or mud-flats. These are areas where tidal flushing keeps the water and sediment well aerated. Loss of eelgrass production can only reduce the productivity of the associated food web.

In Denmark, early workers had developed the hypothesis that eelgrass was the key primary producer of coastal waters. When the eelgrass died, a catastrophic collapse of fisheries was predicted but did not materialize. This led to widespread rejection of the hypothesis that eelgrass productivity was important (see Rasmussen 1977). However, the view, quoted earlier, of Harrison and Mann (1975b) is that eelgrass leaves form a large reservoir of slowly decomposing organic matter which would not be expected to change very much in response to year-to-year changes in productivity. More will be said about this in the chapter on detritus and decomposition (Chapter 5).

2.3   MANGROVE SYSTEMS OR MANGALS

Of all the marine macrophyte systems, the mangroves are the only ones characterized by storage of aerial biomass, so that the individual plants are trees or shrubs and the whole takes on the aspect of a forest. They are found from the highest level of spring tides down almost to mean sea level, on sheltered sedimented shores throughout the tropics and some distance into the subtropical latitudes. They occur in fully saline waters but also penetrate considerable distances into estuaries. Large numbers of crabs, molluscs and other invertebrates are permanent inhabitants of the system, while shrimps, prawns and fish move in and out with the tides. The upper canopy supports a rich insect fauna, together with insectivorous and fish-eating birds, and often provides roosts for large populations of bats.

The word mangrove has traditionally been used to describe either the total community or the individual trees or bushes. More recently, plant ecologists have tended to use mangrove for individual plants and mangal for the community. Biogeographers recognise two main vegetation groups. The Old World mangal contains about 60 species, while the New World mangal contains only about 10 species. It is inferred that adaptation of forest trees to saline water-logged conditions probably first occurred in the Indo-Malaysian area, and that mangrove species spread and evolved from that centre. As we noted for salt-marshes, the communities tend to be simpler in the New World, and there has been more work on ecological processes in this area. Hence, it seems best to illustrate functional aspects of a mangrove system by reference to a rather simple mangal in Puerto Rico (Golley *et al.* 1962). On the seaward side, extending inwards from open water is a distinct zone dominated by the red mangrove *Rhizophora mangle*. This tree has extensive prop roots which emerge from the trunk high above the ground and arch downwards. They form a dense, almost impenetrable tangle which traps sediment (Fig. 2.11). Except for red mangrove seedlings, there is no other vegetation on the forest floor. Numerous sessile marine organisms attach to the prop roots. Moving towards the land, the next zone is dominated by black mangrove, *Avicennia tomentosa*. Tidal inundation is less frequent, but the sediment is dark and anaerobic. The underground system sends vast numbers of breathing roots or pneumatophores vertically upwards, so that they extend well above the forest floor (Fig. 2.11). A few

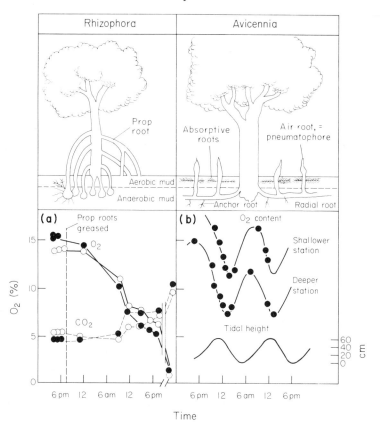

Fig. 2.11 Upper: Diagram of root systems of *Rhizophora* and *Avicennia*.
Lower: Changes in O_2 and CO_2 concentrations (a) when prop roots of *Rhizophora* were
covered in grease, and (b) when aerial roots of *Avicennia* were covered at high tide.

herbaceous plants may be present in this zone. The third and highest mangrove zone is dominated by white mangrove, *Laguncularia racemosa*, which
occurs in more open communities with ferns and grasses growing beneath. A
second species, the button mangrove *Conocarpus erectus* is also found in this
zone or adjacent to it.

As with *Spartina*, the physiological adaptations of mangroves are of two
kinds: to salinity stress and to growth in waterlogged, anaerobic mud. The
question of salinity relations was examined by Scholander *et al.* (1962) and
Scholander (1968). One group of mangroves, including *Avicennia*, *Aegiceras*
and *Aegialitis* have salt-secreting glands on their leaves. The sap which
passes up their xylem contains 0·2–0·5% sodium chloride. Another group,
including *Rhizophora*, *Bruguiera* and *Sonneratia* lack the salt-secreting
glands and the concentration of salt in their sap is only about one tenth that

of the other group. In both cases the osmotic pressure of the cell sap is nowhere near that of the sea-water. How, then, do they take up water? Using a pressure-bomb technique, Scholander (1968) showed that xylem sap is at a negative hydrostatic pressure of -28 to -58 atm, which is more than enough to compensate for the osmotic pressure of sea water (about 25 atm). This negative pressure is generated by the high osmotic pressure of the leaf cells, some 10–30 atm above that of sea-water. When high hydrostatic pressure was applied around the roots of a decapitated seedling, there was a flow of nearly fresh water from the cut surface, and this continued in spite of chilling or poisoning, showing that the separation of fresh water from salt was a simple non-metabolic ultrafiltration process. The normal processes of transpiration accounted for the flow of water through the plant. The main difference between mangroves and other plants is that the mangroves have an unusually high osmotic pressure in the leaf cell sap. They also have a relatively low rate of transpiration. Kuenzler (1974) suggested that this implies a relatively high nutrient content of the water around the roots.

The prop roots and pneumatophores serve the purpose of aerating the underground tissues which are unable to obtain oxygen from the water-logged soil. Scholander *et al.* (1955) found that the upper parts of the prop roots of *Rhizophora* have lenticels which connect by way of air spaces with the lower ends. The latter are spongy structures embedded in anaerobic mud. When the lenticels were blocked with grease their gas content changed from 15% O_2 to less than 2% O_2 within 48 h (Fig. 2.11). In *Avicennia* there are radially arranged spongy gas-filled roots running horizontally in the anaerobic mud. The air roots or pneumatophores project vertically upwards through the mud surface, to a height which depends on depth of submergence. Those furthest down the shore, which were covered by 60 cm of water at low tide, grew to a height of 20–50 cm, while those near high tide level grew to only 10–20 cm. These air roots also had lenticels connecting by way of air spaces with the root tissues. When all the air roots of a plant were cut and blocked with grease, the oxygen content in the radial roots fell from 10–15% to less than 1% in two days. In the normal tidal rhythm, partial pressure of oxygen falls when the air roots are covered by water. The CO_2 released at this time is readily soluble and does not compensate for the oxygen used. As a result, there is an overall negative pressure developed in the air spaces during submergence. When the tide recedes there is a relatively rapid 'inhalation' of air, as gas pressure is equalized through the lenticels.

2.3.1 Primary productivity

Mangroves grow in areas of high solar radiation and have the ability to take up fresh water from salt, so they are in an excellent position to achieve high primary productivity. However, the difficulties of working among the dense growths of prop roots and branches have proved a deterrent and we have rather few production estimates. Golley *et al.* (1962) made some of the first. They worked in the Puerto Rican mangal but only in the month of May. They found a gross photosynthesis of about 8 g C m^{-2} day^{-1}, but total community respiration was at a similar level. Nevertheless, they observed an export of particulate matter in tidal flow amounting to 1·1 g C m^{-2} day^{-1}. Miller (1972) made a very detailed model of leaf production in terms of solar radiation and the associated temperature, transpiration, respiration and gross and net photosynthesis of both sunlit and shaded leaves. He used the experimental data of Golley *et al.* (1962) to derive his equations for the relationship between light and photosynthesis, but he made explicit allowance for variations in photosynthesis and respiration at different levels of the canopy according to leaf temperature and water relations. He found that leaf water stress induced stomatal closure at the top of the canopy on clear, sunny days, so that maximum production occurred in the middle levels of the canopy. The average net production rate for red mangrove in Florida was calculated as 2·8 g organic matter m^{-2} day^{-1} (about 400 g C m^{-2} yr^{-1}). When Miller's model was applied to the mangal studied by Golley *et al.* (1962) it predicted a net photosynthesis of 3·4 g organic matter m^{-2} day^{-1}, about 14% higher than the Florida mangal. Heald (1969) measured the amount of organic matter dropping from Red Mangrove in Florida. His figure for leaf production was similar to that of Golley *et al.* (1962), but when scales and twig debris were included, the estimate of organic matter produced annually increased to about 350 g C m^{-2} yr^{-1}. Lugo and Snedaker (1974), in a review, listed sites where net production varied from zero (respiration equal to gross production) to 7·5 g C m^{-2} day^{-1}. If figures of 350–500 g C m^{-2} yr^{-1} are typical of the net production provided to coastal waters by mangals on a large proportion of the tropical coastline, it is easy to see that this is highly important compared with phytoplankton production. Many of these waters are nutrient-deficient and liable to produce no more than 50–75 g C m^{-2} yr^{-1} in the phytoplankton.

2.3.2 Heterotrophs in the mangal

The most detailed study of consumers in a mangrove system is by Odum and Heald (1975). Heald (1969) had shown that an estimated 5·1% of the total leaf production of Red Mangrove in Florida is consumed by terrestrial grazers. The remainder enters the aquatic system as debris. Leaves on the tree had 6·1% of the ash-free dry weight as protein. At leaf fall this had dropped to 3·1%, but as decomposition progressed (see Chapter 5) the detritus particles became enriched with nitrogen until after 12 months they had 22% protein. Clearly, this is a nutritious food source for a variety of

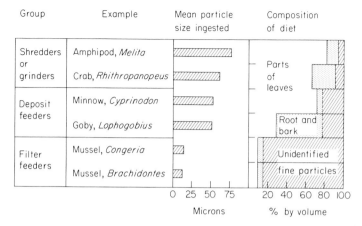

Fig. 2.12 Analysis of the diet of three types of detritivore from a Florida mangrove estuary. (From data in Odum and Heald 1975.)

animals. To establish the importance of detritus in the diet of fish and invertebrates of the North River system in Florida, they analysed the stomach contents of 10 000 animals belonging to 120 species. They defined a detritus consumer as a species whose digestive-tract contents averaged at least 20% vascular plant detritus by volume on an annual basis. They found that roughly one third of the species encountered were in this category: six species of fish, two polychaete worms, one crab, three kinds of chironomid midge larvae and a long list of other crustaceans, including cumaceans, mysids, harpacticoid and calanoid copepods, amphipods, ostracods and three kinds of shrimps. They found that the detritivores could be placed in three functional groups: (1) grinders (also known as shredders) which take large leaf particles and chew them; (2) deposit feeders, which selected smaller leaf particles deposited on the sediment surface; and (3) filter feeders, taking fine particles from suspension in the water column (Fig. 2.12). They found that almost all animals except the filter feeders routinely ingested faecal pellets. The authors emphasized that the organisms in the food web could not be rigidly grouped in trophic levels, but usually combined a diet of detritus with various mixtures of living plant or animal tissue. Nevertheless, the mangrove leaf fall constituted the major source of nutrients and energy for a very productive system. Their pictorial summary is given in Fig. 2.13.

Turning from the Caribbean to the Old World, we find richer species diversity, but a similarity to the Caribbean systems is evident. For example, Watson (1928), a pioneer of Malayan mangrove ecology, produced the diagram in Fig. 2.14 and he recognized five zones based on frequency of inundation. Beginning at the lowest level these are: (1) Species growing on land

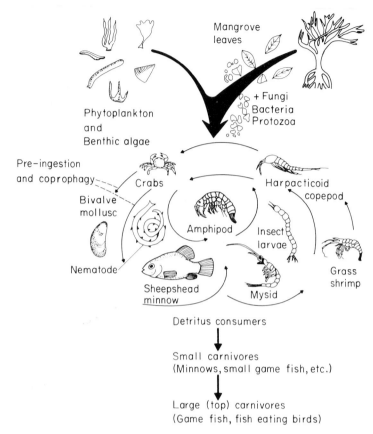

Fig. 2.13 Diagram summarizing the flow of energy and materials through a detritus-consuming omnivorous system in the North River Estuary, Florida. The cyclical nature of the diagram depicts the utilization of detritus particles in the form of faecal material. (From Odum and Heald 1975.)

flooded at all tides: no species normally exists under these conditions but *Rhizophora mucronata* will do so exceptionally; (2) Species on land *flooded by medium high tides*: species of *Avicennia, Sonneratia griffithii*, and, bordering rivers, *Rhizophora mucronata*; (3) Species on land *flooded by normal high tides*: most mangroves, but *Rhizophora* tends to become dominant; (4) Species on land *flooded by spring tides only*: *Bruguiera gymnorhiza* and *B. cylindrica*; (5) Species on land *flooded by equinoctial or other exceptional tides only*: *B. gymnorhiza* dominant but *Rhizophora apiculata* and *Xylocarpus granatus* survive.

The macroscopic animal associations of Indo-Pacific mangrove communities have been well reviewed by Macnae (1968). At the landward side

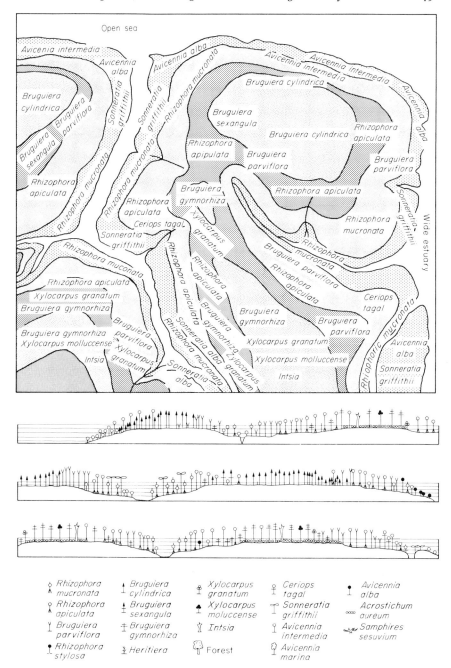

Fig. 2.14   A diagram showing the typical distribution of mangrove trees on the Malayan west coast. (From Macnae (1968) after Watson (1928).)

crabs of the genera *Sesarma* and *Uca* are very abundant. In moist climates they are associated with prosobranch and pulmonate snails. In the *Bruguiera* forests (flooded at spring tides) crabs run everywhere, and in many localities mud lobsters *Thalassina* live in burrows with conspicuous heaps of soil at the entrance. Numerous gastropods are found, often in clumps on the tree trunks. In the main *Rhizophora* zone (flooded by normal tides) the sediment is soft and a bright blue crab, *Metopograpsus*, runs around on the prop roots, while a snapping prawn moves in the mud. In the seaward fringe and on channel banks gobioid fish known as mud-skippers are very abundant. They are characterized by having the eyes placed at the very top of the head rather like frogs and by the use of the pectoral fins for locomotion over the mud surface. One species is able to climb into the mangroves and cling to the branches with a sucker formed from fused pelvic fins. Some of these fish are carnivorous, but others take algae and detritus from the mud surface. The other major components of the fauna at the seaward edge are crabs, gastropods, and bivalve molluscs. While some of the crabs are carnivorous, it appears that the majority feed by sorting detritus from the mud surface. Some of the gastropods rasp algae from the prop roots, but the majority appear to ingest sediment. The bivalves are, of course, filter feeders. Penaeid prawns move in and out with the tides, and traditionally are caught for human consumption by placing traps in the drainage channels, on moonless nights, after spring tides. The details of the natural history of the mangal fauna, so well documented by Macnae (1968) make fascinating reading.

While much remains to be discovered about the nutrient dynamics of mangal systems, it is clear from the information available that they are well adapted to maintaining a high gloss primary production in tropical intertidal environments. Community respiration, of which plant respiration is a major component, varies from one site to another and Lugo and Snedaker (1974) have suggested that it may be related to the degree of salinity stress which the mangroves have to tolerate. Their production is passed on to a rich invertebrate fauna dominated by crustaceans, many of which feed directly on the leaf and twig debris. They provide a sheltered and food-rich habitat for migratory young stages of fish and shrimp, in waters which otherwise tend to be nutrient-poor and unproductive.

2.4   DISCUSSION

All the marine flowering plants have the tendency to form dense, low-diversity stands which act as traps for sediment. An important role which should not be overlooked is that of protection from coastal erosion. The massive amounts of sediment and the plant biomass associated with them serve very efficiently as buffers between the open sea and the dry land, owing to their capacity to absorb wave energy. Chapman (1977) contains numerous references to this property. Mangals are deliberately cultivated for their shoreline stabilizing properties in Thailand, Florida, and elsewhere. Planting of marsh grasses has been shown to reduce coastal erosion, and conversely removal of shoreline vegetation has been found almost invariably to lead to an increased rate of erosion. These effects are readily visible and can be assigned an economic value.

The effects which I wish to emphasize in this book are more indirect, less easy to verify, but are nevertheless very real. All the evidence points to salt-marshes, seagrass beds and mangals being sites of higher biological productivity than the open water adjacent to them. While the range for coastal phytoplankton production in areas not subjected to special upwelling effects is about 50–250 g C m^{-2} yr^{-1}, the range for the marine flowering plant communities is about 300–1000 g C m^{-2} yr^{-1}. Moreover, the plants provide a sheltered habitat for young animals and a surface for attachment and growth of abundant epiphytic communities. Total secondary production in these habitats has seldom been measured, but biomass data indicate that it, too, is substantially higher than in the surrounding coastal waters. The site of secondary production varies according to local topography. Sometimes it occurs within the macrophyte stands, especially in the seaward parts of mangals and in the seagrass beds that have adequate throughflow of water. Alternatively, macrophyte detritus may be transported considerable distances by tidal currents and consumed elsewhere.

For those wishing to dredge, fill, or otherwise modify coastal macrophyte systems, it is easy to take the view that the high productivity is confined to a relatively narrow coastal belt, and can therefore be regarded as trivial when averaged over the whole continental shelf, where most of the commercially valuable fish stocks occur. However, that argument certainly does not apply to the south-eastern part of the USA, as Peters and Schaaf (unpublished) showed. They estimated that about two thirds of the total US commercial fish landings are taken within five miles of shore, and computed the relative contributions of macrophytes and phytoplankton to a strip five miles wide extending from Long Island, New York, to Southern Georgia. They calculated that salt-marshes had a total area of $8\cdot3 \times 10^9$ m^2, and produced on average 1200 g dry weight m^{-2} yr^{-1}, for a total of $9\cdot9 \times 10^9$ kg; seagrass beds occupied $1\cdot3 \times 10^9$ m^2, with an average annual production of 600 g dry weight m^{-2}, yielding a total of $0\cdot8 \times 10^9$ kg; and phytoplankton plus benthic diatoms were found in an area 33×10^9 m^2, at an average productivity of 200 g organic matter m^{-2} yr^{-1}, for a total of $6\cdot6 \times 10^9$ kg. Thus, macrophytes contributed $10\cdot7 \times 10^9$ kg of organic matter, compared with $6\cdot6 \times 10^9$ kg from the planktonic algae. As we have seen, the details of how macrophyte material enters detrital food chains is still not fully understood, but there is plenty of evidence that it is used in a variety of ways. In any case, coastal macrophyte systems are unique in providing a sheltered, food-rich habitat which is essential to the growth of many valuable species, either in the juvenile stages, as in the case of many shrimps and fish species, or throughout life as in the case of various kinds of shellfish. If we add to these considerations the value of coastal marshes, seagrass beds and mangrove forests as habitats for ducks and geese, waders and fish-eating birds, the case for protection of these systems is very strong indeed.

CHAPTER 3
SEAWEED-BASED SYSTEMS

3.1 INTRODUCTION

The theme of this chapter is illustrated rather strikingly by these excerpts from a Government of Canada translation of Vozzhinskaya (1972). Referring to the coast of the USSR she says:

> The coastal zones contain enormously rich underwater 'cornfields'. Our country is especially rich in marine algae: our shores are washed by 14 seas and are fringed with extensive algal belts containing hundreds of species of marine plants. . . . Large algae provide numerous invertebrates and fish with nourishment and protection, especially their young individuals. And we shall not be wrong, if we say that the existence of all living creatures in water depends directly or indirectly on the algae. . . . Submarine forests formed by brown laminarian algae resemble a jungle and stretch for hundreds of kilometers. . . . The density and width of such forests depend on the coastal outline and the geomorphology of the bottom. As far as the coastal zone is concerned, the leading role of the phytobenthos in

the creation of organic matter, and hence of all forms of life, is beyond doubt.

The macroalgae differ from the flowering plants in having no roots. They attach themselves to solid objects by means of a holdfast. As a result, the flowering plants colonize soft, sedimenting shores while the macroalgae colonize rocky shores. In quiet waters the algae can manage to stay in position if they have small pebbles (about 2 cm upwards) for their attachment. In a few rather specialized areas unattached forms, known as 'ecads', may be locally abundant (Brinkhuis 1976). In general, however, we may say that seaweed systems are characteristic of rocky shores, and that they reach their maximum development in cool temperate regions. A taxonomic account of world seaweed distribution would be extremely complex and difficult to unravel, but from the point of view of system function a survey based on the possibilities for commercial exploitation of biomass (Michanek 1975) gives a good indication of the relative importance of the various species (Fig. 3.1). The diagram gives FAO estimates of the potential annual harvest of brown algae. Most of the biomass is made up of kelps (Laminariales) which live subtidally and rockweeds (Fucales) which are predominantly intertidal. They are harvested chiefly for their alginate content, but *Laminaria* is used as food in China and Japan.

An interesting functional interpretation of the morphology of benthic marine algae is given by Neushul (1972). He recognizes four types of water motion which algae experience. At the stage of being a microscopic spore they are attached to a surface and experience only the relatively still water of the laminar sub-layer, with water movements of the order of $\cdot 01$ m sec^{-1}. As germlings they protrude to the edge of the boundary layer and experience water movements of the order of $0\cdot 1$ m sec^{-1}. Larger plants protrude into the surge zone, where wave action causes oscillatory water movements of the order of 1 m sec^{-1}. The largest plants reaching to the limits of the community, may also experience unidirectional flows of the order of 1 m sec^{-1}. The structure of the plants reflects these changing stresses. For those living in the relatively still water close to the surface, there is a wide variety of shapes including encrusting, filamentous and those with broad, thin blades. The development of filaments or thin laminar structures may be seen as adaptation to increasing surface area for uptake of nutrients and gas exchange. However, when plants become large enough to protrude into the surge zone there is one basic structural type which recurs frequently in the large brown algae; its components are a strong holdfast, a tough, flexible stipe, and a single, elongate blade. This structure is well adapted to withstand constant wave-induced oscillatory action. It is the form retained by *Laminaria*, *Agarum* and *Dictyoneuropsis* throughout life. The young stages of other important brown algae such as *Macrocystis*, *Ecklonia*, *Egregia*, *Pelagophycus*, *Pterygophora* and *Eisenia* pass through this stage during

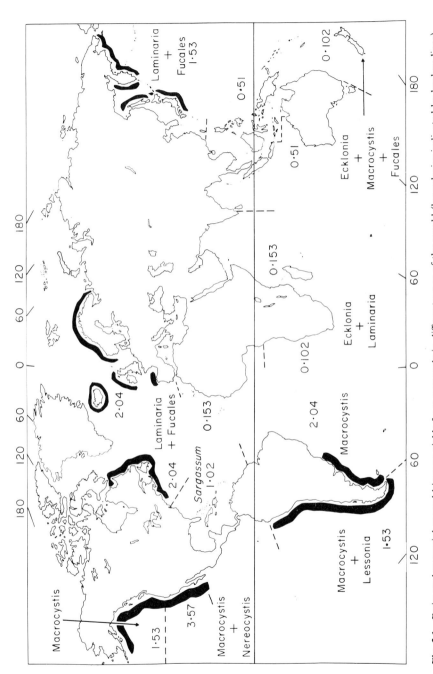

Fig. 3.1 Estimated potential annual biomass yields from seaweeds in different areas of the world (boundaries indicated by broken lines). Figures are millions of tonnes fresh weight. Areas yielding over 1 million tonnes have been shaded. Names of dominant genera are given. (Data from Michanek (1977) and Chapman (1970).)

development. Many of them grow upwards to inhabit the surface waters and unidirectional currents. To do this, they develop gas bladders for flotation, and commonly have various devices such as corrugations or extensive subdivision of blades, to maximize turbulence at their surfaces and increase surface area for photosynthesis and nutrient uptake.

This functional interpretation of structure in the algae, while serving to increase our understanding, cannot be taken too literally. In most situations, in this author's experience, there is very little separation between zones of oscillatory wave action and unidirectional current, or if there is, the separation is horizontal rather than vertical. On shores exposed to swells from the open ocean, there is an oscillatory movement of water at all depths, and any unidirectional current is superimposed on it. However, in areas of considerable rise and fall of the tide, the most marked unidirectional currents are of tidal origin. They are liable to reach maximum velocity in places where tidal currents sweep round headlands and islands, or are channelled through narrow passages. In these situations unidirectional currents (subject to reversal at about 6-hour intervals) are liable to be the dominant influence even close to the bottom, and occur in many situations sheltered from heavy wave action.

If we place less emphasis than Neushul (1972) on the separation between surge-zone plants and current-zone plants, it makes more sense to interpret the flotation devices as adaptations which enable the plants to reach upwards to the zone of maximum light intensity. Just as the upward growth of trees by the production of woody tissue can be interpreted as one of the strategies employed in competition for light as a limiting resource, so the upward movement of algae by the use of flotation devices can be interpreted as a way of maximizing light received while shading out competitors.

Objective measurement of turbulent water movement on a scale appropriate to the understanding of the functioning of marine algae is still in its infancy. Nevertheless, it appears that adaptation to vigorous water movement on eroding rather than sedimenting shores has enabled the macrophytic algae to benefit from very high levels of turbulent diffusion, which in turn permit very high levels of nutrient uptake, photosynthesis and growth. The large algae are probably the most productive plants in the sea.

3.2 KELP ECOSYSTEMS

Kelp is a general term for large brown algae of the Laminariales. If we try to simplify the picture and characterize the kelp beds of the world by their dominant genera, as in Fig. 3.1, we can recognise three groups, dominated by *Laminaria*, *Ecklonia* and *Macrocystis* respectively.

Laminaria is the old-world kelp, valued from ancient times for its mineral content and for its value as a mulch or fertilizer. Many species have a simple,

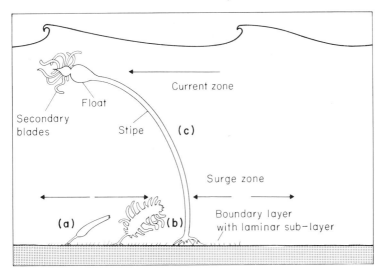

Fig. 3.2 Three stages in the development of *Ecklonia maxima*. The first stage (not shown) is microscopic and inhabits the boundary layer. The next stage (a) is a simple blade, like the mature frond of many *Laminaria* spp. Stage (b) has lateral growths and resembles the mature form of *Ecklonia radiata*. The final stage (c) has an elongated stipe and a float to raise it to the surface. Stages (a) and (b) inhabit the surge zone (Neushul 1972) while stage (c) is exposed to undirectional current.

short, solid stipe and ribbon-shaped blade (Fig. 3.2(a)), while others have a hollow stipe inflated near the junction with the blade, which lifts the plant towards the light. Some have digitate, divided blades. *Laminaria* species are found in many parts of the world, but they are the dominant genus on both sides of the Atlantic and around the coasts of China and Japan.

Ecklonia radiata, common in Australia, has when young a blade resembling a simple *Laminaria* blade. It later develops lateral, or secondary blades (Fig. 3.2(b); Mann & Kirkman 1981). *Ecklonia maxima* passes through both of these stages, and then the stipe elongates enormously, and becomes hollow, with an inflated portion at the apex, which carries the plant up to the sea surface. A much foreshortened primary blade carries secondary lateral blades, which in turn develop tertiary branches, the whole forming a writhing, tangled mass at the sea surface (Mann *et al.* 1979).

Macrocystis is known as the giant kelp. The stipes elongate until they reach the sea surface, where they are held up by gas bladders at the bases of the blades. A number of stipes originate from one holdfast. During elongation, a young frond can grow 45 cm per day (Clendenning 1964), and fully grown fronds can extend up to 60 m, trailing downstream at the surface.

3.2.1 *Laminaria* productivity

In the North Atlantic and on the coasts of China and Japan, the subtidal forests are dominated by *Laminaria* and related genera, which are characterized by having relatively short stipes, usually no more than 1 m long, and single, strap-shaped or fan-shaped blades. The coast of Nova Scotia described by Michanek (1975) as 'one of the richest in seaweeds in the world' is an example of a *Laminaria*-dominated system. In 1968, St. Margaret's Bay (about 10 km × 14 km) was selected as a study site and biomass was measured at frequent intervals on 24 transects. It was found (Mann 1972 a,b) that the total biomass averaged almost 1·5 tonnes per m of shore line, and that of this 84% was in the zones dominated by *Laminaria* or *Agarum*. The intertidal rockweeds contributed only 8·7%. Productivity of this community was measured by determining the amount of new tissue added to the base of the blade, adjacent to the meristem, at intervals of about one month. It was found that, averaged over the seaweed zone, this amounted to 1750 g C m^{-2} yr^{-1}. Averaged over the whole of the bay it was 603 g C m^{-2} yr^{-1}, compared with about 200 g C m^{-2} yr^{-1} for the phytoplankton (Platt & Irwin 1971). In other words, the algal macrophytes were contributing about 75% of the total productivity of the bay.

This rate of production is within the range of estimates made by Westlake (1963) in his review of earlier literature. He suggested that production of seaweeds lay in the range 400–1900 g C m^{-2} yr^{-1}. Field *et al.* (1977) in a preliminary report on production by *Laminaria* in South Africa gave an estimate of 1330 g C m^{-2} yr^{-1}, and Bellamy *et al.* (1968) suggested that the most favourable depth *Laminaria hypoborea* in south-west England produced about 1225 g C m^{-2} yr^{-1}. On the other hand, Johnston *et al.* (1977) chose an extremely sheltered site in a Scottish sea-loch for their study of a carbon budget for *Laminaria saccharina* and found that net productivity was only 120 g C m^{-2} yr^{-1}. These plants were almost certainly limited by the lack of turbulent diffusion in their vicinity.

As new material is added to the base of the blades, old material erodes from the tips, so that the tissue of the blade is gradually replaced. In Nova Scotia the blades were replaced something like five times a year in actively growing plants (Mann 1972b). In south-west England, Parke (1948) said that the average age of tissue at the tips of the blades was between five and seven months, implying a replacement rate of twice per year. However, her study area was at the lower intertidal, which is not an optimum habitat for *Laminaria* (Bellamy *et al.* 1968). In all these examples the new tissue that is produced at the base of the blade is eventually eroded at the tip. The process occurs at all times of the year, so that *Laminaria* beds are more or less continuous producers of large quantities of algal detritus. This detritus is readily attacked by bacteria and fungi, and passes quickly into detritus food webs (see below).

3.2.2 *Macrocystis* beds

Macrocystis or giant kelp, is of the type that develops flotation organs, grows to the surface of the sea, and spreads its canopy in the upper metre or so of the water. It is found in dense beds on the Pacific coast of North America, on the Pacific shores of South America, and on the Patagonia and Tierra del Fuego coasts of the South Atlantic up to the Falkland Islands. Towle and Pearse (1973) measured ^{14}C uptake of the blades of *Macrocystis* in the field in California and reviewed earlier attempts to measure productivity. They found that photosynthesis was greatest near the surface of the water, reducing to 5–20% of the surface value at a depth of 4 m, and 0·5–2% of surface values at 8 m. In other words, the surface canopy intercepted most of the light and carried out most of the photosynthesis. Biomass was measured in the densest part of a bed, and worked out at 5·9 kg fresh weight per m^2 of bottom. When rate of ^{14}C fixation was applied to this biomass it gave an estimated total blade production of 6·8 g C m^{-2} day^{-1}, of which 98% occurred in the canopy. However, their estimates were for a 12 h period of daylight, and they did not calculate what proportion of the carbon fixed was respired at night.

Wheeler (1978) approached the question of productivity in *Macrocystis* in two distinct ways: by measuring photosynthesis per unit area of blade, and by measuring growth. He concluded that net production has a maximum value of 6% of biomass per day, but that sustained growth rates of whole plants are more like 1–4% of biomass per day. Taking 4 kg m^{-2} as an average biomass, this gives a net production of 40–160 g fresh weight m^{-2} day^{-1}, about 1–4 g C m^{-2} day^{-1}, or 350–1500 g C m^{-2} yr^{-1}. A rough estimate of the average productivity of *Macrocystis* beds might therefore be taken as 800–1000 g C m^{-2} yr^{-1}, depending perhaps on latitude and nutrient supply, and the production to biomass ratio (P/B) as about 1·0. It seems that gross productivity is higher than in *Laminaria*, but the maintenance of such plants requires the diversion of large amounts of fixed carbon and energy for respiration and structural repair. Hence the production to biomass ratio of 1·0 is lower than for *Laminaria*, which is in the range of 2–7. If a *Macrocystis* bed is like a forest, then a *Laminaria* bed is like a cornfield, as Vozzhinskaya (1972) suggested.

3.2.3 *Ecklonia*-dominated systems

In Australia, South Africa and various other parts of the Southern Hemisphere, there are algal beds dominated by *Ecklonia*. For example, in the Benguela upwelling system near Cape Town, Velimirov *et al.* (1977) showed that there was a biomass averaging 7 kg m^{-2} fresh weight in a kelp bed. Inshore, to a depth of 8 m the dominant biomass was *Ecklonia maxima*, while from 8–20 m *Laminaria pallida* was dominant. In Australia, Shepherd and Womersley (1976) showed that at various sites in the Great Australian Bight the species contributing the greatest biomass were *Ecklonia radiata* and a fucoid *Scytothalia*. On the west coast of Australia there are shallow limestone reefs running parallel with the coast for hundreds of miles, and the tops of these have dense growths of *Ecklonia radiata* (Mann & Kirkman 1981).

There are very few estimates of the productivity of these systems. A preliminary estimate by Velimirov *et al.* (1977) for production by the *Ecklonia–Laminaria* community near Cape Town is about 620 g C m^{-2} yr^{-1}. Mann and Kirkman (1981) estimated the production of *Ecklonia radiata* in Western Australia over a 30 day period in spring, and found it to be approximately 3·2 g C m^{-2} day^{-1}, which could be tentatively extrapolated to about 1000 g C m^{-2} yr^{-1}. There was evidence that this system was severely nutrient limited (see below).

Reviewing briefly the productivity of kelp, we see that it is of the order of magnitude of 1000 g C m^{-2} yr^{-1}. The very large kelps which put a large proportion of their fixed carbon and energy into maintenance of biomass, have net production usually less than 1000 g C m^{-2} yr^{-1}, whereas the *Laminaria* communities have smaller individual plants and a more rapid turnover, leading to a higher P/B ratio and net production well in excess of 1000 g C m^{-2} yr^{-1}.

3.2.4 Production of dissolved organic matter

The net production figures discussed above refer only to visible, measurable growth of new biomass. There is, in addition, production of not inconsiderable amounts of dissolved organic matter, most of which is rapidly taken up by bacteria, thus adding to the production of particulate organic matter.

Sieburth (1969) measured the production of dissolved organic matter (DOM) by *Laminaria* in the laboratory. To overcome the problem of uptake by bacteria he used millipore-filtered sea-water and a flowing water system. In this way, DOM was carried away from the plant before the bacteria on its surface could take it up. He came to the astonishing conclusion that *Laminaria* may exude 40% of the net carbon fixed. It is difficult to understand what possible adaptive advantage to the plant could ensue from the process of fixing carbon and releasing almost half of it as DOM. Hence, there has been great caution among marine ecologists in accepting these findings. It has been thought by many that the high rate of production of DOM was a laboratory artifact, and that no plant that leaked carbon and energy at this rate could survive in nature. The dilemma was heightened by the appearance of a paper in the same year from the laboratory of Khailov and Burlakova (1969) in Sevastopol reporting that DOM equivalent to 39% of gross production was released by brown algae. The data were mostly obtained from

Fucus and *Ascophyllum*, and the rates of DOM production by *Laminaria* were lower than average. Nevertheless, their results tended to confirm those of Sieburth (1969).

There is a considerable amount of further work with *Fucus* and *Ascophyllum* which will be considered later. The most relevant subsequent work on kelps is that of Fankboner and de Burgh (1977). Working with *Macrocystis integrifolia* on the west coast of Canada, they placed plastic bags around large but immature blades and connected them to a surface float by small-bore, polyethylene tubing. Na H $^{14}CO_3$ was injected into five replicate bags and incubated for 24 h. The blades were washed for 2 h, then enclosed in fresh plastic bags and incubated for a further 24 h. Samples were taken at 2 h intervals during both incubations and analysed for labelled dissolved and particulate organic carbon. The authors suggested that if DOM were being taken up by bacteria, it would appear as particulate matter in their samples. Their conclusion was that production of DOM by these blades amounted to no more than 0·002% of carbon fixed. They pointed out that handling caused a temporary increase in DOM release, and suggested that the high exudation rates of earlier workers may be the result of mechanical or physiological stress, or of decomposition of senescent tissue.

Hatcher *et al.* (1977) constructed an annual carbon budget for *Laminaria longicrurus* in Nova Scotia. Of the net carbon assimulated during the year, it was found that 57% appeared in the frond and 8% in the stipe, but 35% was unaccounted for and was presumed lost as DOM. The gap between carbon fixed and carbon retained in tissues was very large indeed during June and July, when photosynthetic rate was at a maximum but growth was limited by lack of nutrients (see below). It seems possible that production of DOM shows marked seasonal fluctuations, and that discrepancies between the results of various workers may reflect different patterns of photosynthesis and nutrient availability. It has been noted for the phytoplankton that production of DOM reaches a maximum in waters of low nutrient concentration (Thomas 1971). Roughly speaking, it seems possible that, given CO_2 and light, carbon fixation proceeds automatically, but if low nutrient concentrations are limiting to cell division and growth the plants may not be able to use the organic carbon, which is then exuded.

It should be noted that the results of Hatcher *et al.* (1977) do not specifically distinguish between exudation of DOM from healthy tissues and leakage from decomposing tissue at the tips of the blades although by implication DOM leaked from decomposing tissue had earlier been accounted for as organic carbon stored in the blade. Fankboner and de Burgh (1977) on the other hand, specifically excluded leakage from decomposing tissue by picking immature blades for their experiments. Johnston *et al.* (1977) were able to separate exudation and leakage from decomposing tissue, and estimated that 20% of net production exuded from healthy cells, while a further 16% was lost in solution from the decomposing tips of the blades. The remaining 64% was eventually contributed to detritus food chains as particulate matter.

In summary, there is now fairly convincing evidence that in the course of a year the visible net production of *Laminaria* is passed on to heterotrophs as about two-thirds particulate matter and one-third dissolved. We do not have such clear evidence for *Macrocystis* or *Ecklonia*. However, this is not the only point in contention. It would be helpful to know whether, in addition to the net production observed as visible increase in biomass, there is a substantial invisible component given out as DOM from actively photosynthesizing cells. Present evidence suggests that under conditions of nutrient limitation there is such a component, and that it may well be of the order of 20% of net production, as shown by Johnston *et al.* (1977), or even 35% as suggested by Hatcher *et al.* (1977) and Sieburth (1969).

3.2.5   Sea-urchins and their predators

Without a doubt, the most important herbivores in kelp beds are sea-urchins. The literature on them is so abundant that Lawrence (1975) was able to publish a 74 page review, with over 250 references. The impact of the urchins on the kelp communities varies from place to place. In some situations they appear to subsist mainly on detritus which settles to the bottom. For example, Velimirov *et al.* (1977) writing of the sea-urchin *Parechinus angulosus* in the kelp beds near Cape Town stated, ' *Parechinus* is knocked off large plants swaying in prevailing swells, and probably only significantly affects kelp populations by grazing on newly settled plants'. Rosenthal *et al.* (1974) after a five year study of a *Macrocystis pyrifera* stand in southern California stated that foraging movements on attached kelp were not seen, and *Strongylocentrotus francisciamus* fed on detached pieces of macroalgae that drifted along the sea floor.

In other places it has been shown that sea-urchins influence the species mix in the algal community. Paine and Vadas (1969) removed *Strongylocentrotus franciscianus* from subtidal rocks in the Pacific at Friday Harbour at monthly intervals and found that there was a rapid increase in species diversity, followed by a domination by *Laminaria complanata* or *L. groenlandica*. In control areas having urchins at densities of 6 or 7 m^{-2} the only macroscopic algae were *Lithothamnion* and *Ulva* or *Monostroma*. Similar increases in species diversity and biomass following removal were noted by Jones and Kain (1967) in Britain, and Breen and Mann (1976b) in eastern Canada. Foreman (1977) described a situation in which an unusually heavy settlement of *Stronglylocentrotus droebachiensis* on the west coast of Canada led to (1) a great reduction in speces diversity and biomass, then (2) an increase in biomass resulting from the growth of transient species and later (3) an increase of species diversity. However, after four years the species diversity had not reached its earlier level, although the biomass was close to the pre-disturbance level. By this time, the dense population of sea-urchins had dispersed.

There are some areas, however, where sea-urchins have been responsible for almost total destruction of the kelp beds. Leighton (1971) reported the reduction of *Macrocystis* beds at Point Loma, California from 15·5 km² to 0·22 km² between 1911 and 1960, and this was attributed to dense bands of *Strongylocentrotus franciscanus* and *S. purpuratus* which at times advanced through the bed at 10·2 m per month, grazing on stipes and holdfasts and causing the plants to drift away. In eastern Canada, Breen and Mann (1976a) reported large scale destruction of *Laminaria* beds by *S. droebach-iensis*, a process that has now spread over hundreds of km of coast of Nova Scotia (Wharton & Mann 1981).

In many cases, such as the one documented by Foreman (1977) the interaction between the sea-urchins and the kelp has been obviously transitory or cyclical in nature, but in California and in Nova Scotia the situation of sea-urchin dominance and absence of kelp has been found to persist for long periods (Leighton *et al.* 1966; Mann 1977). In California the situation has often been reversed by killing sea-urchins with quicklime, but in Nova Scotia the 'sea-urchin dominated barren grounds' have persisted with no sign of kelp regeneration for over 12 years. Organic pollution was blamed for the persistence of dense urchin populations after kelp-bed destruction in California (Pearse *et al.* 1970), but the waters of Nova Scotia are relatively free of pollution, and it seems as if there are two equilibrium conditions between sea-urchins and kelp: either the urchins live in a dense kelp bed and feed on the detritus, or they destroy the kelp and live by grazing corallines and other small algae, together with any detritus from nearby kelp beds that drifts in their direction.

If the foregoing statement is true, we may ask what determines the switch fom one equilibrium to another. The situation in the Aleutian Islands is interesting from this point of view. The sea otter, *Enhydra lutris* was once abundant round the North Pacific rim from northern Japan to California (Fig. 3.3), but is now reduced to isolated populations in the Kuril, Commander and Aleutian Islands, parts of south-eastern Alaska, and to some places in British Columbia, Washington, Oregon and California where populations have been re-introduced. It is known to feed voraciously on sea-urchins. Estes and Palmisano (1974) compared two Aleutian islands, one with abundant otters and one without (Fig. 3.3). At Amchitka, where otters are abundant, there were far fewer sea-urchins (*Strongylocentrotus sp.*) and those that were present grew to larger size. At this island there was an extremely dense, almost complete cover of kelps, while at the other island there was very little macrophytic vegetation subtidally, and in many areas sea-urchins almost

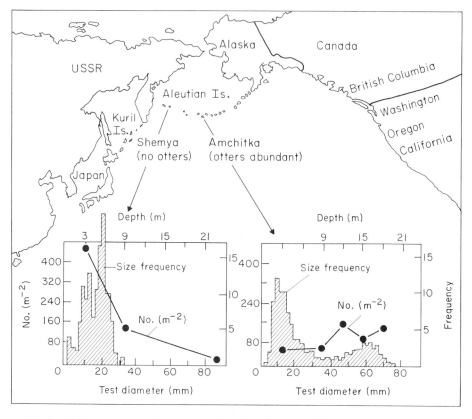

Fig. 3.3 Map to show the Aleutian Islands, and to show population density and size frequency of sea-urchins on islands with and without sea otters. (After Estes & Palmisano 1974.)

completely carpeted the bottom adjacent to the littoral zone. Dayton (1975) investigated competitive interactions between *Alaria*, *Laminaria* and *Agarum* on Amchitka, and reinforced the idea that sea otters have a powerful influence on the structure of nearshore communities. He also drew attention to the fact that these beds were once the grazing grounds of the Steller's Sea Cow (see Chapter 2) and suggested that by keeping down the sea-urchin population the otters probably made possible the high algal productivity needed to support the sea cows.

In Nova Scotia, Breen and Mann (1976a) showed that destruction of kelp beds in Nova Scotia was accompanied by a decline in biomass of the lobster *Homarus americanus*, and showed that, since lobsters are major predators of sea-urchins, it was highly probable that removal of predation pressure had led to the switch from one equilibrium condition to another, i.e.

from urchins staying under the rocks in dense kelp beds and feeding on detritus, to urchins destroying the kelp and then living on relatively barren rock. The situation is not as clear-cut as the relationship between otters and sea-urchins. Lobsters feed on a very wide range of invertebrates and as scavengers, and their population density in any given place is more difficult to determine than is the population density of otters. However, laboratory and field experiments have shown that sea-urchins and crabs are preferred over other invertebrate food, and that since in nature sea-urchins are much more abundant than crabs, sea-urchins are taken most frequently (Evans & Mann 1977). Moreover, Wharton and Mann (1981) have shown for a number of widely separated areas of Nova Scotia that high population densities of lobsters (inferred from high catches per unit effort) are associated with dense kelp beds, while low population densities are associated with urchin-dominated barren grounds. It seems that release of predator pressure leads first to increase in urchin abundance, then leads to a change in behaviour of the urchins, from cryptic detritivores to active herbivores. This would parallel the situation in the Pacific, for Lowry and Pearse (1973) showed that in an area of California where sea otters have been protected for 10 years, the kelp beds are dense and the sea-urchins live in crevices and feed on drift algae. Yet in 1962 it had been reported, for the same area, that the rocks were 'covered with urchins and abalone spaced only a few feet apart . . . and the general appearance of these rocks is barren'.

To summarize this section, it appears that in many parts of the world there is a close association between kelp beds and sea-urchins. In the presence of abundant predators, the sea-urchins live in crevices and feed on drifting pieces of kelp, together with encrusting or transient algae from the rock surfaces. When predator pressure is removed, the urchins emerge onto the upper surfaces of the rocks, collectively browse on the macroalgae, and after these have been consumed or drifted away, continue living on the tops of the rocks browsing on encrusting forms and pieces of drifting macrophyte material. The latter will now be less abundant, but the urchins can compensate to some extent by taking sporelings, corallines, diatoms, etc., from a larger surface area since they are no longer confined to crevices. Mattison *et al.* (1977) showed that urchins inside a *Macrocystis* bed moved about less, and are more often hidden, than those living on the rocks beyond the kelp bed.

3.2.6   The food webs leading to lobsters

When sea-urchins have been taken into account, there are few herbivores of importance in most kelp beds. Abalone (*Haliotis*) may occasionally rival urchins in abundance, and feed on drifting algal pieces. Some gastropods, such as *Littorina*, *Lacuna*, and *Astraea* may scrape with their radulae at the kelp tissue, but their impact is seldom very great. Hence, we find that as in seagrass beds, most of the plant biomass enters detritus food webs. Prominent in the consumer biomass of most kelp systems are the filter feeders. Rosenthal *et al.* (1974) found ascidians, *Styela motereyensis*, gorgonians, *Muricea californica*, a bivalve, *Parapholas*, an anemone, *Tealia*, and a sponge *Tethya* to be the most abundant filter feeders in their Californian *Macrocystis* bed. In the Cape Town *Ecklonia-Laminaria* bed, mussels *Aulacomya*, made up the largest biomass, followed by sponges and the holothurian *Pentacta* (Field *et al.* 1977). In the Nova Scotia *Laminaria* beds mussels of the genera *Mytilus* and *Modiolus* were the most important filter feeders (Miller *et al.* 1971). Remembering that in kelp beds the major source of primary production is macrophyte material, it is probable that the filter feeders ingest mainly kelp detritus and bacteria.

At the next trophic level are to be found various predators: starfishes, carnivorous gastropods, and sometimes octopus. Finally, there are the 'top predators', or second order carnivores, which are normally decapod crustaceans and fish. The fish component is often diverse and abundant, for example, Rosenthal *et al.* (1974) recorded 38 species. But in terms of the next trophic level, man, the most interesting carnivores undoubtedly are the lobsters. In the North Atlantic these are predominantly *Homarus*, a clawed lobster. The Canadian catch alone amounts to 14–24 million kg, worth something like $100 million. A high proportion of the catch is taken in kelp systems. In South Africa and Australia the chief catch is of 'spiny lobsters' or 'rock lobsters', which lack the large claws. In the South African kelp beds the rock lobster *Jasus lalandii* is the largest biomass of carnivore, and it feeds principally on the ribbed mussel *Aulacomya ater*. Field *et al.* (1977) give the revenue from this species at 11 million rand. In Western Australia there is a prosperous fishery for *Panulirus longipes cygnus*. The juveniles of this species are concentrated mainly on shallow (1–9 m) limestone reefs on which are abundant growths of *Ecklonia radiata*. On the sheltered side of the reefs there are also rich growths of seagrasses. Although the main commercial fishery for this species is in deeper water, 27–155 m (Chittleborough 1970), it is clear that the food chains supporting the population during its period of maximum growth of the individual lobsters is based on *Ecklonia* and seagrasses.

3.2.7 Total system function

Almost all the processes discussed in the kelp section so far have been trophic transfers—primary production, grazing, filter feeding, and predation. However, the system can only be understood properly if it is remembered that kelp plants are growing in exposed places and are in almost constant motion, driven by wind and waves. Velimirov *et al.* (1977) show diagrammatically how wind and waves affect the trophic processes

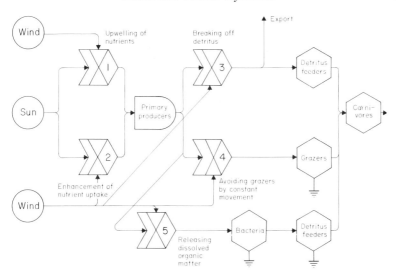

Fig. 3.4 Diagram to show work gates (labelled 1 to 5) at which wind action stimulates ecosystem function (see text). (After Velimirov *et al.* 1977.)

(Fig. 3.4). They use Odum's symbol of a workgate, in which an energy subsidy controls the main biological flow of energy by 'opening and closing the tap'. At workgate 1, offshore winds promote the upwelling of nutrient-rich water for the primary producers. At workgate 2, the waves cause water movements over the kelp surface to increase turbulent diffusion of gases and nutrient salts. At workgate 3, the waves break pieces off the plants or uproot them, thereby transferring them to detritus food webs and making open areas for growth of young plants. Workgate 4 is the effect of waves on grazers—it restricts the ability of grazers to attack the plants by keeping them constantly in motion; on the other hand it may bend the plants so that *Haliotis* can trap a frond underfoot. Finally, workgate 5 is the place where wave action erodes the tips of fronds, releasing dissolved organic matter for bacteria to use, and fine particulate detritus for the benefit of filter feeders. The details of how some of these workgates operate will be the subject of section 3.4.

3.3 ROCKWEED SYSTEMS

Rockweed is the common name for brown algae of the Fucales which are the dominant forms of the rocky intertidal zone in many parts of the world. In the Northern Hemisphere *Fucus*, *Ascophyllum* and *Cystoseira* are common and abundant. Michanek (1975) states, 'Rockweed of the genera *Fucus* and *Cystoseira* are among the richest producers if we estimate the bulk of seaweed in the ocean, but it is not yet solved how to use them'. In the Southern Hemisphere the intertidal tends to be dominated by animals and the fucoids are most commonly found in the sublittoral (Chapman & Chapman 1973). Nevertheless, the few places where quantitative studies have been made, submerged fucoids such as *Scytothalia* and *Sargassum* make major contributions to productivity (Shepherd & Womersley 1970, 1976). In tropical and sub-tropical waters *Sargassum* spp. are often prominent on coral reefs and rocky shores. Their taxonomy is very complex; according to Chapman and Chapman (1973) there are about 150 species. The best known is *S. natans* which is floating throughout life and gives its name to the Sargasso Sea, centred about 1000 km north of the eastern Caribbean. One observer estimated the area of the Sargasso Sea as 5 million km^2 and the amount of *S. natans* as 4–11 million tonnes. Michanek (1975) estimates the harvestable yield as at least 1 million tonnes (Fig. 3.1).

3.3.1 Productivity by intertidal algae and submerged fucoids

Two papers which drew attention to the great potential productivity of intertidal algae were Blinks (1955) and Kanwisher (1966). The former gave growth estimates for *Fucus* of 19–42 g m^{-2} day^{-1}. The latter measured oxygen production of clumps of *Fucus* under a bell jar, and showed that in full sunshine there was a net fixation of about 12 g C m^{-2} day^{-1} (or 20 g C m^{-2} day^{-1} gross). Wassman and Ramus (1973) studied the green seaweed *Codium fragile* which occurs in great quantities in the littoral and sublittoral zones of Long Island Sound, USA. They found that the maximum production potential was similar to that of *Fucus*, 22 g C m^{-2} day^{-1} gross.

Sargassum spp. are often major producers on shallow reef communities in the tropics. Wanders (1976) showed that near Curaçao there is a solid limestone submarine plateau at depths of 2–10 m covered by dense growths of brown algae, mainly *Sargassum platycarpum*. He estimated the yearly net production as 2550 g C m^{-2}. The author has seen similar *Sargassum* beds along the edges of coral reefs in Australia, and it is probable that they are major contributors to the primary production of reef areas (see Chapter 6).

In southern California, Littler and Murray (1974) briefly studied the productivity of 18 intertidal algae from a variety of taxonomic groups. They used the light and dark bottle technique, and integrated the results on production with those obtained from a separate study of percentage cover by each species, to give a daily net production rate (in May) of 1·3 g C m^{-2}. Of this, they found that 46% was contributed by red algae, 36% by browns, and 16% by the blue-greens. Johnston (1969) measured algal productivity in the eastern Canary Islands. He found that the intertidal zone was rather barren, but that *Cystoseira*-dominated communities were present in the sublittoral zone. In favourable sites the biomass was 1·0–1·6 kg dry weight and the net productivity up to 10.5 g C m^{-2} day^{-1}, but over much of the area the biomass was only 200–400 g m^{-2}, and the net production 1.5–3.0 g C m^{-2} day^{-1}.

There is, however, a big difference between potential production and realized production, especially in the intertidal zone. The plants are subject to longer or shorter periods of exposure to the atmosphere, and in the various types of climate this may involve stresses such as desiccation, freezing, or low salinity following heavy rainfall. Sieburth (1969) in the same series of experiments in which he reported large exudations of DOM from *Laminaria* reported that *Fucus* released about 40% of its net production in soluble form, and that *Ascophyllum* behaved similarly, though with more variability. Sieburth (1969) also subjected algae to heating, freezing, desiccation, and spraying with fresh water. Desiccation led to major losses of DOM on dehydration, the other stresses had less effect. Moebus and Johnson (1974) attempted to verify Sieburth's results with *Ascophyllum* but failed to get significant exudation from healthy, intact plants. However, when *Ascophyllum* was caused to lose more than 70% of its original water content, there was a loss of about 2 g C per 100 g organic matter; at lower levels of desiccation the losses were 1–2 orders of magnitude lower. *Fucus* had even higher rates of loss of DOM after desiccation. Since these rockweeds are exposed to some degree of desiccation every day, it seems likely that exudation of DOM, (and its uptake by bacteria) is a major component of rockweed productivity.

One of the factors that make production by rockweeds extremely variable and unpredicatble is grazing and other kinds of interactions with animals. It has long been known that the intertidal rocky shore is an area of great species diversity and marked zonation. In recent years, rocky shores have become increasingly used for experiments on grazing and competitive interactions between species. Insofar as these interactions affect the structure and functioning of the total system, they are of great interest to us, and will be considered in the next section.

3.3.2 Ecological interactions on rocky shores

The pioneer of recent experimental investigations of species interactions on rocky shores is Robert Paine, who recently reviewed progress in this field (Paine 1977). In it, he states, 'The results of experimental manipulations show conclusively that the herbivores control not only the level of production but also the species composition and structure of the attached vegetation'. The herbivores most often quoted are sea-urchins, and their activities in the intertidal zone are similar to those we reviewed earlier in the section on subtidal kelps. However, important controls by grazing have also been attributed to limpets, chitons, littorinids and fish. Black (1976) showed in California that a species of *Acmaea* which lives its entire life on the kelp

Egregia, and feeds on the tissues of the rachis and stipe, has the effect of severely weakening these structures so that they break off and drift away. He showed that plants growing crowded together were particularly susceptible to damage by *Acmaea*, and likened the activity of the limpet to a kind of pruning of the plant. Kelps which were not pruned in this way became so large that they were eventually torn from the substrate by wave action. In Europe, it is well known that the limpet *Patella* grazes on settling algal spores and sporelings, and that removal of limpets results in heavy growths of algae (Southward 1953; Jones 1948). Dayton (1971) obtained a similar result when he excluded *Acmea spp.* limpets from experimental areas on the coast of Washington, in the north-western USA. The initial algal growth was of diatoms, followed by *Porphyra*, *Enteromorpha* and *Ulva*, and after three years there was a community dominated by *Fucus*.

It has been possible to show that not only are the algae of rocky shores in dynamic equilibrium with their grazers, but the populations of grazers and detritivores are themselves subject to the most remarkable interactions with other animals and with the physical environment. For example, Paine (1974) found that when the starfish *Pisaster ochraceus* was removed from a particular intertidal zone, the community changed from one in which 30 species were present, to one totally dominated by mussels, *Mytilus californianus*. He referred to a predator which preferentially consumes a prey that is competitively dominant as a keystone species, in view of the great influence it exerts on the pattern and structure of the whole community. In other situations Dayton (1971) showed that the barnacle *Balanus cariosus* is the competitive dominant, and that it is prevented from monopolizing the avilable space by interference from limpets, by predation by the gastropod *Thais*, and by various random effects such as the impact of floating logs. Using Paine's terminology, we can see that there is little doubt that, in the rocky subtidal, sea-urchins are the competitively dominant invertebrates and that it requires predators such as sea otters or lobsters to maintain a good species diversity, including a canopy of large brown algae.

To summarize, the rocky intertidal zone is an ideal place for studying evolution in action. It provides considerable insights into mechanisms by which individual species succeed in establishing themselves and either persist or are pushed to extinction. It shows how key predators, by taking competitively dominant species, can influence the species diversity of the whole community. If, however, we treat intertidal and subtidal as part of the same system, it is not unusual to find that the rocky subtidal has far greater biomass and productivity. Although intertidal algae have the potential for very high rates of production we find that in the tropics most of the fucoids are in the subtidal possibly because alternating desiccation and downpouring freshwater makes the intertidal a difficult habitat for them. In the arctic and subarctic areas freezing and ice rafting limit fucoid performance, and in the temperate zone, where fucoids reach their full potential, there is competition for primary space with sessile animals such as barnacles and mussels.

Although there are favourable areas where rockweed production reaches or exceeds 1000 g C m^{-2} yr^{-1}, a rough estimate of the average production of the rocky intertidal areas of the world would be nearer 100 g C m^{-2} yr^{-1}.

3.4 FACTORS INFLUENCING PRODUCTIVITY OF ALGAL SYSTEMS

3.4.1 Nutrient relations

The bulk of the evidence points to marine macroalgae being limited in their growth by shortage of dissolved combined nitrogen, at least during part of each year. What is more, it appears that they are able to evolve a strategy which minimizes this limitation. The situation is best understood in the case of *Laminaria longicruris* on the coast of Nova Scotia. In 1968–70, when Mann (1972a,b) investigated the annual pattern of growth he found a marked seasonal rhythm in which growth was minimal in July, August and September, accelerated through October, November and December, reached a peak some time between January and May, then declined sharply to the summer low (Fig. 3.5(a)). Two things seemed remarkable about these results: that growth should accelerate at a time of falling temperature and reducing solar radiation, and that the peak growth rate should occur at a time when the sea-water temperature was close to 0°C.

The idea that combined nitrogen availability might be the determining factor was suggested by Platt and Irwin's (1971) data on the seasonal change

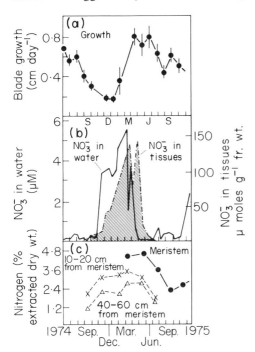

Fig. 3.5 Interactions between *Laminaria longicruris* and external and internal amounts of nitrogen. (a) Growth at the meristem, (b) seasonal variations in NO$_3^-$, (c) seasonal variation in total organic N in various parts of the blade. (After Chapman and Craigie 1977.)

in nitrate in the water of the study area, St. Margaret's Bay. There is a peak concentration in the winter (Fig. 3.5(b)). Could it be that the growth in winter was an adaptation to making maximum use of the high nutrient levels present at that time? Before that question could be settled, it was necessary to show that the observed growth was a result of active photosynthesis, and not just an elongation in certain parts of the plant as a result of food reserves being translocated from storage organs. Earlier work by Lüning (1969, 1971) had shown that for *Laminaria hypoborea* growth in spring is dependent on translocation of material stored in the overwintering frond. However, in the case of *L. longicruris* in Nova Scotia this seemed not to be the case, for growth in winter and spring was so great that the total amount of tissue formed was several times greater than the amount present at the beginning of winter.

Hatcher (1977) devised an ingenious 'underwater laboratory' for measuring the photosynthesis and respiration of *Laminaria*, in position on the sea floor. It consisted of two chambers, one light and one dark, each about 1 m tall, in which oxygen change could be monitored every 4 h for 24 h. There were three important provisions: a submerged pump for producing rapid water movement in the chamber, a set of filters for removing all phytoplankton, zooplankton and a good proportion of the bacteria from the water in the incubation chambers, and thirdly a provision for purging with nitrogen to reduce the oxygen content of the water before an experiment. Measurements were made for 24 hours once every two weeks for a year. The rigours of making the measurements in winter at night with ice on the water and a good wind blowing were very considerable but a complete year's data were obtained (Hatcher *et al.* 1977). They showed that there was a photosynthetic surplus in every month of the year except one, and that the photosynthetic surplus was enough to account for all the carbon in new tissue, except in October, November and December. During these months the plants presumably drew on stored carbon accumulated during summer. The important point was that during the period of rapid growth, January to May, the plants had a photosynthetic surplus, showing that they were adapted to taking up carbon dioxide and nutrients, even at a temperature of 0–1 C.

The question of nutrient relations was taken up by Chapman and Craigie (1977). They followed concentrations of nitrate in the water, and nitrate and organic nitrogen in the tissues throughout the seasons, and found that *Laminaria longicruis* accumulated nitrate in its tissues throughout the period when it was abundant in the water. Then, when the spring growth of phytoplankton depleted the nitrate in the sea-water, the *Laminaria* plants drew on the internal reserves (Fig. 3.5(c)). In this way they were able to maintain growth at a declining rate until mid-summer. During June and July organic nitrogen reserves were also depleted. At the peak of storage, the concentration of nitrate in the plant tissues was about 28 000 times the concentration in sea-water. Fertilization of a *Laminaria* bed with sodium nitrate in summer resulted in doubling of the growth rate.

Throughout these experiments the level of ammonium in the water was below the limits of measurement. It is, however, possible that it was being generated by excretion of animals and bacteria and was being taken up as fast as it was produced. This would partly explain the continuation of growth in summer, when nitrate was at extremely low levels.

The strategy of the species is now clear. Summer is a time when photosynthesis is most active and carbon is stored, although as we discussed earlier, much dissolved organic carbon may be released at this time. Autumn is a time when nitrate becomes available in sea-water and growth takes place using stored carbon reserves. In winter there is both a photosynthetic surplus and an accumulation of nitrate. In spring, growth depends on using nitrogen reserves. At the southern tip of Nova Scotia, near the mouth of the Bay of Fundy, there is an area of upwelling which augments the supply of nitrogen to the surface waters. The *Laminaria* plants which grow there have a higher growth rate and a longer period of rapid growth (Gagné & Mann 1981). This is additional evidence that the supply of nitrogen limits the growth of kelps.

A study of nutrient concentrations in the water surrounding a California *Macrocystis* bed (Jackson 1977) showed that for most of the year the concentration of nitrate near the surface, where most of the photosynthesis takes place, was less than 1 μM, but that at depths greater than 4·5 m they were usually greater than 1 μM, reaching a peak of 10 μM at the time of upwelling in May. Jackson (1977) concluded that to carry out the observed production, the *Macrocystis* would need to take up nitrogen from the lower levels and translocate it to the upper parts of the plants. He suggested that the 'summer die-back' observed in surface tissues (previously attributed to high temperatures) could equally well be caused by nitrogen starvation, since the nutrient concentrations near the bases of the plants are minimal at this time. Wheeler (1978) made physiological measurements of nutrient uptake by *Macrocystis*. He found that the plants took up nitrate and ammonium simultaneously, but did not take up nitrite. The uptake of nitrate, but not of ammonium or phosphate, increased when photosynthesis increased. As with *Laminaria*, it appears that the growth of *Macrocystis* in nature is influenced particularly by the availability of nitrate.

Investigation of the nitrogen relation of *Fucus* growing in Massachusetts (Topinka 1975) again gave evidence of nitrogen limitation in summer. The annual pattern of nitrate concentration in sea-water was similar to that in Fig. 3.5(b). Ammonium concentration was in the range 1–3 μg atoms per litre. As in *Laminaria*, the nitrogen content of the tissue increased during the winter and was depleted through the summer. *Fucus* differed from *Laminaria* in having a low growth rate in winter and early spring; acceleration of growth did not begin until April (1973) or June (1974) and after a peak in early summer, declined steadily until the following spring. A little further south, in New Hampshire, Niemeck and Mathieson (1976) found that although there was a growth increment during every month of the year, the average size of *Fucus* plants in the population decreased from July to January. This was attributable to the breaking free of larger plants, which took place at a high rate in autumn, after spore production. A second period of heavy loss was associated with late winter storms and ice scouring.

Topinka and Robins (1976) developed a laboratory index of nitrogen stress in *Fucus*. It was the stimulation of respiration resulting from the addition of 35 μg atoms $NH_4^+1^{-1}$. When the plants were in normal sea water (1·7 μg at 1^{-1} NH_4^+), this treatment resulted in a 38% rise in rate of repiration. When the plants had been growing in abundant NO_3^- or NH_4^+, the effect was greatly reduced. In a second study, the test was routinely applied to *Fucus* taken from the field. The increase in respiration was low when NO_3^+ was abundant in the sea-water, and highest in late summer. This was taken to mean that the plants were suffering from nitrogen limitation in summer.

3.4.2   Nitrogen relations of algal herbivores

We have seen (p. 62) that sea-urchins are the prime consumers of algal production in coastal waters. There is, however, reason to believe that algae are a poor source of protein for animals. Russell-Hunter (1970) calculated that most animals need a C:N ratio of 17:1 or better in their diet to provide a suitable balance between their requirements of protein for tissue maintenance and carbohydrates for energy. Analyses of 31 samples of *Laminaria longicruris* and *L.digitata* gave C:N ratios from 13·8–27·2 (Mann 1972a) showing that some plants, at some times of year, are very deficient in protein indeed. In fact, as later work showed, a considerable proportion of the nitrogen may be in the inorganic form. One hypothesis put forward to account for the sea-urchins' ability to thrive on a diet of *Laminaria* was that they had mechnisms for retaining nitrogen while giving off dissolved organic carbon (DOC). Field (1972) tested this hypothesis and found that the urchin *Stronglylocentrotus droebachiensis* did indeed give off dissolved organic carbon, at a rate that increased with temperature and was much greater for animals that had been actively feeding than for those that had not. At higher temperatures the amount of carbon exuded was greater than the amount ingested and respired.

A different perspective on the problem was obtained when it was discovered (Guerinot *et al.* 1977) that the same species of urchin had in their guts microorganisms capable of fixing dissolved N_2 from the sea-water. Subsequently it was shown (Guerinot 1979) that the nitrogen thus fixed was

Table 3.1 Occurrence of ^{14}C-label in amino acids of body protein of sea-urchins fed with labelled glucose, phenylalanine, or cellulose, with gut flora normal, or suppressed by antimicrobial substances. (From Fong & Mann 1980.)

	Gut flora inhibited		Gut flora normal		
	^{14}C Glucose supplied	^{14}C Phenyl-alanine supplied	^{14}C Glucose supplied	^{14}C Cellulose supplied	Status (E = Essential NE = Non-essential)
Aspartic acid	+		+	+	NE
Threonine			+	+	E
Serine	+		+	+	NE
Glutamic acid	+		+	+	NE
Proline	+		+	+	NE
Glycine	+		+	+	NE
Alanine	+		+	+	NE
Valine			+	+	E
Methionine			+	+	E
Cystine	+		trace	trace	NE
Isoleucine			+	+	E
Leucine			+	+	E
Tyrosine		+	+	+	NE
Phenylalanine		+	+	+	E
Tryptophan			+	+	E
Lysine			+	+	E
Histidine			+	+	E
Arginine			+	+	E

incorporated in the tissues of the sea-urchin. The rate of fixation was inversely proportional to the nitrogen content of the food.

Once it has been established that the sea-urchins had a rich gut flora, a more detailed study of its role was undertaken (Fong & Mann 1980). It was shown that urchins with the gut flora inhibited were incapable of synthesizing a number of amino acids (Table 3.1), so these were 'essential' amino acids in the dietary sense of the term. However, when ^{14}C glucose was fed to urchins with the gut flora intact, the label appeared in the essential amino acids of the urchin's tissue, showing that these had been synthesized by the gut flora and ingested by the urchins. Fong and Mann (1980) also showed that the gut flora had a spectrum of amino acids which corresponded more closely to that of of the urchins than did the amino acid spectrum of the *Laminaria*. Hence, it was concluded that *Strongylocentrotus* is nitrogen limited in its diet, that it supplements its intake of nitrogen by nitrogen fixation in the gut, and finally that the gut flora, by digesting plant proteins and synthesizing new ones, aids the urchins in making the most efficient use of the limited quantities of amino acids in the seaweeds.

The idea that nitrogen, rather than phosphorus, limits the productivity of phytoplankton in coastal waters was put forward by Ryther and Dunstan (1971). The evidence reviewed earlier for marine macrophytes shows without doubt that nitrogen also limits their productivity. The idea that the productivity of herbivores in the coastal waters may also be nitrogen limited is rather recent, having first been put forward by Mann (1979).

3.4.3 The effect of water movement on algal productivity

It was mentioned (p. 54) that the high productivity of marine macrophytes is in part a function of their ability to remain attached in one place while tidal and wind-driven currents move over them, constantly renewing the supply of CO_2 and nutrients in their vicinity. The best analysis of this phenomenon is given by Wheeler (1978), and the discussion which follows draws freely on his exposition. Let us first consider his empirical results (Fig. 3.6) which show that photosynthesis and nutrient uptake in discs of tissue from *Macrocystis pyrifera* blades were dependent on current speed, and that all processes fell off rapidly as the current decreased below 3–5 cm s^{-1}. Since it has been shown that in some southern California kelp beds the current velocity is generally less than 5 cm s^{-1} and frequently less than 1 cm s^{-1}, it is probable that the overall productivity of these beds is severely limited by water movement.

A theoretical analysis of the problem serves to illuminate both the results quoted above, and the earlier discussion (p. 56) about the adaptation of algae to life in different water movement regimes. Let us begin with the concept of a zone of free-stream water movement and a plant surface, and between them a thin layer, the boundary layer, which may be laminar or turbulent, in which water velocity is reduced and through which momentum, heat and mass are transported from the fluid stream to the plant surface. In quantifying this transport it is useful to think of a boundary layer resistance (R) which is a function of boundary layer thickness (T) and the diffusion constant (D) for the item being transported. The relation between them is:

$$R = TD^{-1} \tag{3.1}$$

and for a given concentration of a substance in the fluid stream, uptake by the plant will be highest when R is minimal. The boundary layer thickness, T, is a function of the skin friction drag coefficient (c_f), the Reynolds number (Re), and various other terms which for our purposes can be taken as constants, i.e.

$$T = (\text{various constants}) \times c_f \cdot Re^{-1} \tag{3.2}$$

The Reynolds number is a mathematical relation between fluid velocity (U), fluid kinematic viscosity (n) and the plant dimension (X), which in this

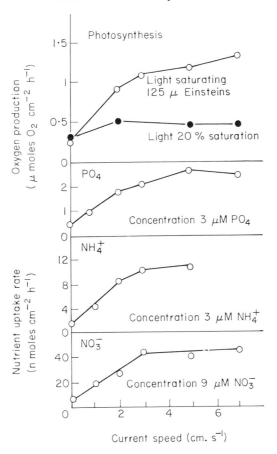

Fig. 3.6 Relationship of photosynthesis and nutrient uptake by discs from blades of *Macrocystis* to current speed in laboratory experiments. (From Wheeler 1978.)

case is distance along the blade, from the leading edge on which the current impinges:

$$Re_x = X . Un^{-1} \tag{3.3}$$

Equations 3.1–3.3 show that for a given substance, such as bicarbonate, with a known diffusion constant, R is minimal when T is minimal, and for a given skin friction drag coefficient T is minimal when the Reynolds number is maximal. The kinematic viscosity of sea-water can be taken as constant, so that the Reynolds number is proportional to the current velocity and the distance along a *Macrocystis* blade. Hence, for a given position on a blade, boundary layer resistance is minimal when the current is maximal.

Wheeler (1978) measured boundary layer thicknesses around *Macrocystis*

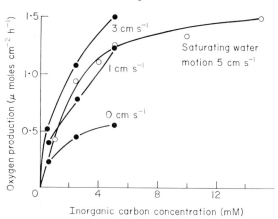

Fig. 3.7 Relation of photosynthetic oxygen production to inorganic carbon concentration in the water at various levels of reduced water motion. (From Wheeler 1978.)

blades in a water tunnel and showed that they were consistent with the presence of a turbulent boundary layer. He also studied the relationship of photosynthetic oxygen production to irradiance, concentration of inorganic carbon, and water movement (Fig. 3.7). Photosynthetic rate was close to maximum when irradiance was 125 μEinsteins m^{-2} s^{-1}, inorganic carbon was 6 mM, and current speed was 5 cm s^{-1}. When any of these variables was reduced, the rate of photosynthesis decreased. A theoretical calculation along the lines of equations 3.1–3.3 above, and incorporating some reasonable assumptions, showed that the values obtained experimentally were in agreement with theoretical prediction.

Hence, for a typical blade of *Macrocystis*, the current beyond the boundary layer should be about 5 cm s^{-1} for optimum photosynthesis and nutrient uptake. However, it should also be noted that within a given species of alga, blade shape tends to be different in different environments. In *Macrocystis*, blades of plants growing in quiet waters are more rugose than those from more turbulent conditions, and have spines which protrude further from the margin. These can be seen as adaptations to increasing turbulent diffusion in the boundary layer around the bade. In *Laminaria longicruris*, plants in sheltered localities develop thinner, wider, more frilly blades (Fig. 3.8) which probably have the same effect of increasing turbulence in the boundary layer (Gerard & Mann 1979).

Before the publication of Wheeler's (1978) results on *Macrocystis*, a field study had been initiated on the effect of water movement on growth and productivity in *Laminaria* at a site in Nova Scotia (Gerard & Mann 1979). A very exposed habitat was selected on the Atlantic coast of Nova Scotia, and

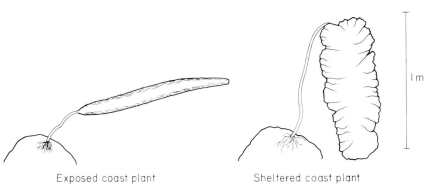

Exposed coast plant   Sheltered coast plant

Fig. 3.8 *Laminaria longicruris.* Morphology of blades of plants from sheltered and exposed sites. (From Gerard and Mann 1979.)

the performance of the *Laminaria* was compared with that at a station on the sheltered side of an island. Attempts were made to transplant individuals between sites. Those taken from the exposed site to the sheltered site survived but those taken from the sheltered site to the exposed site did not. This was because the plants growing in the sheltered site had much thinner blades which were soon torn by wave action after transplanting. On the other hand, the plants with thick blades from the exposed site began to grow new tissue from the meristem that was in the form of a wide, thin blade, showing that this was a phenotypic response to environmental conditions.

The hypothesis being tested was that water movement enhances growth and production, and it was expected that these would be higher at the exposed site. In fact, they were not. In spring, the rate of blade elongation was similar at the two sites (Fig. 3.9), but in summer and autumn the plants at the sheltered site grew about twice as fast as those at the exposed site, and had a lower ash content. The seasonal pattern of availability of nitrate and nitrite was similar at the two sites, but productivity per m^2 was considerably higher at the sheltered site. In the light of Wheeler's (1978) work it appears that the sheltered site had enough water movement to provide for the needs of the plants, for, although it was sheltered from wave action, there was a good tidal flow over the kelp bed, with semi-diurnal tides of amplitude 1–2 m. It appears that the plants at the exposed site were in fact stressed by the water movement and reacted to it by developing narrow, thick blades which had a poorer surface-to-volume ratio, and a smaller area for uptake of carbon dioxide and nutrients. In considering the effect of water movement as a 'work gate' controlling the rate of primary production, we should probably think of a dome-shaped curve. Low current speeds, below about 5 cm s^{-1}, lead to reduced rates of photosynthesis and growth. In the middle range of currents, of the order of 10 cm s^{-1}, photosynthesis and growth are

Chapter 3

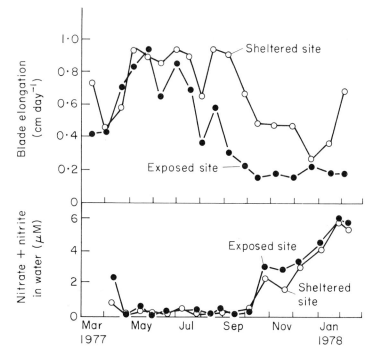

Fig. 3.9 Rate of blade elongation at the meristem of *Laminaria longicruris* and nitrate plus nitrite in the water, at a sheltered and an exposed site. (From Gerard and Mann 1979.)

optimal, but in very rough water the plants must devote more of their resources to the production of strengthening tissue, and reduce their surface area. At this level, water movement constitutes a stress.

3.4.4 The effect of light on macrophytic algal productivity

It has long been known that when algae are exposed to a range of light fluxes (photon flux densities) the form of the photosynthetic response differs from one species to another, so that, for example, the light environment required to saturate the photosynthetic mechanism is higher in *Fucus* than in *Chondrus* (Fig. 3.10). Early workers attributed the zonation of subtidal algae to their differing ability to grow in low levels of illumination. However, it must be remembered that as light penetrates water, different wavelengths are absorbed at different rates, with the red end of the spectrum being absorbed most rapidly. A later view was that seaweeds growing at depth have chromatic adaptations, being endowed with pigments which enable them to use more efficiently the light at the green end of the spectrum. Recently, Ramus

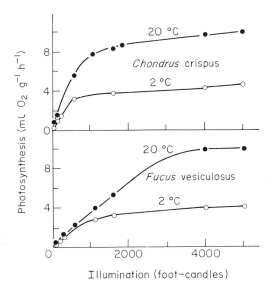

Fig. 3.10 Effect of light intensity on photosynthesis at two temperatures for *Chondrus* and *Fucus*. (From Kanwisher 1966.)

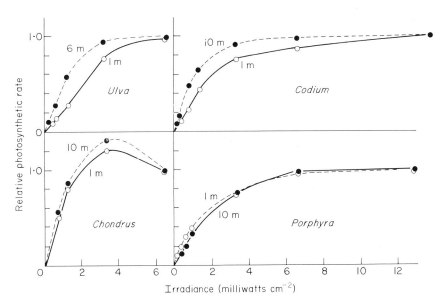

Fig. 3.11 Effect of acclimation at different depths on the photosynthesis versus light curve for four genera of marine algae. (From Ramus *et al.* 1976b.)

et al. (1976a,b) have shown that when individual species are incubated at different depths, they have the capacity to increase both total amount of pigment and the relative amounts of accessory pigments with increasing depth. This has the effect of enabling them to saturate their photosynthetic mechanisms at lower light intensities (Fig. 3.11). As a result of this work, the authors support the idea that chromatic adaptation is important, but do not consider that phylogenetic differences between species are suffcient to explain zonation with depth.

While this type of work illuminates our understanding of the ecological relationships of different species, it enables us to say very little about the effect of light on the whole ecosystem. It is clear that, as on land, light is a limiting resource in the competition between species. For example, Dayton (1975) showed how in the Aleutian Islands *Laminaria* which has an erect stipe can shade out the almost prostrate competitor, *Agarum*, and when both these genera are removed there is a bloom of red algal turf and *Alaria fistulosa*. However, it also seems to be true that the total algal community can adapt to the light regime at a range of depths, performing as effectively at 12 m as at 5 m, in fairly clear water (Mann 1972b). Kain (1966) found that the light requirements of early developmental stages of *Laminaria* spp. were higher than for the sporophytes, and suggested that this factor determined the lower limits of penetration of the kelp.

The reliance of all algae on incident light is sufficiently obvious that we may conclude that a source of pollution or disturbance which caused increased turbidity and reduced light penetration would automatically reduce primary productivity, but there appears to be no experimental demonstration of the phenomenon.

CHAPTER 4
PHYTOPLANKTON-BASED SYSTEMS

4.1   THE PRIMARY PRODUCERS

Phytoplankton is ubiquitous throughout the oceans and is the subject of an enormous scientific literature. To analyse that literature in the same degree of detail as the literature of the macrophytes (Chapters 2 and 3) is beyond the scope of this volume. Hence, attention will be concentrated on a few topics particularly relevant to the understanding of planktonic systems in coastal waters.

The obvious difference in size of the producing organisms can be seen as an adaptation to mode of life. Macrophytes owe their success to their ability to resist the movement of water and stay attached in one place. In doing so, they greatly increase turbulent diffusion over their surfaces and achieve high rates of carbon fixation and growth (section 3.4.3). Phytoplankton offer very slight resistance to water movement, but achieve the necessary uptake of carbon and nutrients by remaining small, thus increasing the ratio of surface area to volume.

It is becoming increasingly obvious that strategies of resistance to the effects of grazers are part of the overall fitness of plants. Macrophytes have two defences: their structural materials tend to be resistant to digestion by animals, and the plants often produce chemical substances which render them unpalatable. Phytoplankton have different strategies: by remaining small and well dispersed in the water they increase the difficulty experienced by larger herbivores of filtering them from the water in sufficient numbers, and by reproducing their biomass rapidly they quickly offset the losses inflicted by the smaller herbivores. A limited number of phytoplankton types also produce chemical defences.

Phytoplankton is divided for practical purposes into net plankton, retained by the finest nets that can be conveniently towed (about 64 μm apertures), and nannoplankton which passes through those nets. The net plankton in coastal waters tends to be dominated by diatoms and dinoflagellates but the nannoplankton contains large numbers of coccolithophores and a variety of other flagellate forms such as Chrysophyceae and Cryptophyceae, together with small species of diatoms. Up to the present, by far the most attention has been paid to the net phytoplankton. Many nannoplankton organisms are extremely fragile, and for many years their importance as producers was underestimated (Pomeroy 1974; McCarthy *et al.* 1974).

It has been found (Smayda 1970) that the rate of sinking of phytoplankton cells increases with cell size (Fig. 4.1). Sinking presents the cell with advantages and disadvantages. The advantage is that movement through the water column increases diffusion at the cell surface and aids the uptake of nutrients. The disadvantage is that unless checked by upward water movement, the cell will soon be carried below the euphotic zone. The idea then arose that large diatoms, which have a relatively low ratio of surface area to volume can only flourish in conditions where there is upwelling water and an abundance of nutrients. When nutrients are scarce and upwelling ceases, small cells, especially the flagellate forms which can create their own movement relative to the water by their locomotory efforts, are more successful.

Parsons and Takahashi (1973) tested this hypothesis by comparing the physiological properties of a large cell, *Ditylum brightwelli*, and a small nannoplankton cell *Coccolithus huxleyi*. They integrated the effects of

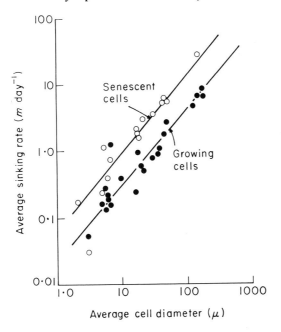

Fig. 4.1 Average sinking rate of various sizes of phytoplankton cells grown in culture and measured in the laboratory. (After Smayda 1970.)

nutrient concentration, average light, rate of sinking, rate of upwelling and mixed layer depth in an expression for relative growth rate:

$$\mu = \mu_{\max}\left(\frac{I}{K_I + I}\right)\left(\frac{[N]}{K_N + [N]}\right) - \frac{S - U}{D} \qquad (4.1)$$

where μ is the instantaneous growth rate and $\mu_{\max}$ is the maximum for the species, $[N]$ is the nitrate concentration, S is the sinking rate, U is the rate of upwelling, and D is the mixed layer depth. K_I and K_N are Michaelis–Menten constants characteristic of the nutrient response of the species or size group and I is the average photosynthetic light intensity in the water column. They were able to show that the population of large cells would have a growth rate higher than the population of small cells only in conditions of relatively high light, nutrients and upwelling. A particularly high value of one variable could compensate for a lower value in another.

4.1.1 The distribution of phytoplankton biomass

A survey of the distribution of marine algal biomass (Table 4.1) shows that two-thirds of the world's total is in the macrophytes of estuaries and coastal algal beds. The plankton biomass on the continental shelves and upwelling

Chapter 4

Table 4.1 Marine algal biomass. (From Whittle 1977.)

Province	Area (10^6 km^2)	Dry matter Mean (g/m^2)	Dry matter Total (10^6 tonnes)	Organic carbon total (10^6 tonnes)	Chlorophyll Mean (g/m^2)	Chlorophyll Total (10^6 tonnes)	Ratio carbon chlorophyll
Open ocean	332·0	3	1000	455	0·03	10	46
Upwelling zones	0·4	20	8	3·6	0·3	0·1	36
Continental shelf	26·6	1	270	123	0·2	5·3	23
Algal beds and reefs	0·6	2000	1200	545	2·0	1·2	454
Estuaries (excluding marsh)	1·4	1000	1400	636	1·0	1·4	454
Total	361·0	10	3900	1773	0·05	18·0	99

zones is less than 8% of the total. The distribution of production is quite another matter (Table 4.2), for the phytoplankton biomass turns over much more rapidly than the macrophytes. In various coastal situations it has been shown that the biomass of the nannoplankton is less variable through the year than that of the net plankton and in many cases it constitutes more than half the biomass. Places where this has been demonstrated include Scoresby Sound, East Greenland (Digby 1953), Long Island Sound (Riley 1941), Vineyard Sound (Yentsch & Ryther 1959), and the Caribbean and Pacific coastal waters of Central America (Malone 1971).

Observations on the distribution of biomass by direct counting of cells is extremely tedious, and investigators have resorted to the measurement of chlorophyll concentrations in sea-water as an index of phytoplankton

Table 4.2 Marine algal productivity. (From Whittle 1977.)

Province	Area (%)	Dry matter Normal range (g/m^2 yr)	Dry matter Mean (g/m^2 yr)	Dry matter Total (10^6 tonnes/yr)	Organic carbon Mean (g/m^2 yr)	Organic carbon Total (10^6 tonnes/yr)
Open ocean	91·9	2–400	125	41 500	56·8	18 900
Upwelling zones	0·1	400–1000	500	200	227·3	90
Continental shelf	7·4	200–600	360	9600	163·6	4400
Algal beds and reefs	0·2	500–4000	2500	1600	1136·4	700
Estuaries (excluding marsh)	0·4	200–4000	1500	2100	681·8	950
Total	100	—	155	55 000	70·5	25 000

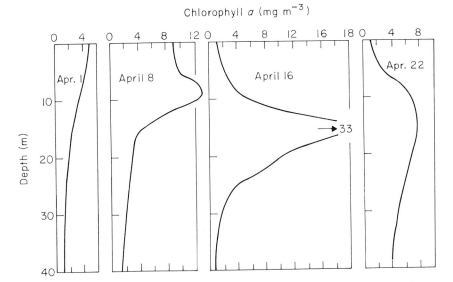

Fig. 4.2 Distribution of cholorophyll with depth in St. Margaret's Bay, Nova Scotia, showing formation and sinking of spring diatom maximum. (From data in Platt & Subba Rao 1970.)

biomass. Conversion from chlorophyll *a* measurements to carbon or dry organic matter is not simple, as the range of carbon/chlorophyll *a* ratios extends from 33 in deep, nitrate-containing waters to 100 in surface waters with no measurable nitrate (Strickland 1972). Even so, under a set of reasonably constant conditions of light and nutrients (as in a transect at constant depth over a limited geographical area) the density of chlorophyll *a* is a reasonably good index of phytoplankton biomass.

Table 4.1 shows that on the continental shelves the average amount of chlorophyll in the water column is 200 mg m^{-2}. However, except in very well mixed, shallow, coastal waters, there is a large difference in biomass distribution with depth, and a large variation on the horizontal plane as well. Most waters have a time of rapid development of a bloom of phytoplankton, and it is common to find that the chlorophyll maximum forms at or near the surface and progressively sinks as the bloom activity declines (Fig. 4.2). The dynamics of bloom formation will be discussed below (section 4.8). In the horizontal plane it has been reported (Lorenzen 1971) that there are large areas of the open ocean with nearly uniform concentrations of chlorophyll, but distribution becomes much more variable in coastal areas influenced by river runoff, strong tidal action and upwelled water. Lorenzen showed for example that one could travel long distances (tens of km) in the open ocean monitoring chlorophyll continuously and find that it always lay below 0·1 mg m^{-3}, while in the Peruvian upwelling area values ranged from under 4 to over 9 mg m^{-3} and fluctuated strongly. It is now recognized that in coastal waters patches of high phytoplankton density tend to occur with diameters of the order of 10–100 km (Steele 1976) and that their existence is of crucial importance to higher trophic levels. Zooplankton and larval fish which depend on phytoplankton for food have often been shown to need a certain critical density of food in order to survive (e.g. Mullin & Brooks 1976; Lasker 1975) (see section 4.7). That critical density often occurs within phytoplankton patches but not outside them. Hence, an understanding of the mechanisms of patch formation and persistence is necessary for an understanding of food webs in the plankton. Discussion of this subject will be deferred until we have considered the dynamics of phytoplankton production.

4.2 PHYTOPLANKTON PRODUCTION

When working with macrophytes, measurement of net biomass increase is the least ambiguous and most useful index of plant productivity (Chapters 2 and 3). In the plankton, as we have seen, estimation of biomass is itself a difficult business, and when we also consider that grazing by zooplankton is going on continuously, net biomass change is not a good guide to rate of primary production. The alternatives are to measure one of the fluxes associated with primary production, either CO_2 uptake or O_2 evolution. The oxygen method is less sensitive but in many ways easier to interpret. The radiocarbon method is more sensitive and has been widely adopted, so that comparable data are available from many parts of the world. Details of the techniques are in a manual edited by Vollenweider (1974). However, the results of ^{14}C uptake experiments are difficult to interpret, since labelled products may be released in dissolved form in the surrounding water and escape the counting procedure, and nannoplankton production may conceivably be consumed and metabolized to CO_2 before the end of an incubation. Both types of problem are more likely to be important in open-ocean, oligotrophic waters than in coastal waters, but the difficulties should be mentioned in connection with planktonic food-chains in general.

A recent contribution to the problem, with references to earlier work, is that of Gieskes *et al.* (1979). The group found that when they carried out standard ^{14}C incubations in 100 ml bottles for 12 hours (on a transect at 20°N in the Pacific) they obtained production values ranging from 20 to 265 mg C m^{-2} d^{-1}. When they reduced bottle size to 30 ml they obtained much lower, even negative results (dark fixation in excess of light fixation) and when they increased the bottle size to 3800 ml they obtained estimates 4–10 times higher than those obtained with 100 ml bottles. When they compared the results of six 2-h incubations with one 12-h incubation they found that the summed short incubations gave much higher estimates. From all this they concluded that incubation in small bottles causes significant algal mortality, and that incubations of more than two hours allow ^{14}C fixed in photosynthesis to be passed to heterotrophs and respired. When both effects are taken into consideration, they suggested that the ^{14}C incubations normally used in oligotrophic waters may underestimate primary production 5–15 times. Results which supported this view had earlier been obtained by Sheldon and Sutcliffe (1978) and Sheldon *et al.* (1973).

However, the results obtained, if true, seem to apply mainly to open-ocean situations with negligible upwelling of nutrients. The community seems to have evolved in such a way that primary production is dominated by small cells which divide rapidly using nutrients regenerated by heterotrophs living in the euphotic part of the water column. As far as we know, the phenomenon is not widespread in coastal waters. In the sections that follow, results obtained from standard ^{14}C experiments will be quoted unless otherwise stated.

A recent review of estimates of global marine phytoplankton productivity (Platt & Subba Rao 1975) set it at 31×10^9 t C yr^{-1}, of which 4×10^9 t C is thought to be fixed annually on the continental shelves and upwelling areas. The figure used to arrive at shelf productivity was 183 g C m^{-2} yr^{-1}, a year-round average of about 0·5 g C m^{-2} d^{-1}. The way in

Table 4.3 Average daily rate of phytoplankton production in continental shelf waters of various oceans, and in various areas of upwelling. (After Platt & Subba Rao 1975 and Cushing 1971b.)

Area	Primary production (g C m^{-2} d^{-1})
*Continental Shelves:**	
Atlantic Ocean	0·41
Pacific Ocean	0·52
Indian Ocean	0·71
Antarctic	0·89
Upwelling Areas:†	
Peru (1) Canary (1) Benguela (2), S. Arabia, Vietnam, Gulf of Thailand	1·0
Peru (2) Canary (3) Benguela (1) Somali, Guinea Dome, Madagascar Wedge, Orissa coast, Java, Ceylon, Flores, Banda, E. Arafura	0·3–1·0
California, Costa Rica Dome, Chile, Benguela (3), New Guinea, Andaman Is., N.W. Australia	0·3

* Upwelling areas included.
† For details of location, see Cushing (1971a).

which this daily average varies among oceans and at different areas of upwelling is shown in Table 4.3. It should be noted that none of these figures include soluble organic products released into the water (see section 4.6).

Seasonal variation in the intensity of primary production follows a pattern which varies according to latitude (Cushing 1959). In temperate waters there is normally a peak of growth and biomass in spring, which declines in summer and may be followed by a secondary peak in autumn. In arctic areas the peak is delayed until early summer and there is no second peak. In tropical waters there are usually minor variations in an otherwise fairly constant level of biomass and production. The mechanisms controlling the seasonal pattern are complex and will be discussed in section 4.8. It should be noted at once that areas with distinctive hydrological regimes, such as well mixed estuaries, or upwelling areas, depart from the general pattern mentioned above.

4.3   THE RELATION OF PHYTOPLANKTON PRODUCTION TO LIGHT

Since light is the energy source for photosynthesis, marine ecologists have long sought a method of predicting phytoplankton production from radiant energy and some easily measured parameter, such as chlorophyll. Under laboratory conditions, phytoplankton photosynthesis increases with light intensity in a more or less linear manner until a maximum value (P_{max}) is reached, the light saturation value. At high light intensities photosynthesis decreases, and this is known as light inhibition of photosynthesis. In nature, since light intensity decreases exponentially with depth in optically uniform water, the rate of photosynthesis in bright sunshine will be below maximum at the surface, increase to a maximum, and then decrease until the point is reached where photosynthesis just balances respiration (the compensation point). This occurs around the depth at which light intensity is 1% of the surface value, and may be at 100 m in clear water, but only a few cm in really turbid water.

Comparisons can be made between the P_{max} values in different laboratory and *in situ* experiments if the rate of photosynthesis is expressed in terms of mg C fixed per unit of chlorophyll *a* per hour, the assimilation number. Platt and Subba Rao (1975) have summarized the literature and shown that the values range over an order of magnitude, most lying between 1 and 10 mg C mg chl a^{-1} h^{-1}. In oceanic water Thomas (1970) found that the values in nitrogen-rich water were approximately double those in nitrogen-poor water, and Caperon *et al.* (1971) showed that the value doubled in a coastal inlet as a result of eutrophication.

In a systematic attempt to discover the extent of the variance in light–photosynthesis relations of natural assemblages of phytoplankton, Platt and

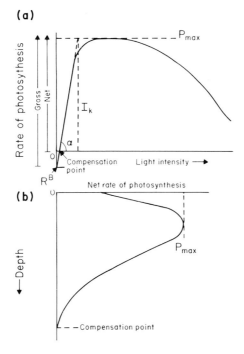

Fig. 4.3 (a) Diagram showing how net and gross photosynthesis vary with light intensity under laboratory conditions. (b) Showing the pattern of variation of net photosynthesis with depth in the sea, when surface light has sufficient intensity to be inhibiting.

Jassby (1976) determined the light saturation curves for 188 samples from three stations in Nova Scotia coastal waters. They found that they could define those curves by three parameters, α (see Fig. 4.3(a)) in mg C mg chl a^{-1} W^{-1} m^2, the assimilation number P_m^B in mg C mg chl a^{-1} h^{-1}, and R^B (in the same units), the intercept at zero irradiance. They found that both α and P_m^B varied about five-fold during the year, and both tended to decrease with depth. Hence, only the roughest kind of prediction could be made if the values were assumed to be constant. They found that α was correlated with the mean solar radiation over the three days prior to the experiment, but uncorrelated with temperature, while the reverse was true for P_m^B. These correlations did not by any means explain all the variance, and the authors concluded that information was needed on the effects of nutrients, cell size and morphology, and the time required for cells to adapt to a changing environment.

An interesting approach to a synoptic picture of the effects of light, temperature and nutrients is that of Takahashi *et al.* (1973). Using a limited amount of field data and some assumptions, they constructed model curves

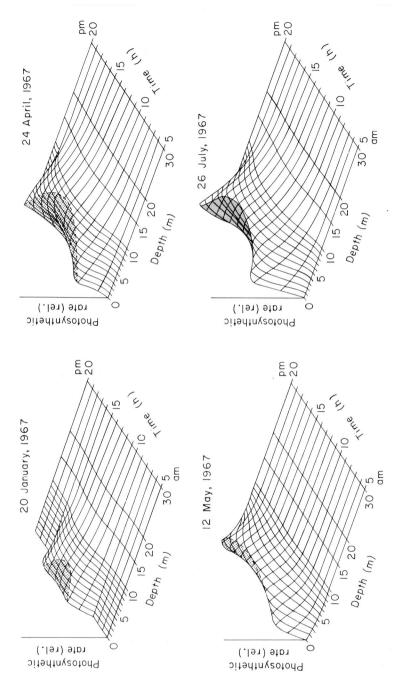

Fig. 4.4 Diagrams illustrating output of the model of Takahashi *et al.* (1973). Diurnal changes in relative photosynthetic rate, at various depths, on four different dates. The photoinhibition on July 26 was associated with low nutrients, on the other dates it was associated with low temperatures.

for the response of phytoplankton production in the Fraser River Estuary to light, temperature, nitrate and phosphate. They then measured those environmental variables, and modelled the vertical profiles for photosynthesis on an hourly basis, in different seasons. The results (Fig. 4.4) illustrate vividly the daily change in the vertical production profile, in January, April, May and July. They concluded that surface photoinhibition was associated with low temperatures in three of the four months, and with low nutrients in summer.

4   PHYTOPLANKTON PRODUCTION AND NUTRIENTS

Photosynthesis can take place for a time if a cell is provided only with light, water and carbon dioxide, but growth and hence production is dependent on the availability of various mineral nutrients (Fogg 1975). Without them, cells cannot divide, and they eventually become senescent. When nutrients are provided, the population of cells begins to increase. At least 18 minerals and various organic growth factors have been shown to be necessary for phytoplankton growth (Fogg 1975) and in theory any one of them could be in short supply and act as a bottle-neck restricting the growth process. However, the fact that nutrients are regenerated from decomposing organic matter probably means that they are supplied more or less in the proportion in which they occur in protoplasm. Hence, there is justification for discussing nutrient limitation as a general phenomenon, without specifying all of the nutrients involved. In practice, since nitrogen and phosphorus are taken up in the greatest amounts, most investigations have been into requirements for these two elements. In lakes, it has been shown that phosphorus is most commonly the dominant limiting element (e.g. Edmondson 1970), but Ryther and Dunstan (1971) suggested that nitrogen was most often limiting in coastal waters, and subsequent work has tended to confirm this.

4.4.1   Nitrogen relations

Different species react differently to changes in concentrations of nutrients; some are able to scavenge their nutrients from low concentrations, while others flourish when nutrients are abundant. A useful way of quantifying this property is by evaluating K_s, the concentration at which uptake is at half of the maximum rate when light is not limiting. It has been found that in culture, the K_s for nitrate uptake is higher for larger cells, and for those with longer generation times. It is positively correlated with the K_s for ammonium uptake. Species in coastal waters tend to have higher values than oceanic species (Eppley *et al.* 1969). MacIsaac and Dugdale (1969) made some of the earliest determinations of K_s for natural phytoplankton populations and found that the value for nitrate uptake was about 1·0 μg at l^{-1} for coastal populations and 0.2 μg at l^{-1} for open ocean populations. Eppley *et al.* (1969) also found that it is more efficient for phytoplankton cells to take up ammonia than to take up nitrate, and assimilation of nitrate tends to be inhibited by concentrations of ammonia greater than 0.5–1 μg at l^{-1}. Conway (1977) confirmed this, and postulated a mechanism.

Given phytoplankton cells and solar radiation, it might be expected that production would be proportional to the supply of nutrients, and that it might be a fairly straightforward matter to determine nutrient supply for a given area then use it as a prediction of primary production. This is not the case. In waters that are stratified to form an upper mixed layer and a separate lower layer there are two sources of nutrients, those that are regenerated in the water column in the mixed layer, so that they are rapidly made available to the phytoplankton, and those that have been regenerated in the lower layer (often on the bottom) and must await some upwelling of deep water before they are made available to the plants in the euphotic zone. From the point of view of the community in the euphotic zone, it is reasonable to refer to the first source as regenerated nutrients, and the second as new nutrients (Dugdale & Goering 1967). In the case of nitrogen, the authors suggested that the regenerated form is mostly ammonia and urea, while the new nitrogen comes as nitrate. In experiments designed to establish how much of each type of nitrogen was being used by the phytoplankton, Dugdale and Goering (1967) found that in coastal waters 60–80% of that used was ammonium, whereas in the open ocean this figure rose to over 90%. In an upwelling system off North-west Africa, Smith and Whitledge (1977) found that zooplankton excretion supplied about 25% of the nitrogen requirements of the phytoplankton. They speculated that if nutrient regeneration by benthos on the shelf and by nekton were taken into account, 75% of the nitrogen requirements of the phytoplankton might be met by nutrient regeneration rather than from nitrate supplied from deep water beyond the shelf. In Chapter 7 we shall see that the nitrogen regenerated by the benthos in coastal waters is mainly in the form of ammonia. Yet, during summer stratification, this ammonia accumulates near the bottom, and must wait for an upwelling event before it is made available to the phytoplankton. Hence, the distinction between 'regenerated' and 'new' nitrogen is rather blurred in the coastal zone.

Yentsch *et al.* (1977) devised a procedure for demonstrating nitrogen deficiency in phytoplankton populations. They found that under laboratory conditions phytoplankton that had been grown in the light under conditions of nitrogen deficiency would take up large amounts of ^{14}C if placed in the dark and given a supply of ammonium. They called this phenomenon ammonium enhancement. They followed an inshore phytoplankton population in the Gulf of Maine for a year, and showed that there were three blooms: a bloom of the diatom *Chaetoceros* in April, a bloom of the diatom *Skeleton-*

ema in July, and a bloom of the toxic dinoflagellate *Gonyaulax* in September. The phytoplankton exhibited symptoms of nitrogen deficiency only in the bloom periods. They postulated that at this time, under the stimulus of upwelled nitrate, the cells grew and divided more rapidly than nitrogen could be replaced, and developed severe nitrogen deficiency, which helped terminate the bloom. They suggested that populations existing between blooms were in equilibrium with the supply of recycled nitrogen, and that there were two distinct sets of nitrogen kinetics to be studied, those associated with bloom conditions and those associated with basal conditions. The former utilized mainly upwelled nitrate while the latter utilized mainly ammonium. Earlier observations on the relative proportions of nitrate and ammonium used by different populations might be explained by the relative frequency and intensity of upwelling.

It will be shown in Chapter 5 that bacteria using plant detritus as a carbon source actively take up nitrogen and phosphorus from the water. Thayer (1974), working in shallow estuaries near Beaufort, North Carolina, showed that nitrogen frequently (and phosphorus occasionally) was limiting to phytoplankton production and that the nutrient requirements of bacteria attached to detritus particles were a major factor in the nutrient budget of the estuary. In this sense detritus is a competitor with phytoplankton for limiting nutrients.

4.4.2 Silicate relations

Diatoms have silicon skeletons, and hence populations dominated by diatoms need a supply of silicon if they are to produce new cells. Dugdale (1972) reported that the K_s value for silicon was about 1 μg at l^{-1} and that in an upwelling system off Peru it was observed that silicate was used more rapidly than nitrate, and was probably limiting production (Fig. 4.5). Compared with nitrogen, silicon appeared to be regenerated much more slowly in the surface layers (the silicon frustules were probably enclosed in zooplankton faecal pellets and had a high sinking rate). Dugdale (1972) suggest that silicon limitation on nitrogen uptake may be a phenomenon worth closer investigation.

4.4.3 Phosphorus dynamics

Phytoplankton cells vary a great deal in their content of nitrogen and phosphorus, but Ryther and Dunstan (1971) suggested that as an approximation, they take up nitrogen and phosphorus in the ratio 10 : 1. In general, the ratio of N : P in the oceans is similar to the ratio in organisms but in almost every case where studies of nutrient uptake have been made, nitrogen has reached limiting values while phosphorus levels were still above limiting.

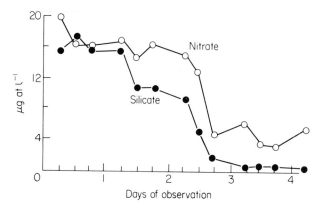

Fig. 4.5 Changes in nitrate and silicate as a ship followed a water mass for five days in the Peruvian upwelling system. (After Dugdale 1972.)

Ryther and Dunstan (1971) proposed two mechanisms leading to this state of affairs. In open oceans where upwelling is infrequent and not very intense, most nutrients are regenerated in the euphotic zone, and phosphorus regenerates faster than nitrogen. In coastal situations there appears to be a small excess in the phosphorus supply, derived from the land. Nevertheless, some interesting questions may be illuminated by the study of phosphorus

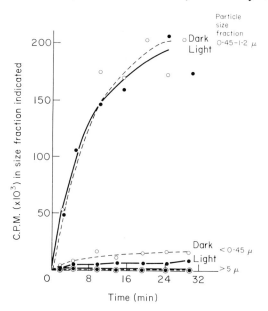

Fig. 4.6 Time course of ^{32}P uptake in various size fractions of phytoplankton from Chesapeake Bay. (After Correll *et al.* 1975.)

dynamics. A question currently being investigated is the relative importance of bacteria and phytoplankton in the uptake of phosphate from sea-water. In Chesapeake Bay, Corell *et al.* (1975) used a variety of labelling techniques to unravel a very complex set of interacting processes, but concluded that the bacteria were responsible for most of the orthophosphate uptake, and that nannoplankton were far more active in taking up orthophosphate than net plankton. Fig. 4.6 shows that most of the activity was in the organisms passing a $1·2$ μ filter but retained by an $0·45$ μ filter. Since light had little effect on the process, it was concluded that it was due to heterotrophic organisms. In contrast to this result, Harrison *et al.* (1977) found that when they incubated water from Saanich Inlet, British Columbia, and measured ^{33}P activity on particles retained by $0·45$ μ filter, the uptake in the light was approximately double the uptake in the dark. Addition of an antibiotic (Garamycin) reduced the phosphate assimilation by about 50%. Differences between these results may reflect differences in the biomasses and activities of autotrophs and heterotrophs in different waters, but there were other factors that were different; for example the ambient levels of phosphate were higher in Saanich Inlet than in Chesapeake Bay.

4.4.4 Organic and inorganic growth promoters

Two thirds of the phytoplankton species investigated have been found to have vitamin requirements, but in general it seems that the supply of vitamins is not important in controlling and limiting production (Williams 1975). Barber and Ryther (1969) found a situation in which the addition of a chelator EDTA, or of a filtered extract of zooplankton, greatly enhanced primary productivity of upwelling water. They were working on an area off Peru, where the water had high levels of N, P and Si, but the productivity was low, only $0·67$ g C m^{-2} day^{-1}. Addition of inorganic nutrients, trace metals, vitamins or amino acids did not improve productivity but EDTA or zooplankton extract did (Fig. 4.7). At $1°$ latitude on either side of the upwelling, primary production was as high as in the experiments with the zooplankton extract, suggesting that natural organic chelators had been added by the time the upwelled water reached these stations. Barber *et al.* (1971) obtained similar results on another study of Peruvian upwelling. The manner in which chelating agents work is not clear. They may immobilize toxic heavy metals, or they could concentrate essential trace elements, facilitating their uptake. Prakash (1971) showed that humic substances entering the sea with land drainage favour primary production, and suggested that they might be acting as chelating agents.

Walsh *et al.* (1974) tried using EDTA to enhance production in surface waters at the beginning of the Baja California upwelling and got negative results. Exposure of surface waters to ultraviolet light reduced their ability

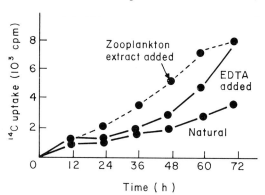

Fig. 4.7 Time course of ^{14}C uptake experiments with water from the Peruvian upwelling. (After Barber & Ryther 1969.)

to support phytoplankton growth, presumably because some organic growth factor had been destroyed. They postulated that the change from flagellate dominated phytoplankton to a diatom community, which occurs as an upwelling system develops, results from dilution of the factor present in surface waters which favoured dinoflagellates.

Yet another view of the relationship between surface and deep waters was put forward by Platt *et al.* (1977). They found in a coastal inlet that addition of less than 1% by volume of deep water to surface waters enhanced surface production by a factor of 4. Addition of greater amounts caused less enhancement (Fig. 4.8). They pointed out that such small additions of deep water could not possibly make a significant difference to the nutrient concentrations. When the deep water was shaken with activated charcoal, its property of enhancing production disappeared. Hence, there seems to be some factor in the deep water that needs to be diluted over 100 times by surface water before its effect on production is optimized. Platt *et al.* (1977) pointed out that the results of others who have worked in upwelling areas could at least partially be explained by *dilution* of upwelled water just as well as by the 'conditioning' resulting from the *addition* of some element in the surface water.

4.5   TURBULENCE AND PHYTOPLANKTON PRODUCTION

In a body of water strongly heated from above and subject to low levels of wind stress, there is stratification to form an upper, warm, mixed layer overlying a cooler, lower layer, with a layer of rapid temperature change, the thermocline, between the two. The temperature profile is as in Fig. 4.9(a). Primary production has the distribution shown in 4.9(b), with the result that

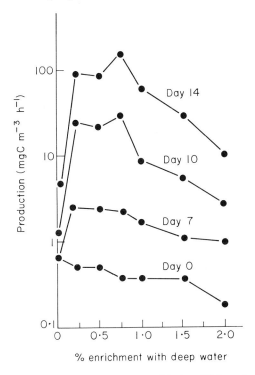

Fig. 4.8 Changes in productivity of surface waters with the addition of various percentages of deep water. (After Platt *et al.* 1977.)

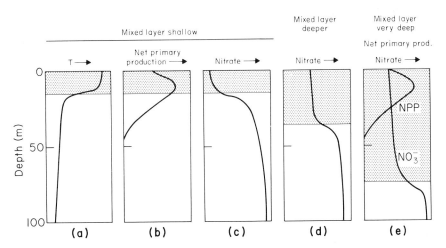

Fig. 4.9 Diagram illustrating the effect of increasing mixed layer depth on net primary production. For explanation see text.

nutrients in the mixed layer are soon depleted, giving the nutrient distribution shown in 4.9(c). Now consider the situation in which wind stress increases. Turbulent mixing in the upper waters greatly increases, causing an increase in the depth of the mixed layer, and a change in nitrate profile to that shown in 4.9(d). If the phytoplankton in the euphotic zone was nitrogen limited, it can now be expected to respond with a burst of new growth.

Next consider the situation in which the mixed layer extends to a depth of say, 75 m. Individual phytoplankton cells are now being circulated by turbulence and caused to spend much of their time below the compensation depth. The population of the mixed layer is now expending more energy on respiration than it is capturing in photosynthesis. From this we can see that turbulence in the vertical scale has two antagonistic effects. It enhances production by causing the upwelling of nutrients, but when it causes the mixed layer depth to exceed the compensation depth it decreases primary production. The balance of these two effects is the strongest factor determining the level of primary production in coastal waters. For any given level of solar radiation and turbidity of water, a critical depth can be defined at which the photosynthesis in the water column above is equal to the respiration. In open waters in winter the depth of mixing usually exceeds the critical depth and phytoplankton does not grow, but in sheltered and shallow waters the depth of mixing is usually less than the critical depth, and growth continues throughout winter. In the tropics, in most situations, there is permanent stratification with a low level of vertical mixing, and primary production is nutrient limited. The same situation applies in many temperate waters throughout the summer.

In coastal waters there are other forces besides wind, acting to create vertical mixing. One is freshwater runoff from the land. Many estuaries (see Chapter 8) become stratified with an upper, low salinity layer flowing away from the land. The shear between this layer and the salt water below causes turbulent mixing at the boundary, with the result that a proportion of the salt water is carried out to sea, and has to be replaced by deeper, nutrient-rich layers. There is, in effect, an upwelling of nutrient-rich water driven by river runoff. Tidal currents are also powerful forces generating turbulent mixing in estuaries and embayments. The end result is that in many nearshore situations the upwelling of nutrients from deeper waters is an almost continuous process. Phytoplankton biomass may be very high, and the extinction of light with depth very rapid. Nevertheless these waters are the sites of unusually intense phytoplankton production.

4.6 THE RELEASE OF DISSOLVED ORGANIC MATTER

It is now known that under certain circumstances phytoplankton cells release a considerable fraction of their photosynthate as dissolved organic matter (DOM). The released material is rapidly taken up by bacteria, and this fact, often overlooked, goes a long way towards explaining the history of conflicting data on this topic. Since the assay of ^{14}C uptake by phytoplankton normally involves counting only the particulate matter present in the incubation chamber at the end of the experiment, most of our data on phytoplankton production provide no information on carbon fixation resulting in labelled DOM at the end of the incubation.

An important paper reporting the production of large amounts of dissolved extracellular products by phytoplankton was that of Fogg *et al.* (1965). The quantitative work was carried out in fresh water, and only qualitative confirmation was obtained from the sea. The dissolved carbon in the water after 3–24 h of incubation was estimated as between 7 and 50% of the total carbon fixed in the photic zone of the water column. Since that time Thomas (1971), Choi (1972), and Berman and Holm-Hansen (1974) have reported amounts within this range released from marine algae. In general, it has been shown that the more nutrient-depleted the water, the greater the percentage of photosynthate released. None of these studies made any measurement of the uptake of the photosynthate by bacteria or other heterotrophs.

Details of attempts to measure the productivity of bacteria are discussed in Chapter 5. However, Wiebe and Smith (1977) devised ingenious techniques for simultaneously monitoring production of photosynthetic dissolved organic carbon (PDOC) and its uptake by microheterotrophs. Their approach differs from all others in two respects: (1) they devised a technique of preparing and storing labelled PDOC, so that they could introduce it into an experiment and examine its uptake and respiration without it being confused with the pathways of inorganic ^{14}C in the system and (2) they designed their experiments and analysed their results in the light of the best recent developments in tracer kinetics. The essence of the method is shown in Fig. 4.10. The system is treated as three compartments with fluxes between them. The time varying radioactivity in the three compartments PDOC, POC and DIC are determined, and from these the fluxes between them can be calculated. In a separate experiment ^{14}C-labelled DIC was used to measure rates of PDOC formation from natural plankton. The overall conclusion from two experiments with phytoplankton from an Australian estuary was that PDOC was being produced at a rate of 0·10–0·13 mg C m^{-3} h^{-1} and that it was being taken up by microheterotrophs at essentially the same rate. The rate at which labelled PDOC was being respired was only 1–3% of its

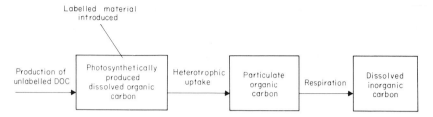

Fig. 4.10 Design of a kinetic tracer incorporation experiment to determine heterotrophic uptake and respiration of photosynthetically produced dissolved organic carbon. By following sizes of the pools the fluxes can be calculated. (From information in Wiebe & Smith 1977.)

rate of uptake. PDOC production was associated mainly with organisms in the range 20–63 μm, while maximum uptake of PDOC was in the size range 106–124 μm. The authors interpreted the latter process as uptake by bacteria attached to fairly large particles. An important aspect of their findings was that the PDOC was only about 0·1% of the total DOC. It constituted a pool of measurable size which was in steady state, with inputs of newly synthesized PDOC being balanced by incorporation. In the light of these experiments, observations on percentage of gross photosynthesis appearing in dissolved and particulate form, with no information on uptake by heterotrophs, are seen to be of limited usefulness. On the other hand, in many of the earlier measurements of ^{14}C uptake, it is possible that DOM was formed, taken up by bacteria, and these were retained on filters and counted. In that case, our data on primary production may not be too much in error, but in experiments designed to measure PDOC production, the total amount produced during incubation may have been even greater than the figures given in the literature. Iturriaga and Hoppe (1977) used antibiotics to control uptake of PDOC by bacteria. They found that bacteria were assimilating about 17% per hour of the photosynthate in solution, and that when corrections were made for this, PDOC production in Kiel Fjord and the Kiel Bight amounted to 2–21% of carbon fixed in photosynthesis. Conversion to bacterial biomass was fairly efficient, for respiration was 0·2–6% of the rate of uptake.

4.7 THE CONSUMPTION OF PHYTOPLANKTON IN THE WATER COLUMN

We saw earlier that in many situations net phytoplankton may play a minor part in primary production when compared with the nannoplankton. Similarly, it is possible that in many situations the net zooplankton are not the major consumers of organic matter (Pomeroy 1974, 1979). Nevertheless, heterotrophic consumption by microorganisms will be dealt with in Chapter 5, and we shall confine our attention in this chapter to net zooplankton. In numbers and biomass, the net zooplankton is normally dominated by copepods, especially calanoids (Raymont 1963). This point is well illustrated by some classic data from the English Channel (Fig. 4.11). The biomass is normally highest in inshore waters, decreasing as one passes towards the open sea (Table 4.4), although there may be an increase in biomass just at the edge of the shelf.

Copepods feed in two ways: by filtering the water or by seizing individual particles. The former method is most commonly used to collect phytoplankton, the latter for preying on other zooplankton. Since seizing a particle implies that it has first been perceived in some way, various writers distinguish between non-perceptive and perceptive feeding (e.g. Conover

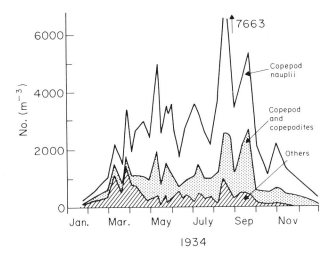

Fig. 4.11 Numbers of zooplankton caught in the English Channel between surface and 45 m, grouped as (1) copepods and copepodites, (2) copepod nauplii and (3) others. (From Harvey *et al.* 1935.)

Table 4.4 Summary of published values of zooplankton biomass and production. (Latter calculated from model given in Conover unpublished.)

Location	Mean depth (m)	No. of investigations	Biomass† (dry mg m⁻³)	Production (Kcal m⁻² yr⁻¹)
Inshore waters	1–30	5	121·6	182·9
Continental shelf	30	5	24·5	77·0
Edge of shelf	200	1	108·2	66·2
Open sea	200*	3	20·2	67·8

* Depth to which sampled.
† Salps not included.

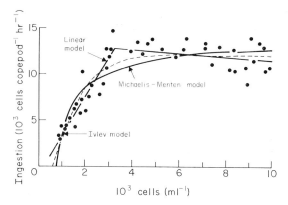

Fig. 4.12 Ingestion of *Thalassiosira* by *Calanus*. Analysis of data in terms of three models. (By Mullin *et al.* 1975.)

1978). Ideas about non-perceptive feeding have recently undergone rather radical changes (Conover 1978). In earlier work, filtration was regarded as a rather automatic process, characterized by the volume of water that an animal could sweep clear in a given time. This was not, of course, measured directly, but calculated from the number of cells ingested and their concentration in the water. In general, and not surprisingly, it was found that the food intake increased with increasing food density, until a level was reached at which the animal could feed no faster, and feeding rate was independent of food concentration (Fig. 4.12). Mullin *et al.* (1975) reviewed data on food ingestion as a function of food concentration and concluded that there was no significant difference in the fit of three models that have been used to describe such results, namely:

(1) The Ivlev equation,

$$I = I_m[1 - e^{-\delta(p - p')}] \tag{4.2}$$

where I is the rate of ingestion, I_m is the maximum rate, p is the concentration of phytoplankton, δ is a constant and p' is the concentration (if any) at which ingestion ceases;

(2) The Michaelis–Menten equation,

$$I = \frac{I_m(p - p')}{K + (p - p')} \tag{4.3}$$

where K is the half-saturation constant;

or (3) Two linear regression equations; one to fit the data in the region where feeding rate increases with increasing food concentration, and one to fit the region of saturation (see Fig. 4.12).

A feature common to almost all data sets is a threshold concentration,

Table 4.5 Critical food density below which *Calanus pacificus* begins to filter at a significantly depressed rate, given for diatoms of different sizes. (From Frost 1975.)

Food species	Mean cell diam. (μm)	Critical food density		Ingestion rate (μg C copepod^{-1} h^{-1})
		(cells ml^{-1})	(μg C l^{-1})	
Thalassiosira fluviatilis	11	1010	95	0·34
Thalassiosira fluviatilis	13	200	27	0·14
Coscinodiscus angstii	35	23	19	0·10
Coscinodiscus eccentricus	75	11	18	0·11
Coscinodiscus angstii	87	4	13	0·11

below which feeding ceases. Steele (1974) stressed the importance of feeding thresholds, since they protect phytoplankton cells from grazing to extinction and confer stability on the total system. Frost (1975) examined carefully the factors influencing the threshold feeding behaviour of *Calanus pacificus*, and found that the animals always showed a measurable feeding rate, but that there was a food concentration below which their feeding effort was less than maximal. It was dependent on the size of the food particles. When particles were large, the animals would continue feeding at a maximum rate down to a lower food density than when the cells were small (Table 4.5).

Another feature of the older view of how copepods filtered was the observation that large particles are ingested in preference to small ones, and the suggestion that this could be explained mechanistically by treating the mouthparts as a simple (but leaky) sieve (Boyd 1976). However, Conover (1978), as a result of extensive experimental investigation of the response of copepods to changing particle-size spectra, concluded that 'feeding by non-perceptive grazers on natural food does not readily lend itself to simple mechanistic analogy'. In his experiments, the animals appeared to be able to slowly increase their rate of feeding and digestion to accommodate all natural concentrations of particles without exhibiting saturation. Conover suggested that saturation phenomena are the result of exposing animals to concentrations higher than those occurring in the animal's environment, or to sudden increases without time for acclimation of the metabolic rate. He found that copepods could feed on larger ($> 70\ \mu$) particles and smaller (20–$30\ \mu$) particles, while particles of intermediate size could be excluded, and suggested that the abundance of chemoreceptors on the mouthparts (Friedman & Strickler 1975) was important in particle selection. Richman *et al.* (1977) reached similar conclusions. To sum up, Conover (1978) suggested that 'the grazers so nearly completely adapt to the prevailing food environment that resource utilization is in direct proportionality with its concentration, depending only on the concentration of the grazers, temperature and probably a few other measurable variables'. If this is true, models of transfer from net phytoplankton to net zooplankton can be made much simpler than at present. Poulet (1978) demonstrated the ability to adapt grazing pressure from one size range to another, according to food availability, in five coexisting species of copepod. He inferred that there were several instances of interspecific competition for food, but thought that coexistence of the five species was made possible by the heterogeneous nature of their environment (see section 4.8).

Conover's (1978) view that a simple mechanistic explanation of selective grazing is inadequate was supported by Donaghay and Small (1979). The estuarine copepod *Acartia clausi* was capable of selectively rejecting plastic spheres intermediate in size between the sizes of diatoms being offered, either ingesting particles on either side of the spheres or taking only the diatoms larger than the spheres. The pattern of selection depended on the size of food particles used for preconditioning.

Meanwhile, the validity of the techniques used in many grazing experiments has been challenged by Deason (1980) and by Harbison and Mc-Alister (1980). Both papers mention the possibility that the breakage of cells or colonies during feeding may change the shape of the particle spectrum and give rise to erroneous conclusions about grazing. Harbison and Mc-Alister (1980) also emphasize that the particular particle counters used size particles on the basis of their volume, while sieving apparatuses may remove particles on the basis of their linear dimensions. Hence, if a collection of phytoplankton of assorted sizes and shapes is analysed by a particle-counter, sieved, and re-analysed, the sieve may have appeared to selectively retain certain size classes in a non-mechanical manner. The debate continues, but Conover (personal communication) is confident that the general results on selective feeding will not be invalidated.

4.7.1   The significance of vertical migration

Diurnal vertical migrations in the plankton are well documented but poorly understood. It is generally agreed that the proximate stimulus for vertical migration is the level of ambient illumination, most migrating organisms tending to rise as light levels decrease, and sink as the light increases. In the open ocean it has been possible to show that layers of migrating organisms, detectable with sonic depth recorders, followed very precisely a particular level of illumination as it changed depth at dawn and dusk (Boden & Kampa 1967).

Longhurst (1976) in a review has suggested that we should recognize a diversity of benefits from vertical migration rather than search for a single unifying hypothesis. Among the possible benefits are avoidance of predation, maximization of food intake and utilization, maximization of fecundity, and finally various strategies associated with horizontal dispersion and tran-sport. In very few cases do we have experimental evidence to enable us to assess the relative importance of these benefits.

Avoidance of predation has been widely discussed in both marine and freshwater literature. Some recent papers which include a discussion of ear-lier work may be mentioned. Zaret and Suffern (1976) showed for a lake in Panama that the dominant planktivore was the fish *Melaniris chagresi*, that it can and does prey on *Diaptomus* adults when given the opportunity, but that the *Diaptomus* adults effectively escape predation by coming to the surface only at night. Turning to a totally different habitat, Robertson and Howard (1978) studied the feeding of 11 species of planktivorous fishes on a seagrass bed where the water depth was about 2·0 m at high tide and 0·3 m at low tide. By day, copepods and decapod larvae were in the water column but were aggregated near the sediment surface in low levels of illumination. By night they swam freely in surface waters and were joined by amphipods and ostracods which had spent the day buried in the sediments. Stomach contents of fish indicated: (1) a preference for the largest organisms, the amphipods, which were available only at night and were successfully taken in only low numbers relative to their abundance; and (2) a preference for the larger decapod larvae which were extremely transparent, and appeared to rely on this factor and proximity to the bottom as strategies for minimizing predatory loss. Arguments against regarding predator avoidance as the sole reason for vertical migration are summarized by Longhurst (1976). They are: (i) downward migration may stop at a depth where light is still sufficient for location by predators; (ii) other migrants go deeper than they need, to avoid visual predation; (iii) many migrants bioluminesce at night and this would seem to invite predation; (iv) many transparent forms which might be thought to be well protected from predation, undergo vertical migration. Some of these are predators themselves.

One of the prime defenders of the idea of benefits in terms of metabolism and fecundity has been McLaren (1963, 1974). In his earlier paper he sug-gested that if the animals were migrating through thermally stratified water they would feed rapidly at the higher temperatures near the surface, but in the cooler, lower layers use the food intake more efficiently to promote growth and fecundity. A consequence of the theory was that body size of animals experiencing alternating temperatures should be greater than of those experiencing a constant temperature, but when this was tested exper-imentally it was found not to be the case (Lock & McLaren 1970). In the later paper (McLaren 1974) the author pointed out that metabolic consider-ations could be rendered unnecessary by direct observation of fecundity and development rates at various temperatures. He showed for *Pseudocalanus minutus* that lower temperatures increased development times, adult size, and fecundity. He then worked out the demographic effects of vertical

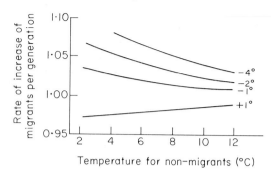

Fig. 4.13 *Pseudocalanus minutus*. Effect of lower average temperature experienced by migrants during development from stage III copepodite to maturity. Rate of population increase is given relative to equilibrium populations of non-migrants living at the temperature indicated. Early mortality (up to stage III) is assumed to be four times late mortality. (From McLaren 1974.)

migration in thermally stratified waters and showed that, with some reasonable assumptions, there was a demographic advantage in undertaking the migrations (Fig. 4.13).

It is a common, though not necessary, concomitant of vertical migration that zooplankton grazing occurs mainly at night. McAllister (1969, 1970, 1971) explored experimentally and by means of computer simulations the effects of continuous versus nocturnal grazing patterns. He showed that absence of grazing during daylight hours permits a greater phytoplankton production and hence, overall, a greater supply of food to the zooplankton. This effect may be one of the benefits attending vertical migration.

There has been controversy about the amount of energy required to make the vertical migration. Some have argued that it is so large as to nullify any feeding or metabolic advantages. Vlymen (1970) proposed that the drag coefficient C_D applicable to a leaping calanoid copepod could be expressed as a function of the Reynolds number Re, as follows.

$$C_D = K(Re)^{-n} \qquad (4.4)$$

where K and n are constants.

By photographing deceleration patterns following each leap by *Labidocera trispinosa*, he was able to quantify the drag coefficient and show that at the swimming speeds used during vertical migration the rate of energy expended for movement was no more than 0·3% of the basal metabolic rate. From this we may conclude that even quite small metabolic gains accruing from vertical migration will lead to a substantial advantage for the migrating animal. Enright (1977a,b) attempted to combine in one hypothesis the metabolic advantages to the zooplankton gained from spending time in cooler deep waters with the advantages to the phytoplankton of not being grazed during the day. He calculated that maximum net gain to the zooplankton would accrue if they migrated upwards and began feeding well before sunset. Moreover, if they did so, it would suggest that metabolic advantages were more important than predator avoidance. Enright and Honneger (1977) undertook three field experiments, each of three days duration, to find out whether the zooplankton did in fact move upwards before sunset. They obtained different results on different occasions. The results were the subject of a lively series of comments in *Limnology and Oceanography* **24** (4) but no firm conclusions were reached.

In the open ocean, there are many examples of planktonic organisms using currents at different depths as an aid to horizontal transport. In coastal waters, with their complex network of currents driven by winds, tides, and river runoff, there are fewer well-documented examples. Yet in stratified estuaries (see Chapter 8) the contrast between low-salinity water moving offshore and a compensatory shorewind flow of salt water is often very marked. Grindley (1964) showed that *Pseudodiaptomus* in an estuary migrated downwards during the day and upwards at night, except that its upward movement was halted by salinities in the range 8·5–19·0 parts per thousand. He suggested that the vertical migrations served to maintain the population in the estuary at times of normal river runoff. At times of river flood the animals were saved from being washed out to sea by their avoidance of low salinities.

To summarize, it seems probable that at different times and places vertical migration confers different advantages on those zooplankton which undertake it. Nocturnal feeding followed by a period of assimilation in cooler water appears to confer advantages in terms of greater food production and more effective utilization. Exposure to lower temperatures appears to confer advantages in terms of fecundity of adult zooplankton, and movement from one level to another is a mechanism by which various species maintain position in an estuary or carry out migrations which are an integral part of their life histories. There appears to be a component of predator-avoidance which, at least in some circumstances, may be of major importance.

4.8 THE DYNAMICS OF PHYTOPLANKTON PATCHES

Phytoplankton distribution is far from uniform (section 4.1.1) and an understanding of the mechanisms of formation and persistence of patches of high phytoplankton density is of the greatest importance for further work in food chain dynamics. High variance in phytoplankton biomass is particularly characteristic of the coastal zone, where differing degrees of vertical mixing induced by river runoff, tidal currents and wind-induced turbulence, interacting with seasonal changes in solar radiation, lead to bursts of phytoplankton production that are variable both in space and time (section 4.5). The net result of this complex set of interactions is a mosaic of diverse habitats for phytoplankton, each with its characteristic species assemblage and growth pattern. At any given time, some patches are in bloom condition, with opportunistic species (*r*-strategists) dividing rapidly; others are at the stage where nutrients have been exhausted and cells are becoming senescent and tending to sink. Still others are in temporary equilibrium with the supply of nutrients derived from heterotroph excretion, and under these conditions species adapted to thriving on low concentrations of nutrients (*K*-strategists) tend to predominate. Hutchinson (1961) in a classic paper, 'The Paradox of the Plankton', pointed out that one might expect that in a particular water mass one or a few species would eliminate all others according to the 'competitive exclusion principle', but Richerson *et al.* (1970) offered an explanation in terms of 'contemporaneous disequilibrium', suggesting that the water masses are mixed, eroded or otherwise obliterated frequently enough to prevent the exclusive occupation of each by a single species. These ideas have led to investigations of the various mechanisms, biological and physical, tending to promote or destroy the integrity of a phytoplankton patch.

4.8.1 The influence of grazing

An early contribution to the subject was that of Hardy and Gunther (1935), who noticed that there was a tendency for zooplankton to be less abundant in areas of dense phytoplankton abundance, and suggested that if, in the course of vertical migration, zooplankton encountered dense phytoplankton patches they stayed below them until currents in the deeper water carried them away from the dense patches. They called this the animal exclusion theory. By implication, then, a patch persisted because it excluded grazers. No convincing direct evidence that zooplankton are repelled from phytoplankton patches has been produced however, and the idea has not gained general acceptance. Riley and Bumpus (1946) opted for a straightforward grazing theory, suggesting that the negative correlation between zooplankton bundance and phytoplankton abundance was caused simply by zooplankton grazing. In a recent development of his grazing theory, Riley (1976) proposed that the interactions between diel migration, ordinary tidal currents and non-tidal drift could serve to perpetuate a state of patchiness. Using a vector diagram of hypothetical rotary tidal currents together with a non-tidal drift, and assuming that both are reduced at depth (say 75–100 m) Riley showed that a zooplankton population spending 9 h at the surface and 15 h at depth will have an uneven effect on the phytoplankton in the euphotic zone, grazing in some areas only once before moving on, but grazing other areas for 2–5 successive nights. He emphasized that no exclusion principle was called for, only zooplankton grazing and vertical migration under the influence of physical forcing factors. Old data from Riley and Bumpus (1946) were capable of interpretation in the light of the model, but Riley suggested that comprehensive programmes of physical and biological oceanography might be needed to test the model.

4.8.2 The influence of turbulence

The idea that a patch of phytoplankton will be subject to destruction by turbulent diffusion at its edges was used in the work of Kierstead and Slobodkin (1953). They recognized that two opposing influences were at work: (1) the reproduction of the algae giving rise to a rate of increase of the population, b, and (2) turbulent diffusivity, D. They showed that there was a critical length of patch, L_c, above which the patch could maintain itself because growth would exceed loss by turbulent diffusion. L_c was defined by the equation:

$$L_c = \pi(D/b)^{1/2} \tag{4.5}$$

For oceanic conditions some representative values might be $b = 10^{-5}$ sec^{-1} and $D = 10^6$ cm^2 sec^{-1}, in which case the critical length is of the order of 10 km. Bainbridge (1957) reviewed the evidence available at that time and concluded that the mean size of phytoplankton patches in the sea was about 16 km × 64 km. More recently, Platt and Denman (1975) developed the Kierstead and Slobodkin (1953) equation to include the effect of grazing. Their formulation was:

$$L_c = 2\pi[D/(b - R_m\lambda)]^{1/2} \tag{4.6}$$

where R_m is the maximum herbivore ration and λ is the Ivlev constant in an equation relating grazing to the concentration of phytoplankton P,

$$gP = Rm\{1 - \exp[-\lambda(P - P_T)]\} \tag{4.7}$$

P_T being the threshold below which zooplankton stop grazing.

The effect of the revised formulation is rather slight when grazing is small compared to phytoplankton growth, but becomes very important when grazing and growth are nearly in balance, i.e. $b - R_m$ approaches zero. Under these conditions, which may be approached as a zooplankton population grows rapidly after a phytoplankton bloom, the critical patch length increases rapidly. Of course, if the grazing factor R_m exceeds the growth rate b, the patch begins to decrease in concentration. In general, the effect of adding the grazing term is to somewhat increase the critical length of a patch for a particular diffusivity value. Platt and Denman (1975) extended their mathematical treatment to include the vertical dimension with a separate vertical coefficient of diffusion, and with cell division rates having a light dependent variation with depth. Solving the equation for a cell-division rate of once per day, they found the critical length to be in the range of $10-10^2$ m, except in the situation where the grazing rate is large compared with phytoplankton growth, where the critical length quickly increases to 10^3 m.

This formulation appears to be an important contribution to our understanding of the formation and maintenance of phytoplankton patches. The authors drew attention to some of the problems hindering further advance along this line. One is a lack of data on the way the eddy coefficient of turbulent diffusion responds to changes in wind stress, currents, etc., and another is lack of any explicit relationship to the supply of nutrients, the diurnal periodicity of grazing and other more subtle biological variables.

At a more empirical level, it has been found that strong wind over a water surface may produce 'windrows', or lines of floating particles parallel to wind direction, separated by distances ranging from a few cm to hundreds of metres. They were first investigated by Langmuir (1938) who found that the windrows were regions of convergence and sinking, while between them were regions of upwelling and divergence, and that they were manifestations of pairs of right and left helical vortices with axes parallel to the wind. Smayda (1970) showed that such a pattern of turbulence would tend to sort phytoplankton according to their sinking rate (positive or negative). The most obvious case is that organisms with a strong tendency to float, e.g. seaweeds and some blue-green algae, will accumulate over the convergences at the surface. However, other effects are possible. Algae whose sinking rate approximates to the rate of upwelling may accumulate in the upwelling regions. Since large diatoms tend to sink more rapidly than small naked cells, the former may be concentrated in upwelling areas while the latter are more abundant in the downwelling. Stavn (1971) observed the behavioural response of zooplankton (*Daphnia*) in upwelling and downwelling conditions and concluded that they would be concentrated in downwellings when current velocities are low, but in upwellings when current velocities are high. Leadbetter (1979) modelled the distribution of phytoplankton, herbivorous zooplankton and carnivorous zooplankton in Langmuir circulations, and showed that the patchy distribution of zooplankton led to patchy distribution of the diatoms through a complex series of trophic interactions. The model clearly showed that the distribution of organisms would change with time after the onset of the strong wind, and that the pattern would change between daylight and dark according to the diurnal behaviour of the zooplankton. Nevertheless, it is now clear that Langmuir circulations are important determinants of plankton patchiness.

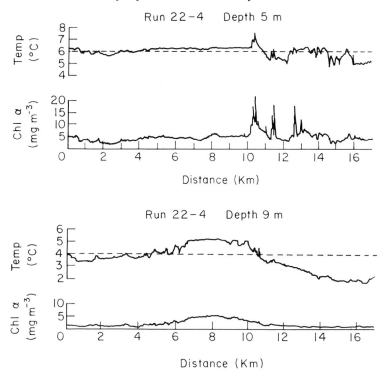

Fig. 4.14 Series of chlorophyll *a* and temperature obtained simultaneously at depths of 5 m and 9 m along a 17 km horizontal transect. (From Denman 1976.)

4.8.3 The approach through spectral analysis

New approaches to the study of phytoplankton patchiness were made possible by the introduction of a technique for continuously measuring chlorophyll concentration from a moving ship (Lorenzen 1966). In spite of the problems of converting chlorophyll to phytoplankton biomass, there has grown up a body of knowledge about the distribution of chlorophyll *per se*, which gives valuable insights into the mechanisms governing patch formation and persistence. If a ship travels a track while recording chlorophyll, a continuous record may be produced (Fig. 4.14) with distance as the horizontal axis. However, it must be remembered that the observations are not truly synoptic, and that both time and space are variables in the record. In fact, a similar record might have been obtained by anchoring the ship in one place for a considerable period and making measurements as the water flowed past. Some rough observations may be made by examining a graphical display. For example, in Fig. 4.14 it may seem that there is a similarity

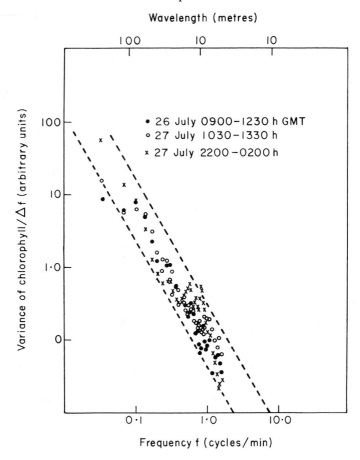

Fig. 4.15 Power spectral distribution of chlorophyll concentration in the mixed layer. Dashed lines forming envelope to data points have slope of −1.66, obtained from least-squares fit to all data points. (From Platt 1972.)

between patterns of temperature and chlorophyll. However, a far more powerful method of analysis is the statistical technique known as spectral analysis. Platt and Denman (1980) likened it to an analysis of variance where the total variance of the chlorophyll is partitioned among contributions with different characteristic scales (of space and time). A plot of partial variance against scale is called a power spectrum. When Platt (1972) analysed data obtained over three days from a ship anchored in the Gulf of St. Lawrence (Fig. 4.15) he found that a log plot of the power spectrum had a slope of −1·66. The range of his observations corresponded to length scales of approximately 10 m–1000 m. This led to the important new idea that phytoplankton abundance on these scales was controlled by turbulence, for Kolmogorov (1941) had shown that under ideal conditions the log plot of the power spectrum of velocity fluctuations should be a straight line with a slope of -1.66. Subsequent work (e.g. Denman & Platt 1975; Fasham & Pugh 1976) confirmed the initial idea of a relationship between chlorophyll and turbulence. For example, Denman and Platt (1975) showed a high level of coherence between chlorophyll and temperature over the scales of 50 m to several km. They regarded temperature as a 'passive scalar' or 'indicator' of horizontal turbulence, and concluded that the distribution of chlorophyll, like that of temperature, was governed by turbulence at these scales.

In a subsequent development of the theory (Denman & Platt 1976) the power spectrum was divided into two parts, separated by a wave number around 1 km^{-1}. At higher wave numbers (smaller space scales) the findings mentioned above hold true, but at smaller wave numbers (larger space scales) the turbulent eddies are liable to persist long enough for phytoplankton reproduction to be important in maintaining the patch. Denman and Platt concluded that in this part of the power spectrum, the slope of a log plot would be -1.

The picture that emerges from the various lines of work on patchiness is that there is a strong tendency for patches smaller than about 1 km to be formed primarily under the influence of turbulence, but for larger patches to be subject to strong biological influences tending to accentuate them, while turbulent processes are tending to erode them. Since turbulence is a function of wind speed, we shall see in the next section that the effect of turbulence can vary from day to day according to the strength of the wind.

4.8.4 Interacting physical and biological processes

Under some circumstances, point sampling is the best method of studying mechanisms underlying phytoplankton patchiness. Therriault and Platt (1978) selected an area of 12 km^2 in an exposed marine bay and chose at random six sampling stations. On 30 occasions during a year they measured chlorophyll, phaeopigments, ^{14}C fixation, ATP, carbon and nitrogen in the plankton, plus nutrients and salinity in the water. Since their stations were 1–5 km apart, they put forward the hypothesis that most of the time biological factors would determine spatial patterns of distribution, but that during wind storms physical factors might predominate. Analysis of the data revealed that there were significant correlations in the spatial organization of the phaeopigments with those of production, ammonia, biomass estimates, chlorophyll and ATP. It was thought that the phaeopigments resulted mainly from zooplankton grazing, and this was confirmed by the positive correlation between phaeopigments and ammonia, the latter presumably originating from zooplankton excretion. Hence, it was concluded that differential grazing by zooplankton was an important factor in creating phytoplankton patchiness.

Turning to physical factors at the same site, Therriault *et al* (1978) showed that during a two month period in which wind and currents were measured continuously, wind stress was a satisfactory index of turbulence as measured by high frequency current fluctuations. Wind stress measured over a whole year was then used to examine the dependence of patchiness on physical phenomena. It was found that physical processes dominated over biological and chemical processes in controlling phytoplankton variability when wind velocities were over 5 m s^{-1}. This occurred 40% of the time.

This study demonstrates the futility of trying to find a single mechanism to explain phytoplankton patchiness. There is a good deal of evidence that for scales less than about 1 km, turbulence is normally the strongest factor influencing spatial distributions of chlorophyll, but that at scales above about 1 km biological processes are important. In this study it seems likely that in the mesoscale (1–5 km), biological processes such as zooplankton grazing and phytoplankton growth are predominant for perhaps 60% of the time, but in the other 40% of the time physical processes take over and tend to smooth out the previously formed variability.

The topic of patchiness in the plankton has come to occupy a central position in our present understanding of the functioning of pelagic ecosystems. Advanced explorations of this difficult subject are to be found in Steele (1978).

4.9 SECONDARY PRODUCTION BY ZOOPLANKTON

From a system point of view we may think of zooplankton organisms as performing two major roles. First, they convert the organic matter of phytoplankton, which occurs in rather small particles of the order of ·01–0·1 mm, to larger particles of the order of 1–10 mm, thus facilitating movement of energy and materials along food chains. Second, they excrete inorganic substances such as ammonia and phosphorus, returning nutrients to the water column for use by the phytoplankton. These two roles will be considered separately.

One of the areas in which a revolutionary new method, a 'breakthrough', is badly needed, is in the measurement of secondary production by zooplankton. For convenience, sensitivity and precision there is nothing at the secondary production level that corresponds to the ^{14}C method of estimating primary production. Those estimates of zooplankton production that are found in the literature have been obtained by one of three methods. The first involves direct estimation of numbers present and organismal growth rates. The second involves calculation of the ratio of production to biomass

Table 4.6 Daily production/biomass (P/B) ratios, daily production rates, and production efficiency (total herbivore production/total primary production) for some named species of marine copepods and for some total communities. (From Conover 1974.)

Species	Locality	Season	Daily P/B	Production* mg C m^{-2} d^{-1}	Production efficiency
Calanus					
finmarchicus	Barents Sea	Year	0·019	7·8	
C. plumchrus	Georgia Strait	Feb–May	0·035–0·14	23·3	
C. helgolandicus	Off California	Apr–Sept	0·11–0·16	4–172	
Acartia tonsa	Patuxent River	July–Sept	0·50	77	
A. clausi	Black Sea	Year	0·035	0·38	
A. clausi	English Channel	Year	0·034	0·72	
A. clausi	Black Sea	Year	0·040–0·175	0·92	
Pseudocalanus					
elongatus	Black Sea	Year	0·104–0·203	2·57	
P. elongatus	Ogac Lake	June–Sept	0·033	4·55–5·67	
Oithona minuta	Black Sea	Year	0·050–0·144	1·82	
O. similis	Black Sea	Year	0·069–0·179	0·60	
O. similis	Ogac Sea	June–Sept	0·033	2·24–3·86	
Total communities	English Channel	Year	0·10	75	0·30
	North Sea	Jan–June	0·08	4·9	0·14
	North Sea	Mar–June	0·10	46	0·20
	Ogac Lake	June–Sept	0·03	11	0·07
	Pacific, Station P	Year	0·12	35·6	0·27
	Black Sea (epiplankton)	Year	0·07	25·8	0·29
	Black Sea (bathyplankton)	Year	0·12	53·2	0·17
	Ionian Sea	Summer	0·18	22·0	1·33
	Equatorial Atlantic	Spring	0·15	13·8	0·38

* Carbon assumed to be 5% wet weight in some instances.

(P/B), so that from a knowledge of biomass one may estimate production. The third approach is from metabolic considerations. Knowing something of relationships among feeding, respiration, and growth, under various environmental conditions, one seeks to predict growth, and hence production.

Methods for direct estimation of secondary production from zooplankton samples have been reviewed many times (e.g. Mann 1969; Edmondson & Winberg 1971; Conover 1974; Tranter 1976). All require an estimate of numbers present and rate of growth for each species, cohort, or life history stage that is considered to be worthy of separate consideration. In a community dominated by a small number of species with simple life histories this may be fairly straightforward, but in many cases it is extremely difficult. Table 4.6 gives some representative estimates of secondary production by named species and by whole communities. Most temperate neritic species produce between 1 and 10 mg C m^{-2} day^{-1} but the work with *Calanus helgolandicus* and *Acartia tonsa* shows that for short periods under favourable circumstances the rates of production may be an order of magnitude greater. The data for whole communities are undoubtedly very approximate, incorporating many assumptions. Yet their spread is less than for individual species, and suggests that most communities produce between 10 and 50 mg C m^{-2} day^{-1}, on average.

The ratios of daily production to biomass are also given in Table 4.6. Since biomass is much more easily measured than production, it has been hoped that some rules governing P/B ratios might be elucidated, so that measurements of biomass could be used to predict production. The range for communities is from 3% per day in Ogac Lake (a marine inlet in the Arctic) to 18% per day in the Ionian Sea in summer, with the North Sea data indicating 8–10% per day. There is little doubt that temperature plays an important role in determining P/B ratios, but much more information is needed before any attempt is made to use them for predictive purposes.

Figures in the last column of Table 4.6 suggest that zooplankton production is normally between 10 and 40% of primary production. The very high figure for the Ionian Sea can only be explained by an import to the system of primary production generated elsewhere, or by the production of a large amount of dissolved organic matter, which was not measured. Production efficiency has two major components, a grazing efficiency and a growth efficiency. That is to say, the secondary production depends on what proportion of the primary production is taken up by the zooplankton, and with what efficiency the food is converted to zooplankton tissue. It was shown in section 4.7 that according to a recent view the zooplankton, given time to adjust, can graze all the primary production more or less without limit. There are circumstances that might prevent this; for example sudden large pulses of primary production, very intensive predation on the zooplankton, or inhibition of zooplankton metabolism by low temperatures. Growth efficiency, defined as units of growth per 100 units of food consumed, has been reviewed for marine zooplankton by Corner and Davies (1971). They found that the range was from under 10% to a maximum of 50%, with considerable variation according to the stage of development. Integrated estimates for growth from egg to adult (including egg production) are most commonly of the order of 28–40%. Hence, the product of grazing efficiency and growth efficiency might well be of the order of 10–40% as Table 4.6 suggests.

Steele (1974) considered levels of primary production and fish production in the North Sea and other locations and concluded that an ecological efficiency of 20–25% was required at the herbivore level. Since the ecological efficiency of terrestrial herbivores is much lower, around 2–5%, Steele (1974) speculated that perhaps the energy of the turbulent diffusion somehow enables zooplankton to attain levels of ecological efficiency not matched in any other situation.

A rather different approach to the estimation of zooplankton production was tried out by Conover (unpublished). There were three elements in his calculation: (1) biomass data from different environments where the temperature regime is known; (2) a multiple linear regression equation for respiration, in terms of temperature and biomass; and (3) an equation linking population respiration to population production. The respiration equation was calculated by Conover and Mayzaud (1975) from 36 sets of measurements on a mixed zooplankton population at different times of year. It was:

$$\log R = 0.032T - 0.565 \log W + 2.402 \qquad (4.8)$$

where R is respiration in μl O_2 (mg dry wt)$^{-1}$ day^{-1}, T is temperature in °C, and W is dry weight per animal in μg.

The production equation was the well-known McNeill–Lawton (1970) formulation:

$$\log P = 0.8262 \log R - 0.0948 \qquad (4.9)$$

Where P is annual population production, in kcal m^{-2} yr^{-1} and R is annual population respiration in the same units. Estimates ranged from 8.4 to 483 kcal m^{-2} yr^{-1}, equivalent to 0.5–33 g C m^{-2} yr^{-1}. Average values for each type of water are given in Table 4.4. One may note that both regression equations were in the logarithmic form, so that confidence limits on the estimated production would be very wide indeed. Nevertheless, the trend to higher productivity in inshore waters is clear.

Ikeda and Motoda (1978) converted extensive zooplankton biomass data from the Kuroshio and adjacent seas off Japan to estimates of production using a slightly less sophisticated technique than Conover. Using the equation from Winberg (1956):

$$P = K_r R/(A - K_r) \qquad (4.10)$$

where P is production, R is respiration, A is the assimilation efficiency and K_r is the gross growth efficiency, they chose values of 70% for A and 30% for K_r, which gives $P = 0.75R$. This led to production estimates ranging from 10 to 60 mg C m^{-2} day^{-1} for various stations. They also calculated zooplankton excretion rates (see section 4.10).

4.10 THE ROLE OF ZOOPLANKTON IN NUTRIENT REGENERATION

The physiology of nitrogen and phosphorus excretion by zooplankton has been reviewed by Corner and Davies (1971). Nitrogen excretion varies with food-level, temperature, salinity, season and body-size. Rates are high compared with other invertebrates. Whereas crabs have been shown to excrete 0.044 μg N mg^{-1} day^{-1}, and amphipods 0.002 μg N mg^{-1} day^{-1}, zooplankton have been found to have rates of nitrogen excretion which are commonly in the range 1–10 μg mg^{-1} day^{-1} and sometimes between 10 and 50 μg mg^{-1} day^{-1}. When both phosphorus and nitrogen excretion have been studied, the rate of phosphorus excretion is commonly an order of magnitude lower than the rate for nitrogen.

Broadly speaking, there are three sources of nutrients for phytoplankton growth: those upwelled from below the euphotic zone, those regenerated by zooplankton and those regenerated by microorganisms. The relative importance of each varies from place to place and from season to season. For example, in tropical and sub-tropical waters which are thermally stratified throughout the year, upwelling is of minor importance and primary production is in balance with regeneration in the mixed layer. Under these conditions regeneration by zooplankton will be a very important factor.

McCarthy and Goldman (1979) pointed out that many phytoplankton populations seem to thrive in extremely low concentrations of nutrients, and suggested that they might be encountering minute 'patches' of higher nutrient concentrations caused by the excretion of individual zooplankters. Lehman (1980) showed that the rate of uptake by phytoplankton cells also depends on their nutrient status, and nutrient-deficient cells might be capable of very rapid uptake when they encountered such 'patches'. Jackson (1980) thought that molecular diffusion would quickly disperse the patches of high nutrient concentration, and suggested that phytoplankton of nutrient-deficient waters are adapted to meeting their growth needs with nannomolar ammonia concentrations. It should also be mentioned that in nutrient-deficient waters there may be significant numbers of algae such as *Trichodesmium* that are capable of nitrogen fixation, using gaseous nitrogen as a nutrient source.

It will be shown in Chapter 5 that bacteria provided with a carbon source may actually compete with phytoplankton for the uptake of nutrients, and are an unlikely source for regenerated nitrogen. Ciliates, on the other hand, though not classified with the net zooplankton, are important consumers of bacteria and nannoplankton, and probably contribute a considerable amount of regenerated nitrogen.

In temperate latitudes there is a seasonal alternation between what Yentsch *et al.* (1977) called bloom conditions and basal conditions, with upwelled nitrate being a major source of nutrients during the early phase of a bloom, and regenerated ammonium predominating between blooms. There have been very few attempts to determine the contribution of the zooplankton on a year round basis. Harris (1959) estimated that in Long Island Sound the net zooplankton contributed 77% of the nitrogen required by phytoplankton in one year and 66% and 43% in two others. In Naragansett Bay, which is very well mixed from top to bottom, Martin (1968) found that the contribution of the zooplankton ranged from only 2·5% of the phytoplankton requirements during spring, to more than 100% during autumn. Even in major upwelling areas, where high productivity is stimulated by the upwelled nutrients, zooplankton populations contribute around 25% of the phytoplankton requirements (see section 4.4.1).

4.11 TOTAL PLANKTONIC SYSTEM DYNAMICS

We have discussed phytoplankton production and herbivore grazing and production. We have seen that phytoplankton tends to be patchy in its distribution and that there is evidence that only in the more dense aggregations do some zooplankton find enough food to thrive and grow. The next question is, how significant is all this structure for the productivity of fish, and for total stability of the whole system? It is a very difficult topic for which we have only fragmentary answers.

A very striking example of the dependence of young fish on plankton patches was provided by Lasker (1975). He showed that first feeding larvae of the northern anchovy *Engraulis mordax* were able to feed and thrive on phytoplankton, specifically *Gymnodinium splendens*, provided the concentration of food particles was above a threshold level. The greater the concentration the more frequent were the feeding strikes and the greater the capture success. When laboratory-reared larvae were taken into the field and placed in water samples to test their feeding ability, their food intake was minimal until a dense patch of phytoplankton about 100 km long was encountered. This patch contained enough food to sustain vigorous growth of the larvae. When the patch was mixed to a depth of 20 m by a passing storm, the water was no longer suitable for rapid feeding by the larvae. Once the larvae are ready to start feeding, they must encounter good feeding conditions within 2·5 days or perish. The storm eliminated those conditions in that area and served to emphasize the critical balance that must exist between the organization of the pelagic system and the commercially important fish stocks. There is further discussion of this topic in section 9.6.

The North Sea is one of the most intensively studied bodies of salt water in the world, yet when Steele (1974) reviewed the productivity data for the planktonic and pelagic components, he was forced to state that the values were so tentative 'they must be considered as an attempt to define problems rather than to provide answers'. He noted that annual primary production ranged from 90 g C m^{-2} close inshore to 70 g C m^{-2} in the middle of the North Sea, so 80 g C m^{-2} was taken as a mean. He allowed only a 10% increase for production by way of DOM and bacteria, giving 90 g C m^{-2} yr^{-1}, or 900 kcal m^{-2} yr^{-1} as the total particulate production available to metazoan herbivores. The average zooplankton biomass was thought to be about 25 kcal m^{-2} with three generations per year and a P/B ratio of 2–3 for each generation. This led to a rough estimate of herbivore production of 175 kcal m^{-2} yr^{-1}, which is 19% of the primary production.

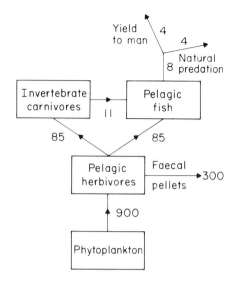

Fig. 4.16   Tentative estimates of energy flow in the North Sea pelagic ecosystem, in kcal m^{-2}yr^{-1}. (After Steele 1974.)

Steele (1974) suggested that the herbivore production was probably divided about equally between harvestable species of fish and other predators, including invertebrates. On this basis, the estimated food requirements and production of pelagic fish in the North Sea can be accounted for (Fig. 4.16).

Using these data, Steele (1974) constructed a 'rough simulation of conditions in the North Sea'. It included vertical mixing, nutrient dynamics in the mixed layer, phytoplankton production, zooplankton grazing and production, and predation on the zooplankton by fish. One of his major conclusions was that threshold feeding behaviour—cessation of feeding below a certain food density—was critical to the stability of the planktonic system. The generality of this conclusion was challenged by Landry (1976), who constructed a revised model in which thresholds were not essential for long-term stability, provided that the young stages of herbivorous zooplankton were subjected to a moderate rate of predation. Considering that neither model incorporated plankton patchiness, which we have seen can be of critical importance, we can only regard the present discussion of stability in the plankton as an early stage in a long and difficult search for understanding.

An alternative type of exploration of the properties of planktonic/pelagic ecosystems takes a more holistic approach than anything we have discussed hitherto. The view is taken that if we wish to make predictions that are valid at the ecosystem level we should try to make observations and develop hypotheses about the whole ecosystem. The problem is, that most people do not know what properties of ecosystems to study. One rather revolutionary possibility is to treat all organisms in the plankton as particles characterized by their dimensions, without regard for their taxonomic position or mode of life, and try to deduce rules governing the formation and distribution of such particles. Using the Coulter counter, Sheldon and Parsons (1967) developed the techniques for doing just this, and Sheldon *et al.* (1972), after examining the frequency distributions of particles between about 1 μ and 100 μ in many parts of the Atlantic and Pacific Oceans, put forward the hypothesis that if particles are arranged in logarithmically equal size groups, roughly equal concentrations of material occur in all groups from 1 μ to about 10^6 μ i.e. from bacteria to whales. This idea was later coupled with the idea of production (Sheldon *et al.* 1973). In the long term, biomasses in each size class remain fairly constant. Yet bacteria reproduce in a matter of hours while fish require months or years to reproduce their biomass. Hence, production in each successively larger size class should be less than in the preceding ones, and a state of balance is preserved by transferring biomass from smaller particles to larger ones in the course of feeding.

Sheldon *et al.* (1973) illustrated this point rather elegantly by showing that particle growth (measured by Coulter counter) was inversely proportional to the size of the container in which the incubation was carried out (Fig. 4.17). The suggested explanation was that large containers held a full complement of consumers, so that particle production and consumption were in balance, but small containers (50 ml) did not, since the herbivores were present in the sea at a density of about three per litre, and an average 50 ml sample did not contain any. The same rate of production as in the 50 ml bottle is in fact going on in the 20 l bottle, but it is being consumed by herbivores.

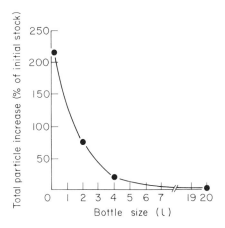

Fig. 4.17   The increase of particles in bottles of different sizes, after 24 h incubation in natural light. Particle size range 1–40 μ. (From Sheldon *et al.* 1973.)

Starting from the ideas of Sheldon *et al.* (1972, 1973) Platt and Denman (1977) developed a steady-state theory of organization in the pelagic ecosystem of the open ocean. They arranged the size classes of particles in the spectrum in an increasing octave-scale, i.e. so that the characteristic weight of a size class is double that of its smaller neighbour and half that of its larger neighbour. They then analysed the biomass flow from one size class to another in terms of turnover, metabolic losses and losses to the decomposer food chain through unassimilated ration. For the open ocean (with a deep water column) they found the latter to be negligible, and, using metabolic and growth data for multicellular heterotherms, concluded that the biomass spectrum should have a slope, on a logarithmic plot, of about -0.22. In that part of the spectrum occupied by unicellular organisms, Platt and Denman (1977) used a different set of metabolic parameters and came to the conclusion that the slope would be less negative. In general, these conclusions were in harmony with the empirical data of Sheldon *et al.* (1972, 1973).

At the time of writing, this approach has not been developed beyond the steady-state conditions which might be approximated in a relatively aseasonal, open ocean such as the Sargasso Sea. The topic is included here to introduce one of the possible future approaches to a theory of pelagic ecosystem structure in the coastal zone. More will be said about various models of ecosystem function in Chapters 9 and 10.

CHAPTER 5
THE ROLE OF MICROORGANISMS
IN COASTAL WATERS

5.1 INTRODUCTION

It is now thought that, in terfns of total energy flow, the processes in the ocean mediated by microorganisms are at least as important as those mediated by net plankton and larger organisms. Morita (1977) stated that the biomass of the bacteria in the total system may approach that of the entire fauna. Since turnover of microbial biomass is much faster than the turnover of macroscopic biomass, it follows that the flux of energy and materials is likely to be greater. Pomeroy (1974) discussed this question and suggested that something like half of the ocean's total primary production is being processed by microbes. It is probable that microbial processes are even more important in coastal waters than in the open ocean, so the views of Morita (1977) and Pomeroy (1974) are almost certainly true for the coastal zone.

The chief processes in which microorganisms are involved are the following: (1) release of much of the primary production of plankton and macrophytes as dissolved organic matter (DOM) or as dead particulate organic matter (POM) and colonization of the latter by microbes; (2) uptake of DOM by bacteria with production of living and dead POM; (3) decomposition of the less refractory portions of POM of plant origin by microorganisms; (4) consumption of bacteria in large quantities by protozoa, planktonic filter feeders and benthic detritivores; (5) conversion of some DOM to particulate form by physicochemical processes, and subsequent colonization by microorganisms; (6) sedimentation of the POM to the sea floor and subsequent incorporation into aerobic food chains on the sediment surface, or decomposition by anaerobic organisms in the deeper layers of sediment. In this chapter we shall consider the sizes of the pools of particulate and dissolved organic matter, the sources and magnitudes of the inputs, removal by microbial processes, and transfers to higher trophic levels.

5.2 PARTICULATE AND DISSOLVED ORGANIC MATTER

Differentiation between particulate and dissolved organic matter is purely operational, depending on the size of filter used. A continuum exists from organic matter in true solution, through macromolecules, colloids, and true particles which will undergo gravitational sinking. In the world's ocean, the dissolved organic carbon is thought to average 700 μg l^{-1} and to amount in total to about 1×10^{18} g C (Williams 1975) which is of the same order of magnitude as the total terrestrial biomass and very much greater than the biomass of the marine organisms. Concentrations in coastal waters are well above the average for the oceans, often in the range 1000–2000 μg l^{-1} (Fredericks & Sackett 1970). However, not much can be inferred from these figures alone; one fraction of the marine DOC is resistant to chemical change and appears to play very little part in ecosystem processes, while another fraction is extremely active and appears to turn over rapidly (Andrews & Williams 1971).

The biomass of POM in the ocean is on average only about 3% of the biomass of DOM, averaging about 20 μg C l^{-1} (Williams 1975). However, the concentration in coastal waters is generally one to two orders of magnitude greater than in oceanic waters (Parsons 1975), and is thus of the same order of magnitude as the DOM.

5.2.1 Inputs of particulate and dissolved organic matter

In Chapters 2, 3 and 4 we saw that a considerable proportion of primary production escapes the grazers and thus remains as dead particulate or dissolved organic matter. In many situations over 90% of macrophyte production travels this pathway, approximately one-third as DOM and two-thirds as POM. As we move away from the coastline phytoplankton production assumes increasing relative importance, and it seems that in reasonably productive areas, such as the continental shelves in temperate latitudes, about 10% of carbon fixed by phytoplankton is released in soluble form (Thomas 1971; Fogg 1975) (see Chapter 4). In unproductive waters the percentage is higher.

There is also a substantial input from the land by way of rivers, and this component is especially important in coastal waters. Federicks and Sackett (1970) estimated that the DOC added annually to the Gulf of Mexico by runoff was 0.6×10^{13} g C, about two-thirds of the total phytoplankton production in the area. In South India, Qasim and Sankaranarayanan (1972) found that detritus derived from terrestrial and aquatic macrophytes constituted the greater part of POC in suspension in an estuary, the contribution from phytoplankton being less than 1%. In western Canada, Naiman and Sibert (1979) made a budget for the carbon inputs to the intertidal mudflats of an estuary. River inputs predominated from October to January, epibenthic algae and phytoplankton were important during summer, and products of seagrass decomposition were available from late summer onwards. However, the inputs from the river (1956 g C dissolved and 56 g C particulate for every square metre of the mud flats) were much larger than any primary production in the estuary.

Wangersky (1977) considers that river outflow is a minor source of organic matter outside of the estuary itself, since almost all of the particulate matter sediments within the estuary as a result of changing surface charge. In his opinion, most organic particles in the sea are formed not by fragmentation of plant tissues but by conversion of DOM to particulate form. There is a variety of mechanisms that bring this about, all of them involving the collection of surface-active material at a gas–liquid interface and compression of the interface. The surfaces of bubbles and the surface film of the sea itself are sites of aggregation of surface-active molecules, and breaking waves are excellent sites for producing the necessary force of compression. Frequently, inorganic particles act as a focus for the condensation of DOM to POM. There is as yet, no unanimity about the relative importance of the various mechanisms, but it does seem clear that there is a complex equilibrium DOC–POC which often leads to the formation of amorphous organic particles. The subject was reviewed in detail by Riley (1970). Gordon (1970) recognised four categories of particles: aggregated which were chiefly carbohydrates, flakes which were mostly protein, fragments which were entirely carbohydrate, and finally unclassifiable particles.

A more recent development of our thinking about how DOM is converted to particulate form arises from the observation in lakes (Paerl 1974 1978) that bacteria form large quantities of extracellular particulate organic matter, and that they may constantly scavenge DOM from low concentrations and use it to produce new fibrils of colloidal material. Details of the morphology of the fibrils were given by Massalski and Leppard (1979). They suggested that they are used to bring about adhesion of bacteria in clumps, and adhesion of bacteria to algae, and also thought it probable that the structures recorded by Paerl were 'rope-like aggregates of the fine fibrils revealed by transmission electron microscopy'. Paerl's (1978) conclusion is that 'a small living bacterial population can turn over quite rapidly, leaving behind a larger quantity of particulate materials which have been laid down by extracellular secretion and cellular death'.

Another recent development of ideas about the origin of amorphous organic aggregates in the sea comes from Pomeroy and Deibel (1980). They showed that the faecal pellets of pelagic tunicates pass through several stages of degradation in which they ressemble various kinds of aggregates that have previously been described, but whose origin was unknown. They suggested that the tunicates may play an important role in marine planktonic food webs (see also section 9.3).

There is a positive correlation between the concentration of POC in an area and the plankton productivity of that area (Wangersky 1977), but the peak of the POC concentration usually occurs a considerable time after the bloom of phytoplankton, suggesting that the phytoplankton production augments the pool of DOC, after which a conversion of DOC to POC occurs. This sequence of events was demonstrated by Parsons *et al.* (1970) in the Strait of Georgia, on the west coast of Canada, and led him to postulate the general sequence of events shown in Fig. 5.1.

In summarizing the situation regarding DOM and POM, we may say that the total amounts in solution range from less than 0.5 mg C l^{-1} off-

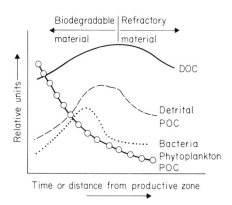

Fig. 5.1 Schematic diagram showing peaks of DOC, POC and bacteria, all occurring after the phytoplankton maximum. (After Parsons 1975.)

shore to over 2 mg C l⁻¹ close to shore. The range is not very great, because a large proportion of the substances coming into solution are readily transformed by bacteria. The concentration of POM in suspension has a greater range, from 0·01–2·0 mg C l⁻¹, with higher concentrations in estuaries and coastal waters generally.

5.2.2 Sedimentation of particulate organic matter

In general, the place to look for the greatest concentration of particulate organic matter is at the sediment–water interface. Almost all non-living particles tend to sink, and unless consumed, continue to do so until they reach the sediment. It has been shown that for various coastal waters that there is relationship between primary production in the water column and the flux of carbon to the sediment surface (Hargrave 1973, 1975). However, the relationship is not a simple one. The greater the depth of the water column, the greater the proportion of organic matter is decomposed before it reaches the bottom. Furthermore, the greater the depth of the mixed layer, the greater the amount of mineralization occurring in the water column. Hargrave (1980) made a detailed analysis of the sedimentation process as mixed-layer depth changed with season, and the results are summarized in Fig. 5.2. In winter, when the water is not stratified and the mixed layer is

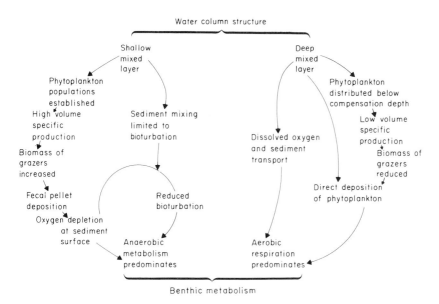

Fig. 5.2 Diagram illustrating the two main pathways by which organic matter is supplied to the sediments, according to whether the mixed layer is deep or shallow. (From Hargrave 1980.)

deep, phytoplankton is distributed below the mixed layer depth and productivity is low. The biomass of grazers is low, and the chief mode of sedimentation is by direct sinking of phytoplankton. In summer, when water is stratified and the mixed layer is shallow, phytoplankton blooms occur, populations of zooplankton increase, and the main method of sedimentation is by the sinking of zooplankton faecal pellets.

This seasonal pattern is modified in other locations by pulses of input from river runoff, transport of detritus from macrophyte beds, and the sinking of the amorphous organic particles described earlier. Detailed consideration of these factors will be given in the chapter on benthic systems. The main point to establish at this stage is that particulate and dissolved organic matter occurs throughout the water column, but that particularly high concentrations occur on and in the sediments. In the discussion of microbial processes that follows, the water column and the sediments will be treated separately.

5.3   MICROBIAL PROCESSES IN THE WATER COLUMN

It has proved difficult to get accurate measurements of either the biomass or the activity of microorganisms in the water column. Early attempts to determine bacterial numbers in sea-water relied on culturing on agar plates and counting colonies. However, the diversity of bacterial types in the sea is very great, and any one culture technique permits the detection of only a small fraction of the total (Morita 1977). Direct counting by epifluorescent microscopy is thought to be reliable, but the problems of concentrating the organisms that are free-living in sea-water makes the use of the method extremely tedious. Morita (1977) and Sieburth (1976) both give estimates of bacterial numbers in the euphotic zone as 10^4–10^5 ml^{-1}. Sieburth (1976) states that this is equivalent to a biomass of 1·5–8 mg C m^{-3}. Ferguson and Rublee (1976) found concentrations of bacteria averaging $6·6 \times 10^5$ cells ml^{-1} in coastal water off Carolina, and commented that several other workers had found 10^5 ml^{-1} to be characteristic of coastal waters. In the nearby Newport River Estuary, Palumbo and Ferguson (1978) found 10^6–10^7 ml^{-1}. Hoppé (1978) used autoradiography to distinguish active from inactive bacteria and found that in the Baltic the annual average number of *active* bacteria ranged from $4·5 \times 10^5$ ml^{-1} in offshore water to $9·5 \times 10^5$ ml^{-1} in polluted costal waters. The percentage of those present that were active ranged from 10% in winter to 56% in summer.

Most investigators have found that roughly 80% of the bacteria in the water column of the open ocean are to be found floating freely, but Wangersky (1977) argues that those attached to particulate matter are much more likely to be metabolically active. Those floating freely are so close to the specific gravity of sea-water that they are likely to move with the water at all times and have no effective mechanism for overcoming boundary layer resistance (see pp. 76 and 84). Those attached to particles are likely to move either faster or slower than the surrounding water and are thus constantly exposed to new water. This should enable them to take up organic matter more rapidly. However, this conclusion is at variance with the results of Williams (1970) who, when working on rates of substrate utilization (see below), found that the most active organisms passed through a 1·2 μm mean pore size filter.

Hanson and Wiebe (1977) suggested that there may be differences between inshore and offshore waters in respect of the proportion of bacteria attached to detritus particles. As an index of bacterial activity they used the rate of uptake of ^{14}C-glucose. On the edge of the continental shelf of the south-eastern USA they found that 80% of the uptake was by particles less than 3 μm diameter, and 93% was by particles less than 8 μm. Hence, they showed that the bacteria not attached to particles comprise 80% of the *activity*, which is in conflict with the views of Wangersky quoted above. When Hanson and Wiebe (1977) sampled about 8 km from shore they found that particles under 8 μm accounted for only 35–45% of the uptake. At 4 km from shore, and in tidal creeks, over 80% of the activity was associated with particles greater than 3 μm in diameter. Almost all the uptake by this fraction was found to be carried out by bacteria attached to detritus. There were marked tidal cycles, with the greatest activity occurring near low ebb tide (Fig. 5.3). The authors were aware of one problem with these experiments which they stated as follows:

> It is possible that many of the bacteria in the sea do not utilize glucose, or utilize it at very low rates, and that the bacteria which actively take up glucose are preferentially attached to particles. This would alter the picture we have described, and it would be well to keep this possibility in mind.

5.3.1   Measures of microbial activity

One approach to understanding the relative importance of microorganisms in the water column is to separate various size classes from the plankton and measure their rates of respiration. To do this, it is first necessary to concentrate organisms from a large volume of water, without impairing the metabolism of the organisms. Pomeroy and Johannes (1966, 1968) succeeded in doing this and found that the respiration of the microorganisms (bacteria and Protista) accounted for over 90% of the total plankton respiration. This result has been confirmed in various parts of the world (Pomeroy 1974). The method does not, of course, distinguish between respiration due to autotrophic and that due to heterotrophic organisms. If a large proportion of the

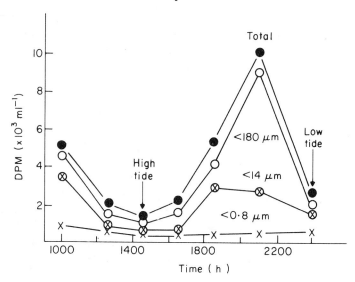

Fig. 5.3 Heterotrophic activity in creek water in various size fractions over one tidal cycle. (From Hanson & Wiebe 1977.)

autotrophs were nannoplankton, such as very small flagellates, these could account for much of the observed respiration.

Another approach to the problem is to add ^{14}C-labelled soluble organic material to sea-water and study its removal by heterotrophs. Andrews and Williams (1971) added labelled glucose and labelled amino acids to sea-water from the English Channel and measured the amount of labelled CO_2 produced. They concluded from this and previous work that probably about 50% of the net photosynthetic production is taken up by heterotrophs in the size range 1–8 μm. They showed that while heterotrophic activity varied seasonally, substrate concentrations varied very little, presumably because any increase in concentration was taken up rapidly by the microorganisms. The result should not be taken to imply that 50% of net phytosynthetic production is released by the producers in soluble form. Feeding, excretion and egestion by herbivores and their predators will all give rise to soluble organic material, and a proportion of those phytoplankton organisms which escape the grazers will undergo autolysis in the water column. In a subsequent study of these relationships in water off the Bahamas, Williams and Yentsch (1976) estimated that phytoplankton excretion supplied no more than half the DOM required to sustain the observed heterotrophic uptake, and concluded that zooplankton excretion, decay of plant and animal material (including faecal pellets) and losses from algal cells during grazing probably accounted for the remainder of the DOM supply.

In yet another approach to understanding the role of microheterotrophs in coastal waters, Derenbach and Williams (1974) collected natural plankton populations, removed the net zooplankton, and incubated with NaH $^{14}CO_3$ in the usual way. Instead of counting radioactivity on a single filter, they compared the counts of samples filtered at 3·0 μm and at 0·45 μm. They aimed to retain mainly the photosynthetic component on the coarser filters and the photosynthetic component plus the heterotrophs on the fine filters. By testing each fraction for photosynthetic and heterotrophic activity, and by treatment with antibiotics they showed that their method worked. They assumed that any counts attributable to the heterotrophs resulted from secretion of DOM by the autotrophs, followed by uptake by bacteria. Their results showed that between 1% and 30% of primary production was passed on by this route during a 4–6 hour incubation, and further uptake of DOM occurred during a succeeding period of darkness. They estimated that for the English Channel waters, daily averages of bacterial production may be as high as 20% of the total primary production. In some experiments the figure was as high as 50%.

Still more recently, Taguchi and Platt (1977) have studied uptake of $^{14}CO_2$ in the dark, from waters of a small enriched coastal inlet in Nova Scotia, and estimated the annual uptake to be about 50 g C m^{-2} yr^{-1}, which is about 25% of annual photosynthetic production. They were extremely cautious in their interpretation of the data, suggesting that no one can do so without a great many more experiments and observations.

5.3.2   The structure of planktonic food webs

It is very important to know whether the bacteria are able to grow and divide fairly rapidly, or whether they spend long periods in a food-limited condition, converting the carbon they have absorbed to CO_2. Similar questions need answering in respect of the next trophic level. If both the bacteria and their predators are normally in a state of active growth and reproduction, then DOM is being converted to biomass which is usable by large zooplankton. If either the bacteria or their predators spend long periods in food-limited inactivity then the energy and materials they consume get used up in respiration and are in effect being shunted away from the food chains leading to higher trophic levels. The overall efficiency with which marine systems produce fish biomass from primary production (see Chapter 9) suggests that DOM is being utilized effectively rather than simply respired by microorganisms. Wiebe and Smith (1977) showed that in kinetic tracer experiments of about 10 h duration, DOM was converted to microbial biomass with an efficiency of about 97–99%.

Pomeroy (1974) has drawn attention to the possibility that Protista are major consumers of bacteria in the sea. Organisms that filter-feed using very fine mucus nets (salps and some pteropods, for example) may also be able to take bacteria quite effectively. Support for Pomeroy's view comes from several sources. Eriksson *et al.* (1977) found that ciliates, microrotifers and nauplii constituted 15% of the biomass of zooplankton in a shallow coastal area off Sweden, but estimated that their energy requirements were 65% of the total. Beers and Stewart, (1971) reached similar conclusions regarding two sites in the Pacific Ocean, and Margalef (1967) had earlier suggested that ciliates contribute as much or more to organic production as do the net zooplankton. Since ciliates are well equipped to take bacteria as food, it is possible that they are an important step in the food chain beginning with DOM and bacteria, and going on to larger zooplankton. Sorokin (1971a) has suggested that bacteria in the sea normally occur in aggregates large enough for net zooplankton to feed on directly.

In a more recent development of his views, Pomeroy (1979) presented a compartmental model of energy flow through a continental shelf ecosystem, in which he demonstrated the various pathways by which energy may pass from primary producers to terminal consumers, and showed that there is no underlying reason why pathways involving dead organic matter, bacteria and their predators (ciliates or mucus-net feeders) should not be a major pathway. The structure of his model is shown in Fig. 5.4; it involves abandoning classical ideas of trophic levels and regarding food webs as anastomosing structures that defy classification under trophic levels. By varying the proportion of primary production flowing to (1) zooplankton by grazing, (2) mucus-net feeders (taking nannoplankton) and (3) bacteria by way of DOM and detritus, Pomeroy (1979) showed that it is possible for sufficient energy to flow through either the grazers or the alternate pathways to support all the major trophic groups at a reasonable level, and to maintain fish production at about the levels that commonly occur. More will be said about this model in Chapter 9.

To conclude this section, reference will be made to some strange data which at the time of writing cannot be explained. Sorokin, in a series of papers (e.g. Sorokin 1971a, b) gave estimates for heterotrophic bacterial production, obtained by measuring dark assimilation of $^{14}CO_2$ and taking this as 6% of newly synthesized bacterial carbon. His estimates were well in excess of phytoplankton production at the same sites. For example, at a station in the Solomon Sea he obtained a ^{14}C fixation by phytoplankton equivalent to 1 mg C m^{-3} day^{-1}, and a bacterial heterotrophic production of 3·5 m C m^{-3} day^{-1}. He postulated that the bacterial carbon was obtained from upwelling DOM. Banse (1974) discussed the oceanography of the area and showed that there was no known source of DOM that could support such a bacterial production, and concluded that Sorokin's estimates were an order of magnitude too high. If we assume that Sorokin's measurements of $^{14}CO_2$ uptake were not in error, the most probable source of difficulty seems to be

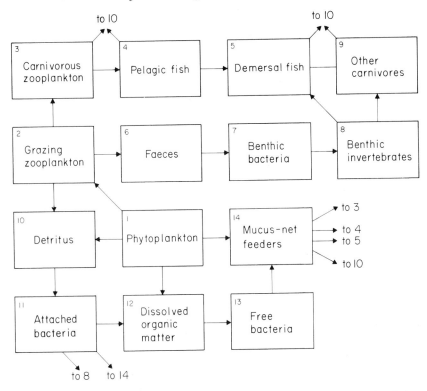

Fig. 5.4 Structure of a model of energy flux in a continental shelf community. For description, see text. (After Pomeroy 1979.)

the assumption that there is a ratio of 100 : 6 between the uptake of CO_2 and the synthesis of new bacterial carbon. This is apparently attributable to earlier work by Romanenko, quoted in Sorokin (1965). The matter might have rested there, had not Joiris (1977) found that in the North Sea plankton respiration exceeded apparent ^{14}C fixation by an order of magnitude, and Sieburth (1977) reviewed evidence suggesting that levels of microbial production even higher than Sorokin's have been observed in the Atlantic. The conclusion of Sieburth's review was that there is a possibility that present estimates of photosynthesis by phytoplankton are too low; that a great deal of carbon is fixed, passed out as DOC, taken up rapidly by microbes, and not recognized as fixed carbon in any of the procedures at present being used. This is, of course, a highly contentious suggestion, and must remain an open question for the present.

5.4   MICROBIAL PROCESSES IN THE BENTHOS

There are still many big question marks associated with the role of bacteria in the water column, but our knowledge of events in the benthos is a little further advanced. For benthic communities below the photic zone, the only method of acquiring energy and materials for biological processes is from material settled from the water column. It is a mixture of living cells and dead organic matter, the proportion varying with the season and with depth, as described in section 5.2.2. The dead material is an excellent substrate for growth of bacteria and fungi; the complex of dead organic matter and microbes is referred to as detritus. In the course of being acted upon by microorganisms, the plant or animal matter is broken down into simpler substances, and eventually is reduced to its mineral constituents. For this reason, the microorganisms have become known as decomposers. However, there is a sense in which every heterotrophic organism that takes in organic food and excretes minerals is a decomposer, so that it may be misleading to associate this function mainly with microbes.

Conversely, in terms of ecosystem function, zooplankton, benthos and fish are often referred to as secondary producers. However, bacteria which have an adequate food supply and can maintain active growth are important secondary producers, and their production is used by filter feeders in the water column and a variety of detritivores in the benthos. Hence, the conventional distinction between animals as producers and microbes as decomposers is subject to many exceptions. In the sections that follow, this point should be kept in mind, even when the conventional terms are used.

5.4.1   Processing of marine macrophyte detritus at the sediment surface

The colonization of marine macrophytes by bacteria and fungi begins when the plants are still living and growing. Gessner *et al.* (1972) showed that the internodes of the lower stems of *Spartina alterniflora* were colonised by the fungus *Sphaerulina pedicellata*, and that this biomass supported a variety of bacteria and grazing animals such as nematodes and mites. Meyers (1974) emphasized the role of various marine fungi (*Lulworthia*, *Leptosphaeria*) in association with more terrestrial genera (*Fusarium*, *Cephalosporium*) in helping to decompose *Spartina* tissue in Louisiana. The moulds colonized the plants while they were still actively growing, but during dieback various yeasts became prominent and were thought to be particularly active in decomposing cellulose. On *Thalassia*, Fenchel (1970) counted bacteria on intact dead leaves and on particles of various sizes, and found that the numbers were always between 1 and 9×10^6 cm^{-2}. Associated with them were flagellates (10^4 cm^{-2}), ciliates (about 65 cm^{-2}) and diatoms (10^4 to 10^5 cm^{-2}).

In a study of the bacterial flora of the surfaces of *Laminaria* fronds, Laycock (1974) used plate counting techniques and, as expected, obtained lower numbers than others had obtained by direct counting. She was, however, able to show that there was a distinct seasonal succession of bacterial types, and that there were consistent differences between different parts of the plant (Fig. 5.5). The tips of the fronds had the highest counts (10^3–10^5 cm^{-2}) while the meristems had the lowest (10–10^3 cm^{-2}). Psychrophilic bacteria dominated at all levels from November to April. The bacteria capable of hydrolysing mannitol, alginate and protein were abundant at the tips of the blades, where tissue is continually breaking down, at all times of the year. At the meristems and the middle parts of the blades bacterial density was inversely proportional to growth rate, falling to very low levels when growth was most rapid in spring (Fig. 5.6). It is reasonable to presume from this information that there is a seasonal succession of bacterial types equipped to exploit the abundant dissolved and particulate organic matter generated by *Laminaria* (see Chapter 3), and that the plant fragments eroded from the tips of the blades by wave action are richly colonized by bacteria before they break free.

As we mentioned earlier, detritus derived from marine macrophytes tends to accumulate at the sediment surface. Here it is attacked by a variety of animals which functionally may be called 'shredders'. Fenchel (1970) observed the feeding activities of the amphipod *Parhyalella whelpleyi* on detritus derived from *Thalassia* and found that these animals shredded the material, ingesting some particles and rejecting others. The faecal pellets were found to contain bits of detritus that were almost completely undigested, but freshly formed faecal pellets were almost devoid of microorganisms. It seemed that the amphipods digested the microbes but not the plant tissues. When the faecal pellets were kept in Millipore-filtered sea-water, a microbial community typical of the detritus was restored in about four days. Similar results were obtained from invertebrates filtering detritus from suspension, and from deposit-feeding gastropods and worms (see Fenchel 1977). It appears that most of these detritivores are unable to digest the structural components (cellulose, etc.,) of the detritus, but readily assimilate the attached microbes, which act as an intermediary in the process of transferring nutrients and energy from the macrophytes to the invertebrates. Furthermore the plant material, having been ingested and passed out again in a faecal pellet, may be repeatedly colonized by microbes and ingested by an invertebrate. This process, first demonstrated by Newell (1965) for the detritus-feeding molluscs *Hydrobia* and *Macoma*, has been confirmed for other organisms (Hargrave 1976).

Recently, Valiela *et al.* (1979) showed that the rate of decomposition of

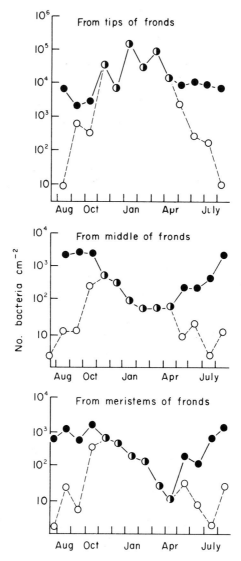

Fig. 5.5 Numbers of bacteria per cm² of blade of *Laminaria longicruris* as determined by incubation of plates at ambient temperature (solid line) and 3°C (broken line). (After Laycock 1974.)

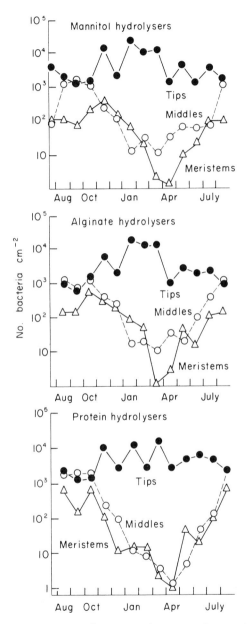

Fig. 5.6 Numbers of bacteria per cm² of blades of *Laminaria longicruris* as determined by incubation on media containing substances indicated. (After Laycock 1974.)

Spartina detritus is strongly influenced by its content of substances distasteful to invertebrate grazers and shredders. They showed that newly dead *Spartina* contains considerable amounts of ferulic and coumaric acids, and that the amount present decreases during nine months of aging. When 9-month-old *Spartina* detritus was modified by adding differing amounts of the acids, its palatability to the amphipod *Orchestia grillus* and the snail *Melampus bidentalus* was decreased. Since, as we have seen, invertebrate detritivores accelerate the decomposition of macrophyte material by reducing its particle size and increasing its exposure to microorganisms, any substance which deters the invertebrates is likely to reduce rates of decomposition.

Close study of the colonization of macrophyte detritus by bacteria reveals that only 2–10% of the surface is normally occupied by bacteria. The reason is not entirely clear, but it does seem that there is an upper limit to the area available for colonization. Hence, every process tending to reduce the particle size of detritus will increase the surface-to-volume ratio and hence the ratio of bacterial biomass to detrital biomass. This is confirmed by noting the rate of oxygen consumption of detritus particles in different size ranges. Fig. 5.7 uses data from Fenchel (1970) to show that as particle size decreases both the oxygen uptake and the numbers of microorganisms per unit weight in detritus increase markedly.

One consequence of the increase in microbial biomass is that the protein content of the detritus also increases with decreasing particle size. Hence, for benthic invertebrates, many of which are nitrogen-limited in their diet (see p. 74) the detritus that has been processed several times with particle-size reduction at each stage is more nutritious than the original plant material. If this is so, there must have been uptake of nitrogen from some source other than the plant detritus. For example, the C/N ratio of fresh and of recently dead leaves of *Zostera* are about 8 and 15 respectively in spring, but about 30 and 40 respectively in autumn, and shed leaves have a seasonal range of 18–30 (Harrison & Mann 1975a). Bacteria have a C/N ratio of about 5·7, and to decompose, plant detritus must take up nitrogen and other nutrients from the water. It has been shown many times that addition of nutrients to cultures increases the rate of decomposition. One of the most precise experiments (Fenchel 1977) involved adding uniformly ^{14}C-labelled hay to sea-water and collecting the $^{14}CO_2$ (Fig. 5.8). There was a lag period of 50–100 h during which the material was colonized by microbes. After that, decomposition was rapid. In sea-water it was about 2% per 100 h at 22°C; phosphate enrichment increased it to 5%, nitrate enrichment to 11%, and the two combined to 21% per 100 h. In the light of these findings, it is clear that particulate organic detritus is a net consumer of nutrients, and when held in suspension by water turbulence may even be a competitor with phytoplankton for limiting nutrients (Parker *et al.* 1975). This aspect of microbial activity is very different from the conventional view of microbes as

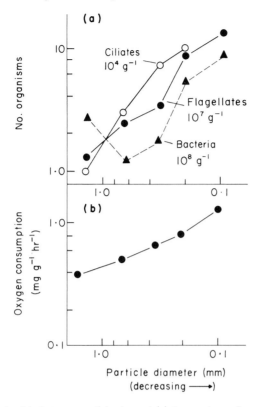

Fig. 5.7 The relationship between particle size and (a) the numbers of organisms on their surfaces and (b) the oxygen uptake of the detritus. (From data in Fenchel 1970.)

primarily responsible for nutrient regeneration. This topic will be further discussed below (p. 206).

The rate of decomposition of plant material is increased if protozoa are present to graze the bacteria (Fig. 5.9). Early theories put forward to explain this (Johannes 1965) emphasized the high rate of phosphorus excretion by the protozoa. As we have seen, bacterial activity is enhanced by increased availability of phosphorus. However, more recent work (Barsdate *et al.* 1974) utilizing ^{32}P has shown that although grazed systems have higher phosphorus turnover rates than ungrazed ones, this is mostly due to higher rates of phosphate uptake and release by the bacteria. Hence, it is concluded that the grazed bacteria are more active in decomposition because of the relief of some density-dependent limitation other than nutrient availability; space, perhaps, or the enhancement of uptake caused by the stirring action of the protozoans.

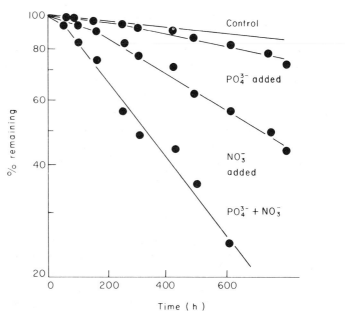

Fig. 5.8 Breakdown rates of water-extracted ^{14}C-labelled hay in sea-water with different mineral enrichments. PO_4^{3-} was added as 25 mg KH_2PO_4 l^{-1} and NO_3^- as 100 mg $NaNO_3$ l^{-1}. (After Fenchel 1977.)

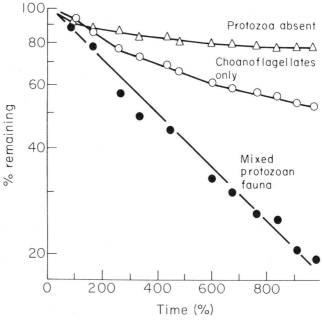

Fig. 5.9 Rates of decomposition of ^{14}C-labelled hay in sea-water with bacteria only or with bacteria plus various protozoa. (From Fenchel & Harrison 1976.)

In addition to protozoans, marine macrophyte detritus normally contains rotifers, turbellarians, nematodes, and small crustaceans. Fenchel (1977) has calculated that the biomass of this group of animals is of the same order of magnitude as that of the bacteria, so that they constitute an important food source for the detritivores. Their movements can be expected to help break down diffusion gradients of oxygen and nutrients around the bacteria, and thus hasten decomposition. Similar advantages result from the activities of larger animals, including the snail *Hydrobia* (Fenchel 1972) and the amphipod *Parhyalella* (Fenchel 1970).

5.4.2 Processes occurring within bottom sediments

Detritus, in various states of colonization by microbes, is transported laterally by currents but eventually sediments to the bottom. Included in it are living and recently dead plant fragments, detritus in an advanced stage of colonization, amorphous organic matter derived from DOM, bacteria free in the water, and faecal pellets of planktonic and benthic animals. Various invertebrates use this material as a food source. Some, like the amphipods, process the material at the surface, but others cause it to be buried in the sediments. Filter feeding bivalves, for example, may filter particles from water taken at, or a little above, the sediment surface, then egest faeces below the surface. Detritus also becomes buried when animals such as polychaetes ingest subsurface sediments, retain a large proportion of the organic matter, and defaecate considerable amounts of mainly inorganic material at the surface. This process, known as bioturbation, leads to an intimate mix of organic and inorganic particles in the sediment. Dale (1974) showed that bacterial numbers, estimated by direct counting, varied from 1×10^8 to almost 1×10^{10} g^{-1} of sediment, in an estuary in Nova Scotia. There was a highly significant negative correlation between numbers and mean grain size (Fig. 5.10) suggesting that the surface area of the grains was important for the development of a dense bacterial population. There was a highly significant positive correlation of numbers with sediment organic carbon and organic nitrogen content, but these factors were in turn strongly correlated with grain size. Nevertheless, in a partial correlation analysis, there was a significant variance attributable to carbon and nitrogen, after grain size had been accounted for. Hence, we are given the outlines of a situation in which bacteria attach themselves not only to organic matter in the sediment but also to the inorganic particles where they benefit, presumably, from soluble organic matter released from the organic particles by bacterial activity. Lopez and Levinton (1978) have suggested that microorganisms attached firmly to sediment particles may survive the passage through the gut of a gastropod such as *Hydrobia*. In sediments having a dense population of such deposit-feeders, there may be natural selection in favour of

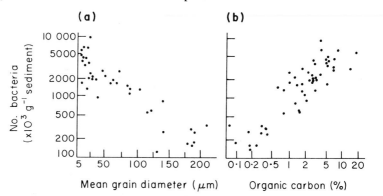

Fig. 5.10 Relationship of bacterial numbers per g of sediment to (a) mean grain diameter and (b) organic carbon content. (From Dale 1974.)

organisms tending to attach to sediment particles. Dale (1974) calculated that the biomass of bacteria in the sediments was of the same order of magnitude as that of the animals (up to 30 g m^{-2} dry weight) and suggested that they might well process the greater part of the carbon entering the sediment.

The metabolism of the organisms in the sediment gives rise to an oxygen demand, but dissolved oxygen from the surface penetrates only a limited distance varying from a few mm in fine-grained, carbon-rich sediments to many cm in a coarse sediment, depending on the degree of turbulence at the sediment–water interface. For example, penetration is deep on beaches exposed to a strong surf. Beneath the oxidized layer the sediment is anaerobic and chemically reducing (Fenchel & Riedl 1971). Dale (1974) found no correlation between bacterial numbers and Eh of the sediments, and concluded that in the deeper layers aerobic bacteria were replaced by an equivalent number of anaerobes (the number depending on particle size and carbon content). The initial stages of anaerobic decomposition of organic detritus are often fermentative, giving rise to such substances as lactate and acetate. These tend to diffuse upwards to the aerobic zone where they are oxidised by aerobic, chemoheterotrophic bacteria (Fenchel 1977), or are used as hydrogen donors by photoautotrophic bacteria near the surface.

Another method for carrying out decomposition in the anaerobic zone is for bacteria to use sulphate, nitrate or carbon dioxide as hydrogen acceptors, leading to the formation of H_2S, NH_3 or CH_4. Of these processes, quantitatively the most important is sulphate reduction, since sulphate is abundant in sea-water. Hence, the anaerobic zone is characterized by the production of hydrogen sulphide, which is precipitated as black ferrous sulphide. The reduction of iron from the ferric to the ferrous state leads to the liberation of adsorbed phosphates—a mechanism that is of important in nutrient regen-

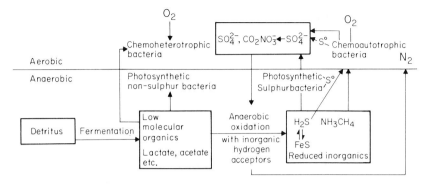

Fig. 5.11 Diagram representing pathways of energy and matter decomposition processes within a sediment. (From Fenchel 1977.)

eration (see section 7.8). Sulphide can be oxidized by white sulphur bacteria or by green and purple photosynthetic bacteria, and the end result is the formation of elemental sulphur and sulphate. Hence, sulphate (and to a lesser extent nitrate and carbon dioxide) may be regarded as alternatives to oxygen in mediating the oxidation of organic matter in the sediments. Figure 5.11 from Fenchel (1977) summarizes these processes.

Jørgensen and Fenchel (1974) set up a microcosm with sand and *Zostera* detritus, matching the organic matter content to natural sediment. They measured oxygen consumption, rate of sulphate reduction and the concentrations of SO_4^{2-}, HS^-, FeS, and sulphur at different depths, and were able to assess the magnitude of the sulphate reduction system. They followed the processes for seven months, during which the system changed from oxidized to strongly reducing, then slowly reoxidized. In the first month sulphate reduction processes caused much more mineralization of organic matter than did oxygen uptake processes. The situation was slowly reversed, but over the whole period more than half of the mineralization of organic detritus was catalyzed via the sulphur cycle.

In an attempt to verify this result in a natural habitat Jørgensen (1977) made a budget of the sulphur cycle at nine stations in a shallow coastal sediment in Denmark. He found (Fig. 5.12) that oxygen uptake and sulphate reduction changed in parallel through the seasons. The weighted average daily rate of oxygen uptake for the area was 34 mmol O_2 m^{-2}, and the average daily rate of sulphate reduction was 9·5 mmol SO_4^{2-} m^{-2}, made up of 6·2 mmol in the upper 10 cm and the 3·3 mmol in deeper sediments. However, 1 mole of sulphate oxidizes twice as much organic carbon to CO_2 as does 1 mole of oxygen. For example:

$$2 \text{ lactate} + SO_4^{2-} \rightarrow 2 \text{ acetate} + 2CO_2 + H_2O + S^{2-}$$

$$(CH_2O) + O_2 \rightarrow CO_2 + H_2O \tag{5.1}$$

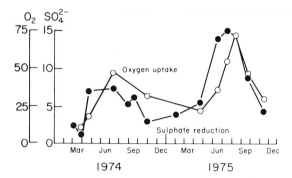

Fig. 5.12 Seasonal variation in rate of sulphate reduction in the upper 10 cm of sediment, and rate of oxygen uptake, averaged for ten stations in the Limfjorden, Denmark. (After Jørgensen 1977.)

Hence we might conclude that a total of 34 mmol of organic carbon per m² was oxidized daily, with $9.5 \times 2 = 19$ mmol being oxidized by sulphate reducing bacteria, the remainder by processes in the aerobic zone. However, it was found that 10% of the sulphide produced remained in the sediments, indicating a further 2 mmol of organic carbon per m² being oxidized and not leading to oxygen uptake. Hence, it was concluded that the proportion of carbon oxidation being catalysed by sulphate-reducing bacteria was $(19/36) \times 100 = 53\%$. A budget for the sulphur cycle in the sediments is given in Fig. 5.13.

Exploration of the deeper marine sediments reveals that at a depth of 30–50 cm significant amounts of methane are present, showing that the use

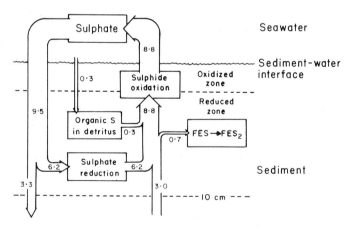

Fig. 5.13 Transfer rates of sulphur in a marine sediment. Weighted average for nine stations over two years. (From Jørgensen 1977.)

Table 5.1 Concentrations of sulphate, sulphide and methane, and rates of methane production and oxidation in sediments of Santa Barbara Basin, California. (From Kosiur & Walford 1979.)

Depth (cm)	SO_4^{2-} (mM)	Sulphide (mM)	CH_4 (mM)	CH_4 production rate (μmol l^{-1} yr^{-1})	CH_4 oxidation rate (μmol l^{-1} yr^{-1})
0–25	28·3	trace	n.d.*	20·5	
30–35	21·8	0·4	n.d.	21·4	357·6
35–40	20·5	0·6	n.d.	24·1	
110–120	10·3	3·7	0·2	5·0	
120–130	6·5	3·6	0·2	5·2	139·7
150–160	n.d.	3·8	0·6	5·1	8·3
265–270	2·9	3·9	9·5	12·0	7·6
275–280	n.d.	3·6	8·9	20·3	
285–330	1·8	n.d.	7·3	41·5	
335–340	1·3	1·4	7·0	34·3	

* n.d. = not determined.

of CO_2 as a hydrogen acceptor is important at this level. Beyond 50 cm depth the amount of methane usually increases steadily, with concentrations up to 10 or 15 mM in some places. The increase in methane coincides with the decrease of sulphate in solution, and two theories have been put forward to explain the relationship. Working with freshwater sediments, Cappenberg (1975) found that the methane producers were inhibited by hydrogen sulphide, and suggested that the sulphate reducers effectively excluded methane producers at depths where sulphate was available. However, Kosiur and Warford (1979) found that in the sediments of the anoxic Santa Barbara Basin of the Southern California continental shelf, methane production was occurring in the upper zone where sulphate was present. However, methane oxidation (probably by sulphate reducing bacteria) was going on simultaneously (see Table 5.1). The rate of methane oxidation appeared to be high enough to account for the methane diffusing upwards, in addition to that being generated in the upper sediments. Hence, there appears to be a multistage mechanism for oxidizing deep sediments, in which organic matter is oxidized by methane-producing bacteria; the methane diffuses upwards and is oxidized by sulphate-reducing bacteria; the sulphide thus produced is finally oxidized to sulphate and returned to the water column. It is interesting to note from Table 5.1 that the zone in which methane-oxidizing bacteria are active has very little sulphide, so that Cappenberg's (1975) findings may apply even in this situation.

A different approach to the measurement of rates of bacterial degradation of organic matter in sediments was used by Vosjan and Olanczuk-

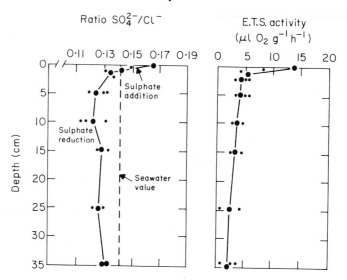

Fig. 5.14 Sulphide/chloride ratios and activity of the electron transport system (ETS) in a tidal flat sediment of the Dutch Wadden Sea. (From Vosjan & Olanczuk-Neyman 1977.)

Neyman (1977). They employed a new technique for measuring the activity of the respiratory electron transport system of bacteria in sediments, noting that is applied equally to aerobic and anaerobic processes, but they expressed their results in oxygen equivalents. They found (Fig. 5.14) that the highest activities occurred at the surface of a tidal sediment flat and decreased rapidly in the first 2 cm. Below that depth there was a slow decrease. Considering a zone 35 cm deep, 10% of all activity was found in the upper 1 cm. A study of sulphate/chlorinity ratios showed that sulphate reduction was occurring at all depths of the anaerobic layer, but that sulphide was being converted to sulphate only in the upper few mm of sediment.

Wiebe (1979) reviewed the importance of anaerobic processes, especially sulphate reduction and methane production as one moves from a Georgia estuary out onto the continental shelf. He concluded that in an estuary with salt marshes anaerobic processes are of great importance even in the upper 20 cm. They give rise to a constant flow of dissolved organic carbon compounds which can be utilized by aerobic heterotrophs. In the nearshore environment (shallow coastal waters to a depth of about 15 m) methane and sulphide concentrations in the top 20 cm of sediments are only about 10% of those found in salt-marshes, indicating a much reduced anaerobic metabolism. In the coastal zone beyond the nearshore waters Wiebe reported that methane and sulphide concentrations in the upper 20 cm of sediment were barely detectable and that nutrient regeneration was mainly caused by animals feeding on the benthic microflora. These topics are discussed further in Chapter 7.

5.5 CONSUMPTION OF MICROORGANISMS AND DETRITUS BY ANIMALS

5.5.1 Consumption in the plankton

The views of Pomeroy (1974) and others that protozoa are major consumers of bacteria has been discussed in section 5.3.2. This section deals with the mechanisms by which dissolved and dead particulate organic matter generated by primary producers is used in support of secondary production by invertebrates and fish. Considering first the zooplankton, the question resolves itself into a consideration of whether bacteria or protozoa, individually, in clumps, or attached to particulate organic matter, constitute an important source of food for the net plankton.

One of the best documented studies of this question has been made in the Patuxent River Estuary, Maryland, USA, a tributary of Chesapeake Bay (Heinle & Flemer 1975; Heinle *et al.* 1977). A carbon budget was constructed for a population of the copepod *Eurytemora affinis* and it was found that during March, April and May the carbon demands of the copepods greatly exceeded primary production (Fig. 5.15). During April, the carbon demands exceeded supply by factors of 5 to 75. Since at that time the standing crop of detritus greatly exceeded that of phytoplankton, the authors concluded that the detritus must be a food supply for the copepods. The hypothesis was tested by attempting to rear copepods on standardized rations of detritus with and without microorganisms, using cultures of copepods grown on algal food as controls. Such experiments are notoriously difficult and tedious, owing to the difficulties of working with copepods in the laboratory. The conclusions from a set of mixed results was that copepods could grow and produce eggs on a diet of detritus when abundant microorganisms were present, or on a mixed diet of algae and detritus, but they did not thrive on a diet of detritus which had been autoclaved to control the microbial flora. The results also suggested that the copepods could do very well on a diet of ciliates.

The controversial nature of Sorokin's (1971) estimates of bacterial production in tropical oceans has been discussed in section 5.3.2. Nevertheless, his work on the consumption of the bacteria by zooplankton may be considered separately. He added to natural water samples 50–100 μg C l^{-1} of 'strongly labelled dissolved organic matter'. After allowing time for incorporation of the label in bacteria, he estimated their numbers by direct counting, and allowed various planktonic organisms to feed on them. Ingestion

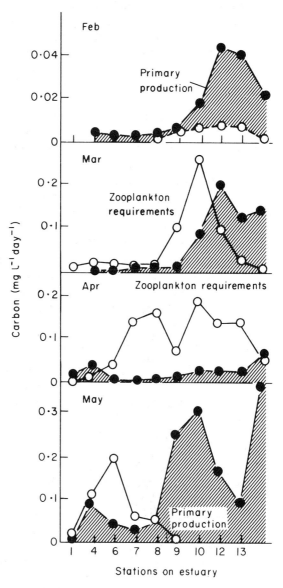

Fig. 5.15 Primary production and estimated carbon requirements of the zooplankton at various stations in the Patuxent River estuary. (After Heinle & Flemer 1975.)

and assimilation were estimated from counts of radioactivity after shorter (20–40 min) and longer (1·5–2 hrs) periods of feeding. He found that the appendicularian *Oikopleura* could take up to 100% of its body weight a day from bacteria, and cladoceran *Penilia* could take about 55%, at an assimilation efficiency of about 35%. He also found a small but significant uptake of bacterial biomass by the copepods *Eucalanus* and *Paracalanus* and suggested that they were able to filter from the water the 20–30% of bacteria that are in aggregates.

The question of how effectively planktonic animals use dead particulate organic matter as food has been under consideration ever since Baylor and Sutcliffe (1963) showed that the brine shrimp *Artemia salina* would live and grow on a diet of organic particles produced by bubbling air through filtered sea-water, and Riley (1963) pointed out that 'the combination of organic aggregates and phytoplankton provides a more nearly uniform source of sustenance (for the zooplankton) than either one by itself'. Since dead particulate organic matter normally has bacteria attached, the controversy is intimately bound up with questions of how effectively zooplankton utilize bacteria. Work since 1963 has tended to indicate that there are important trophic pathways involved, but the evidence is still inconclusive. In particular, more work is needed on the idea that protozoa are an important link between particulate organic matter, bacteria and net zooplankton.

5.5.2 Consumption by shredders and deposit feeders

Odum and Heald (1975) divided detrivores functionally into (1) shredders and grinders which chew detritus particles, (2) deposit feeders which select small detritus particles from the sediment and (3) filter feeders. We saw in section 5.4.1 that shredders and deposit feeders ingest detritus particles consisting of dead organic matter coated with bacteria, and appear to retain mainly the bacteria. When Kristensen (1972) examined the carbohydrases of a variety of marine invertebrates he concluded that they were, on the whole, not equipped to digest structural polysaccharides such as cellulose derived from macrophytes. From this we might conclude that between marine macrophytes and benthic invertebrates there is an essential intermediate trophic level, dominated by microorganisms. To put it in a very simple way, marine invertebrates do not consume macrophyte structural material; microorganisms consume it and invertebrates consume the microorganisms.

Of course, not all of the macrophyte material is structural carbohydrate. There are proteins, simple carbohydrates and fats. However, when macrophyte material dies and becomes detritus, it is highly probable that the bacteria assimilate these substances before the animals get at them. Hence, the detritivores at the sediment surface are presented with a mixture of indigestible carbohydrates and microorganisms.

The situation invites comparison with terrestrial plant–herbivore relations. Most terrestrial plants have a high content of structural carbohydrates such as cellulose, which are resistant to the digestive enzymes of animals. Among the more successful terrestrial herbivores are the ruminants, such as deer or goats, which have an expanded anterior part of the stomach, the rumen, and this holds a culture of microorganisms many of which are able to digest cellulose. Rumen fluid commonly contains about 10^{10} bacteria and up to 10^6 protozoa g^{-1}. Fermentation of cellulose leads to formation of volatile fatty acids, which are a major source of energy to the ruminant. Proteins are degraded to peptides, amino acids and ammonia, and are re-synthesized as microbial proteins with a different amino acid spectrum, to be digested and absorbed by the host animal in the small intestine. Another group of herbivores, such as horses or rabbits, have a cellulose-digesting microflora in the hind gut. This arrangement is less efficient than the rumen, but its effectiveness is sometimes enhanced by re-ingestion of faecal pellets, as for example by rabbits, mice and guinea-pigs. In addition to their function in cellulose digestion, gut floras enhance the efficiency of nitrogen utilization by converting ammonia and urea to microbial protein, and by synthesizing vitamins.

It is now clear that both in the sea and on land, microorganisms play an important part in transferring energy and nutrients from plants to animals. Their role is especially important in relation to those plants having a large component of structural carbohydrates. In the sea, the flowering plants such as mangroves, marsh grasses and seagrasses are particularly well endowed with structural materials. We can therefore regard the microflora which colonizes the detritus from these sources as functionally analogous to those in the guts of terrestrial herbivores.

In the past much has been made of the distinction between grazing food chains and detritus food chains, but the foregoing shows that terrestrial herbivores and aquatic detritivores have much in common. Both rely, for the most part, on the activities of microorganisms to make the plant food available to them. Furthermore, the so-called large herbivores of the semi-arid plains of the world consume large amounts of herbage that is dry and brown, and it could be said that they switch from being herbivore to detritivore according to the season. The distinction between grazing food chains and detritus food chains is very tenuous indeed.

It has recently been shown that some species of marine invertebrate have gut floras which perform functions very similar to those of the ruminants. The ability of mysid shrimps, to digest cellulose derived from particles of *Zostera* detritus was discussed in section 2.2.3. Reference has also been made (section 3.4.2) to the rich gut flora of the sea urchin *Strongylocentrotus droebachiensis* and its role in the nitrogen metabolism of the animal. It was mentioned that when the animals were given ^{14}C glucose, the gut flora used the labelled carbon atoms in the synthesis of amino acids which were eventually incorporated into the tissues of the urchins (Fong & Mann 1980). An interesting sideline of this study was that the experiment was repeated, but the urchins were induced to consume ^{14}C labelled cellulose. Once again the ^{14}C label appeared in the proteins of the urchins, showing that the gut flora contains organsims able to digest cellulose. Hence, the gut flora of *Strongylocentrotus* has been shown to be capable of synthesis of proteins from non-protein nitrogen, fixation of N_2, and digestion of cellulose. The parallel with ruminants is very close indeed.

Tenore and his colleagues set up an experimental system for the study of the conversion of detritus to invertebrate biomass. (Tenore 1977a,b; Tenore *et al.* 1977). The polychaete *Capitella capitella* was cultured on detritus of marsh grass, seagrass, *Fucus* or *Gracilaria*, at three different food levels. The biomass of worms that was present after three months was taken to be the equilibrium value that could be supported by the food supply. It was found (Fig. 5.16) that the biomass produced was proportional to the nitrogen content of the food, up to about 3·5%, above which additional nitrogen made no difference. This is additional evidence for the view (p. 76) that many marine invertebrates are nitrogen limited in their growth and production. Tenore went on to select a nitrogen-poor (*Zostera*) and a nitrogen-rich (*Gracilaria*) food source, cultured them in $NaH^{14}CO_3$ until they were well labelled, freeze-dried them, ground them and used them in experiments designed to find out how 'aging' (i.e. exposure to colonization by bacteria in a nutrient-enriched medium) affected their value as food for *Capitella*. He found (Table 5.2) that *Gracilaria* was taken up at the maximum rate of 91 μg dry wt. per mg of worm per day after 14 days of 'aging' whereas *Zostera* was

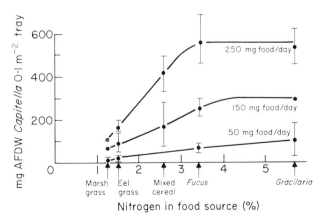

Fig. 5.16 Biomass of *Capitella* resulting from culture on five different foods at three levels of ration. (From Tenore 1977.)

Table 5.2 Effect of aging and of presence or absence of *Capitella* on rates of oxidation (mg dry wt. day^{-1}) and rates of incorporation into *Capitella* tissue (μg dry wt. per mg worm day^{-1}). (From Tenore 1977b.)

Aging time	Process	*Gracilaria* detritus		*Zostera* detritus	
		No *Capitella*	*Capitella*	No *Capitella*	*Capitella*
5 days	Oxidation	52·1	64·0	23·6	
	Incorporation	—	58·1	—	
14 days	Oxidation	59·3	61·6	24·9	25·9
	Incorporation	—	91·0	—	37·3
30 days	Oxidation	61·0	58·7	27·6	26·9
	Incorporation	—	73·5	—	41·3
60 days	Oxidation	44·5	55·3	34·0	39·0
	Incorporation	—	45·0	—	70·7
120 days	Oxidation			37·3	32·5
	Incorporation			—	123·7
180 days	Oxidation			59·9	74·5
	Incorporation			—	375·4

taken up at rates which increased steadily, reaching a value of 375 μg mg^{-1} day^{-1} at 180 days, when the experiment ended. Tenore concluded that natural detritus probably consists of different pools of fast-decomposing and slowly-decomposing detritus, thus damping out any fluctuations in food supply to detritivores caused by fluctuations in primary production. He further suggested that from the system point of view, the slower rate of decomposition of *Zostera* might be an advantage. At the time of optimum utilization by the polychaete it was incorporated in its tissues much more effectively than was the *Gracilaria*. The ease with which *Gracilaria* was decomposed might lead to a high proportion of its carbon being converted to CO_2 by bacteria, before the detritus was consumed by an invertebrate.

Looking for a moment at the effect of the worms on the decomposition process, it seems that there was no significant difference in rate of decomposition, whether *Capitella* was present or not (Table 5.2). However, when labelled *Spartina* detritus was aged for five months and cultured (1) with microbenthos alone, (2) with the addition of the polychaete *Nephthys incisa* and (3) with *Nephthys incisa* and a fixed meiobenthos dominated by nematodes, the culture with meiobenthos had almost twice the rate of oxidation and twice the rate of incorporation into the polychaete. Clearly, the meiobenthos plays an important part in accelerating microbial decomposition of detritus. These experiments are very illuminating, but the results were always expressed as the equilibrium biomass of worm resulting from a particular treatment. We still lack any measure of the actual rate of production or turnover of *Capitella* or *Nephthys* tissue, and thus cannot make estimates of food chain efficiency.

The range of marine animals that has been shown experimentally to benefit by feeding on deposits of detritus and ingesting the bacteria now includes annelids (Tenore 1977a,b), gastropods (Newell 1965), sea-urchins (Fong & Mann 1980), amphipods (Fenchel 1970), mysids (Foulds & Mann 1978), prawns (Moriarty 1976, 1977) and fish (Moriarty 1976). Questions of food uptake by benthic animals will be considered more fully in Chapter 7, but some studies in which the assimilation of bacteria was particularly emphasized may be mentioned here.

Moriarty (1976, 1977) used the muramic acid method to determine the biomass of bacteria ingested by five species of prawns and by mullet. He found that the prawns were opportunistic omnivores, taking detritus and some living animals. On average, bacterial carbon constituted 10–20% of the organic carbon in their foreguts, and in animals where the foregut contained mostly detritus, bacterial carbon constituted up to 30% of the organic carbon. This proportion was much higher than the average for detritus in the environment, so the prawns were probably selecting food with a high bacterial content. The ratio of bacterial carbon to ash was much lower in the hindgut than in the foregut, indicating that the bacteria were being efficiently digested. Moriarty's (1976) results on mullet (*Mugil cephalus*) confirmed that these fish, well known as consumers of detritus, were selectively taking particles less than 100 μm in diameter and were deriving 20–30% of their carbon intake from bacteria. The selection of small particles is, in effect, a selection for high-protein food.

A detailed carbon budget for the mud snail *Nassarius obsoletus* living on a Georgia salt-marsh (Wetzel 1976) showed that it was unable to utilize insoluble carbon from *Spartina* detritus, but ^{14}C from bacteria was taken up and retained with an efficiency of 46%. *Nassarius* has in the past been regarded as a deposit-feeding detritivore, but Wetzel's study demonstrated that two-thirds of its carbon supply could be derived by selectively grazing algae on the mud surface. Another interesting point to emerge was that more than half of the carbon loss by *Nassarius* was in the form of dissolved organic matter. Since this material could well be assimilated by bacteria, there is a distinct possibility of carbon recycling in the system.

Fundulus spp. are small minnow-like fish which are very abundant in the shallow waters of estuaries of eastern North America. Two studies of their feeding have yielded apparently conflicting results. Jefferies (1972) compared the fatty acid content of their stomach contents with the fatty acid content of *Spartina*, of *Spartina* detritus, of the fish muscle, and of various other marine animals. He found that whereas the fish and other animals were rich in acids with 20–22 C atoms, the *Spartina* was rich in 16–18 C fatty acids. During detritus formation many of the 18 C compounds were lost but the 16 C fatty acids remained, and characterized the detritus. In order to account for the spectrum of fatty acids found in the fish guts, Jefferies postulated that they were consuming five parts of detritus to one part of animal food.

Prinslow *et al.* (1974) tested this hypothesis by feeding *Fundulus* on various amounts of a diet consisting of one part commercial food and five parts detritus. They compared the growth, at each level of feeding, with the growth of fish which received the same amount of commercial fish food, but no detritus. There was no significant difference; the detritus did not improve the growth of the fish at all. What is the explanation of the conflicting results? One possibility is that in nature *Fundulus* selects detritus rich in bacterial protein, as Moriarty's (1976) prawns did. Such a diet might be qualitatively quite different from the one used by Prinslow *et al.* (1974), for they obtained their detritus by skimming it from the surface of the water in the creeks of a salt-marsh. Tenore *et al.* (1977) found that the degree of microbial colonization (aging) was critical in determining how efficiently detritus was used by *Capitella*. This question should be investigated more closely before we conclude that *Fundulus* does not derive nourishment from salt-marsh detritus.

5.5.3 Consumption by benthic filter feeders

Bacteria and detritus which settle at the sediment surface are easily brought into suspension a few cm above the sediment surface by currents, wave action, or turbulence produced by the movements of animals. Hence, filtering suspended particles from just above the sediment surface is a very good way of obtaining food. It is practiced by a wide variety of benthic invertebrates including sponges, coelenterates, polychaetes, crustaceans, bivalve molluscs, some gastropods, holothurians, and ascidians. Many of these have been shown to be capable of retaining particles down to a diameter of 1 or 2 μm, (Jørgensen 1966) and under laboratory conditions will readily filter out small detritus particles and even bacteria. Oysters, mussels, sponges and brine shrimps have been shown to grow under laboratory conditions on a diet of bacteria, but in rather few cases has the relative importance of detritus and bacteria been assessed in relation to the other sorts of food available, such as flagellates, diatoms, etc. One of the more careful and critical studies along these lines was carried out with sponges by Reiswig (1971). He analysed samples of inhalent and exhalent water from sponges growing *in situ* on the north coast of Jamaica. The water samples were individually analysed for plankton by direct microscopy after filtering (0·22 μm) and staining, and for total particulate organic carbon by chemical analysis. He calculated the POC attributable to four microscopically identifiable fractions which he called bacteria, armoured cells (fungi, diatoms, dinoflagellates, coccolithophores, etc.), unarmoured cells (recognized on filters only as flattened ghosts) and finally detritus, narrowly defined as discrete organic particles such as cellular debris and amorphous flakes. There was a large and highly significant difference between total POC determined by the acid dichromate method and the amount of POC attributable to the microscopically identifiable fractions. He called the material making up the difference, unresolvable particulate organic carbon (URPOC). It comprised 80% of the total POC in the water taken in by the sponges.

The efficiency of removal of the various fractions as they passed through the sponges was approximately as follows: bacteria 96%, unarmoured cells 89%, armoured cells 69%. The detritus concentration was higher in the exhalent water than in the inhalent, possibility due to egestion of indigestible parts of the cells. URPOC was retained with a 35% efficiency. The conclusion from this study was that there are two mechanisms for particle retention in these sponges: a system attributable to the amoebocytes lining the inhalent canals, which traps and ingests larger particles (5 μm upwards), and the choanocyte system which traps bacteria, nannoplankton, and probably the URPOC. Reiswig (1971) concluded that in the net diet of the sponges, 80% of the carbon was derived from URPOC for, although it was retained with only 35% efficiency, it was much more abundant than other types of POC. He discussed its origin and concluded that it was part of 'a continuous spectrum of quasi-particulate organic aggregates extending from isolated truly dissolved molecules to discrete detrital flakes'. He continued, 'The material is therefore hypothesized to exist in a state of physico-chemical equilibrium with truly dissolved material, from which it is generated and from which it is separated only by an arbitrary effective pore size'.

While questions may arise about the effectiveness of the technique for quantitative assessment of bacteria, ciliates, flagellates, etc., the interesting points for this discussion are (1) that sponges appear to be very efficient filters for bacteria and (2) that sponges can apparently filter out very small particles of organic matter which are part of the POC $\rightleftharpoons$ DOC equilibrium. In fact, the sponges may be indirectly drawing on the very large stocks of DOM discussed earlier in this chapter. This may prove to be one of the first verifications of the idea first put forward by Darnell (1967) that colloidal organic matter is an ecologically important food source in the coastal zone.

On the other hand, it seems doubtful that filter feeders are able to meet their nutritional requirements by filtering macrophyte detritus with attached microflora. Kirby-Smith (1976) collected *Spartina* leaves, dried them, ground them to 200 μ or less, aged the material in sea-water for 6 months, and cultured bay scallops (*Argopecten irradians*) in a suspension of about 5% (by weight) of this material in sea-water. In an 18 day experiment the scallops showed no shell growth after the first 7 days, and their tissue weight decreased by 9–20%. In parallel experiments, scallops fed fresh detritus

Table 5.3 Results of feeding common coral reef animals with bacteria. (From Sorokin 1973.)

Animal	Daily intake, as % of body organic matter	Ratio of food assimilated to food consumed (%)
Gastropod veligers	51	61
Hydroid *Pennaria*	43·5	74
Annelid Serpulidae	7·8	73
Coral *Pocillopora*	5·5	76
Coral *Montipora*	5·8	82
Sponge *Toxadocea*	3·4	82
Tunicate *Ascidia*	1·6	83
Holothurian *Ophiodesoma*	10·4	22
Gastropod *Nerita*	9·4	20
Lamellibranch *Grossostrea*	2·2	68

increased tissue weight up to 17%, and scallops fed phytoplankton increased tissue weight 18–26%. Kirby-Smith concluded that in the North Carolina estuaries phytoplankton is the only major energy source for filter feeders. He suggested that deposit feeders are well adapted to using the microbes on macrophyte detritus but the filter feeders are not.

Sorokin (1973) used isotope techniques to make measurements of the ability of various common coral reef animals to filter, ingest and assimilate bacteria (Table 5.3). He used as the food source, water with bacterial biomass equivalent to those found in water over coral reefs, $(20–80 \text{ mg C m}^{-3})$ and assessed the rate of metabolizing bacteria from the rate of evolution of $^{14}CO_2$. In spite of the controversy about some of Sorokin's results on bacterial production (see section 5.3.2) it does seem probable that a wide variety of organisms on coral reefs obtain a significant proportion of their organic carbon from bacterial biomass.

5.5.4 Consumption by animals living and feeding within the sediments

We have discussed the role of surface-feeding and filter-feeding benthic animals. Their remain two groups of infaunal animals: the macrofauna that live by ingesting large amounts of sediment, and the meiofauna that live and feed in the spaces between the particles. There are many studies relating the distribution of macrofauna to particle size and organic content of the sediment, but very few that throw light on the question of what these animals actually assimilate. Longbottom (1970) measured organic carbon and nitrogen in the faeces of *Arenicola*, and showed that both values were much lower than in the surrounding sediment which the animal was ingesting.

However, when the faecal material was held in clean sea-water and stirred (either in the dark or in the light) the nitrogen content of the material increased rapidly. There was a small increase in carbon content. This suggests that the worms had assimilated bacterial biomass, which was restored on exposure to sea-water; in this respect it is similar to the results obtained for deposit-feeding animals by Newell (1965).

The role of the meiofauna as consumers of bacteria seems to be better documented. We saw earlier that Tenore *et al.* (1977) found that the presence of meiobenthic organisms speeded the breakdown of detritus and uptake of detrital carbon by a polchaete worm. Coull (1973) summarized the evidence that oligochaetes, polychaetes, nematodes and a variety of small crustaceans (especially harpacticoid copepods), feed on bacteria. Rather remarkable multiple-choice experiments have shown that various meiofaunal animals are attracted to certain species of bacteria not to others. Detailed discussion of processes mediated by benthic organisms is given in Chapter 7.

CHAPTER 6
CORAL REEFS

A coral reef is one of the most spectacular of nature's marvels. Viewed from beneath the water, a reef front offers a variety and abundance of plant and animal life that has few parallels. Yet coral reefs are found in waters that are usually poor in nutrients and have very little primary or secondary production. For example, Rongelap Atoll, in the Marshall Islands, has a gross production estimated at $1800 \text{ g C m}^{-2} \text{ yr}^{-1}$ (Sargent & Austin 1954; modified by Kohn & Helfrich 1957) while the surrounding waters produce only $28 \text{ g C m}^{-2} \text{ yr}^{-1}$ (Steeman-Nielsen 1954). Hence from the system point of view, the intriguing questions are: What are the primary producers? How do they get their nutrients? How is the reef structure built? What are the important trophic links which permit such a profusion of animal life, yet ensure conservation of the nutrients?

6.1. CHARACTERISTIC ORGANISMS

The hermatypic or reef-building corals are anthozoan coelenterates of the class Scleractinia. They are distinguished by their ability to produce an external skeleton of calcium carbonate, which grows in a cumulative manner, giving rise to massive formations, and by having unicellular algae, the zooxanthellae, living internally in their tissues. It has been shown (Goreau 1961) that the zooxanthellae are an essential factor in the calcification process, since there is a correlation between photosynthetic rate and calcification rate. According to Goreau (1963) the primary reef framework is formed in shallow, well-illuminated, turbulent water by the scleractinian corals, assisted by hydrocoralline and alcyonarian corals, which also have zooxanthellae, and by calcareous algae. Under the conditions of stress imposed by the mechanical forces of the sea, the primary framework develops stable structures capable of dissipating those forces, for example spurs and buttresses separated by surge channels (Yonge 1972). With the passage of time, the primary framework becomes cemented and slowly filled by the activities of secondary hermatypes and 'sand formers'. The latter comprise a diverse assemblage of algae, foraminifera and higher animals, many of which contain symbiotic algae, and all of which are capable of secreting lime. In deeper water there are secondary, or detrital reefs composed largely of uncemented material derived from the primary reef, interspersed with some growing corals, algae and (in the Atlantic) gorgonians.

The dependence of corals on photosynthesis is reflected in their depth distribution. Most grow at depths less than 25 m, and maximum growth occurs at depths less than 10 m. In general, reef-building corals are confined to the tropics and sub-tropics. Vaughan (1919) concluded that reefs do not grow if the annual mean temperature is below 18°C, and they grow best at 25–29°C. The richest assemblages of corals are found in the Melanesian–South-east Asian area, where there are over 50 genera and 700 species. The Atlantic is less rich, the best area being the Caribbean with about 26 genera and less than 100 species (Stoddart 1969; Glynn 1973).

6.2.   THE GEOMORPHOLOGY OF REEFS

There are three main types of reef (Fig. 6.1): fringing reefs, barrier reefs and atolls. Fringing reefs, as their name implies, are found growing as a fringe to a land mass. The longest stretch of reef in the world is a fringing reef in the Red Sea. According to Ladd (1977) it would, if straightened into a single line, exceed 2500 miles. The aridity of the surrounding land makes this a particularly favourable habitat, for there are no floods of fresh water or deposition of river silt to harm the corals. Barrier reefs are also related to coastlines, but occur some distance out to sea, and have a relatively shallow lagoon between the reef and the land. The best known example is the Great Barrier Reef, off the north-east coast of Australia. It stretches more than

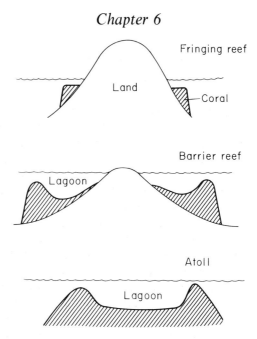

Fringing reef

Land

Coral

Barrier reef

Lagoon

Atoll

Lagoon

Fig. 6.1 Diagram illustrating structure of the three main types of reef. For details see text.

1200 miles, but is far from being a continuous barrier. It is composed of many reefs of different sizes and shapes, with considerable spaces between. Atolls are isolated structures surrounded by deep water. They tend to form a ring of coral with a central shallow lagoon.

In 1842 Darwin published *The Structure* and *Distribution of Coral Reefs*, and put forward his Subsidence Theory, according to which atolls were formed from fringing reefs on the shores of islands which were subsiding. Upward growth of the reef was able to keep pace with the island subsidence, and when the land mass finally disappeared beneath the sea, the reef remained as a ring structure. A consequence of this theory, which Darwin was unable to test, was that the living coral of an atoll rested on a layer of dead coral extending far below the depth at which coral can carry on growth. Subsequent drillings have confirmed this. Darwin suggested that barrier reefs had been formed in an analogous manner, the land mass remaining visible, but bores on the Great Barrier Reef and elsewhere show that modern reef growth has taken place on old limestone surfaces, during the last 17 000 years when sea levels have been rising in the aftermath of the Glacial periods. The Glacial Control Theory, originally proposed by Daly as an alternative to Darwin's subsidence theory, is now accepted in modified form as an explanation of the morphology of many barrier and fringing reefs.

6.3. THE CALCIFICATION PROCESS

Individual coral polyps are measured in millimetres, yet coral reefs measure tens of kilometres. The minute organisms are capable of a calcification process that proceeds for thousands, even millions of years, and is integrated into structures that are capable of withstanding both hurricanes and the insidious effects of countless boring and grazing organisms. What factors make possible this impressive activity? As was mentioned earlier, reef-building corals require sunlight, warm water, and an internal flora of unicellular algae, the zooxanthellae. Unless all these conditions are present, the reef does not grow. The role of the zooxanthellae has been a matter of debate for more than 50 years (see section 6.5) but Goreau (1959) and Goreau and Goreau (1959) showed very clearly that the zooxanthellae are an essential factor in the calcification process. Using ^{45}Ca as a tracer, they showed both in the laboratory and in the field that the growth rate of most corals in the light was considerably higher than in the dark (Fig. 6.2; Table 6.1). When corals were held in darkness for several weeks they extruded their zooxanthellae, though the polyps remained apparently healthy and active in food collection. Corals treated in this way had much reduced rates of calcification, even in the light.

The relationship of calcification to zooxanthellae must be indirect, for the large apical polyps of some corals have very few zooxanthellae, yet

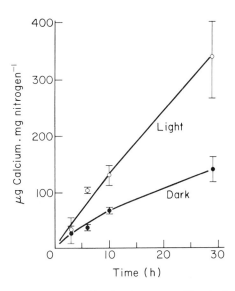

Fig. 6.2 Time course of calcium deposition in *Acropora prolifera* in the light and in the dark. (From Goreau 1959.)

Table 6.1 (a) Laboratory data. Calcification rates in the apical polyps of branching coral species, in μg Ca . mg N^{-1} . hr^{-1}. Number of samples in brackets.

Species	Calcification in light	Calcification in dark
Cladocora arbuscula	$6\cdot3 \pm 1\cdot58$ (9)	$6\cdot1 \pm 0\cdot20$ (10)
Porites divaricata	$9\cdot8 \pm 0\cdot54$ (10)	$5\cdot0 \pm 1\cdot00$ (8)
Porites compressa	$7\cdot8 \pm 1\cdot70$ (11)	$7\cdot4 \pm 2\cdot10$ (7)
Acropora prolifera	$12\cdot4 \pm 6\cdot50$ (12)	$7\cdot2 \pm 5\cdot00$ (11)
Montipora verrucosa	$11\cdot9 \pm 5\cdot60$ (9)	$9\cdot7 \pm 3\cdot4$ (10)
Pocillopora damicornis	$10\cdot3 \pm 3\cdot90$ (11)	$6\cdot8 \pm 2\cdot1$ (10)
Oculina diffusa	$1\cdot6 \pm 0\cdot38$ (7)	$0\cdot8 \pm 0\cdot15$ (9)
Porolithon sp.	$8\cdot8 \pm 0\cdot58$ (11)	$3\cdot3 \pm 0\cdot55$ (13)

(b) Field data. Calcium uptake of pieces of coral incubated under water close to the reef, in μg Ca . mg N^{-1} . hr^{-1}.

Species	Sunshine	Cloudy	Darkness
Acropora palmata	$43\cdot6 \pm 9\cdot81$ (8)	$26\cdot3 \pm 7\cdot5$ (10)	$3\cdot2 \pm 0\cdot64$ (7)
Acropora cervicornis	$53\cdot7 \pm 7\cdot34$ (9)	$39\cdot4 \pm 8\cdot65$ (7)	$8\cdot4 \pm 0\cdot66$ (6)
	$71\cdot5 \pm 12\cdot92$ (5)	$33\cdot2 \pm 6\cdot80$ (6)	$4\cdot1 \pm 0\cdot35$ (8)
Millepora complanata	$35\cdot7 \pm 3\cdot89$ (9)	$24\cdot6 \pm 5\cdot52$ (9)	$4\cdot7 \pm 0\cdot36$ (10)

calcification proceeds most rapidly at the tips of the branches. Pearse and Muscatine (1971) carried out ^{45}Ca experiments with staghorn coral *Acropora cervicornis* and showed that the light enhancement of calcification at the tips of the branches was related to photosynthesis by zooxanthellae further down the branch. They suggested that algal products of photosynthesis were translocated to the tips of the branches and used somehow to enhance calcification rates. Vandermeulen *et al.* (1972) confirmed that the calcification process is dependent on photosynthesis rather than on some other photobiological effect. Using *Pocillopora damicornis* they showed that the photosynthetic inhibitor DCMU at a concentration of 5×10^{-4} M was effective in blocking the uptake of ^{14}C both by complete branches of coral and isolated zooxanthellae, but the effect was totally reversible in 1–3 h after removal of the inhibitors. They then went on to show that there was a similar effect on light-enhanced ^{45}Ca incorporation. The level of calcification in the light when DCMU was present, was similar to the level observed in the dark.

Various hypotheses have been put forward to account for the relationship between photosynthesis and calcification. Pearse and Muscatine (1971) suggested, in effect, that the zooxanthellae provided organic material for the construction of a skeletal matrix. Barnes and Taylor (1973) emphasized

energy budget considerations and suggested the symbionts provide photosynthate to satisfy the energy requirements of the calcification process.
Crossland and Barnes (1974), taking their cue from literature on
calcification in molluscs and in hens' eggs, suggested that urea metabolism
might be involved. They incubated pieces of the staghorn coral *Acropora
acuminata* with ^{14}C-urea and found that the label was incorporated into
skeletal carbonate. Various other lines of investigation suggested that the
zooxanthellae provide glycolate, which is converted to glyoxylate and
combined with urea to form allantoic acid. The authors proposed that allan-
toins are the medium by which calcium and CO_2 are transported to sites of
calcification. Details of the proposed mechanism are shown in Fig. 6.3.

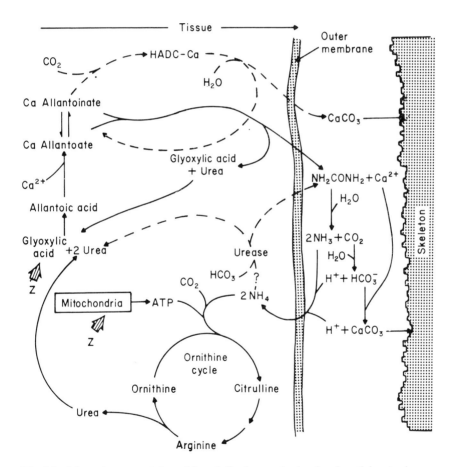

Fig. 6.3 Schematic representation of the calcification mechanism in scleractinian corals.
Broad, striped arrows (Z) represent probable sites of stimulation by products of zooxanthellae.
HAD-Ca is a calcium salt of hydroxyacetylene diureide carboxylic acid. (From Crossland
& Barnes 1974.)

A relatively simple method of monitoring calcification in nature was developed by Smith and Kinsey (1978). CO_2 is monitored, and its flux determined, by measuring pH, total alkalinity, salinity and temperature. The total alkalinity change enables one to calculate how much CO_2 change is due to calcification. The remainder is attributable to photosynthesis and respiration. When this technique was applied in the field, it was found that a very rich community of corals had about the same calcification rate as an alga-covered reef flat, while a zone of alga-encrusted rubble and small coral heads had an even higher rate of calcification (LIMER Expedition Team 1975). This serves to remind us that while hermatypic corals are the characteristic organisms of the reef, many other organisms, especially coralline algae, play a key role in calcium deposition.

6.4. THE FUNCTIONAL ZONES OF A REEF

While the details of structure and composition of reef communities vary enormously from place to place, there is a tendency for a certain general pattern to occur. The following account, which is taken mainly from Milliman (1974) and Orme (1977), applies particularly to Indo-Pacific reefs. (In the Atlantic, most corals are found in the Caribbean region. Those in the warmer, southern part have similar zones, but those in the northern part, especially in Florida and the Bahamas, tend to be smaller and simpler.) In areas where the wind direction is more or less constant throughout the year, there is a very well marked windward *reef front* (Fig. 6.4). In coastal areas the reef front develops on the seaward side regardless of wind direction. The front is characterized by vigorous development of coral in the form of spurs projecting seaward, alternating with deep grooves. This formation allows waves to dissipate their energy by surging up the channels between the spurs. As the water washes back it tends to carry a load of sediment and to accentuate the grooves by erosion. The reef front generally drops quite steeply to a depth of 5–15 m, and then gently to about 18 m. Below this level

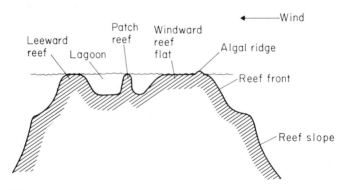

Fig. 6.4 Diagrammatic section through an atoll to show the chief zones of a reef complex.

the gradient is much steeper, and in some places is almost vertical. A platform at 18 m depth is characteristic of numerous localities, and is thought to have been formed in the Pleistocene when sea levels were much lower than at present. Some writers consider this platform to mark the lower limit of the reef front, and refer to the zone below it as the *reef slope*. Some corals can grow as deep as 40 m, but there is little doubt that the main growth occurs in the upper 18 m.

Behind the front is found the *windward reef flat*. Many Pacific reefs have on the outer flat an *algal ridge*, formed from crustose coralline algae. Development of this ridge depends on there being a prevailing wind, constant in direction and never failing, which enables the algae to grow as much as 100 cm above low tide level, moistened by the surge and splash of the waves. These conditions are characteristic of much of the tropical Pacific, but less so of the Indian Ocean. In the southern Caribbean some similar ridges have been found, but containing a mixture of corals, soft corals and algae. In the Indo-Pacific area the main reef flat is often paved with coralline algae, whereas in the Caribbean, corals are much more important and the surface is more irregular. In protected environments on the inner reef flat, benthic formaminifera are often particularly abundant.

Inside the reef flat is the *lagoon*. In the Caribbean the lagoon depth is almost always in the range 5–15 m, but in the Indo-Pacific Atolls lagoon depth is related to size of atoll, and may be as much as 70 m. The lagoon floor is composed mainly of sediment derived from erosion of the windward reef, and this becomes colonized by a variety of macrophytes and invertebrates. Rising from the lagoon floor are various coral reefs varying in size from low knolls to large patch reefs which may resemble miniature atolls. Some lagoons have few patch reefs, while others may be liberally dotted with them.

On the leeward side of the lagoon, an atoll has a *leeward reef*. Here, zonation may be similar to that on the windward reef, but in the absence of heavy wave action the algal ridge is weak or absent. In the Caribbean the leeward reef is usually poorly defined, and may consist of anastomosing patch reefs. In barrier reefs the inner margin of the lagoon is usually the land mass.

6.5 THE NUTRITION OF CORALS

After many years of debate, it now seems to be fairly well agreed that corals obtain their nutrition from several sources: from the extracellular products of their zooxanthellae; from the capture of particles in the water, especially zooplankton but probably also bacteria and phytoplankton; and from particles scavenged from the substrate and possibly from dissolved organic matter in the water. The subject has been well reviewed by Muscatine (1973) and Muscatine and Porter (1977).

6.5.1   Contribution from zooplankton

As a result of his work on the Great Barrier Reef Expedition in 1928–29, Sir Maurice Yonge (1930) suggested that corals obtained most of their nutrition by capturing zooplankton. He pointed out that their oral surface is adapted to prey capture and that its surface area in relation to the volume of the polyp is extremely high. Mechanisms of capture include the raptorial use of tentacles bearing nematocysts, the use of mucus as a trap, with ciliary currents to carry the trapped particles to the mouth, and the extrusion of mesenterial filaments through the mouth.

This view of coral nutrition was difficult to reconcile with the low density of zooplankton and other particles in the water surrounding the reefs. In an attempt to test the hypothesis Johannes and Tepley (1974) used time-lapse cinematography to estimate the zooplankton ingestion rate and concluded that not more than 10% of the daily energy requirement came from this source. Land *et al.* (1975) showed that the ratio of $^{13}C/^{12}C$ in the total soft tissue of Jamaican corals was very close to the ratio in isolated zooxanthellae, and different from the ratio in zooplankton caught nearby in the water column. They therefore concluded that zooxanthellae were the prime source of carbon for the corals. Porter (1974) syringed gut contents from individual polyps and found a wide variety of planktonic and demersal organisms, but concluded that these organisms accounted for no more than 20% of the energy requirements of the coral.

The argument about the amount of zooplankton available to corals has been modified by recent discoveries of a zooplankton fauna peculiar to the reef and distinct from that of the surrounding oceanic water. (Sale *et al.* 1976, 1978). The density is of the order of 700 organisms m^{-3} with at least 180 taxa represented. Many of the organisms are demersal or epibenthic in habit, but can be taken with the aid of a light trap. Alldredge and King (1977) identified a dersal component which hides within the reef by day and emerges at night. It consisted of cumaceans, mysids, ostracods, shrimps, isopods, amphipods, crustacean larvae, polychaetes, foraminiferans and copepods, at a mean density of 2510 m^{-2} of substrate. However, the density of organisms emerging specifically from coral was over 11 000 m^{-2}, and the average density over the reef face (all types of substrate) was 7900 m^{-2}, composed mainly of copepods. Still more recently it has been shown that very dense aggregations (up to 3·3 million m^{-3}) of single species of copepods could be found during the day on the lagoon side of windward reefs, and adjacent to coral outcrops in the lagoons (Hammer & Carleton 1979). This had led to the suggestion that random sampling for zooplankton may greatly underestimate its true abundance. Nevertheless, there is a general consensus that while zooplankton may be a major component of the diet of the species of coral that are voracious carnivores, it is unlikely that it provides more than a fraction of the metabolic needs of the whole community.

Table 6.2   A tentative carbon budget for a *Pocillopora* coral head of 30–50 g wet weight.

Daily respiration of zooxanthellae plus animal	11·71 mg C
Daily respiration of animal component	11·12 mg C
Net carbon fixed by zooxanthellae in 24 h	24·12 mg C
Amount of carbon translocated to animal component	9·65 mg C
Proportion of respiratory need supplied by translocation	86·8%

6.5.2   Contribution from zooxanthellae

We have already seen that the rate of deposition of calcium is dependent on the photosynthesis of zooxanthellae. It is now fairly clear that the soft tissues of corals take up the photosynthetic products of the zooxanthellae. For example, Muscatine and Cernichiari (1969) incubated pieces of *Pocillopora damicornis* with $Na_2{}^{14}CO_3$ both in the laboratory and *in situ* on the reef. After 24 h incubation, 35–50% of the total ^{14}C fixed appeared in the animal tissue as lipid and protein. Muscatine and Porter (1977) put together a tentative carbon budget for *Pocillopora* (Table 6.2) and showed that photosynthesis of the zooxanthellae was potentially able to provide for most of the carbon requirements of the coral tissue. They went on to suggest that there is a spectrum of coral types ranging from the voracious carnivore to the mainly autotrophic. The carnivores are characterized by having large polyps and a low surface/volume ratio, while specialized autotrophs have branching or plated forms which are efficient for light interception and are characterized by a high surface/volume ratio. When Caribbean reef corals are plotted on the two axes of surface/volume ratio and polyp diameter (Fig. 6.5) the points can be fitted to the equation:

$$S/V = 1·89(P.D)^{-0·8} \qquad (6.1)$$

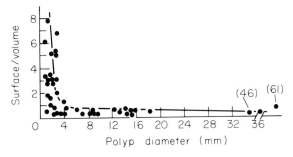

Fig. 6.5   The surface/volume ratio of each of the Caribbean reef-building coral species plotted against polyp diameter. For explanation see text. (After Porter 1976.)

and show a rather even distribution over the range of types. Each species seems to have defined its unique niche in terms of the relative importance to it of plankton or of photosynthesis as an energy source.

Coral polyps differ in their diurnal rhythms of activity, and it has been suggested that those relying mainly on photosynthesis may expand their polyps by day, whereas those relying more on zooplankton may expand at night when the crustaceans emerge from the crevices and sediment. Semens and De Riemer (1977) tested the hypothesis as it applies to 14 sea anemone species at 9 sites on Caribbean reefs. They found that tentacles containing dense populations of zooxanthellae expanded during the day as well as the night, while those with few zooxanthellae contracted during the day, but expanded at night. Some species had their zooxanthellae mainly in auxilliary structures of the column. They tended to expand the auxiliiary structures during the day, but expanded the tentacles only at night. The authors concluded that contraction of tentacles when not in use conserves energy and nitrogen. These observations, made on anemones, may well apply equally to coral polyps.

6.6   THE NUTRIENT BUDGETS OF CORALS

The early work of Sir Maurice Yonge and his collaborators emphasized phosphorus budgets. They showed that the presence of zooxanthellae was associated with a reduced rate of phosphorus excretion, and postulated that the zooxanthellae benefited the corals by taking up phosphate, thus functioning as 'automatic organs of excretion' (Yonge 1940) and helping to make possible the high level of growth and calcium deposition characteristic of corals. In recent years it has become generally agreed that nitrogen, not phosphorus, is the nutrient most often limiting, especially in the tropics. D'Elia and Webb (1977) showed that *Pocillopora elegans* colonies actively take up nitrate from sea-water, both in the light and in the dark. The Michaelis–Menten kinetic constants for uptake were:

$$V_{max} = 5 \cdot 69 \pm 1 \cdot 11 \text{ ng atoms . mg atom N}^{-1} . \text{min}^{-1}$$

$$K = 249 \pm 247 \text{ nM} \qquad S_0 = 57 \pm 47 \text{ nM} \qquad (6.2)$$

where S_0 is the threshold concentration below which uptake of nitrate did not occur. The authors also referred to unpublished work on the uptake of ammonium, in which the V_{max} appeared to be almost twice as high as for nitrate. Combining the two sets of results, they concluded that *Pocillopora* probably obtains its nitrogen two-thirds from ammonium and one-third from nitrate, and showed that the ratio of N uptake to P uptake is consistent with the 16:1 ratio of Redfield *et al.* (1963), suggesting that the zooxanthellae are responsible for the uptake. However, preliminary observations on loss of organic nitrogen, and on the rate of turnover in the biomass, suggest that uptake of inorganic nitrogen is a minor part of the nitrogen budget of the corals. They must rely to a large extent on the capture of particulate organic nitrogen.

Summarizing to this point, we see that photosynthesis is probably an important factor in providing for the carbon and energy needs of corals, but that capture of zooplankton and detritus is probably the main method by which they obtain nitrogen. Hence, the statement at the beginning of section 6.5 indicating that corals obtain their nutrient from a variety of trophic levels is amply justified.

6.7 THE METABOLISM OF A REEF

The pioneers of the whole-ecosystem approach to coral reefs were Howard T. Odum and Eugene P. Odum (1955) who in the summer of 1954 undertook the daunting task of determining the biomass of primary producers, herbivores and carnivores in five distinct zones and the production and respiration of the total community on a transect. They showed that it was indeed possible to study the system in its totality. Although the details of their work have been improved upon by separate studies of each process, the paper stands as a landmark in the history of coral reef ecosystem studies.

6.7.1 Primary production

Reviews of the methods used and the values obtained for primary production of total reef communities have been published by Lewis (1977) and Sournia (1977). One of the most striking points to emerge is that every conceivable type of primary producer makes a contribution: zooxanthellae, which are symbiotic dinoflagellates; filamentous chlorophyceans attached to the coral skeleton; macrophytic brown and red algae; coralline algae; seagrasses; benthic diatoms, and phytoplankton. The gross primary production of the total community is as high as any in the world, often in the range $2–5000$ g C m^{-2} yr^{-1} (Table 6.3). However, the respiration of the community is also high, and net community production is low, indicating that most of what is produced is also consumed within the community.

Studies of photosynthesis by corals are often expressed in terms of tissue weight, or tissue area, but for comparative purposes the most useful figures are in g C m^{-2} of reef surface. Kanwisher and Wainwright (1967) reported on 14 species of Florida reef corals, and gave figures of $2·7–10·2$ g C m^{-2} day, equivalent to $985–3723$ g C m^{-2} yr^{-1}. From the time constants of the response to changed light intensity, they concluded that the zooxanthellae were responsible for the observed photosynthesis, and that the filamentous green algae located deep in the coral skeleton were contributing little.

Table 6.3 Comparison of estimates of primary production of coral reefs, atolls and seagrass beds made by different authors. (From Lewis 1977.)

Locality	Gross production (g C/m²/year)	Community respiration (g C/m²/year)	P/R	Authors
Hawaiian coral reef, Coconut Island	7300	12 370	0·59	Gordon & Kelly (1962)
Fringing coral reef, North Kapaa, Hawaii	2427	2200	1·1	Kohn & Helfrich (1957)
Eniwetok Atoll, Marshall Islands	4200	4200	1·0	Odum & Odum (1955)
El Mario reefs, Puerto Rico	4450	4100	1·1	Odum, Burkholder & Rivero (1959)
Eastern Reef, Rongelap Atoll, Marshall Islands	1250	1090	1·1	Sargent & Austin (1954)
Kavaratti lagoon, Laccadives	4715	3482	1·3	Qasim & Sankaranarayanan (1970)
Bimini lagoon, British West Indies	319	205	1·5	Odum & Hoskin (1958)
Kavaratti reef, Laccadives	2250	880	2·5	Qasim & Sankaranarayanan (1970)
Turtle grass bed, Long Key, Florida	3880	2740	1·4	Odum (1957)
Turtle grass bed, West La Gata reef, Puerto Rico	980	1290	0·8	Odum, Burkholder & Rivero (1959)
Turtle grass bed, Isla Magueyes, Puerto Rico	1350	1500	0·9	Odum, Burkholder & Rivero (1959)
Eniwetok Atoll, algal flat	4234	2190	1·9	Smith & Marsh (1973)
One Tree Island, lagoon reef	1387	1314	1·1	Kinsey (1972)
Eniwetok Atoll, coral algal flat	2190	2190	1·0	Smith & Marsh (1973)
Guam, reef flat	6900	2600	2·6	Marsh (1974)
Eniwetok Atoll, windward reef flat	3285	2190	1·5	Smith (1974)
Eniwetok Atoll, algal flat	5329	2190	2·4	Smith (1974)

Hence, we may conclude that zooxanthellae are among the major primary producers of a reef. Scott and Jitts (1977) estimated that zooxanthellae at Lizard Island, Barrier Reef were fixing carbon at about 0.9 g C m^{-2} day^{-1}.

The role of benthic algae (other than corallines) on coral reefs has not yet been clarified. Odum and Odum (1955) recognized seven types on Eniwetok Atoll: (1) filamentous algae boring into coral; (2) algae matted as an encrustation on and in the dead rigid porous reef substrate; (3) encrusting fleshy green types, with encrusting reds mostly beneath the greens; (4) small algae in and on loose coral pieces; (5) small filamentous algae in and on dead coral heads; (6) large conspicuous branching algae attached around dead heads; and (7) microscopic algae in the coral sand. They estimated biomass by chlorophyll extraction and concluded that the reef had a rather uniform algal component, averaging 703 g dry organic weight per m^{-2} of surface area, with different components in different areas. Wanders (1976a,b, 1977) has documented the role of benthic algae on the Caribbean island of Curacao. *Sargassum* is a common and abundant fleshy alga in the Caribbean (Chapter 3) and Wanders showed that it forms highly productive beds on the north-east coast of Curacao. He drew attention to the importance of fish grazing in controlling the growth of fleshy algae on the coral reef. When cages were erected to exclude grazers, the filamentous and fleshy algae became abundant and out-competed the corallines. On dead coral the carpet of grazed filamentous algae had a very high production/biomass ratio. It seems probable from several indirect lines of evidence (Bakus 1966; Vine 1974) that macroalgae on coral reefs are very intensely grazed by fishes and invertebrates, and that they constitute a rather inconspicuous but nevertheless highly productive 'algal turf'. Johannes *et al.* (1972) showed that at Eniwetok the gross primary productivity on a transect with negligible coral heads but dominated by algae was about 10 g C m^{-2} day^{-1}, a figure that was much higher than that found on the coral-dominated transects.

In contrast to the fleshy algae, the coralline algae are very conspicuous on a coral reef. Marsh (1970) found that the reef building algae on Eniwetok had a production of about 550 g C m^{-2} yr^{-1} gross, and 240 g C m^{-2} yr^{-1} net. He suggested that their role as reef-builders was more important than their role as primary producers. Wanders (1976a) gave production of 890 g C gross and 370 g C m^{-2} yr^{-1} net for coralline algae on Curacao. In general, the corallines are seen to be less important as primary producers than are the algal turfs. This is understandable in view of their role in calcification.

Seagrasses such as *Thalassia testudinum* are frequently found in sheltered lagoonal areas, where they grow rooted in coral sediment, and make an important contribution to detritus food chains. Net production is in the range 400–4000 g C m^{-2} yr^{-1} (Lewis 1977). The ecology of seagrasses has been discussed in Chapter 2.

Primary production on the lagoon floor is apparently quite high when the bottom consists of coarse coral rubble with filamentous algae attached (Johannes *et al.* 1972) but less high on sandy bottoms. Sournia (1976) found that on Takapoto Atoll (French Polynesia) the sandy bottom included large numbers of foraminifera with algal symbionts, and that these could yield a net production of 0·43–1·33 g C m^{-2} day^{-1}.

In general, then, the overall gross primary productivity of a reef appears to be very high, in the range 2000–5000 g C m^{-2} yr^{-1}. Attempts to break this down to the components responsible for the production lead to no firm conclusions, since each reef is a complex mosaic of producers. The indications are that corals themselves may fix over 3000 g C m^{-2} yr^{-1} through their zooxanthellae and that coralline algae may fix rather less rapidly. It seems probable, but has not been clearly demonstrated, that the most intense primary production is in the turfs of filamentous algae which are intensively grazed by fish and invertebrates, and consequently have an extremely rapid turnover of biomass. The productivity of the total community is often greatly enhanced by the presence of seagrass beds in the sheltered, sedimented sites.

6.7.2 Consumers of primary production

The numbers and taxonomic diversity of animals associated with coral reefs is often extremely great. For example, Grassle (1973) found 1441 polychaetes belonging to 103 species in a single coral head. However, in most cases the biomass of corals is greater than that of other consumers. Odum and Odum (1955) estimated the mean biomass of consumers on Eniwetok as 143 g dry weight of living material m^{-2}, of which one to two-thirds was coral polyp. We have seen that corals receive much of their nutrition from photosynthate translocated from zooxanthellae, and another proportion from zooplankton and other invertebrates. Recent work has suggested that there may be an important food chain involving coral mucus, bacteria, zooplankton and fish. Johannes (1967) reported the release of mucus by corals at Eniwetok at a rate which he estimated at 20 mg m^{-2} hr^{-1}, equivalent to about 40% of coral respiration. He showed that when brine shrimp *Artemia salina* was cultured in the presence of this mucus it grew faster and survived longer than in controls. This mucus is known to be ingested by fish, crabs, and copepods and was shown by Benson and Muscatine (1974) to contain wax esters and triglycerides. Richman *et al.* (1975) showed that the copepod *Acartia negligens* could assimilate up to 50% of the organic matter of the mucus, while Gerber and Marshall (1974) showed that the guts of planktonic organisms in Eniwetok lagoon contained 90–95% detritus, which they thought was derived partly from coral mucus, while another major component originated from algal detritus. Marshal *et al.* (1975) demonstrated a sharp increase in particulate organic matter in the water as it passes from open water over various reef crests, but the increase did not continue across to the back slope of the reef. They suggested that the particles were being trapped and consumed by the reef community.

Recalling what was said in section 6.5 about the recent discovery that zooplankton organisms are very abundant in the interstices of reefs, emerging in great numbers at night, and that single-species swarms of great density occur on the windward side of the lagoons, it seems possible that coral mucus could be an important source of nutrient for these organisms. It is also possible that bacteria play an important part in transforming some soluble or gell-like components of the mucus into particles of filtrable size.

Moriarty (1979) made an intensive study of the biomass of bacteria suspended in water flowing over coral reefs at two locations in the northern

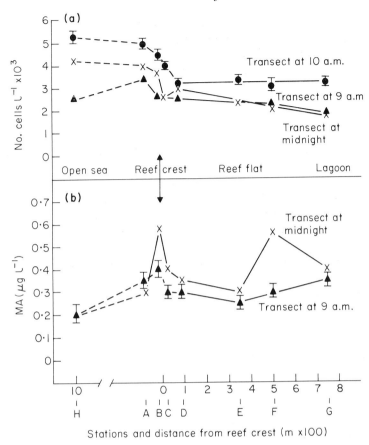

Fig. 6.6 (a) Counts of total free cells and (b) muramic acid values as indices of bacterial biomass, in a transect from open sea across a reef to the lagoon. (From Moriarty 1979.)

Great Barrier Reef. He used two methods: direct counting, which is good for free bacteria but inadequate for bacteria attached to particles, and a muramic acid method which works equally well for bacteria on particles. In samples in which the two methods gave similar results he concluded that most bacteria were free, but when the direct counts gave much lower figures he concluded that many bacteria were attached to particles. Water masses moving across the reef were identified either by a drogue or by fluorescein. He found that water in front of the reef crest had fewer free bacteria than the open sea, but more bacteria attached to particles (Fig. 6.6). He concluded that particulate matter containing bacteria was being thrown up into suspension at the reef front, and was being carried back over the reef flats to the lagoon. The total amount of particulate organic matter in the water was of the order of 100–300 mg m^{-3}, and bacterial carbon was thought to account for 10–15% of it.

An experiment by Smith *et al.* (1979) showed that coral reef zooplankton seldom ingest phytoplankton. The authors suggested instead that they are detritus feeders. Sorokin (1974) showed that many organisms of the reef fauna are capable of efficiently filtering bacteria from sea-water. Evidence from a number of sources adds up to the view that particulate organic matter, originating from algal fragments, coral mucus, etc., and richly colonized by bacteria, is the vehicle by which one of the most important transfers of energy and nutrients takes place within a coral reef ecosystem.

Among the direct consumers of coral reef production, echinoderms are prominent. Sammarco *et al.* (1974) showed how the sea-urchin *Diadema antillarum* modifies a reef community. When these urchins were removed from a patch reef in the Caribbean there was a great increase in macro-algal biomass, with concomitant changes in species composition and species diversity. Dart (1972) showed that in the Red Sea there were two species of urchin *Heterocentrotus mamillatus* and *Diadema setosum* which lived in crevices during the day but emerged at night to graze the algal lawn on areas of open rock. Unlike the fishes (see section 6.7.3) the urchins systematically removed all the algae from an area, often removing rock or dead coral tissue from beneath. It is possible that such areas are prime sites for recolonization by corals.

Where patch reefs occur among seagrass beds in lagoons, there is often a 'halo' of light-coloured coral sand round each reef. This is due to the heavy grazing of seagrasses by sea-urchins, which hide in the reef by day but emerge to forage at night (Ogden *et al.* 1973).

There are numerous examples from many parts of the world (Lawrence 1975) of sea-urchins becoming very abundant and creating 'urchin-dominated barren grounds'. The cause of these population explosions is not entirely clear, but is usually attributed to a reduction in the number of predators. Similar outbreaks have been noted in the numbers of the crown-of-thorns starfish *Acanthaster planci*. This multi-armed species which can grow to a diameter of 60 cm has been recorded in small numbers (about 6 km^{-2}) on most reefs of the Indian Ocean and West Pacific (Endean 1974). It preys chiefly on hard corals, and it has been calculated that each animal requires on average the coral from about 10 m^2 (flat projection) per year. In the decade 1965–1975 there were numerous cases of destruction of large areas of coral by dense aggregations of *Acanthaster* and, as in the cases of urchin aggregations, opinions differed as to the cause of the outbreaks and whether they were due to human interference in the ecosystem. Endean (1977) reviewed the evidence and concluded that the basic cause was removal by man of the natural predators of the starfish, especially the giant triton *Charonia tritonis*. On the other hand, Frankel (1977) inferred from skeletal remains in surface and subsurface sediments that *A. planci* was present in abundance on reefs several hundreds of years ago, and that the aggregations are naturally occurring phenomena. One study (Dana *et al.* 1972) invoked typhoons as the principle agents causing aggregations; another invoked salinity change. The question has not been settled, but the author's own experience with the destruction of kelp beds by sea-urchins (Chapter 3) leads him to favour predator-removal as a major component. It is entirely possible that predator removal combined with natural tendencies to aggregate has led to destruction of coral on an unprecedented scale.

6.7.3 The role of reef fishes

A good review of the role of herbivorous fishes on coral reefs has been published by Ogden and Lobel (1978). In general, it supports the view mentioned earlier (section 6.7.1) that there is intense grazing of fish on algae, resulting in modification of algal community structure and rapid turnover of algal biomass. Most herbivorous fish are active by day and hide within the reef at night. Many are territorial. Damsel fishes (Pomocentridae) defend a territory which is identifiable by a patch of algae of distinctive colour and composition. In areas where pomocentrids are not present, acanthurids (surgeon fishes), scarids, chaetodontids, balistids and siganids keep filamentous algae closely cropped (Vine 1974). When the food preferences of various fishes were reviewed (Ogden & Lobel 1978) it appeared that acanthurids preferred *Polysiphonia* and *Enteromorpha*, scarids preferred *Thalassia*, siganids preferred *Enteromorpha* while pomacanthids preferred *Enteromorpha* and *Codium*. There have been several demonstrations that caging an area of bottom to exclude fish results in a rapid increase in algal biomass and often in the establishment of large fleshy algae which otherwise are restricted to places where it is difficult for fish to graze, such as the wave-washed top of a reef.

Odum and Odum (1955) suggested on the basis of visual census that herbivores predominated on coral reefs, but Goldman and Talbot (1976) considered that more destructive sampling measures such as poisoning or explosives must be used to obtain a balanced picture. They concluded that carnivorous fishes—piscivores, planktivores and benthic invertebrate predators—constitute about 75% of the fish biomass on a reef. In their study of One Tree Island Reef in the Great Barrier Reef, piscivorous forms predominated on the windward reef slopes (64% of the biomass), benthic invertebrate feeders predominated on the reef flat and the community in the leeward reef slopes had all four types, piscivores, planktivores, benthic invertebrate predators and grazers (on algae and corals), about equally represented (Fig. 6.7). The greatest biomass (2000 kg/ha) was found off the reef front, the next largest (1400 kg/ha) on the leeward reef slope, while the windward upper slopes had the least (200 kg/ha).

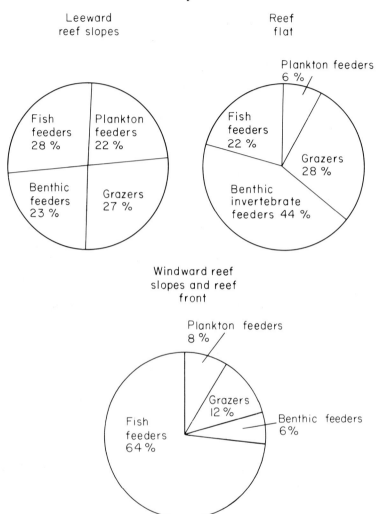

Fig. 6.7 Proportion of total biomass of the four major feeding types of coral reef fishes found on the three main habitats of One Tree Island Reef. (After Goldman and Talbot 1976.)

These figures are impressive and show that fish play a much more important role in system function on a coral reef than they do in almost any other system. It appears that the herbivores consume a high proportion of the plant production, and it is probable that their faeces contribute large amounts to detritus food webs. Carnivores must be active in removing a high proportion of the production of benthic invertebrates and zooplankton. A rough estimate of production based on figures reviewed to this point suggests a primary production of over 2000 g C m^{-2} yr^{-1} supporting by way of a complex network of trophic pathways, a fish biomass averaging perhaps 500 kg/h or 50 g m^{-2}. The annual production of such a stock may well be in the range of 5–10 g C m^{-2} yr^{-1}. However, as we have seen there seems to be little evidence of export of either primary or secondary production from coral reef systems, and the key to understanding system function is to know how materials are so tightly recycled. The next section returns to this topic.

6.7.4 Nutrient dynamics of the total community

We saw in section 6.6 that coral polyps take up nitrate and ammonia from the water but this appears to provide for only a small part of their needs. The remainder must come from feeding on particulate matter, presumably zooplankton, bacteria and detritus. We also saw, earlier in section 6.7, that there is probably a major contribution of primary production by benthic algae, especially by the short turf of filamentous algae which is turning over its biomass rapidly. Algae need nitrogen but the oceanic water that bathes the reef normally contains very little. How does the reef balance its nitrogen budget?

With these questions in mind, Webb *et al.* (1975) measured changes in the concentrations of dissolved and particulate nitrogen in sea-water as it crossed the reef of Eniwetok Atoll. They worked on two transects: one dominated by coralline algae and the other having an algal pavement upstream but rich coral growth in the downstream half. The former transect was a net consumer of nitrate, but the latter showed a 70% increase in nitrate from upstream to downstream. Ammonium remained unchanged over the first transect, but had a 17% increase over the second. Dissolved organic nitrogen (DON) and particulate organic nitrogen (PON) increased along both transects. The source of the nitrogen was found to be gaseous nitrogen fixation by algae, the most important of which was the blue-green *Calothrix crustacea* (Webb *et al.* 1975), growing particularly on the windward slope of the reef flat. Rates of fixation were equivalent to an average rate of 1·8 kg N ha^{-1} day^{-1}, and were enough to account for the net export of nitrogen from the system. Routes by which the nitrogen fixed by the algae entered the rest of the community include: (1) grazing by fish and release of nitrogen in egestion and excretion; (2) breaking off of algal tissue by wave action, with subsequent ingestion by detritivores downstream; (3) release of DOM by the algae.

In their discussion of the significance of these results, Webb *et al.* (1975) remarked that it is usually thought that mature ecosystems (Margalef 1968) have relatively 'closed' nutrient cycles, whereas Eniwetok Atoll was a major exporter of dissolved nitrogen, at least at the time the observations were made. It is probable (Jones & Stewart 1969) that a large proportion of the fixed nitrogen was initially released as DON, yet a considerable amount of the export was in the form of nitrate. This indicates the organic matter must have been deaminated by heterotrophs (bacteria?) to yield NH_4^+, and then nitrified through NO_3^-. This is interesting, since little is known about the microbial processes responsible for formation of the large reservoirs of NO_3^- in the sea.

By contrast, the cycling of phosphorous at Eniwetok Atoll is very tightly closed, with negligible fluxes in or out of the system (Pilson & Betzer 1973). Such a result is not surprising for coral communities (see section 6.6) but it was also found to hold true for transects dominated by algae, with negligible amounts of coral present. The explanation offered was that phosphorus excretion by heterotrophs must be balanced by the phosphorus uptake of autotrophs. Yet in other situations this has been shown to lead to diurnal fluctuations in dissolved phosphorus which were not found in the reef. The authors went on to suggest that the algae may be phosphorus limited during the day, so they continue to take up phosphorus even after dark. When Webb *et al.* (1975) analysed their nitrogen flux data, there was no clear indication of a difference between night and day, but uptake of both NO_3^- and NH_4^+ was significantly higher between noon and midnight than it was between midnight and noon.

6.8   TOTAL SYSTEM FUNCTION

We have now reached the point where our very incomplete knowledge of processes occurring on a coral reef may be integrated to provide a tentative model of system function (Fig. 6.8).

Corals are the organisms whose calcifying activity makes possible the formation of a reef in the first place, but once formed, the coralline algae play a major part in cementing the structure, and filamentous algae contribute a large share of the overall primary production. The concensus seems to be that corals obtain most of their carbon and energy from photosynthesis, but most of their nitrogen from ingestion of zooplankton and other particulate matter. Species differ in the proportion of energy they obtain from internal sources (zooxanthellae) but all rely on external food sources to a greater or lesser extent.

Phosphorus is tightly recycled, both within the coral–zooxanthellae complex and within algal–heterotroph communities, but nitrogen is less tightly recycled, the losses being made up by nitrogen fixation in the algal turf.

Particulate matter in suspension is much more abundant over a reef than in the surrounding water. It originates from coral mucus and from fragments of plant production, and is rapidly colonized by bacteria. Actively growing bacteria scavenge organic and inorganic nitrogen released into the water by

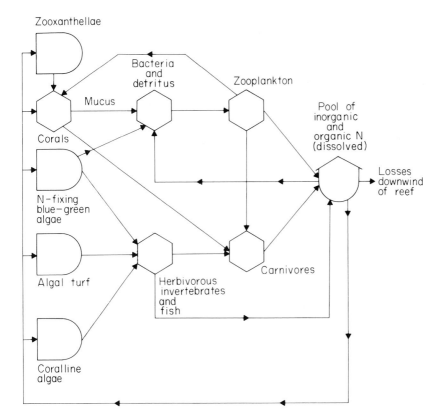

Fig. 6.8 Diagram to show the probable relationships of the functional groups in a coral reef ecosystem. Autotrophs, heterotrophs and reservoirs are each given a distinctively-shaped compartment, as in the Odum energy circuit symbolism.

animal excretion, and detritus with attached bacteria is a major source of food for filter feeders on the reef and in the lagoon.

The paradox which existed for a long time, in which corals were perceived to be zooplankton predators but the water bathing a reef appeared to contain little zooplankton has been resolved by the discovery of a cryptic zooplankton community, living in the interstices of the reef by day, and emerging mainly at night. The prime food source for this community appears to be bacteria and detritus.

The majority of the abundant and diverse fish community consists of carnivores, but a significant minority are voracious herbivores. These, together with invertebrate herbivores such as sea-urchins, graze the algal turf which covers a large proportion of the reef, encouraging the development of small species with high P/B ratios, but discouraging the formation of stands of large fleshy algae.

Finally, the interstices of the reef and the floor of the lagoon is colonized by diatoms, foraminifera, and higher animals, many of which are active in calcification and in carbon fixation through consumers of algae. The sediment associated with the activities of these organisms is usually occupied by seagrasses.

The whole system is abundantly colonized by an amazing diversity of invertebrate animals, far too numerous to mention. Those who specialize in the taxonomy, morphology, physiology or autecology of these organisms will no doubt consider that the chapter is most incomplete without an account of this aspect. It is here that the divergence between the system approach and the approach of the organismal biologist becomes most apparent. The organismal level has had a very considerable amount of attention, and there is an enormous scientific literature. The study of system function is relatively young and our understanding is at best fragmentary. Yet we can make wise decisions about the impact of man's activities only if we are well informed about both aspects. That is the justification for writing the book.

CHAPTER 7
SEDIMENT COMMUNITIES

7.1 INTRODUCTION

Up to this point we have dealt with various coastal ecosystems mainly in the terms of their characteristic primary production, but there are large areas of sea floor which have no primary production of their own, receiving instead quantities of organic matter by sinking and horizontal transport. There are massive exports of detritus from macrophyte beds, and much sinking of phytoplankton cells or zooplankton faeces from the upper layers of the water column. The final resting place of this material is the sediment–water interface. We discussed in Chapter 5 many of the microbial transformations that occur in the sediments. In this chapter we shall concentrate on the total community of the benthic sediments, and try to clarify its roles in ecosystem function.

In the North Sea, which is probably representative of large areas of coastal waters in the temperate zones, catches of bottom-feeding fish constitute 30–50% of the total fish catch (Steele 1974). However, a good proportion of pelagic fish catches are processed for animal feed or fertilizers, so demersal stocks probably produce at least half of our sea food. Seen in this light, a major role of benthic communities is to receive organic detritus and convert it to invertebrate biomass which serves as food for demersal fish and other predators. The conversion process is relatively inefficient, and the by-products include carbon dioxide and inorganic nitrogen, phosphorus, silicon, etc., which are regenerated to the water column and used again in primary production.

7.2   THE INPUT OF ORGANIC MATTER

Sediment surfaces are usually colonized by algae both intertidally and in shallow subtidal areas. It is not unusual for algae on the surfaces of intertidal sediments to fix 100–200 g C m^{-2} yr^{-1}. For subtidal sediments algal production is usually less than 100 g C m^{-2} yr^{-1} and decreases with depth.

Measurement of the amount of material arriving at the sediment surface has proved to be difficult. Sediment traps, usually consisting of cylinders open at the top, reveal that phytoplankton sinking after a bloom in surface waters makes an important contribution; but the traps have also indicated large inputs of organic matter when there was little production in surface waters. This is probably best explained by lateral transport, especially by tidal currents, and by resuspension of material previously settled on the bottom. Resuspension is particularly likely to occur in stormy weather, and probably accounts for the high catches of organic matter recorded in winter. Within the limits of uncertainty just mentioned, Steele and Baird (1972) estimated that input to the sediment in a Scottish inlet was about 30 g C m^{-2} yr^{-1}, mainly in the form of zooplankton faeces; Stephens *et al.* (1967) collected about 200 g C m^{-2} yr^{-1} in a bay on the west coast of Canada, and thought that about half was from terrestrial runoff; Webster *et al.* (1975) collected   164 g C   m^{-2} yr^{-1} in St.   Margaret's   Bay, Nova   Scotia and   concluded   that   the two   main   sources   were   phytoplankton cells and macrophyte detritus. Other examples are given in Parsons *et al.* (1977).

For areas further from land, and thus less under the influence of terrestrial runoff or inshore macrophyte production, an estimate of input to the sediments can be obtained from data on production and consumption in the water column, with the sediments receiving the difference. Riley (1956, 1970) calculated that in the Sargasso Sea, with a low level of phytoplankton production and a water column in excess of 400 m, only 1–2 g C m^{-2} yr^{-1} reached the bottom. The situation in Long Island Sound was quite different, and 60–80 g C m^{-2} yr^{-1} reached the sediments.

Pamatmat (1971) and Hargrave (1973, 1975) used the oxygen consumption of sediments to indicate the rate of metabolism of organic matter. If the assumption is made that metabolism is in balance with supply, this can be used to provide an indirect indication of organic matter input to the sediment. Hargrave found that sedimentation increased with increased primary production, but was inversely proportional to mixed layer depth, according to the equation:

$$S = 4 \cdot 9 + 3 \cdot 9 \left(\frac{C_s}{Z_m} \right) \qquad (7.1)$$

where S is rate of sedimentation in g C m^{-2} yr^{-1}, C_s is the carbon supply from primary production (same units) and Z_m is the mixed layer depth (m). It works out that when the thermocline is at 10–15 m (a fairly common value for coastal waters) 30–40% of the carbon supply is sedimented, whereas for a mixed layer depth over 25 m, carbon input to the bottom amounts to only a small percentage of the supply. The probable explanation is that in a deep mixed layer the phytoplankton remains suspended by turbulence long enough for zooplankton to consume most of it, whereas in a shallow mixed layer a good proportion passes through to the less turbulent waters below the thermocline, and then sinks steadily to the bottom.

If we take coastal phytoplankton production to be 100–200 g C m^{-2} yr^{-1}, we can therefore expect 30–80 g C m^{-2} yr^{-1} to sink to the bottom. In areas close to shore, where terrestrial runoff or macrophyte production augments the supply of organic matter, the amount reaching the sediments may be in the range 100–300 g C m^{-2} yr^{-1}.

7.3 CLASSES OF CONSUMERS IN THE BENTHOS

There is an abundant literature on the distribution and abundance of benthic invertebrates. Those living within the sediments, the infauna, have usually been collected by taking grab samples and sieving them. They are commonly sorted according to size into macrobenthos, meiobenthos and microbenthos, with dividing lines at about 1·0 mm and 0·1 mm mesh, or 10^{-4} and 10^{-10} g wet weight (Fig. 7.1). Invertebrates living on the sediment surface, or just above it, are referred to as epifauna. They are best collected in nets dragged along the surface on sledges. Mills (1975) referred to benthic ecology in these terms:

> Despite more than a century of intensive work on the collection and classification of shallow water benthic animals, much of benthic ecology seems a rather shabby and intellectually suspect branch of biological oceanography. Its methods are, for the most part, those of the nineteenth century; its results, too often, are of interest only to other students of the benthos; and its importance to other branches of biological oceanography has, in my opinion, been proportionately rather small, in spite of one origin of this discipline as a branch of fisheries research.

This is probably an unduly harsh criticism of the field, but the fact

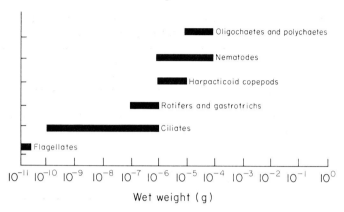

Fig. 7.1 The approximate weight ranges of meiobenthic groups.

remains, as Mills went on to show, that we have rather little information on the details of the processes whereby organic detritus is transformed into invertebrate biomass. There are almost no studies in which all components of the benthos have been determined. In part, this is due to the wide range of techniques needed to collect and separate all components. The great diversity in size means that quite different scales and techniques of sampling are needed for, say, lobsters weighing several kg and harpacticoid copepods weighing only μg. A few authors have attempted to make comparisons. Fenchel (1969) considered separately, bacteria, ciliates, meiobenthos and macrobenthos. He concluded from the literature that in most types of sediment the bacteria were responsible for more than 50% of community respiration. In terms of numbers, the meiobenthos outnumbered the macrobenthos by a factor of 10–100 or even more. In biomass, the situation was reversed, with the macrobenthos having 10–100 times more biomass than the meiofauna. However, Fenchel (1969) compared the metabolism of the various groups and considered that macrofauna, meiofauna and ciliates had roughly equal shares of the metabolism, with different proportions in different types of sediment (Table 7.1). Figures such as this might lead one to conclude that the transformation of dead organic matter into invertebrate biomass was an extremely inefficient process, with a very high proportion of the carbon being converted to CO_2. If, for example, carbon in dead plant remains were all to pass through the food chain:

organic detritus → bacteria → ciliates → meiobenthos → macrobenthos

and if ecological efficiency at each step was particularly high, say 20%, the overall efficiency would still be very low, only 0·16%. However, the available evidence suggests that the situation is really quite different. Steele (1974)

Table 7.1 Ratios between macrofauna, meiofauna and ciliates, on the basis of numbers, biomass and metabolism, at three sites in Denmark. (From Fenchel 1969.)

	Proportions		
Location	Numbers	Biomass	Metabolism
Alsgarde Beach (fine sand 175 μm)	1 : 40 : 1500	190 : 1·5 : 1	2·7 : 1 : 1·4
Helsingør Beach (fine sand 200 μm)	1 : 28 : 3000	3·9 : 1·6 : 1	1 : 3 : 8
Niva Bay (medium sand 350 μm)	1 : 10 : 50	170 : 10 : 1	4 : 2 : 1

showed that it was necessary to assume an overall efficiency of benthic invertebrate production close to 20% in order to account for demersal fish production in the North Sea, and Mills (1975) showed that the situation on the Argentine Shelf seems to be similar, though with higher levels of both primary and tertiary production. In an attempt to resolve this paradox, we must examine more closely the various classes of benthic consumers.

7.4   THE ROLE OF BACTERIA AND PROTOZOA

This topic was developed in some detail in Chapter 5 (section 5.4.2) and will be reviewed briefly here. Early work on the numbers and biomass of bacteria in bottom sediments had used plate counts which seriously and selectively underestimate natural microbial populations. Dale (1974) was one of the first to use direct counting after acridine orange staining as a method of evaluating bacterial biomass in sediments. He showed that bacteria were present to a depth of 10 cm in numbers ranging from $1·17 \times 10^8$ to $9·97 \times 10^9$ g^{-1} of dry sediment, and that they tended to be more abundant in sediments with fine particles and a high organic content. There was no correlation between abundance and Eh, suggesting that the numbers in anaerobic sediments were not significantly different from those in aerobic sediments. When converted from numbers to biomass in the top 10 cm, the estimates ranged from 5·5 g m^{-2} in fine sand to 26·5 g m^{-2} in coarse silt. Sorokin (1971) had reported 9·7 g m^{-2} in lagoon sand in the Pacific, and Zhukova and Fedosov (1963) had estimated 17–57 g m^{-2} in shallow mud of the Sea of Azov. These numbers are in the same range as the biomass of invertebrates in such sediments (Table 7.2) and give a clear indication that the bacteria are likely to be responsible for more than 50% of the metabolism of benthic communities.

In an attempt to demonstrate the metabolic role of bacteria in Castle

Table 7.2 Estimated biomass, turnover and production of various components of the benthos in a generalized silty sand station at a depth of 30 m. (After Gerlach 1978.) Food demand is assumed to be five times production (20% ecological efficiency).

	Mean biomass g m^{-2}	Turnover P/B	Annual production g m^{-2}	Annual food demand g m^{-2}
Bacteria (top 5 cm)	5	(21)	(104)	—
Ciliates and flagellates	trace	?	—	—
Foraminifera	0·5	2	1	5
Meiofauna	1	10	10	50
Macrofauna: total	10			
Subsurface deposit-feeders	6	2	12	60

Harbour, Bermuda, Smith *et al.* (1972) measured total benthic community oxygen demand before and after the addition of streptomycin to inhibit bacterial respiration. They found that respiration dropped by 31·5–35·5%, but suggested that inhibition was only 75% efficient, so the bacteria probably accounted for 42–47% of community respiration. However, Yetka and Wiebe (1974) produced evidence to suggest that antibiotics cannot be used to give a reliable quantitative estimate of bacterial respiration in mixed microbial communities. Even allowing for uncertainties as to the part played by bacteria, the work of Smith *et al.* showed that the total activity of microorganisms was very large indeed. Meiofaunal respiration was estimated at 1·6–1·7% of the total, and macrofaunal respiration 1·9–2·6% of the total. The balance was attributed to microorganisms other than bacteria, and the microorganisms were apparently responsible for over 95% of community respiration.

Several authors have recently emphasized the role of ciliates in marine systems (see Chapter 5). Vernberg and Coull (1974) made a detailed study of ciliate respiration, then recalculated the data of Fenchel (1969) referred to in section 7.3, and concluded that ciliate respiration is greater than that of meiofauna or macrofauna only in habitats, such as exposed beaches, which particularly favour ciliates. Nevertheless, as Fenchel and Harrison (1976) have shown, the presence of ciliates accelerates the rate of decomposition of plant detritus, probably by grazing on the bacterial populations. Hence, the importance of ciliates is not to be measured solely in terms of their population metabolism.

7.5 THE ROLE OF THE MEIOFAUNA

Meiofauna includes a wide assortment of metazoan animals with small elongated bodies adapted to an interstitial mode of life. Fenchel (1978) distinguishes three main faunal assemblages. In well-sorted sands with particles of diameter greater than 100 μm, and having interstices that are filled with water rather than with clay or silt, a rich interstitial fauna is found comprising ciliates, tardigrades, turbellarians, gastrotrichs, oligochaetes, archiannelids, harpacticoids, ostracods and others. In silty and clayey sediments the character of the fauna changes completely, and is dominated by nematodes which are capable of burrowing. However, there is a richer fauna inhabiting the upper 1 mm or so of these silty sediments, and harpacticoids, ostracods, foraminifera, and various annelids, along with nematodes, may be found in abundance. The third meiofaunal community is that inhabiting the anoxic layer of the deeper sediments (see section 5.4.2). Whenever the interstices of this material are sufficiently large, quantities of anaerobic species of ciliates occur, together with a few species of zooflagellates, nematodes, turbellarians, rotifers, gnathostomulids and gastrotrichs. According to Fenchel (1978) it is not known whether these metazoan organisms are permanent residents of the anoxic zone, or whether they make occasional excursions from the upper, oxygenated layers.

The meiofaunal community shows complex ecological properties, with predictable patterns of species composition and abundance in time and space, and with recognizable patterns of resource partitioning. For example, in temperate shallow estuarine communities, the spring diatom bloom is the signal for beginning a succession of peaks in maximum abundance: copepods, followed by oligochaetes, then nematodes, ostracods and finally turbellarians. The species that occur can be seen on close study to have very clear food niches; for example they may take diatoms of different sizes, they may scrape sand grains or chew at organic detritus. In the process they undoubtedly consume considerable amounts of bacterial and ciliate production (Gerlach 1978).

Opinions differ as to the importance of the meiofauna in ecosystem processes. At the end of a 45-page review of the ecology of marine meiobenthos McIntye (1969) concluded that the role was probably an unimportant one, accounting for a rather small proportion of the energy flow in the benthos, and providing for rather limited transfer to higher trophic levels. He thought that regeneration of nutrients for the use of autotrophs was one of the main functions. Gerlach (1971), reviewing data for sublittoral silty sands, concluded that when the meiobenthos are compared with the macrobenthos they account for about 3% of the total biomass but 15% of the production. In a later review (Gerlach 1978) he revised these estimates on the basis of more recent information, and concluded that meiofaunal biomass was about 10% of macrofaunal biomass, but that production of meiofauna and deposit-feeding macrofauna were nearly equal. He argued that there are enough non-selective deposit feeders, ingesting unsorted sediment, to provide predatory control of meiofaunal populations and absorb all their production. Gerlach's analysis resulted in an interesting conclusion regarding bacterial production. He assumed that bacterial production supplied all the food requirements of the meiobenthos, and bacterial production plus meiobenthic production supplied all the food requirements of the macrobenthos (Table 7.2). It turned out that this food could be provided if the annual ratio of bacterial production to biomass was 21. Since, under favourable conditions, bacteria have a doubling time of a few hours, he concluded that 'a rather large part of the bacterial population in the sediment seems to be in the stationary phase in life, and only a fraction of the total population exhibits high metabolic rates and rapid duplications'. He went on further to speculate that one way in which bacteria are switched from a stationary to an actively dividing phase is by the browsing, mixing and excretory activities of meiofauna.

Warwick *et al.* (1979) formulated a steady state model for the benthic community of a mud-flat in an estuary in Cornwall. Respiration rates were measured for a range of meiobenthic animals, and production was inferred from respiration, as in McNeill and Lawton (1970). They concluded that the total annual production of the meiofauna, dominated by small polychaetes, nematodes and copepods was $20 \cdot 17$ g C m^{-2} yr^{-1}, nearly four times as much as the production of the macrofauna ($5 \cdot 46$ g C m^{-2}). They calculated that 16% of the meiofaunal production was used by the macrofauna within the system, leaving $16 \cdot 83$ g C m^{-2}, or three times the production of the macrofauna, available to mobile carnivores, such as fish, birds and crabs.

Clearly, in some situations, meiofaunal production can be equal to or greater than macrofaunal production. Some of this production is consumed within the benthic community, but much remains, and in some situations, such as intertidal mud flats, nematode and harpacticoid production may be the dominant ecological transfer to mobile predators. Feller and Kaczynski (1975) and Sibert *et al.* (1977) have documented cases in which harpacticoid copepods were the principal food of chum salmon during the first critical weeks of estuarine life. In this connection it should be mentioned that there is a distinction to be made between 'psammon'—meiofauna that are small and adapted to an interstitial life among sand grains—and larger, broader forms that live epibenthically or by burrowing in soft mud. It is the latter two types that are the major contributors to the diet of fish predators (Brenda Harrison personal communication).

7.6 THE MACROFAUNA OF BENTHIC SEDIMENTS

There is an enormous literature on the distribution and abundance of benthic macroinvertebrates. Attempts have been made to bring order into the bewildering complexity by naming characteristic associations of animals, either on the basis of subjective observations or after sophisticated analysis.

The field was reviewed by Mills (1969), who concluded that while there may be, in some parts of the world, recognizable communities that can be characterized by certain constantly occurring large and conspicuous species, there are other areas where the communities are extremely diverse and defy classification in this way. No attempt will be made here to develop that subject further. Since our prime interest is in the system functions of the benthic community, we may begin by considering the ways in which benthic macrofauna capture and process a food supply.

7.6.1 Suspension feeders and deposit feeders

Those that utilize the primary carbon source, dead organic matter, do so in one of three ways: they either filter particles that are in suspension in water just above the sediment, browse on particles at the sediment surface, or ingest particles that have been deposited on or in the sediments. Examples of suspension or filter feeders are bivalve molluscs, sponges, ascidians, and fan worms. They all use cilia to create water currents which pass over a filtering surface. Mucus bands, moved by cilia, carry the adhering food particles to the mouth. Ecologically speaking, this is a remarkable process, for it permits very small organic particles to be collected and effectively utilized by relatively large organisms. The size of the package is converted in one trophic step from a scale of μm to a scale of cm, thus greatly facilitating the flow of energy and materials to higher, predatory trophic levels. For a review of mechanisms of filter feeding, see Jørgensen (1966). Many filter feeders live partially buried in the sediments, and protrude only their feeding organs above the surface. In this way, organic matter in suspension gets drawn down into the sediments and incorporated into the bodies of animals. Material that is not assimilated gets deposited in compact pellets as faeces or pseudofaeces.

Browsing animals include those epifaunal animals that move freely over the sediment surface grazing on organic detritus (e.g. amphipods, isopods, and some gastropods) and those that rasp the epibiota from the surfaces of rocks, pebbles or sand grains. The radulae of gastropods are particularly well adapted to the latter type of feeding.

Deposit feeders ingest particles from the sediment surface, or ingest mouthfulls of sediment from lower levels. Annelids are the characteristic deposit feeders, but many bivalves, gastropods, holothurians and crustaceans also live in this way. Most of them deposit faecal pellets at the sediment surface, and in aggregate their activity results in a thorough mixing of the top layers of the sediments. Such activity, known as bioturbation, has important consequences in terms of conditioning the sediments for meiofauna and microfauna, and as a stimulant of nutrient regeneration (see section 7.8).

There is a general tendency for deposit feeders to predominate in clay-silt sediments and filter feeders to predominate in sandy sediments. For example, Sanders (1958) found that in Buzzard's Bay, Massachusetts, the muddy areas were dominated by the lamellibranch *Nucula proxima* and the polychaete *Nephthys incisa*, both of them deposit feeders, while the sandy areas were dominated by filter-feeding species of the tube-building amphipod *Ampelisca*. In muddy areas it is clear that water movements must be small enough to permit the settling of fine particles and abundant organic detritus, hence providing a nutritive medium for deposit feeders. Sandy areas, on the other hand, have enough water movement to remove the fine mineral particles, so organic detritus will tend to be carried in suspension. Under these circumstances there are clear advantages to being a filter feeder. Rhoads and Young (1970) showed how the animals further modify the environment. The muddy sediments were found to have a surface layer of semi-fluid consistency, several cm thick, made up chiefly of faecal pellets of deposit feeders (Fig. 7.2). This material was readily resuspended by very small water movements, and was thought to discourage filter feeders from settling, and reduce their feeding efficiency by clogging the filtering structures. In a later publication Rhoades (1973) reported on the artificial introduction of filter feeders, namely oysters, into this 'turbidity zone'. When supported on racks a few cm above the bottom, the oysters gave a higher meat yield than those grown on shallow-water commercial beds.

Another interesting example of animal–sediment relations was provided by a detailed study of the role of the holothurian *Molpadia aolitica* in the clay-silt muds of Cape Cod Bay, Massachusetts (Rhoads & Young 1971).

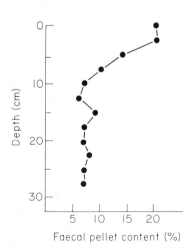

Fig. 7.2 Vertical gradient of faecal pellets in muds from Buzzards Bay, Massachusetts. (From Rhoads 1974.)

The feeding activity of the animal results in the formation of a cone of faecal pellets around the anus, and a ring of unconsolidated sediment in a depression round the cone. Filter feeders are inhibited from colonizing the depression, but colonize the sides of the cone in great numbers. These cones confer a spatial heterogeneity on an otherwise rather uniform environment.

Large deposit feeders such as holothurians, maldanid polychaetes and crustaceans, which feed at depth but defaecate at the surface have been termed by Rhoads (1974) 'conveyor-belt species'. They ingest anaerobic sediments and transfer them to the surface layer where they become oxidized. In this way, organic matter and bacteria from the sulphide zone are brought up and exposed to organisms feeding at the mud–water interface (Fig. 7.3). Rhoads (1974) speculated that this activity may be particularly important at a time of year when sedimentation of organic matter is low, but the magnitude of turnover by populations of conveyor-belt species has not been assessed.

The survival of animals burrowing deep into the anaerobic layer is conditional upon them being able to irrigate (or ventilate) their burrows with a supply of well-oxygenated water from the surface. When an area is artificially enriched with organic matter, as in sewage pollution, the oxygen demand of the sediments and the overlying water increases, and the conveyor-belt species can no longer survive. Such changes have been well documented in pollution studies (see Pearson & Rosenberg 1978). With increasing organic enrichment the animals causing deep bioturbation are eliminated first, followed by those working at intermediate depths. The anaerobic layer comes closer and closer to the surface, while the sediments become less porous. In heavily polluted areas only worms like *Capitella* and *Scolelepis* remain, feeding by ingesting organic matter close to the sediment surface. In grossly polluted areas, there is no macrofauna (Fig. 7.4).

While Rhoads and Young (1970) concentrated their attention on the reworking of sediments, and proposed that the very fluid layer at the surface of many muddy sediments had the effect of excluding filter-feeders, Wildish (1977) has focused attention on the importance of turbulence at the sediment–water interface. He put forward his 'trophic group mutual exclusion hypothesis' which states that: (1) macrobenthic communities are food limited; and (2) the proportion of filter feeders to deposit feeders is determined by the current speed near the bottom, with predominantly deposit feeding communities developing in low current speeds and predominantly filter feeding communities developing in higher current speeds. He suggested that the development of the later stages of deposit-feeding associations would be influenced by current speed through the control of oxygen exchange between sediment and water, and through resuspension of organic matter.

Wildish and Kristmanson (1979) presented the hypothesis in quantitative form. They developed the idea that filter feeding would be expected to lower the concentration of food particles in the water near the bottom, and this would limit the production of filter feeders unless there were sufficient turbulence to break down the gradient of concentration. Factors influencing this turbulence are current velocity and bottom roughness. They showed that the rate (N) at which microbial carbon (measured as ATP-seston) is

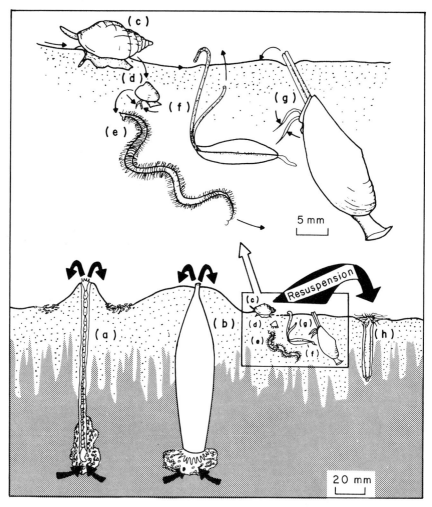

Fig. 7.3 Methods of mixing and recycling of sediment by deposit-feeders: (a) maldanid polychaete; (b) holothurian; (c) gastropod (*Nassarius*); (d) nuculid bivalve (*Nucula* sp.); (e) errant polychaete; (f) tellinid bivalve (*Macoma* sp.); (g) nuculid bivalve (*Yoldia* sp.); (h) anemone (*Cerianthus* sp.). Oxidized mud lightly stippled, reduced mud densely stippled. (From Rhoads 1974.)

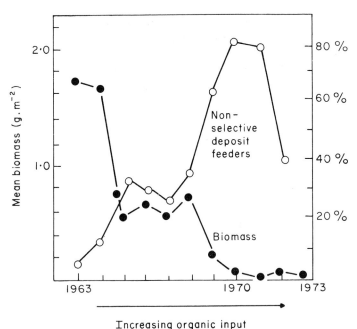

Fig. 7.4 Changes in biomass and in the proportion of non-selective deposit-feeders in the benthos of Loch Eil as a result of increasing organic input, 1963–73. (Modified from Pearson & Rosenberg 1978.)

transferred to suspension feeders is given two equations:

$$N = R\alpha C'P \tag{7.2}$$

$$N = \gamma V(C - C') \tag{7.3}$$

where R is the pumping rate per individual filter feeder $(m^3 . s^{-1})$; α is the filtering efficiency as a proportion of the maximum possible and ranging from 0–1; C is the concentration of ATP-seston, C' is the concentration of ATP-seston just sufficient to meet the maintenance requirements of the population (P), γ is a dimensionless coefficient depending only on bottom roughness, and V is mean tidal current velocity 1–2 m above the sediment–water interface in $m . s^{-1}$.

Combining (7.2) and (7.3), the population density at which mass transfer just becomes limiting is given by

$$P = \frac{\gamma V}{R\alpha} \frac{(C - C')}{C'} \tag{7.4}$$

The usefulness of this formulation was limited by lack of information on C'.

The authors made the assumption that C' lay in the range 0·2–0·8 C, and substituted for other variables values observed at locations off the east coast of Canada. They found that there would be no limitation by mass transfer at two stations, and these were in fact dominated by filter feeders; mass transfer limitation was feasible at three stations, and two of these were dominated by deposit feeders. Two other stations, with very high tidal currents, were judged to be limited by current speed, either because the sediments were unstable or because the current speed inhibited filter feeding. Those stations had an impoverished fauna. In general, there was at least a preliminary indication that turbulence generated by moderate tidal current and bottom roughness is beneficial for filter-feeding benthos. If this view is coupled with the idea that the total community is food-limited, then variation in the proportion of filter feeders in a community may indeed be accounted for by turbulent mass transfer from the water column to the sediment surface.

7.6.2   The role of the predators

Reference was made in section 3.3.2 to the role of predators on rocky shores in influencing the structure of grazing communities. For example, starfish, by preying on competitively dominant species of herbivores, can greatly increase the species diversity of a rocky shore community (Paine 1974). Similar considerations apply to subtidal soft-bottom communities. For example, Sanders (1968) enunciated a 'stability-time hypothesis' according to which organisms in a community that has experienced rather constant environmental conditions for a long time become 'biologically accommodated', permitting a high degree of species diversity. Examples given to illustrate the hypothesis were benthic communities from the deep sea, or from shallow, tropical habitats, which have higher species diversity than communities in shallow, temperate waters. Menge and Sutherland (1976) reinterpreted Sanders' data, suggesting that the communities in more stable environments probably had more predator species, and that the resulting increase in predation led to fewer occurrences of competitive exclusion among the prey species. Hence, there were more species coexisting in the stable environments.

Others have tended to emphasize the role of physical disturbance in maintaining species diversity. Thus Dayton (1971) involved the impact of floating logs at high tide as a factor restricting the competitive dominance of barnacles, and permitting higher species diversity. Connell (1978) went further, and suggested that a highly diverse system such as a coral reef can maintain its diversity only because frequent disruptions such as storm damage or local occurrences of intense predation prevent the reef from attaining an equilibrium condition in which competitive dominance reduces species diversity.

Huston (1979) has combined several of these ideas into a ' dynamic equilibrium model' of species diversity. He reiterated the point made by Connell (1978) that fairly frequent disturbance, resulting in reductions in population densities, appears to be a characteristic of high-diversity systems. However, Huston added a second major point: high diversity systems tend to be characterized by species with low rates of population growth while low diversity systems tend to be colonized by populations having high rates of growth. He suggested that low rates of growth lead to low rates of competitive displacement, and hence a tendency to maintain high species diversity. The two effects and their interaction are illustrated by Fig. 7.5.

There are rather few investigations of these matters on sediment

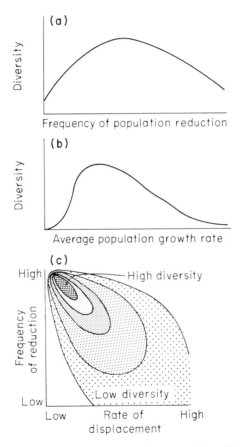

Fig. 7.5 (a) Predicted relationship of diversity to frequency of population reduction. (b) Predicted relationship of diversity to average population growth rate. (c) Contour map of dynamic equilibria between frequency of population reduction and rate of competitive displacement, as reflected in differing degrees of species diversity. (After Huston 1979.)

communities. A good recent example is that of Woodin (1978), who showed that on an intertidal sand flat in Virginia the blue crab *Callinectes* and the horseshoe crab *Limulus* cause important disturbances of the upper layers of sediment and cause mortality of the infauna. During high tide, both species dig pits as they feed in the sediment, and will burrow into the sediment if stranded by the falling tide. Their activities are modified by the presence of an onuphid polychaete, *Dipatra*, which forms a tube about 1 m long, projecting about 5 cm above the sediment surface. If there are six of these tubes in an area of 0·01 m², the abundance of other polychaetes is about twice as high as in areas where tubes were absent, and the species diversity is higher. Hence, the area around *Dipatra* tubes serves as a refuge from predation for the polychaetes, and the tubes enhance both habitat diversity and species diversity. This study provides evidence that predation on the community is considerable, so that competitive exclusion is unlikely to occur.

Peterson (1979) drew attention to the fact that most of the experiments which led to the current view of how marine benthic communities are structured were carried out in hard-bottom communities. He reviewed the rather small body of experimental data on the effect of excluding large predators from unvegetated soft sediments in lagoons or estuaries, by erecting cages. In every case there was, after a time, a higher density of macroinvertebrates inside the cages than outside them, indicating that predation was having a significant effect on the uncaged areas. Furthermore, the caged areas always had more species inside than outside. No matter how long the experiments lasted (the range is two and a half months to two years) there was no evidence of the communities becoming dominated by a few competitively successful species. Yet competitive exclusion effects were observed in three to six month experiments on hard bottoms. Peterson suggested that whereas on rocky shores there is clear evidence of competition for two-dimensional space by lateral pushing or by overgrowth, there is no evidence of this occurring in sediment communities. There is no firm basis of attachment from which to push, and there is a third dimension in which the organisms may distribute themselves. While the forces structuring sediment communities are far from clear, Peterson tended to favour the idea that patches created by the foraging of large predators create opportunities for larval settlement, and the species that establish themselves in the patches are determined by what happens to be available as planktonic larvae ready to settle. The animals living in sediment tend to be sedentary or slow-moving and to grow fairly slowly. As we saw, Huston (1979) suggested that low rates of growth lead to low rates of competitive displacement. There has to be an upper limit to the density of organisms inhabiting a caged area, but it may be that sedimented communities react more slowly than those on hard bottoms, and that none of the predator exclusion experiments have been maintained long enough for competitive interactions to be observed.

7.7 THE BENTHIC PRODUCTION PROCESS

7.7.1 Intertidal mud or sand flats

A mudflat of the Lyhner estuary in Cornwall, England, has been rather intensively studied. Joint (1978) showed that there was a production of 143 g C m^{-2} yr^{-1} by algae on the mud surface, and 82 g C m^{-2} yr^{-1} in the water column when the tide was in. Other sites where these parameters have been measured include the Wadden Sea (100 g C m^{-2} yr^{-1}; Cadée & Hegeman 1974), southern New England (81 g C m^{-2} yr^{-1}; Leach 1970) and Georgia (200 g C m^{-2} yr^{-1}; Pomeroy 1959).

On the same mudflat, Warwick and Price (1975) measured the biomass and production of the macrofauna. They found a mean biomass of 13·2 g m^{-2} ash-free dry weight, and a production of 13·3 g m^{-2} yr^{-1}, so that the P/B ratio was about 1·0 Table 7.3 shows that six species contributed significantly to the production: one carnivore, two suspension feeders and three deposit feeders. The position of *Nephtys* was considered an anomaly. It was thought to be a carnivore, but it was the most important producer, and all the production of the other species would not have been enough to sustain it. Warwick *et al.* (1979) gave additional data on numbers, biomass and rate of respiration of the meiofauna (retained on a 45 μ sieve) and of intermediate sized annelids (retained on a 125 μ sieve). Using various assumptions and literature values they calculated that these two components together produced 20·2 g C m^{-2} yr^{-1}, compared with 5·5 g C m^{-2} produced by the macrofauna, and that the P/B value for the meiofauna was 11·1; with small annelids included it was 7·7.

There is agreement from other studies (McIntyre 1969; Gerlach 1971) that the P/B ratio of the meiofauna is about 10. Warwick *et al.* (1979) pointed out that the meiofaunal densities which they found are not unusual

Table 7.3 Mean biomass production and P/B ratio of the most important macrobenthos species in an estuarine mudflat. (From Warwick & Price 1975.)

Species	Feeding type	Mean biomass g m^{-2}	Production g m^{-2} yr^{-1}	P/B
Nephthys hombergi	Carnivore (?)	3·95	7·34	1·9
Mya arenaria	Suspension feeder	5·54	2·66	0·5
Ampharete acutifrons	Deposit feeder	0·43	2·32	5·5
Scrobicularia plana	Deposit feeder	2·15	0·48	0·2
Macoma balthica	Deposit feeder	0·34	0·31	0·9
Cerastoderma edule (= *Cardium edule*)	Suspension feeder	0·85	0·21	0·2
	Total	13·24	13·31	

for intertidal areas. Hence, the Lynher estuary mudflat may be fairly representative of temperate latitude estuarine areas. The problem of the nutrition of *Nephtys* mentioned earlier was resolved by constructing a simulation model of the system and experimenting with different feeding regimes. The most realistic simulation was obtained by allowing *Nephtys* to feed on phytobenthos, meiofauna and some small species of macrofauna. Using this approach, a steady state energy flow model was constructed (Fig. 7.6). It showed that the total organic input to the invertebrates was 163 g C, and the total production available to mobile carnivores was 16·8 g, giving an ecological efficiency of about 10%. If bacterial respiration were included in the equation, the efficiency of the benthic system would be even lower, hence, it does not come anywhere near the overall efficiency of 20% postulated by Steele (1974) (see section 7.3). However, Steele was discussing systems with little or no benthic primary production. These form the subject of the next section.

7.7.2   Subtidal benthic production

Gerlach (1978) is of the opinion that while the productivity of the subtidal meiobenthos may be of the same order of magnitude as that of the macrobenthos, meiobenthic production is probably consumed in the sediments by the macrobenthos. Hence, for purposes of calculating the production made available to mobile benthic predators, it is probably sufficient to consider only the macrobenthic production. Warwick *et al.* (1978) measured the production of a community at a depth of 17 m in the Severn Estuary, UK, dominated by the bivalve *Pharus legumen*. Total annual production was 25·8 g ash-free dry weight m^{-2} (about 10 g C m^{-2}) with a P/B ratio of 0·56. They reviewed comparable data in the literature (Table 7.4) and concluded that absolute values of production tended to be high in estuaries and decrease as one moved out to deeper water, from 16·5 g C m^{-2} yr^{-1} close inshore, to 0·7 g C m^{-2} yr^{-1} at a depth of 80 m. Steele's (1974) calculations for the North Sea called for an average benthic production of about 5 g C m^{-2} yr^{-1}, which seems feasible on the basis of the data given in Table 7.4. Those figures apply to production measurements on whole benthic communities. There is a much larger data set for production of individual species. The measurement of secondary production (reviewed in Mann 1969) is a tedious business, and various people have tried to find short-cuts by investigating the rules governing P/B ratios. A recent example is Robertson (1979). About 80 estimates of P/B values for marine macrobenthos were analysed. For 49 of these, information was available on the length of life and it was found that the P/B ratio was significantly ($r = 0.835$) correlated with lifespan, according to the equation:

$$\log_{10} P/B = 0.660 - 0.726 \log_{10} L \qquad (7.5)$$

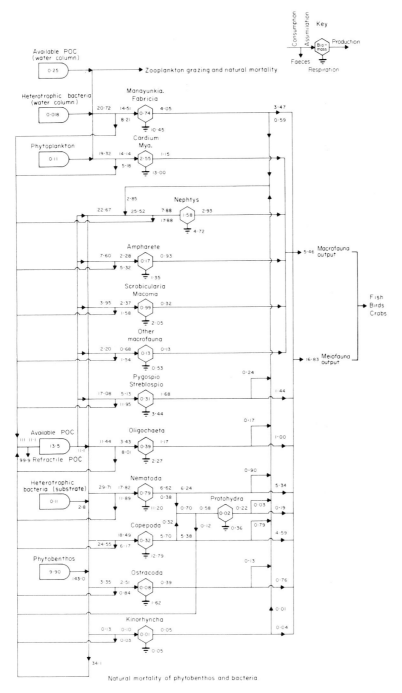

Fig. 7.6 Steady state energy flow model of the benthic community of a mud-flat in the estuary of a river in Cornwall. (From Warwick *et al.* 1979.)

Table 7.4 Production, biomass and P/B ratio for total benthic communities in various locations. Converted from biomass data by assuming carbon is 40% of ash-free dry weight.

Depth (m)	Location	P (g C m^{-2} yr^{-1})	B (g C m^{-2})	P/B	Reference
0	Estuary, Netherlands	16·5	10	1·6	Wolff & de Wolff (1977)
0	Estuary, Cornwall	5·3	5·3	1·0	Warwick & Price (1975)
17	Severn Estuary, UK	10·0	17·0	0·6	Warwick et al. (1978)
18	Long Island Sound, USA	12·0	4·8	2·5*	Sanders (1956)
46	Baltic	2·7	1·7	1·6	Cederwall (1977)
80	North Sea	0·7	1·7	0·4	Buchanan & Warwick (1974)

* Thought to be unduly high, because only organisms under 0·2 g individual weight were considered. Larger organisms would have lower P/B values.

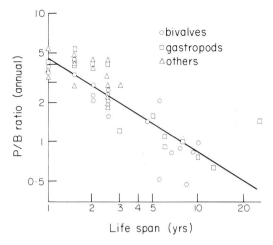

Fig. 7.7 Regression of annual population P/B on life span. (Redrawn after Robertson 1979.)

This accords with common sense. An organism that completes its life history in one year has to turn over its biomass much faster than an organism that lives for ten or more years. However, length of life is not the sole determinant of P/B ratio. Obviously, it must depend on, for example, the availability of food, the temperature regime and the rate of predation on the population. Hence, it is not surprising that for any given length of life there is considerable variation in P/B ratio (Fig. 7.7). The absolute range in Robertson's data is from 5·45 for *Ampharete* in the Lynher Estuary, Cornwall, to 0·12 for a decapod at 80 m depth in the North Sea. However, the latter figure was thought to be inaccurate, as a result of size-selective sampling, and the lowest figure used in Fig. 7.7 was 0·48 for the *Mya arenaria* population in the Lynher estuary. Can we use this information to estimate P/B ratios of whole communities? Gerlach 1978 (see Table 7.2) suggested that subsurface deposit-feeders have an annual P/B of 2. Mann (1976) had earlier suggested that on a global scale the annual production of the benthos might be about twice the biomass. However, the limited data in Table 7.4 suggest that this might be too high a figure. A great deal depends on whether the meiobenthos production is included, for we have seen that meiobenthic organisms have P/B ratios around 10. Inclusion of meiobenthic data would have the effect of extending the line in Fig. 7.7 to the left. If we assume that small mobile predators were using considerable amounts of meiobenthos as food the production to predators by benthic communities might well be two or more times the mean biomass.

7.7.3   Energy flow and production efficiency

The techniques for estimating energy flow through marine benthic populations were reviewed in Mann (1969) and Crisp (1971). Using the simple equation:

$$C = P + R + F + U \tag{7.6}$$

where C is food consumed, P is production, R is respiration, F is faeces and U is urine, all expressed in energy units, one can make energy budgets for populations and arrive at two measures of production efficiency. The ratio P/C gives production as a fraction of total food consumed. However, it is well known that faecal material is used by detritivores, so the ratio of production to energy assimilated (A) which is given by $P/(P + R)$, where $A = P + R$, is probably a more meaningful measure of the ecological efficiency of populations.

There are not many marine benthic populations for which the necessary measurements have been made. Not surprisingly, most of those that have been studied carefully have been the more accessible intertidal species. Dame (1976) studied an extremely dense intertidal oyster population which had a production in excess of 400 g C m^{-2} yr^{-1}. On the basis of earlier measurements of respiration (Dame 1972) he calculated $P/(P + R)$ as 42%. This is the highest figure on record for a benthic herbivore or detritivore population. All others (Table 7.5) are in the range of 10–30%. The study by Miller and Mann (1973) illustrates some of the problems and uncertainties attendant on measurements of energy efficiencies. The figure of 22% given in Table 7.5 for the sea-urchin *Strongylocentrotus droebachiensis* was arrived at from a population production of 49·8 kcal m^{-2} yr^{-1} and a population respiration of 178·5 kcal m^{-2} yr^{-1}. However, when an attempt was made to measure every term in the energy budget including feeding rate (in the laboratory) there proved to be an enormous imbalance. The energy of food assimilated (ingestion minus egestion) exceeded the energy of production plus respiration by 66–72%, and subsequent work (Field 1972) showed that this could be accounted for by loss of dissolved organic matter. Miller and Mann (1973) also showed that there were similar gaps in the energy budgets of half a dozen other marine herbivores. It is not known whether the DOM loss occurred during feeding, during defaecation, or whether DOM diffused through the body surface. Whichever was the case, it could be argued that the DOM was not used by the sea-urchins, but would probably be quickly taken up by bacteria. Hence, the calculation of efficiency from $P/(P + R)$ is ecologically the most meaningful.

McNeill and Lawton (1970) showed that for a range of terrestrial and freshwater poikilotherms, there is a relationship between population production and population respiration. They made an arbitrary distinction

Table 7.5 Some values for population production efficiency of marine benthic animals, calculated as $P/(P + R) \times 100\%$. (Partly after Miller & Mann 1973.)

Species	Type	Habitat	Effi-ciency (%)	Source
Littorina irrorata	Gastropod	Salt-marsh	14	Odum & Smalley (1959)
Modiolus demissus	Bivalve	Salt-marsh	30	Kuenzler (1961)
Scrobicularia plana	Bivalve	Mud flat	21	Hughes (1970)
Tegula funebralis	Gastropod	Rocky shore	15	Paine (1971)
Fissyrella barbadensis	Limpet	Rocky shore	27	Hughes (1971a)
Nerita tessellata	Gastropod	Rocky shore	12	Hughes (1971b)
Nerita versicolor	Gastropod	Rocky shore	13	Hughes (1971b)
Nerita peloronta	Gastropod	Rocky shore	19	Hughes (1971b)
Strongylocentrotus droebachiensis	Sea-urchin	Subtidal	22	Miller & Mann (1973)
Neanthes virens	Polychaete	Mud flat	63*	Kay & Brafield (1973)

* The only carnivore in the list.

between long-lived animals (life span > 2 years) and comparatively short-lived (< 2 years). For the short-lived forms the equation was:

$$\log P = 0.8262 \log R - 0.0948 \tag{7.7}$$

Since the slope of the line is significantly different from 1, the values of $P/(P + R)$ change with changing levels of production from 62% at a production of 0.01 kcal m^{-2} yr^{-1} to 25% at 100 kcal (= 10 g C) m^{-2} yr^{-1}. For those animals having a longer life history, data were less good, but there was an indication that efficiencies would be lower.

Miller and Mann (1973) using a slightly modified version of the McNeill and Lawton equations calculated that production of *Strongylocentrotus* should be 30% of the respiration, whereas field measurements gave 28%, and $P(P + R)$ should be 23%, when the field data gave 22%. Hence, it seems possible that marine invertebrates follow the same trend as freshwater and terrestrial forms, and that it is quite reasonable to expect them to have efficiencies of the order of 25–50% in the transformation of assimilated energy. We have seen that the input of organic matter below the photic zone in coastal waters is probably over 100 g C m^{-2} yr^{-1} in places close to sources of macrophyte detritus and 30–100 g C m^{-2} yr^{-1} in places more remote from macrophytes. Let us assume for the moment that 50% of the carbon is lost in bacterial and meiofaunal respiration, but that the remainder is assimilated by the macrofauna. Then input to macrofauna is in the range 15–50 (or more) g C m^{-2} yr^{-1}, and production in the range 4–25 g C m^{-2} yr^{-1}.

In the benthic production data for 76 individual species populations reviewed by Robertson (1979) there is an enormous range of values, from mysid populations producing only 0.02 g C m^{-2} yr^{-1} to the oyster population (Dame 1976) producing around 400 g C m^{-2} yr^{-1}. However, the mean value is about 24 g C m^{-2} yr^{-1} if three extremely productive bivalve populations are included, or 6.2 g C m^{-2} yr^{-1} if they are excluded. In a mixed community of a sedimented area we might expect to find up to five important species overlapping in range, so that their production could be summed and a total of 6–30 g C m^{-2} yr^{-1} would be expected.

To summarize this section, we may refer again to Steele's observation that to account for the benthic fish production of the North Sea it is necessary to assume a 20% overall efficiency in transformation of energy (and carbon) by the benthos. He postulated an input equivalent to 30 g C m^{-2} yr^{-1} and an output to fish predation of 5 g C. Our review of the literature suggests that input of organic matter to the benthos in coastal waters ranges from about 30 g C m^{-2} yr^{-1} to well over 100 g C m^{-2} yr^{-1}. Although the biomass of bacteria may be of the same order of magnitude as that of the macrobenthos, so that their potential for metabolizing carbon is very high indeed, there is evidence that the bacteria probably spend most of their time in an inactive state. The view of many people at present is that bacteria are food for meiobenthos, and meiobenthos are food for macrobenthos. However, many macrobenthic organisms are capable of filtering the organic matter from suspension in the water, or taking it from the sediment surface, before either bacteria or meiobenthos have had time to extensively metabolize it. Hence, it is possible that the macrobenthos gets about half of the sedimented carbon, and that many species are able to transform it to macrobenthos production with an efficiency around 40%. In that case, an overall benthic transformation efficiency of 20% may be realizable, and yield to fish of 5 g C m^{-2} yr^{-1} be well within the capacity of most benthic communities.

7.8   THE REGENERATION OF NUTRIENTS

It is to be expected that as organic matter sediments to the bottom and is metabolized by heterotrophs there will be a release of not only CO_2 but of compounds of N, P, K, etc., which were constituents of the original organic matter. It would, however, be a mistake to assume that all the sedimenting material is converted in this way. There is a certain amount of organic matter which gets buried in the sediments and a certain amount is incorporated in the tissues of macrobenthos which are consumed by mobile predators and hence removed from the area of study. Finally, it has been shown in both lakes and the sea that under oxidizing conditions inorganic nutrients become adsorbed on ferric compounds. They are not released until conditions become reducing and ferric compounds change to ferrous. It is therefore of interest to ask what proportion of the sedimenting organic matter is mineralized, and how important is the regeneration of nutrients from the benthos compared with regeneration in the water column. Since nitrogen is the nutrient most limiting to coastal productivity, we shall give it most attention.

Rowe *et al.* (1975) reported the first successful attempts to measure directly the nutrient flux from nearshore sediments. They placed over the sediments an opaque bell jar fitted with a stirring motor and oxygen electrode. Periodically, samples of water were removed for nutrient analysis. In Buzzard's Bay, Massachusetts, at a depth of 17 m, the regeneration of N (NH_4^+, NO_2^{2-} and NO_3^{2-}) averaged 81% (36–106%) of that predicted from the rate of oxygen consumption, with NH_4^+ being the most abundant form. Extrapolating from published data on oxygen consumption of benthic sediments, they estimated that the sediments of the New York Bight would regenerate on average 144 μg atom NH_4^+ m^{-2} h^{-1} for a total of $16\cdot8 \times 10^{11}$ μg atom NH_4^+ h^{-1}. This would be an order of magnitude larger than the contribution of river runoff, and more than enough to supply the requirements of the phytoplankton. Hence, the authors concluded, benthic regeneration of nitrogen is a major factor influencing phytoplankton production.

Rowe and Smith (1977) developed the idea further by measuring the nitrogen profile in the water column at 55 stations on the continental shelf of the New York Bight. They found higher concentrations of ammonia near the bottom of almost all stations, and made rough estimates of ammonia flux by using a reasonable assumption about vertical eddy diffusivity. They arrived at an upward flux of the order of 100 μg atom NH_4^+ m^{-2} h^{-1}, which is similar to the rate of assimilation of nitrogen by phytoplankton.

In Naragansett Bay, Rhode Island, Nixon *et al.* (1976) made a year long study of nutrient fluxes and oxygen demand in three different types of benthic community, one dominated by the clam *Mercenaria*, one dominated by the amphipod *Ampelisca*, and one by a mixture of the polychaete *Nephtys* and the bivalve *Nucula*. For all communities, the total annual oxygen consumption was around 370 g O_2 m^{-2} yr^{-1}, equivalent to about 140 g C m^{-2} yr^{-1}. The main nitrogen flux was in the form of NH_4^+ and ranged from 0–400 μg atom m^{-2} h^{-1}. Difference between communities were minor, and the main determinant of flux rate was temperature. When summed for the year and compared with oxygen uptake, NH_4^+ flux accounted for less than half of the expected nitrogen flux. A preliminary study of the production of organic nitrogen suggested that in summer about half the nitrogen flux might be in that form. We noted that in Chapter 5 that regeneration of dissolved organic matter is to be expected from anaerobic sediments.

An alternative approach to benthic nutrient regeneration is through the study of the depth profiles of nutrient concentrations in sediment pore water. A good recent example is Billen's (1978) study in the North Sea off the Belgian coast. He pointed out that earlier workers had estimated nutrient flux from concentration gradients at the sediment–water interface, using Fick's Law and assuming a dispersion coefficient equal to the molecular diffusion coefficient, corrected for porosity and tortuosity. Billen (1978) avoided the necessity of making an assumption about the dispersion coefficient. Instead, he modelled the microbial processes (ammonification, nitrification and dentrification) contributing to the concentration profile, and was able to evaluate the dispersion coefficient by adjusting the theoretical solution to the experimental one.

All three microbial processes had rates that were dependent on the organic content of the sediment, so Billen (1978) went one step further, and estimated rates of NH_4^+ and NO_3^- flux for three types of bottom, having 0–1%, 1–2% and > 2% organic matter. He then calculated the integrated fluxes for a large study area off the Belgian coast (Fig. 7.8). His conclusion was that benthic ammonia and nitrate regeneration would account for 30–52% of the requirements of the phytoplankton in the offshore zone (mean depth about 35 m) and 62–100% of the phytoplankton requirements in the coastal zone (mean depth about 15 m). A very rough calculation of probable nutrient regeneration by meio- and macrofauna suggested that together they would

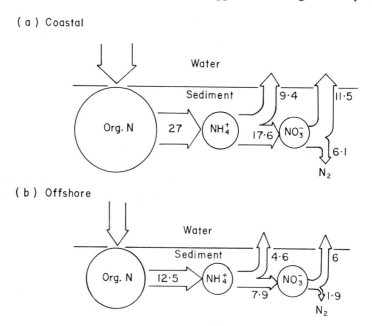

Fig. 7.8 Regeneration of nitrogen from sediments in the North Sea. (a) Coastal (b) Offshore. Fluxes in g N m^{-2}yr^{-1}. (From Billen 1978.)

be responsible for about 20% of the nutrient regeneration; the remainder would be regenerated by microbenthos. Johannes (1968) had earlier shown that bacteria are not particularly active in nutrient regeneration, in fact they are active in its uptake. However, ciliates, which feed on bacterial populations liberate dissolved nitrogen and phosphorus at a remarkably high rate.

As was mentioned earlier in Chapter 4, there is a great deal of interest in the question of to what extent nutrient regeneration takes place in the water column, and to what extent on the bottom. The authors whose work has been reviewed in this section have tended towards the view that the amounts of nitrogen regenerated from the bottom are probably sufficient for the needs of the phytoplankton. By implication, regeneration in the water column is of secondary importance. Kremer and Nixon (1978) integrated the nutrient flux data in a simulation of the whole ecosystem in Naragansett Bay. They found that through most of the year, benthic and zooplankton sources contributed about equal amounts towards the algal demand, but benthic fluxes were slightly higher in winter. Naragansett Bay is shallow and well-mixed, but we should not assume that the benthic community would have the same importance in deeper water, where a smaller proportion of the phytoplankton production reaches the bottom. Even inshore, not all sediments are equally active in nutrient regeneration. Hartwig (1976) studied the fluxes of nitrogen and phosphorus from a siliceous sediment (mean particle diameter 88–105 μm) with very little organic carbon content at a depth of 18 m. He concluded that the sediment supplied only 5% of the phytoplankton requirement for N, and 10% of P. Moreover, since nutrients were constantly being advected into the area, Hartwig judged that the N and P released from the bottom was 'superfluous to the needs of the phytoplankton'.

We may conclude that in coastal waters generally, the nutrients regenerated from benthic sediments are a major factor influencing primary production. Regeneration by zooplankton may be the predominant influence during periods of bloom and in dense zooplankton patches, but regeneration from the benthos is a more continuous process. There is a great deal of activity in the upper, aerobic layers of sediment, and the nutrients released there diffuse and disperse fairly rapidly into the overlying water. However, it is in the anaerobic lower layers that the highest concentrations of ammonia are to be found, and there must be a slow upward diffusion along the concentration gradient. It was once assumed that bacteria were the chief agents of nutrient release, but there is now good evidence that when they have a carbon source they will take up inorganic nitrogen and build it into microbial protein. Bacterial populations are heavily grazed by ciliates, and these have a high rate of excretion of nitrogen and phosphorus compounds. There is a certain amount of evidence that significant amounts of nitrogen and phosphorus may be released from sediments in organic form.

CHAPTER 8
WATER MOVEMENTS
AND PRODUCTIVITY

8.1 ESTUARIES

8.1.1 Types of estuaries

In terms of the units used earlier in the book, for example seagrass-, seaweed-, or phytoplankton-based systems, an estuary is a unit of a higher order, for it commonly includes several of these systems, and will include interactions between them. Ketchum (1951) defined an estuary very simply as a region where river water mixes with, and measurably dilutes, sea-water. Pritchard (1967) wished to exclude large coastal areas such as the Baltic, and large stretches of dilute sea-water off open coasts, such as the New York Bight, so he gave a definition that is widely accepted:

> An estuary is a semi-enclosed coastal body of water which has a free connection with the open sea, and within which sea-water is measurably diluted with freshwater derived from land drainage.

This definition will serve us for the present, but we shall find it expedient later to return to Ketchum's simpler version. The characteristic feature of estuaries is the density gradient between freshwater and salt water, which causes very distinctive patterns of circulation. That circulation is constrained by the shape of the basin, so it is useful to begin by distinguishing four types of estuary on the basis of geomorphology. In the last 20 000 years or so since the last Ice Age there has been a marked rise in sea-water level relative to the land. In places where the sea-water invaded existing river valleys we find *coastal plain estuaries*, or more picturesquely *drowned river valleys*. In places where the valleys were strongly glaciated, giving steep sides and a pile of glacial deposits near the mouth, the estuaries are called *Fjords*, and are characterized by having a submerged sill which restricts circulation at the lower levels. In very flat, low-lying areas, where sand tends to be deposited in bars lying parallel with the coast, we find *bar-built estuaries*. Finally, there is a miscellaneous collection of estuaries formed from faults or folding of the earth's crust. These are known as *tectonic estuaries*.

A very clear account of estuarine circulation patterns is found in Cameron and Pritchard (1963) and in Pritchard and Carter (1971). In relatively narrow drowned river valleys in which the ratio of river flow to tidal flow is relatively large, we find *salt wedge estuaries*, in which a layer of relatively fresh water flows out at the surface. The shear at the boundary between fresh and salt water causes mixing of salt water into the freshwater layer, and we find that the salinity of surface waters tends to increase as we move in a seaward direction. At the same time the surface layer becomes thinner. To compensate for the entrained salt water, there is a slow movement of salt water up the estuary at depth. However, there is no significant amount of mixing of freshwater downward, so salinities at the bottom are close to those of the open sea, all the way up the estuary to the zone where river water is encountered (Fig. 8.1(a)). The distance this salt wedge extends upriver depends on the flow of the river. During flood stages the wedge will retreat, during low flows it will extend further up-river. The mouth of the Mississippi is a classic case of a salt wedge estuary.

In places where the rise and fall of the tide or a constriction in the estuary causes a strong tidal flow, turbulence and mixing are increased and this tends to erase the salt wedge. Salt is mixed upwards but freshwater is also mixed downwards. The river flow entrains 10, 20 or more times its own volume of salt water and moves it seaward. This must be balanced by an equivalent volume of sea-water moving landward near the bottom. The effect of the earth's rotation (Coriolis force) is to cause the surface flow to be stronger on the right hand side facing seaward, or the opposite in the southern hemisphere. The deep flow tends to be stronger on the opposite side, resulting in an asymmetry in salinity profiles. Such a system is called a *partially mixed*, or *moderately stratified estuary* (Fig. 8.1(b)).

It is not difficult to imagine the situation in which tidal flow is strong, river runoff is weak, and all stratification is broken down by the turbulence, so that we have a *vertically homogeneous estuary*, as in Fig. 8.1(c). There is a

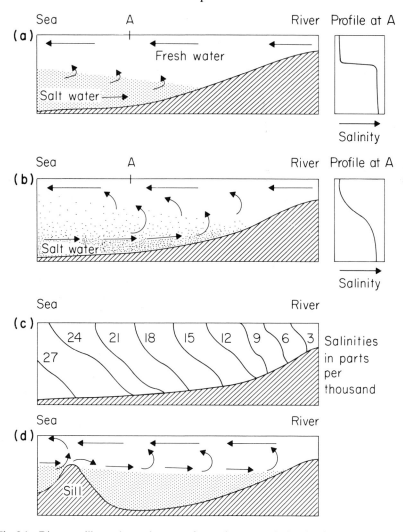

Fig. 8.1 Diagrams illustrating main types of estuaries as seen in longitudinal vertical section. (a) Salt wedge estuary. Salt water is stippled. (b) Moderately stratified estuary. Salt water and freshwater partially mixed by tidal movements and internal waves. (c) Vertically homogeneous estuary. Isolines for salinity are shown. (d) Fjord. Saline water trapped by sill.

longitudinal gradient in salinity which extends to all depths. The Coriolis force carries the river runoff to the right in the Northern Hemisphere so that there is a lower salinity on the right hand side facing seaward.

The fjord-type estuary may be regarded as a partially mixed estuary in which the bottom has been replaced by a basin of undiluted sea-water held in position by a sill at the seaward edge (Fig. 8.1(d)). When entrainment in river flow causes a strong landward flow at the bottom, then water rises over the sill and enters the estuary at an intermediate depth, leaving the deep waters undisturbed. A major storm in conjunction with particular oceanographic conditions may cause an intrusion of cold, saline water which displaces the water in the bottom of the fjord. Otherwise, the density of the deep water decreases slowly over many months, until its replacement becomes inevitable.

8.1.2 Patterns of sedimentation

Particulate matter carried by rivers undergoes a change in surface charge, flocculates and tends to sediment out as it encounters saline water (Wangersky 1977). The pattern of circulation of an estuary enables us to understand the major features of the pattern of sedimentation. For example, in a salt wedge estuary, where river flow predominates but there is a gentle up-estuary movement in the lower layers, particles carried by river water will tend to sediment out to lower layers, and be gently carried upstream as far as the tip of the salt wedge. Since the tip of the wedge may move up and down the estuary according to the strength of river flow (as much as 135 miles in the Mississippi; Ippen 1966) there is a section of the estuary where river-borne particles are particularly likely to accumulate.

Partially mixed estuaries have much more vigorous vertical mixing, and therefore more energy available for resuspension of sediments. Particles which settle out of surface layers into deep water are vigorously carried landward, and resuspended when they come close to the zone of entrainment. They may then be carried seaward in the surface flow and have the whole process repeated. Partially mixed estuaries tend to have a zone of high turbidity in their upper reaches which constitutes a 'sediment trap'. In some cases, the landward flow near the bottom may bring sediment from the mouth of the estuary and add it to the 'sediment trap'. The position of the zone of high turbidity changes with changing strength of river runoff, but the sediment tends to accumulate in a rather narrow zone, as the following example shows.

Nihoul *et al.* (1979) reported on the salinity, turbidity and chemical oxygen demand of the Scheldt Estuary in Belgium. It is partially stratified and in typical summer conditions, the pattern is as shown in Fig. 8.2, with an upstream zone of high turbidity, high chemical oxygen demand, but low salinity. In the region where the salinity reaches a critical level (between 60 and 80 km from the sea) intense flocculation and sedimentation occurs, and there is a rapid change in both turbidity and chemical oxygen demand of the water. The authors reported that the effect of unusually high (or low) flow rates was to shift the pattern about 10 km downstream (or upstream). It was therefore expected that deposition of bottom sediments would occur over a

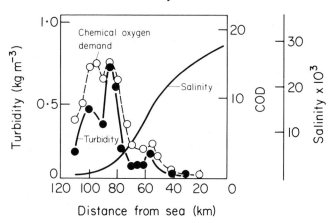

Fig. 8.2 Longitudinal profiles of salinity, turbidity, and chemical oxygen demand in the Scheldt Estuary in a typical summer situation. (Redrawn from Nihoul *et al.* 1979.)

very wide zone, but in fact the zone was narrower than expected. They constructed a two-dimensional width-integrated residual circulation model, and showed (Fig. 8.3) that under average conditions (four times minimum river-flow) there is a net bottom flow upstream as far as salinity level 4×10^3 (approx.), at which point there is zero residual current, and this coincides with the zone of maximum sediment deposition. They expored the position of zero residual flow at maximum and minimum river runoff, but pointed out that the estuary tends to return to average conditions, and sediments deposited higher or lower in the estuary during abnormal conditions will tend to be resuspended and carried to the median zone.

In vertically mixed estuaries, since there is a tendency for there to be a lower salinity on the right hand side facing seaward, this is associated with a slow net seaward flow on the right and a slow net landward flow on the left.

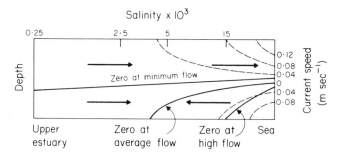

Fig. 8.3 Lines of equal, width-averaged horizontal velocity calculated by the model of the Scheldt Estuary for a typical river flow rate. The positions of lines of zero residual flow at minimum and at maximum runoff are also indicated. (Modified from Nihoul *et al.* 1979.)

Sediment therefore tends to be carried to the limit of salt intrusion on the left hand side. For example, in the Thames Estuary in England, which is vertically mixed there has been found to be a net upstream movement of sediment on the left hand side.

In the intertidal zone, and in shallow water just below it, the accumulation of sediment provides good conditions for the growth of salt-marsh plants and seagrasses (see Chapters 2 and 3).

Hence, estuaries commonly have extensive areas of macrophyte-dominated systems, which contribute to the characteristically high level of primary production.

Most of the literature on estuaries refers to temperate latitudes with a modest seasonal variation in river runoff. However, there are parts of the world where variation in river runoff is so extreme that none of the classifications given above are applicable for the whole year. For example, Hodgkin (1978) has described the Blackwood Estuary in Western Australia where the freshwater flow changes by more than three orders of magnitude, from 10^4 m^3 day^{-1} in summer to well over 10^7 m^3 day^{-1} in winter. When river flow is maximal, the estuary is fresh throughout its length. As flow declines a salt wedge spreads progressively up the estuary to its head, until only a small plume of brackish water spreads over the surface of the fully saline water in the bulk of the estuary, and the only important flows are tidal currents. Such a regime places an enormous strain on the salinity tolerance of sedentary organisms, and results in a very low diveristy of such species. Much of the productivity is attributable to organisms that enter and leave the estuary with the changing physical and chemical conditions.

8.1.3 Phytoplankton production in estuaries

We saw in Chapter 7 that there is normally a large amount of nutrient regeneration from the surface of sediments in shallow waters. Hence, in stratified estuaries the bottom water often has a higher concentration of nutrients than the upper layers. This leads to a situation where the biological flux of nutrients in surface waters is higher in those parts of an estuary where vertical mixing is strongest. This point, and a number of others mentioned in the previous two sections, are well illustrated by work done in the St. Lawrence Estuary and the Gulf of St. Lawrence. The physical oceanography of the area was summarized by Trites (1972). The discharge of the St. Lawrence River (Fig. 8.4) averages 10^4 m^3 s^{-1}, and surface water of low salinity flows primarily along the shore of the Gaspé Peninsula, as the Gaspé Current. Deep water of salinity 34·5 per thousand flows in along the north side of the Laurentian Channel to form a two-layer system. Kranck (1979) has shown that there is a very strong turbidity maximum in summer in the section between Quebec City and Saguenay Fjord. Above Quebec City con-

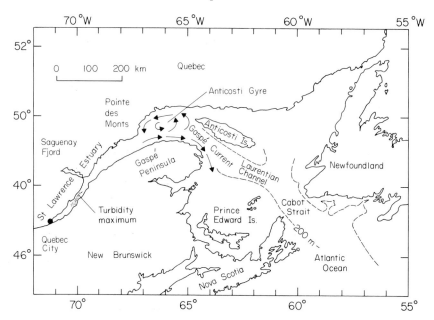

Fig. 8.4 Sketch map of the St. Lawrence Estuary and the Gulf of St. Lawrence showing features mentioned in the text.

centrations of suspended particulate matter are between 5 and 10 parts per million, but over a relatively short distance they rise to more than 50 parts per million, and decline again to about 1 part per million near Saguenay Fjord.

Coote and Yeats (1979) studied nutrient distributions in the Laurentian Channel during both summer and winter. The data for nitrate in summer are shown in Fig. 8.5 and we see that whereas in winter, surface concentrations had been around 10 μg atom 1^{-1} and the layers of equal concentration had

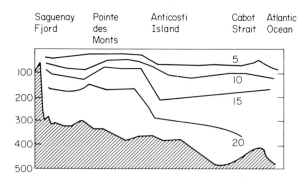

Fig. 8.5 Nitrate isolines in the Laurentian Channel, Gulf of St. Lawrence, July–August. Concentrations in μg at 1^{-1}. (From Coote & Yeats 1979.)

been nearly horizontal, the surface layers in summer had their concentrations greatly reduced and the lines of equal concentration were tilted indicating vertical movement of nutrients in the inner regions of the estuary. In fact, as the authors pointed out, concentrations of nutrients in the deep layers of the estuary are three times as high as concentrations at similar depths in the North Atlantic outside the Gulf, indicating that the Gulf of St. Lawrence is a trap for nutrients. The suggested mechanism is that nutrients flow in with the deep water, are mixed into the surface waters by entrainment, upwelling or other mixing processes, and are taken up by phytoplankton. The phytoplankton move seaward but before reaching the ocean a proportion are either eaten by zooplankton and passed out with zooplankton faeces, or they sink passively to the bottom. In either case, they decompose and release nutrients into deeper water, which is moving upstream into the estuary.

Internal waves and tides have been shown to be responsible for strong vertical oscillations of deep nutrient-rich waters near the head of the estuary, and this is seen as a supplementary mechanism for bringing nutrients into the euphotic zone (Therriault & Lacroix 1976; Muir 1979).

The most comprehensive study of biological production in the Gulf of St. Lawrence was carried out under the International Biological Programme, and reported by Steven (1974). Clear evidence was provided for high levels of phytoplankton production and high phytoplankton biomass in the lower estuary and in the Gaspé Current throughout the growing season. While the open Gulf had a phytoplankton production estimated at 212 g C m^{-2} yr^{-1}, the Gaspé Current had 385 g C m^{-2} yr^{-1} and the lower estuary 509 g C m^{-2} yr^{-1}.

To the north of the Gaspé Current is an anticlockwise pattern of circulation, the Anticosti Gyre. Sevigny *et al.* (1979) made an intensive five day study of the area in July and showed that the isolines for nutrients were dome shaped, indicating upwelling in the centre of the gyre resulting from the cyclonic circulation. However, a strong shallow thermocline prevented nutrient enrichment of surface waters, so that they were characterized by dinoflagellates and microflagellates having a relatively low rate of production. The Gaspé Current, on the other hand, was rich in nutrients and had a dense phytoplankton population dominated by diatoms with a high rate of production. It was inferred that the nutrients reached the Gaspé Current by entrainment, horizontal advection, or a combination of the two.

8.1.4 Secondary production in estuaries

Steven (1974) reported that the highest concentrations of zooplankton were in the southern Gulf of St. Lawrence. He concluded that the Gaspé Current formed a 'plume' which spread over the Magdalen Shallows in the southern Gulf and gave rise to a very high biomass and production of zooplankton in summer.

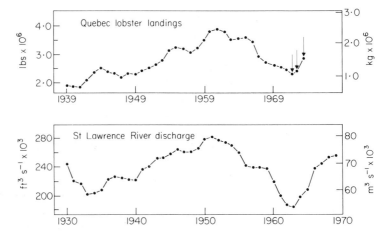

Fig. 8.6 Annual lobster catch from the Province of Quebec and discharge of the St. Lawrence River during the month of April. Both are plotted as three year running means. The time scale of catches is lagged nine years behind the river discharge. Correlation coefficient $r = 0.831$. (Data from Sutcliffe 1973 and Statistics Canada.) Note that the upward trend (marked with arrows) was predicted by Sutcliffe and subsequently verified.

The role of river runoff as a cause of upwelling and thus a stimulator of biological production led Sutcliffe (1972, 1973) to investigate correlations between river runoff and the catch of fish. He allowed a suitable time lag so that fish that had been in the larval stage at the time when runoff was being measured had had time to grow to catchable size. He found good positive correlations of annual runoff of the St. Lawrence River with catch of haddock eight years later, and catch of halibut ten years later. When he considered separately the river runoff for each month, he found that the halibut catch had the best correlation ($r = \cdot855$) with runoff in March. There was a good correlation ($r = \cdot831$) between the discharge in April of any year and the lobster catch nine years later. On the basis of the pattern of river runoff (Fig. 8.6) Sutcliffe was able to predict that the lobster catch would increase in future years. The prediction was subsequently confirmed.

Sutcliffe (1973) mentioned as a possible explanation of his correlations, the chain of events:

increased runoff → increased upwelling →

increased nutrient levels → increased primary production →

improved survival of larval stages of consumers.

Evidence for or against this mechanism is not available, but there is at least one other possible mechanism to be considered: that in years of high river runoff, a larger volume of freshwater will lead to a larger salinity difference between surface and bottom. This in turn will mean a more marked halocline, and probably a more effective warming of surface waters. Elevated temperatures, rather than a better supply of nutrients, could be the cause of enhanced year-class survival among commercially important species.

Summarising to this point, we see from the case history of the St. Lawrence Estuary that river runoff is a major factor influencing upwelling, primary production and secondary production. Since the St. Lawrence is one of the world's major rivers, this effect is particularly well marked, but there is every reason to believe that most rivers produce this effect in some degree. Sutcliffe (1972) also analysed the nitrogen budget of St. Margaret's Bay, Nova Scotia. The volume of the bay is about 4.6×10^9 m^3, and total freshwater runoff about 1.3×10^9 m^3 yr^{-1}. Total primary production was thought to require 62 g N m^{-2} yr^{-1}, of which the rivers supplied directly only about 7 g N m^{-2} yr^{-1}. 26 g N m^{-2} yr^{-1} were thought to be regenerated in the water column, and another 26 g N m^{-2} yr^{-1} supplied by upwelling of nutrient-rich deep water, stimulated by river runoff. Hence, it was the stimulation of upwelling by river runoff, rather than the nutrient content of the river water that enhanced production in St. Margaret's Bay. All over the world there are coastal inlets receiving freshwater runoff, where the productivity is enhanced by a similar mechanism. Moreover, as Sutcliffe showed, it may be the peak runoff at a certain season that is critical to the biological production process, and we should keep this in mind when modifying river flow for purposes of irrigation or power generation. Construction of the Aswan High Dam reduced the flow of the Nile from 42 km^3 yr^{-1} to under 4 km^3, and led to the disappearance of an important sardine fishery in the Eastern Mediterranean. Construction of power dams on the Volga River led to a decline in productivity in the Sea of Azov (Moiseev 1971).

Given that most estuaries are more productive than nearby coastal waters we may ask how much of this production finds its way out of the estuary and onto the continental shelf. This brings us to the question of estuarine flushing.

8.1.5 The effects of estuaries on coastal waters

We are now beginning to realise that major rivers have an effect on coastal waters far beyond the boundaries of the semi-enclosed body of water which we normally regard as the estuary proper. For example, Ketchum (1967) wrote, 'The waters of the New York Bight are measurably diluted by the Hudson and Raritan River waters, so that it may be treated as an estuary, even though the area considered lies outside the geographical boundaries which define what most people would consider the estuary'. He went on to distinguish three types of water in this area: the brackish water showing marked dilution by river water, the surface coastal water entering the area from the east, and the deep ocean water brought in by the countercurrent in the estuarine-type circulation. The estuarine water is characterized by high concentrations of nutrients and suspended detritus, derived chiefly from the sewage wastes of the New York–New Jersey metropolitan area. The total input of inorganic nitrogen to the New York Bight from this source was estimated as $5 \cdot 5 \times 10^7$ kg N yr^{-1} (Garside *et al.* 1976). Malone (1976) showed that over an area of 600 km^2 in the apex of the Bight (close to the estuary proper) phytoplankton production amounted to about 370 g C m^{-2} day^{-1}, compared with 160 g C m^{-2} yr^{-1} near the middle of the Bight and 100 g C m^{-2} yr^{-1} at the edge of the continental shelf. He concluded that the nitrogen from the estuarine waters was sufficient to provide for the high productivity, except in summer months, when ammonia regenerated in the water column was an important subsidiary source. Underneath the area of high primary production, during summer stratification, the oxygen demand generated by decomposing phytoplankton and zooplankton sometimes reduced the oxygen content of the lower layer to 10% of saturation.

The Hudson River system is a spectacular example of a heavily enriched estuary enhancing primary productivity over a considerable distance beyond its mouth. Nevertheless, we have seen that most estuaries have natural mechanisms for enhancing production within their limits, and it would be useful to know to what extent that production is exported to the adjacent coastal waters. Sutcliffe *et al.* (1976, 1977) found evidence that water leaving the Gulf of St. Lawrence by way of the Cabot Strait joins the Nova Scotia Current and moves south-west towards the Gulf of Maine. Fluctuations in the discharge of the St. Lawrence River showed interesting correlations with temperature fluctuations in the waters of Nova Scotia and Maine, when allowance was made for time required for a water mass to move down the coast, and the catches of commercial fishes in turn showed interesting correlations with the sea-water temperature. Sutcliffe *et al.* (1976) were careful to point out that the St. Lawrence River discharge is not the unique determinant of the phenomena observed, but suggested that its importance should not be overlooked.

Turning from large estuaries to small, there is evidence that estuarine water and its associated biological material is moved out to sea not only by the conventional mechanisms of river runoff or tidal flushing, but by water movements on the continental shelf. It has been shown (Platt *et al.* 1972; Heath 1973) that on the east coast of Canada a strong, steady southerly wind can set up currents which are initially parallel with the coast, but because of the Coriolis effect soon turn to the east, as offshore currents. There is a compensatory flow towards shore in deeper waters, and upwelling at the coast. The whole system, Ekman transport, can lead to the total exchange of surface waters simultaneously in numerous inlets along the coast. Vetical profiles of the inlets show upwelling of cold nutrient-rich water and qualitative changes in the planktonic communities, indicating that the biological community previously existing in the mixed layer was transported out to sea.

On the west coast of the USA, Duxbury (1979) observed an analogous process. The flushing rate of Gray's Harbour, Washington, was greatly increased during late summer by the influx at depth of water upwelled along the coast. Since the upwelling was produced by northerly winds creating offshore Ekman transport, it seems as if the mechanism involved is probably very similar to that described by Platt *et al.* (1972) and Heath (1973) for the east coast.

To summarise: estuaries are known to be highly productive, and to act as nutrient traps. In addition, many estuaries are enriched by sewage effluents or agricultural runoff. Stratified estuaries tend to have a net seaward flow of surface water, which produces a steady flow of productive water out to the coastal waters. This flow is often accelerated by wind-induced currents which may cause a relatively rapid and simultaneous exchange of several inlets along a length of coastline.

8.2 UPWELLING SYSTEMS

8.2.1 Physical description

The world's major oceans have large gyres rotating clockwise in the Northern Hemisphere and anticlockwise in the Southern Hemisphere. Because of the rotation of the earth on its axis, the current gyres tend to be displaced towards the west, giving rise to deep, fast-moving currents on the western sides of the ocean basins, and wide, shallow, slow-moving currents on the eastern sides. For example, the Gulf Stream is a large and well-known example of a western boundary current, but there is nothing very spectacular associated with the corresponding eastern boundary current, the Canary Current. Partly on this account, eastern boundary currents are very susceptible to wind-induced vertical movement. For example, as we have seen, when the wind blows from the north along the Oregon coast, the Coriolis effect leads to a movement of surface waters away from the coast, and an upwelling of deeper, nutrient-rich water. The most important areas for upwelling events are in eastern boundary currents off Oregon and California, off Peru, around the Canary Islands off North-west Africa, and in the Benguela Current off southern Africa. There are many areas where upwelling occurs on a smaller scale.

A good example of a documented upwelling event is that which occurred at a latitude of 21°40' off the coast of North-west Africa between the 10th

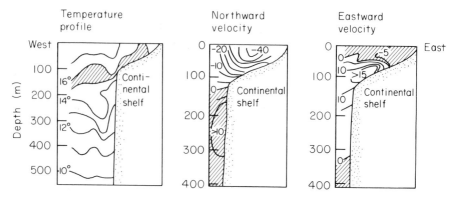

Fig. 8.7   Record of temperature (°C) and northward and eastward velocities (cm s^{-1}) at 21°40′N during an upwelling event off North-west Africa, 13 March 1974. (Modified from Barton *et al.* 1977.)

and 25th of March 1974 (Barton *et al.* 1977). Within 24 h of the onset of a wind from the north, a strong, south-flowing, surface current had developed along the shore, with a component of offshore flow. Profiles taken 3 days after the beginning of the event (Fig. 8.7) showed a southerly flowing surface current of 40 cm s^{-1} with an offshore component of 5 cm s^{-1}. Water at 100 m depth was moving shoreward with a velocity of 15 cm s^{-1} and water of 16 C, which offshore was lying at 150 m, came to the surface close to shore. Deeper water almost invariably has a higher concentration of nitrate than surface waters, so the upwelled water stimulates primary production.

The general picture of such events is given in Fig. 8.8 from Cushing (1971a). As the wind blows parallel to the shore towards the equator, the water is moved offshore by Coriolis force and, because the movement does not extend far in depth, water is drawn from below, near the coast. Since the water is blown offshore at an angle to the coast, it is moved towards

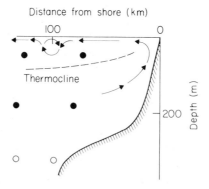

Fig. 8.8   Generalized diagram of an upwelling system. ●● Surface drift towards equator. ○○ Countercurrent towards the pole. (After Cushing 1971a.)

the equator. At about 100 km (it may be as little as 20 km or as much as 200 km) offshore there is often a convergence where the water sinks and, a little further offshore, a divergence generating a secondary source of upwelling above the thermocline. Sverdrup called this region the dynamic boundary and Hart and Currie (1960) called it a 'roller bearing'. The current flowing towards the equator at the surface is compensated by a countercurrent below about 200 m, flowing towards the pole. More information on upwelling is given in section 8.3.2.

8.2.2 The production cycle in an upwelling system

The upwelling regions of the oceans constitute about 0·1% of the world's surface, and can yield up to 50% of the world's fish' catches (Walsh 1976). Hence, there is strong economic motivation for studying production processes in such regions. Cushing (1971a) gives the following generalized picture: upwelling is rather slow, of the order of 1–5 m per day, so phytoplankton rises through the photic zone in the course of many days. As the light intensity increases, the phytoplankton increases its rate of production, since it is bathed in nutrient-rich water. The surface currents are faster than the rate of upwelling, so the upwelled water tends to be carried offshore at an angle. Production along the line of movement is high, and decreases slowly with distance from the point of origin.

There has been much debate (see Chapter 4) about the extent to which the stimulation of phytoplankton production in the plume is due to release from nutrient limitation, to the presence of 'conditioning' substances, or to the regeneration of nutrients by dense populations of consumer organisms. One way of testing rival theories is to construct models based on various assumptions. Walsh (1976) has summarized the results of modelling the Peru, Baja California and North-west Africa upwelling systems. The philosophy of modelling will be discussed in Chapter 10 but we may note that there were state equations for nitrate, ammonia, phosphate and silicate in the water, and for nitrogen content of the biomass of phytoplankton, zooplankton, fish and detritus. The chief processes simulated were upwelling of nutrients, uptake of nutrients by phytoplankton and diurnal migration, grazing and excretion by herbivores. The water was assumed to rise from a depth of 50 m within 1–10 km of the coast, and to drift 100 km downstream along the axis of the main flow. Results were presented (in the 1976 summary) for the distribution of nitrate and phytoplankton nitrogen in a surface layer 10 m deep. The phytoplankton in the Peruvian model were limited by nitrogen inshore and by silica offshore. In the others it was limited by nitrogen at all times. Grazing losses were set to be relatively small inshore but large offshore, on the assumption that it takes time for the grazing population to build up, in a particular water mass, after the increase in primary production.

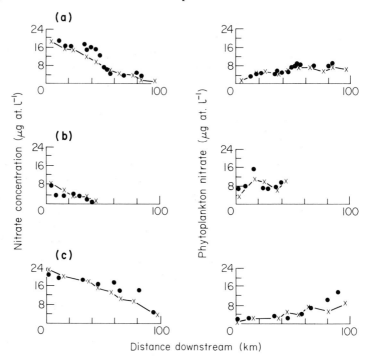

Fig. 8.9 Field data (·) and simulated results (×) for three upwelling systems, (a) Peru, (b) Baja California, (c) North-west Africa. (After Walsh 1976.)

Figure 8.9 shows that Walsh and his colleagues obtained considerable success in simulating the utilization of nitrate and the building of phytoplankton nitrogen in the plumes of all three systems. Walsh pointed out that it is not yet possible to obtain matching quantitative data for zooplankton and fish. Nevertheless, there is good qualitative information about the food chains. An important difference between the Peru system and the others is that upwelling occurs year round off Peru. This may be the reason why a species of fish (*Engraulis ringens*, the Peruvian anchoveta) has been able to evolve the habit of grazing directly on the phytoplankton. In the other upwelling systems which are seasonal and less predictable, zooplankton are always present as trophic intermediaries between phytoplankton and fish.

The Baja California system was observed by Walsh and his colleagues during the early part of its seasonal cycle, and it was found that dinoflagellates predominated in the phytoplankton, rather than diatoms, as in the other systems. Dinoflagellates are capable of diurnal vertical migration, and may take up nitrate below the euphotic zone, so this property was built into the model. During the middle and late parts of the upwelling season, however, the Baja California system resembles the other systems in having phytoplankton dominated by diatoms which, as was shown in Chapter 4, are characteristic of turbulent water.

Production at various trophic levels of upwelling systems has been well reviewed by Cushing (1971a). Primary production is commonly in the range $0.25-2.00$ g C m^{-2} d^{-1}, which is much higher than that of the oligotrophic, tropical water with which the systems are surrounded. Zooplankton production has not been measured in these areas, but Cushing made some reasonable estimates from biomass observations. He concluded that the transfer coefficients between primary and secondary levels ranged from under 5% in the highly productive systems to over 20% in some less productive systems. Tertiary production was estimated by postulating a transfer coefficient of either 1% from primary production or 10% from secondary production, and this led to a global estimate of 76 million tonnes of fish and squid production per year, from upwelling systems. The most important areas for fish production were thought to be the Benguela Current (18.36×10^6 tonnes), the Peru Current (12.24×10^6 tonnes), the Canary Current (8.16×10^6 tonnes) and the California Current (5.1×10^6 tonnes). Anchoveta are dominant in the Peruvian fishery, sardines in the Benguela and Canary systems, anchovy with hake in the California Current. Hence, the fish that have adapted to life in the cold waters of upwelling systems are predominantly clupeoids. In aggregate, they represent a very major contribution to the world fish production. The situation summarized by Walsh (1972) has changed now, on account of a drastic decline in the Peruvian fishery (Idyll 1973) but shows what an enormous production potential exists in these systems (Table 8.1).

8.3   FRONTS IN COASTAL WATERS

If two water masses of distinctly different properties meet at a sharp boundary, the zone of their meeting is termed a front. It has been found that

Table 8.1   Estimated potential yield of fish per year in upwelling ecosystems. (After Walsh 1972.)

Area	Effective period of upwelling (months)	Pelagic fish (10^6 tonnes)	Demersal fish (10^6 tonnes)
Peru–Chile	12	11.73	0.612
Angola–South Africa	9	3.978	1.22
Dakar–Casablanca	8–9	3.06	0.714
Baja California– Cape Mendocino	7–8	3.57	0.408
Arabian Sea	6	3.57	0.714
Oregon–Washington	3–4	0.816	0.612
Gulf of Panama	3–4	9.204	0.102

fronts tend to be areas of enhanced biological productivity, so they merit intensive study of their physical, chemical and biological properties. A good review of contemporary knowledge of coastal marine fronts was given in a volume edited by Bowman and Esaias (1978) and this section relies heavily on that collection of papers. Six types of front were recognized: (1) fronts on a planetary scale, far from major ocean boundaries; (2) fronts at the edge of major western boundary currents; (3) shelf break fronts; (4) upwelling fronts; (5) river plume fronts; and (6) shallow sea fronts commonly located at the boundaries between shallow, mixed, inshore waters and stratified, deeper, offshore waters. The first two types are open-ocean phenomena and need not concern us here; (3)–(6) are important coastal phenomena. Their common feature is that they are all at the boundary between a well mixed and a stratified water mass.

8.3.1 Shelf break fronts

The best documented shelf break fronts are on the east coast of North America (Mooers *et al.* 1978). The simplest structure occurs in winter, between November and March (Fig. 8.10). Over the shelf where the water column is less deep, and therefore holds less heat, cooling occurs more rapidly in autumn and mixing occurs from top to bottom. Offshore, the cooling surface water sinks to a great depth and the surface water remains warmer than on the shelf. For example, south of Rhode Island at the end of winter the inshore water is at about 4°C, water near the edge of the shelf is at about 8°C but slope water offshore of the frontal zone has a surface temperature of 14–16°C. On the other hand the shelf water, under the influence of the river runoff, has a lower salinity than the offshore water with the result that

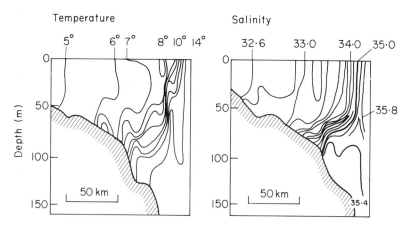

Fig. 8.10 Temperature and salinity profiles south of Rhode Island, April 2–4 1974. (After Flagg & Beardsley 1975.)

the cooler, less saline, inshore water has about the same density as the warmer, more saline, offshore water. The front between the two water masses is always close to the shelf break, where the continental shelf changes to the continental slope.

A shelf front is not a rigid, fixed phenomenon, but under the influence of passing storms has been shown to meander about its mean longshore position, to tilt strongly in the vertical plane under the influence of upwelling events, and to 'calve' off 'bubbles' of shelf water into slope water.

With the onset of spring warming a thermocline forms over both shelf and slope, but below the thermocline a cold water mass remains on the shelf, with a front separating it from the slope water.

8.3.2 Upwelling fronts

Reference was made in section 8.2.1 to the occurrence of convergences and divergences at the seaward boundary of an upwelling region. The process is incompletely understood, but it is a matter of observation that the offshore surface Ekman transport associated with an upwelling area does not move seaward indefinitely. Since it is relatively cool, dense water, it moves seaward until it encounters warm, lighter, offshore water, and at this point it sinks. However, the offshore water is strongly stratified while the inshore water is well mixed. Moreover, the inshore water is moving towards the equator while the offshore water is not. The difference in properties of the water masses results in a sharp front.

8.3.3 River plume fronts

At river plumes, a layer of light, less saline water spreads over more saline water. Because of its buoyancy, the plume is elevated and there is a surface slope towards the sea. Friction at the interface leads to retardation of buoyant spreading, and the formation of a front with the kind of circulation shown in Fig. 8.11. The situation somewhat resembles that found within a salt wedge estuary, except that in a plume front surface water is entrained and mixed downward, whereas in a salt wedge the entrainment is mostly upwards and is attributable to breaking internal waves (Bowman & Iverson 1978).

8.3.4 Shallow sea fronts

Many coastal waters, especially on the continental shelf of Europe, are permanently well mixed by the action of strong tidal currents. Hence, we have the potential for the formation of fronts at the boundaries of vertically mixed and stratified bodies of water. Simpson and Hunter (1974) suggested that the

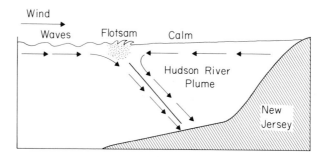

Fig. 8.11 Diagrammatic cross section of the Hudson River plume front. (After Bowman & Iverson 1978.)

presence or absence of stratification can be related to a parameter h/u^3 where h is the water depth and u is the amplitude of the oscillations in the tidal current velocity. Simpson and Pingree (1978) showed that contours of this parameter were indeed good predictors of the occurrence of major fronts in summer, particularly in the Irish Sea, the Celtic Sea and the approaches to the English Channel. The fronts form at boundaries between well stratified conditions offshore and well mixed conditions within much of the Irish Sea, the Bristol Channel and the English Channel. They are of the order of 100 km in length.

Other, smaller scale, frontal structures found in shallow coastal waters include estuarine fronts and headland fronts. In relatively large estuaries on ebbing tides the centre channel may contain well stratified water with a layer of low salinity, warm water moving seaward at the surface. The edges of the estuary may, on the other hand, have shallower, well-mixed water, and fronts develop parallel with the axis of the estuary.

In places where strong tidal streams move parallel to the coastline, projecting headlands cause major deformation of the lines of flow. Pingree *et al.* (1978) list four effects: (1) increased tidal streaming off headlands and weaker flows in bays; (2) jet-like flow off headlands; (3) curvature of flow round headlands resulting in local lowering of sea level caused by centrifugal forces; and (4) vortices in the residual circulation patterns. These effects lead to the formation of fronts of relatively short duration, i.e. during the time of strong tidal flow in one direction.

8.3.5 The effect of fronts on biological productivity

The shelf break areas are well known to fishermen as being highly productive of fish (Fig. 8.12). Fournier *et al.* (1977) studied the distribution of phytoplankton across the Scotian Shelf (off Eastern Canada) on four occasions and showed that there were increases in chlorophyll associated with

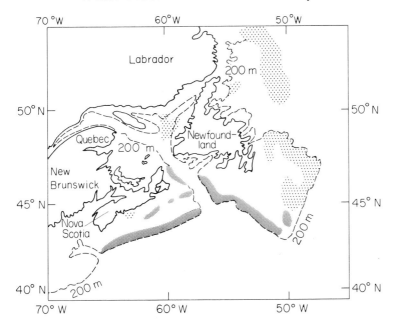

Fig. 8.12 The areas of concentration of foreign fishing vessels off the east coast of Canada. (After Grant & Rygh 1973.)

the shelf break in March, May and August. They later showed that winter conditions are similar to those described in section 8.3.1, with a clearly marked shelf break front (Fournier *et al.* 1979). However, the steepness of the front varied between vertical and almost horizontal. When it was vertical, the mixed layer depth in its vicinity was about 40 m and there was little phytoplankton biomass. When it was horizontal the mixed layer depth was about 8 m and there was greatly enhanced phytoplankton biomass. We saw in Chapter 4 that onset of spring bloom of phytoplankton is associated with reduction in mixed layer depth. Fournier *et al.* (1979) proposed that the shelf break front, when in the tilted position, enhanced phytoplankton production by restricting the mixing depth. Mills and Fournier (1979) concluded that the annual production over the slope was about 127.6 g C m^{-2} yr^{-1} compared with 102.1 g C m^{-2} yr^{-1} over the shelf.

Simpson and Pingree (1978) showed for shallow sea fronts produced by tidal stirring that there is a zone of high phytoplankton biomass on the stratified side of such fronts in summer. The normal state of affairs is that stratified waters are nutrient-depleted at the surface in summer, while mixed waters are richer in nutrients. A transfer of nutrients from the mixed to the stratified waters, across the front, could account for the enhanced phytoplankton biomass and production. On this point, Horne *et al.* (1978) wrote:

A common misunderstanding is that since frontal zones by definition are regions with sharp gradients of properties, they must therefore represent a barrier to mixing between the two juxtaposed water masses. Otherwise, diffusion across the zone would soon dissipate the front and smooth out any horizontal discontinuities. However, in reality the opposite is true. The frontal zone is a region of *intensified* motion and mixing.

Horne *et al.* (1978) put forward a number of plausible hypotheses for mixing across the front, including interleaving of layers of different temperature and salinity, and turbulence generated by different velocities of the two water masses. Since almost all fronts have a vertically mixed layer on one side and a stratified layer on the other, these mechanisms for injecting nutrient-rich water into the surface layer of a stratified water body are probably the cause of enhanced productivity associated with many types of front.

Sinking at the convergence is caused by a phenomenon known as cabbeling. A mixture of two waters of dissimilar temperature and salinity but equal density possesses greater density than the components, and will therefore sink. This means that surface currents move towards a front from both sides, then sink. The front is a place where materials brought by surface currents tends to accumulate. Sea birds are particularly abundant at fronts, and fish, dolphins and whales also tend to aggregate there. While we lack a comprehensive quantitative study of a food chain at a front, it is now clear that they are indeed zones of enhanced biological productivity which merit further attention from coastal oceanographers. Bowman (1978) speculates that the story of the miraculous draft of fishes in the Gospels may refer to a situation on the sea of Galilee when the boat was on a convergence. The disciples had been fishing on the unproductive side of the front, but at the injunction of the Master they cast their nets on the other side—the productive side— and 'when they had this done, they inclosed a great multitude of fishes: and their net brake'.*

8.4   GENERAL CONCLUSIONS

The preceding sections have shown that it is impossible to understand biological processes in coastal waters without understanding the physical oceanography of the system under consideration. As a general rule, nutrients are concentrated in deeper waters while primary producers are concentrated near the surface. The physical mechanisms that transport nutrients from depth to the surface are key factors controlling primary and secondary production. The three chief forcing functions are winds, tides and the runoff of fresh waters from the land. In estuaries we see all three interacting in

---

* Luke, Chapter 5, v.6. King James Version.

complex and fascinating ways. When river runoff is dominant and tidal mixing is slight we find salt wedges which move up and down the estuaries according to the volume of river flow. As tidal mixing increases so does entrainment of salt water in the river runoff, to produce the moderately stratified estuary with its strong inshore flow at depth. Strong tidal flows in relatively shallow waters produce completely mixed waters which may extend well beyond the estuaries onto the continental shelf, as in the English Channel and the Irish Sea.

In stratified waters, wind-induced offshore Ekman transports lead to rapid flushing of bays and estuaries, carrying the fruits of enhanced primary and secondary production out into coastal areas. Finally, we find that some coastal areas have their patterns of productivity dominated by frequent periods of wind-induced upwelling. The plumes of high productivity associated with them support some of the world's richest fisheries.

It would greatly simplify the problems of resource management and environmental protection in the coastal zone if the performance of coastal ecosystems could be predicted. The techniques of modelling will be reviewed in Chapter 10, but at present we may note that the functioning of coastal ecosystems is heavily dependent on meteorological factors such as wind strength and direction, rainfall, snow melt, warming of surface waters, and so on. Even if we understood all the relevant biological interactions and could model them with confidence and accuracy, the predictive value of the models would be no better than our ability to predict the weather.

We are accustomed to thinking of biological processes in terms of energy fluxes such as photosynthesis, respiration, etc., but a truly representative energy model of a coastal ecosystem would also take account of the much larger energy fluxes associated with vertical, wind-induced mixing, the ebb and flow of the tides, and the hydrologic cycle of evaporation and precipitation.

CHAPTER 9
FISH AND SHELLFISH PRODUCTION IN COASTAL ECOSYSTEMS

Although the empirical facts were well known to fishermen and fisheries scientists, it was Ryther (1969) who first provided an ecological basis for the idea that most of the world's fish production takes place in coastal waters and upwelling areas. His calculations were based on the assumptions that primary production is lower and food chains are longer in the open ocean than in coastal waters. Details of this argument have been criticized, but the general conclusion still stands.

Ryther's paper gave prominence to a view that had been gaining ground during the 1960's, which was that those responsible for the management of fisheries had paid too little attention to the food chains on which fish production ultimately depended. Current views on the dynamics of exploited fish populations with particular reference to the North Sea were well summarized in the classic volume by Beverton and Holt (1957). Underlying most of their mathematical models was the assumption that food is not a limiting factor for exploited fish stocks, or that it is in constant supply, so that an increase in population density leads to a proportional decrease in food per fish. An alternative approach had been developed independently by Schaeffer, working in the Pacific, and the two were compared in Schaeffer and Beverton (1963). Schaeffer had used biomass data rather than population numbers, and there was an implication that some factor limited the total biomass of the population, but whether this factor was food, and whether it operated by changing the growth rate or the recruitment was not made explicit.

In the same volume that Schaeffer and Beverton were discussing the merits of their population models, Riley (1963) was reviewing models of phytoplankton production in the sea and extending them to models of higher trophic levels, which he called herbivores, first order carnivores or 'forage animals' and second order carnivores or 'potential tuna'. The models were metabolic in nature. For example, if h is the concentration of herbivore zooplankton, α is a predation coefficient, β is the fraction of food consumed that can be assimilated by the forage fish, γ is basal plus work metabolism, and δ is the fraction of excess food over maintenance that is converted to weight increase, the rate of change of the forage animal biomass F is given by:

$$\frac{\mathrm{d}F}{\mathrm{d}t} = F[\delta(\alpha\beta h - \gamma) - cT] \tag{9.1}$$

where T is biomass of potential tuna, and c is the coefficient of capture.

If F is in steady state, $\mathrm{d}F/\mathrm{d}t = 0$ and

$$T = \frac{\alpha\beta\delta}{c}\left(h - \frac{\delta\gamma}{c}\right) \tag{9.2}$$

Using equations of this sort, Riley pointed out that relationships between trophic levels are non-linear, so that, for example, a fourfold increase in biomass of zooplankton could lead to a fifteen-fold increase in potential tuna, when reasonable assumptions were made about physiological coefficients.

This work made it very plain that we should not expect to find any simple proportionalities between, say, primary production and fish production. Nevertheless, it gave an impetus to the search for connections between fish production and the food chains on which they depend. For example, Dickie (1972) reviewed a number of efforts to estimate global marine fish production from global marine primary production, and concluded that although the estimates varied widely the differences were based on subjective judgements rather than on testable hypotheses. He went on to review current theories of trophic dynamics in the sea and to suggest lines of research that might be expected to clarify food chain relationships and transfer efficiencies.

9.1 FISH PRODUCTION IN THE NORTH SEA

The North Sea is one of the most intensively fished areas in the world, but is also the area with the longest records on the yields of fish (Steele 1974). It is therefore appropriate that pioneering attempts should have been made to relate fish yields to productivity at various trophic levels. The existing information was reviewed in Steele (1974), and was expanded and modified in Jones (1976) and Jones and Richards (1976). Further comments were made in Steele (1979).

The original, tentative food web model took net production of 'particulate organic matter available to the metazoan herbivores' (i.e. average phytoplankton production plus production of bacteria feeding on extracellular production of DOM) as 90 g C m^{-2} yr^{-1} or 900 kcal m^{-2} yr^{-1}. Of this, one third was thought to be incorporated in zooplankton faeces and sedimented to the bottom (Fig. 9.1). Herbivorous zooplankton production was judged to be 170 kcal m^{-2} yr^{-1} and divided equally between pelagic fish and invertebrate carnivores such as chaetognaths.

Steele (1974) drew attention to the extent of our ignorance about the proportion of energy in the benthos that is metabolized by macro-, meio- and microbenthos (cf. Chapter 7) but finally set the production of the macrobenthos at 50 kcal m^{-2} yr^{-1}. Note that in both the zooplankton and the benthos it was thought necessary to assume transfer efficiencies not

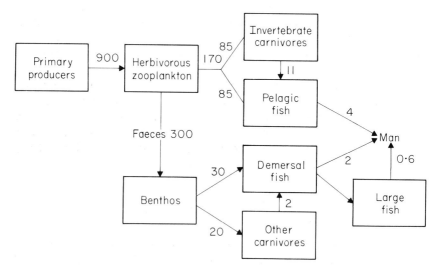

Fig. 9.1 Energy flow in the North Sea ecosystem. Fluxes are kcal m^{-2}yr^{-1}. (After Steele 1974.)

much below 20%. Macrobenthic production was divided 3 : 2 between demersal fish and other carnivores, and the demersal fish were given a production of 2.6 kcal m^{-2} yr^{-1}, which converts to 1.3×10^6 tonnes for the North Sea, and corresponds to a commercial catch of 0.95×10^6 tonnes, plus an allowance for natural mortality. Pelagic fish were given a production of 8 kcal m^{-2} yr^{-1}, divided equally between natural mortality and yield to man. 4 kcal m^{-2} yr^{-1}, which is approximately 4 g m^{-2} yr^{-1} converts 2×10^6 tonnes of yield to man, and corresponds with the catches during the later part of the 1960's, when pelagic catches were particularly high. The overall energy flow diagram is shown in Fig. 9.1.

The tentative estimates given above were modified by Jones and Richards (1976) in the following ways. They noted that between about 1960 and 1970 the biomasses of fish in the North Sea showed a shift, with herring and mackerel decreasing to about one-third of their former value and gadoid groundfish increasing 2–5 times. They calculated the food requirements of the fish stocks, using reasonable physiological parameters, and found they were lower than Steele had suggested. They postulated that the herbivore production not now required by the fish was used by 'other primary carnivores' such as sand-eels, sprats, euphausids, Norway pout, and juvenile stages of demersal fish. They pointed out that euphausids and sand-eels are eaten by mackerel and herring, while demersal fish during part of their life histories take all the primary carnivores they can get. They found that they could balance the energy budget by assuming that the herbivore production released by the decline in herring and mackerel was all taken up by the 'other primary carnivores' and passed to the demersal fish.

From this exercise they concluded that in spite of the heavy fishing pressure on the fish stocks of the North Sea, the available food is being fully utilized, and one cannot assume that a change in fishing pressures will lead to a higher sustainable yield overall. The interesting point for our present discussion is that it shows clearly how seemingly distinct parts of an ecosystem are related in ways that are economically important. No amount of study of the population dynamics of a benthic fish species considered in isolation from the total system, could have explained the increase in stock size which occurred during the 1960's. Only a consideration of interactions of three trophic levels provided the necessary clues.

9.2   FISH PRODUCTION ON THE SCOTIAN SHELF

Mills and Fournier (1979), using a much less complete data set, attempted to document the food web leading to fish on the Scotian Shelf, eastern Canada. Primary production on the shelf (depth range 0–180 m) averaged 102 g C or 1160 kcal m^{-2} yr^{-1}, but the authors noted that their cruises had not included the spring bloom and on this account the estimates might be up to 25% too low. Herbivorous zooplankton production was estimated at 89 kcal m^{-2} yr^{-1}, and food intake by zooplankton at 450 kcal m^{-2} yr^{-1}.

Pelagic fish production was estimated at 3·9 kcal m^{-2} yr^{-1} and food requirements at 46·8. Mills and Fournier found that the pelagic fish common on that part of the shelf (redfish and hake, for example) fed mainly on carnivorous macrozooplankton such as chaetognaths, rather than on herbivorous zooplankton. The food requirements of pelagic fish were then assumed to be satisfied by the production of carnivorous zooplankton. When this was done, there was insufficient production of herbivorous zooplankton to support the pelagic predators. Mills and Fournier (1979) therefore postulated an alternative pathway by way of microzooplankton (see Fig. 9.2).

The benthic food web involved the assumption that a fall-out of phytoplankton cells and zooplankton faeces was processed by bacteria with an efficiency of 45% and that bacterial production was used by a meiofauna/macrofauna community with a transfer efficiency of 10%. The resulting benthic production provided about the right amount of food to supply demersal fish stocks.

A comparable food web was constructed for the shelf slope, where a front is present and primary production is higher (see Chapter 8). The front is highly productive of pelagic fish, and the problem of accounting for this production in pelagic food chains is particularly acute. The authors speculated about the relationships of microzooplankton, salps, chaetognaths, and pelagic fish but were forced to admit that the problem of accounting for pelagic fish production was as yet unsolved. Comparing the Scotian Shelf with the North Sea they noted that while primary production was higher on the Scotian Shelf, production of zooplankton and pelagic fish appeared to be much lower, while demersal fish production was about the same. They concluded:

> We believe that any hypothesis (based on evidence cited by Dickie 1972 and Mills 1975) that the food webs leading to the major commercial fisheries are similarly constructed everywhere is too broad a generalization, and requires major qualification. Detailed regional studies are still needed before predictive modelling of shelf and slope ecosystems can begin.

We saw (Chapter 8) that the physical oceanography of the Scotian Shelf and the North Sea are radically different. Much of the North Sea is strongly mixed by tidal currents. The Scotian Shelf, on the other hand, has a deeper water column, weaker tidal currents, and is strongly stratified in summer. Furthermore, it is probably strongly influenced by the outflow from the Gulf of St. Lawrence (see section 8.4). It is clear that associated with these differences are major differences in the structure of the food webs. Nevertheless,

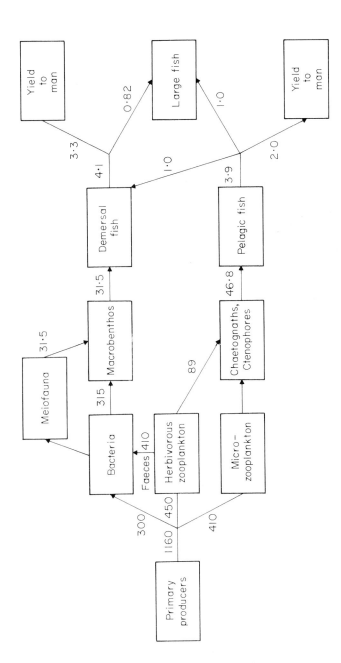

Fig. 9.2 Food web for a fishery at 90 m on the Scotian Shelf, Eastern Canada. Fluxes are kcal m^{-2}yr^{-1}. (After Mills & Fournier 1979.)

our knowledge of the details of those food webs is so inadequate that we can do no more than guess what the differences might be.

9.3 ALTERNATE PATHWAYS TO FISH PRODUCTION IN CONTINENTAL SHELF COMMUNITIES

Mention was made in Chapter 5 of Pomeroy's view that energy fluxes through detritus pathways to bacteria and ciliates and by way of nanno-plankton to mucus-net feeders may be much more important than we have hitherto supposed. We saw in Fig. 5.4 the outline of an energy flow model which included those alternate pathways. Pomeroy (1979) reported on a series of experiments with that model in which he took care to maintain an appropriate relationship between primary production and fish production, but explored the effects of allowing different proportions of energy to flow through the conventional phytoplankton–zooplankton pathway and through alternate pathways.

The 'standard run' of the model had a primary production of 1000 kcal m^{-2} yr^{-1} (approx. 100 g C m^{-2} yr^{-1}) and had the zooplankton removing 700 kcal by grazing. This yielded a pelagic fish production of 8 kcal m^{-2} yr^{-1} and demersal fish production of 3·9 kcal m^{-2} yr^{-1}, values not very different from those in Steele (1974).

The first experiment consisted of passing 70% of the phytoplankton production to mucus-net feeders, on the assumption that the primary producers were nannoplankton, too small for conventional zooplankton to graze. The production of mucus-net feeders was assumed to be taken about equally by pelagic fishes and planktonic carnivores. The lack of zooplankton faecal material resulted in a reduced production of benthic invertebrates and benthic fishes, but overall fish production was reduced by only about 20%.

In another experiment it was assumed that phytoplankton were not eaten by grazers or mucus-net feeders, and that 50% of their production became detritus while a further 30% became DOM. As a result, the flux to planktonic grazers and carnivores was reduced, but production of attached bacteria was high. This was used by the benthic invertebrates giving a benthic fish production which was higher than the standard run, while pelagic fish production was reduced. Total fish production was reduced by about 27%.

Pomeroy (1979) went on to comment on Steele's assumption of a 20% transfer efficiency in zooplankton and benthos. He gave reasons why he thought that in many cases populations achieved energy transfer efficiencies as high as 30%, and went on to give examples of his model with 30% efficiencies for grazers, mucus-net feeders and carnivorous zooplankton. When most of the energy was channelled through zooplankton, fish production was about double that of the standard run, but when alternate pathways were made more important, fish production came back down to the levels quoted by Steele (1974).

In discussion, Pomeroy pointed out that involving alternate pathways of energy flow does make it more difficult to keep an appropriate ratio between primary production and observed fish production. One way of compensating for this is to assume a higher transfer efficiency (which he called gross growth efficiency) for various consumer groups, and the model demonstrated how this might be done. However, another possibility remains. Several workers have suggested that the presently accepted estimates of phytoplankton production, using ^{14}C techniques, are too low on account of methodological problems. There is some discussion of these ideas in sections 4.2 and 5.3.2. However, if phytoplankton production were in general higher than presently believed, there would be less difficulty in balancing primary production and fish production, while allowing for significant energy flow through alternate pathways.

9.4 PELAGIC FISH PRODUCTION: A THEORETICAL APPROACH

Given the difficulties of unravelling the tangled skein of trophic relationships discussed in the previous two sections, it is perhaps not surprising to find that attempts have been made to find some valid simplifying assumptions that could make the problems more tractable. One such attempt is associated with R. W. Sheldon and colleagues. The idea arose from the use of an automatic particle counter to assess the number and size distribution of particles in the plankton. Sheldon *et al.* (1972) reported that when particle concentrations (in parts per million by volume) were grouped in logarithmic size intervals according to a universal grade scale (Sheldon 1969) they were relatively uniform over a wide range of particle diameters ($1-10^6$ μm). Kerr (1974) developed a theoretical model based on trophic processes which supported the idea of particle density in pelagic systems being a linear function of the logarithm of particle size, primarily due to regular prey–predator size relations (see below).

Sheldon *et al.* (1977) carried the analysis one stage further. Pointing out that if one size of organisms provides the food for a size class of larger organisms, the equilibrium condition requires that the production of the prey size class equals the food requirement of the predator size class. Production of a size class is given by

$$P = rS \tag{9.3}$$

where P is production, S is standing stock, and r is the instantaneous growth rate. The relationship between the predator biomass S_c and prey biomass S_p is given by:

$$r_c S_c = r_p S_p \times G_e \times C_e \tag{9.4}$$

or

$$r_c/r_p = S_p/S_c \times G_e \times C_e \tag{9.5}$$

where G_e is the growth efficiency and C_e is the capture efficiency of the predator.

Fenchel (1974) showed that r tends to be smaller for larger animals, and formulated the relationship $r = aW^{-0.275}$. Sheldon *et al.* (1977) produced a relationship involving particle diameter (equivalent spherical diameter) rather than weight, which was $r = bD^{-0.72}$. The ratio of instantaneous growth rates can therefore be expressed as:

$$r_c/r_p = (D_c/D_p)^{-0.72} \tag{9.6}$$

Equations (9.5) and (9.6) can be combined and rearranged to give

$$S_c/S_p = (D_c/D_p)^{0.72} \times G_e \times C_e \tag{9.7}$$

Now $G_e \times C_e$ in equation (9.4) is in effect the transfer efficiency between trophic levels. Setting this efficiency at three 'reasonable' levels enables us to plot the relationship of S_c/S_p to D_c/D_p as in Fig. 9.3.

The final step in the argument is the observation that pelagic aquatic predators all tend to be about the same shape (streamlined) with minimal appendages, seizing their prey by means of their jaws. This imposes a fairly regular relationship between the size of predator and the size of prey.

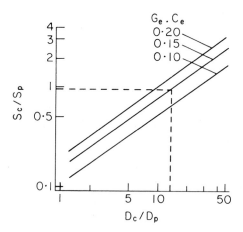

Fig. 9.3 Plots of equation 9.4 (see text), where S is standing stock, D is size, G_e is growth efficiency and C_e is capture efficiency. Subscript c denotes predator and p denotes prey. (After Sheldon *et al.* 1977.)

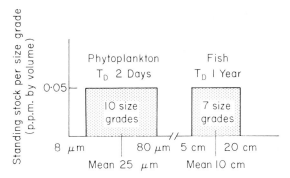

Fig. 9.4 Relationship between size, standing stock and growth rate for phytoplankton and fish in the Gulf of Maine. (Note that for sizes to be compared a common scale is used—the diameter of an equivalent sphere. Actual fish lengths would be three to four times greater, depending on shape). (From Sheldon *et al.* 1977.)

Evidence was produced to show that on average the ratio of sizes D_c/D_p is about $14:1$. When a value of 14 is entered in Fig. 9.3, with a transfer efficiency of 15%, the ratio of standing crops is close to 1. From this, it was concluded that while there will be natural variation, it is reasonable to assume that the idea of equal biomasses in different size classes is a valid one.

Sheldon *et al.* (1977) used this relatively simple concept to show how a knowledge of the production at a trophic level can be predicted from a knowledge of the biomass or production at some other trophic level. They took as their first example the fish yield of the Gulf of Maine, which over many years had been fairly constant at about 3.0 g m^{-2} yr^{-1} (wet wt.). From the literature they concluded that the stock approximately doubles its biomass in a year, so they set the biomass at 3.0 g m^{-2}. The size range of the fish was taken as 5–20 cm, which covers seven size grades on the universal scale. Phytoplankton ranged from 8–80 μm which is ten size grades. Assuming equal biomass in each grade, the biomass of fish should be 70% of the biomass of the plankton (Fig. 9.4). The phytoplankton turns over its biomass about 180 times per year, so that when the biomass difference is taken into account the phytoplankton production should be about 260 times the fish production, i.e. 780 g m^{-2} yr^{-1} wet weight, or 45 g C m^{-2} yr^{-1}. Bearing in mind that fish yield is probably less than half the total natural production of fish, the phytoplankton production in the Gulf of Maine is predicted to be something over 90 g C m^{-2} yr^{-1}, which is reasonably close to measured values. The exercise was repeated using North Sea data as given in Steele (1974) and found to give reasonable agreement with field measurements. Working in the reverse direction along the food chain, primary production in the Peruvian upwelling system was used to predict that fish production should be of the order 10.2×10^6 tonnes. The actual landings of

Table 9.1 Fish production on the east coast of North America, primary production calculated from it by the method of Sheldon *et al.* (1977) and empirical estimates made of primary production. (Adapted from Sherman *et al.* 1978.)

	Fish production (g wet wt. m^{-2} yr^{-1})		Primary production calculated from fish production (g C m^{-2} yr^{-1})		Measured primary production (g C m^{-2} yr^{-1})
	1964–66	1973–75	1964–66	1973–75	
Gulf of Maine	7·0	5·6	109·2	87·3	150–200
George's Bank	17·5	12·7	273·0	198·1	450
Southern New England	9·2	6·8	99·0	73·0	150
Mid-Atlantic Bight	4·1	3·7	123·0	111·0	150–200

anchoveta between 1966 and 1971 were in the range 8·67–12·546 × 10^6 tonnes.

The method was adopted by Sherman *et al.* (1978) in their broad review of the fisheries of eastern North America from the Gulf of Maine to Cape Hatteras. It had earlier been shown that heavy fishing in this area had resulted in a marked drop in biomass of fish, from about 6·12 × 10^6 to about 2·55 × 10^6 tonnes between 1963 and 1974 (Clark & Brown 1977). From these biomass data and best estimates of P/B ratios, fish production was calculated and used to estimate the phytoplankton production needed to support it during periods of high and low fish biomass. The figures are shown in Table 9.1. It seems that even before the recent reduction in fish biomass, there was more primary production than a calculation by the method of Sheldon *et al.* (1977) would lead us to expect, and the difference was even more marked after the fish stocks declined. Sherman *et al.* (1978) concluded that the fish stocks were not food limited (at least not as medium-sized fish, larvae could be another matter) and that there was a surplus of primary production which was being used in food chains leading to organisms not taken commercially.

The Sheldon spectrum model and its derivatives are examples of a class of highly aggregated models which give us totally new insights into the working of ecosystems and help explain why the fish production is of a particular magnitude. It seems probable that with further work and refinement a greater degree of precision will be obtained. Nevertheless, they do not give the kind of fine scale resolution required by managers of particular fish stocks. In the next section we shall deal with attempts to consider several stocks simultaneously at the degree of detail which managers find useful.

9.5 MULTISPECIES INTERACTIONS IN FISH STOCKS

The idea that effective management of fish stocks calls for an appreciation of the complexity of the whole ecosystem of which those stocks are a part, is now being widely discussed (e.g. Edwards 1976; Gulland 1978). However, the preceding sections have shown that predictions made on the basis of the whole system are still in an early stage of development and lack the detail required for practical management. As a compromise between the ecosystem approach and the single stock approach, a number of fishery biologists are now considering interactions between groups of fish species.

The southern Gulf of St. Lawrence is a major spawning ground for both herring (*Clupea harengus harengus*) and mackerel (*Scomber scombrus*), and interactions between these species have been studied by Winters (1976) and Lett and Kohler (1976). In the late 1950's the stocks of herring were at a low level, apparently as a result of a fungus disease. They increased to an estimated biomass of 1.9×10^6 tonnes in 1964, and this led to heavy fishing pressure which again reduced the stocks, this time to 0.36×10^6 tonnes. Mackerel were also reduced in numbers by the fungus, but their numbers remained low until 1967, after which they began to increase rapidly (Fig. 9.5). Clearly, the reciprocal relation between biomasses gives grounds for suspecting a competitive interaction between these two pelagic species, breeding in the same area. Winters (1976) investigated changes in mean length and weight of the spawning groups (ages 3–7 years) and showed that these had an inverse relationship with the total biomass of herring and mackerel in the southern Gulf (correlations of $r = 0.94$ for length and 0.98 for weight) (Fig. 9.6). The timing of the increase in mackerel biomass was thought to be determined by temperature. Mackerel are pelagic spawners requiring a surface temperature of 11–18°C, and the period after 1965 was one of warm summers which favoured mackerel spawning and survival. A plot of log recruitment against log temperature showed a strong positive

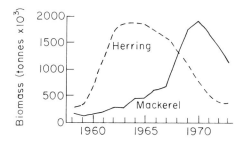

Fig. 9.5 The biomass of herring and mackerel in the Gulf of St. Lawrence, 1958–73. (From Winters 1978.)

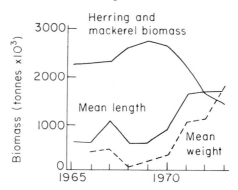

Fig. 9.6 Mean length and mean weight of herring, and total herring and mackerel biomass in the Gulf of St. Lawrence, 1965–73. (From Winters 1976.)

correlation with $r = 0.82$. It was concluded that the carrying capacity of the southern Gulf for pelagic fish is limited, and that growth of herring responds in a density dependent manner to the total biomass of herring and mackerel, while mackerel biomass is determined mainly by temperature in the first year of life.

Lett and Kohler (1976) looked closely at the competitive interactions between the species, paying particular attention to larval interactions, and exploring these by means of a simulation model. They found that the growth of herring age 2–10 could be adequately described by the regression:

$$\log_e G_a = -4.701 \log_e Y_a - 0.161 \log_e MY$$
$$+ (0.827 \log_e Y_a) \times (\log_e T_m) + 6.028 \quad (9.8)$$

where G_a is the instantaneous growth rate of a year class Y_a, MY is the year-class size of age-group 0 mackerel $\times 10^{-6}$, and T_m is the maximum monthly mean temperature for the year. The implication of this expression is that the only significant interspecific competition for food is at age-group 0, which the authors maintained was supported by field data.

Using the instantaneous growth rate calculated as above and numbers in each year class, the production P of the adult population in any year was calculated, and it was found that larval abundance could be fitted to a regression on adult production and temperature, such that when temperature was held constant at 10°C there was an extremely close correlation between adult production and larval abundance (Fig. 9.7).

The year class size for herring Y_R was then related to larval abundance L_R, and total pelagic biomass B_{Tp}, by the equation:

$$\log_e Y_R = 2.679 \log_e L_R - 5.000 \times 10^{-5}(\log_e L_R)^2$$
$$\times B_{Tp} - 0.165(\log_e L_R)^2 \quad (9.9)$$

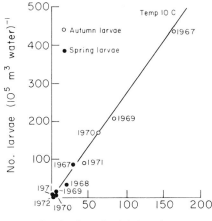

Fig. 9.7   Effect in a simulation model of the production of the adult stock on the abundance of herring larvae, when temperature is held constant at 10°C. (From Lett & Kohler 1976.)

which implies that predation by mackerel and cannibalism by older herring is a major factor influencing year class strength of juvenile herring.

The relationship between herring larvae and their competitors (0-group mackerel), their predators (larger herring and mackerel) and the water temperature were then used in a stochastic simulation model to predict herring biomass in the southern Gulf of St. Lawrence. It was shown that in the absence of mackerel the herring population could be expected to oscillate about a value of 2.0×10^6 tonnes, but in the presence of 1×10^6 tonnes of mackerel there would be two differences: the herring population would be much more stable, and the biomass would be about 0.8×10^6 tonnes (Fig. 9.8). A plot of herring biomass against mackerel biomass (Fig. 9.9) shows that the real values and simulated values follow the same trend, in spite of the perturbations introduced by changing fishing effort.

The results in Fig. 9.8 are based on a changing biomass of large mackerel predators, but a constant size class of 0-group mackerel competing with the herring. If mackerel were to be exploited in an optimal manner the year class sizes of 0-group mackerel would tend to increase, and their competition could cause recruitment failure in the herring stocks. Lett and Kohler (1976) concluded that if their model is correct, mackerel should be either under-exploited or over-exploited, in order to protect the herring. This may sound strange, until one remembers that the stocks evolved together as unexploited species, until comparatively recently. Such insight can only be obtained from

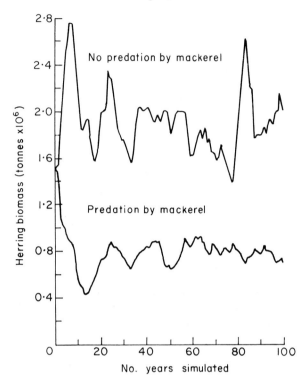

Fig. 9.8 Simulated pattern of herring biomass over time when mackerel biomass is 10⁶ tonnes and when mackerel are absent from the Gulf of St. Lawrence. (From Lett & Kohler 1976.)

quite detailed considerations of interactions between species, and not at all from intensive study of species in isolation.

More recently, Lett (1980) looked closely at the interaction between mackerel and cod in the Gulf of St. Lawrence. Cod larvae are abundant when mackerel are recovering from spawning and are eating voraciously, so these were good grounds for supposing that mackerel population density is a factor influencing the survival of cod. The details of the model, which was built in a manner analogous to that described above for herring and mackerel, are too complex to review here. However, one of the main findings was that when the biomass of mackerel is varied between 0·5 and 1·5 × 10⁶ tonnes, there is a marked influence on the predicted relationship between biomass and catch of cod (Fig. 9.10). Factors such as this are thought to be at least partly responsible for the inverse relationship between cod and mackerel biomasses in the Gulf between 1950 and 1980 (Fig. 9.11).

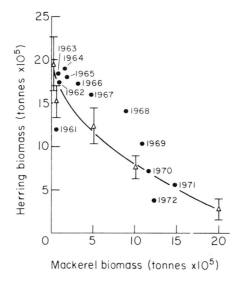

Fig. 9.9 Simulated trade-off between herring and mackerel in the Gulf of St. Lawrence. Data points represent real values since 1961 (these values are somewhat confounded by the effect of exploitation). (From Lett & Kohler 1976.)

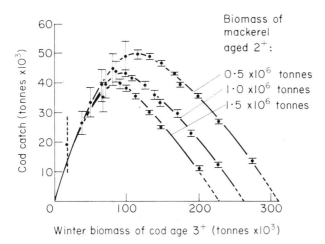

Fig. 9.10 Predicted relationship between biomass and catch of cod, when biomass of mackerel is varied. (From Lett 1980.)

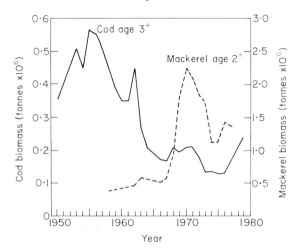

Fig. 9.11   Relationship between cod and mackerel biomasses in the Gulf between 1950 and 1980. (From Lett 1980.)

9.6   LARVAL FISH AS A CRITICAL STAGE

Reference was made in Chapter 1 to the decline of the Pacific sardine (*Sardinops caerulea*) and the increase of the northern anchovy (*Engraulis mordax*) off the west coast of the USA beginning about 1945. Vrooman and Smith (1970) calculated that between 1950 and 1965 the spawning biomass of anchovies increased from about 0.7×10^6 tonnes to nearly 8×10^6 tonnes. The mean total biomass for the period 1962–66 was estimated at 6.2×10^6 tonnes, divided into three sub-populations: a central stock of 4.8×10^6 tonnes off southern California, a northern stock of 0.27×10^6 tonnes extending along the coast of northern California and southern Oregon, and a southern stock of 1.1×10^6 tonnes off Baja California. The spectacular increase in anchovy biomass at a time when sardine biomass was decreasing strongly suggests a competitive interaction between the two species, but Smith (1972) concluded that neither the feeding of anchovy and sardine nor the population dynamics of the food organisms was well enough understood for firm statements to be made about competition. He pointed out that size frequency curves of larvae show little change, and suggested that competition would occur in juvenile and pre-recruit stages, if at all.

In the last decade Lasker (1975, 1978) has made an intensive study of the feeding of anchovy larvae. He spawned anchovy in the laboratory, hatched the eggs, and first studied larval feeding in the laboratory. He found that when they take their first meal (at a length of about 3·5 mm) their mouths are small and most of the food consists of particles between 60 and 80 μm in diameter. They are relatively inefficient, capturing successfully only about one in ten of the food organisms they attack, and therefore needing a fairly high concentration of food in their environment in order to stay alive. As the food concentration increases, the rate of ingestion increases, but not all organisms in the appropriate size range are acceptable as food. Of a range of phytoplankton species tested, only the dinoflagellate *Gymnodium spendens* supported growth. Various zooplankton species were acceptable, but it seemed that none were present in nature in sufficient concentration to support growth.

The next stage of the investigation was to take larvae in first-feeding condition out to sea and expose them to food organisms in natural sea-water samples. It was found that for successful feeding it was necessary to have in every ml of the water at least 20–30 phytoplankton cells of a minimum diameter of 30 μm. The larvae fed well on blooms of *Gymnodinium spendens*, but would not take *Chaetoceros* sp. or *Thalassiosira* sp. Suitable concentrations of phytoplankton were found in chlorophyll maxima which, in April 1974, occurred at a depth of 15–20 m along the California coast. A storm which caused mixing of the upper 20 m of water destroyed this layer of high phytoplankton concentration, and probably caused heavy mortality among first-feeding larvae.

Using this information, oceanographic conditions in the Southern California Bight were monitored throughout the 1975 spawning season of the anchovy (January–May). Suitable food was found to be abundant within the chlorophyll maximum layer in January, but strong upwelling began in February and after brief interruption in early March, was renewed in April and continued well beyond the end of the spawning season (Lasker 1978). The effect of the upwelling was to dissipate the dinoflagellate blooms and replace them by a variety of small diatoms which are not suitable food for the fish. As a result, Lasker predicted that the 1975 year class of northern anchovy would be a poor one.

The general conclusion from this type of work is that survival and growth of newly hatched anchovies is an extremely risky business, because conditions which provide enough of the right kind of food depend on the occurrence of a dinoflagellate bloom in relatively calm conditions. Strong winds from the north, which cause upwelling, or strong winds from other directions which mix the upper layers of the ocean, lead to the dispersal of the all important dinoflagellate blooms. This is a particular case of the theory of Hjort (1914) which states that the success of a year class of fish depends primarily on there being adequate concentrations of the right food present during the critical first-feeding stage. One is left wondering why the biomass of anchovies has increased so spectacularly since 1950.

A partial explanation is found in the recent paper by Methot and Kramer (1979). Using a newly developed technique for recognizing daily growth rings in sagittal otoliths, the authors determined the growth rates of larval northern anchovies less than one month old, from twelve stations off Los Angeles. They found that at nine stations growth was similar, ranging from 0·34 to 0·40 mm per day for fish 8 mm long, while at the remaining three stations growth was better, 0·47–0·55 mm per day. The values obtained corresponded to growth rates obtained in the laboratory under conditions of abundant food. The authors therefore concluded that anchovy larvae which obtain enough food to survive, apparently obtain enough to grow rapidly. They asked whether the survival of these larvae was determined primarily by food or by predation, but were unable to supply the answer. In general, it appears that studies of the biology of the northern anchovy are moving away from strict single-stock population dynamics to a consideration of feeding relationships, but that information is at present much more restricted than the knowledge we have of food chain relationships of some pelagic stocks in the Atlantic.

9.7   MAMMALS AND BIRDS IN COMPETITION WITH MAN

There are now several fish stocks for which we have an idea of the magnitude of predation by birds and/or mammals. Such information alerts us to the idea that man is in competition with other warm-blooded animals for fish production, and both are part of the same ecosystem. In the heyday of the anchoveta fishery in the Peru Current, Schaeffer (1970) estimated that the maximum sustainable yield of the combined fishery was about 10×10^6 tonnes, which was at that time divided $9·3 \times 10^6$ tonnes to man and $0·7 \times 10^6$ tonnes to the local population of 'guano birds' (cormorants, boobies and pelicans).

Historically, production of anchoveta stocks has been adversely affected by El Niño, a periodic interruption of the upwelling process, and there has been a consequent crash in bird numbers. In 1956 their numbers were estimated at more than 25 million, but the El Niño of 1957 reduced them to about 6 million. They increased again to over 15 million in 1961–64, but El Niño reappeared in 1965, reducing them to under 5 million. By this time the fishery had greatly expanded, and between 1965 and 1971 the bird population remained below 5 million. Idyll (1973) reported yet another El Niño in 1972 (Fig. 9.12) and speculated that the guano-bird population might be further reduced or even eliminated.

A still greater impact of mammals and birds on a fish stock was documented by Laevastu and Favorite (1978). They calculated that the consumption of herring by mammals and birds in the eastern Bering Sea was 431×10^3 tonnes, which is ten times the catch by man (43×10^3 tonnes in 1973). However, herring is not the most sought-after species in the eastern Bering Sea. Since 1960 there has been a spectacular increase in the catch of

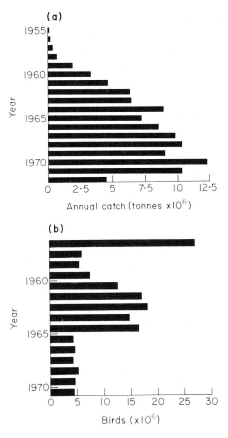

Fig. 9.12 (a) Anchovy catch in the Peru Current, 1955–72; (b) guano bird population over approximately the same period. (Both from Idyll 1975.)

Pacific pollock, *Theragro chalcogramma*. In 1973, after the collapse of the Peruvian anchoveta fishery, the Pacific pollock fishery became the world's largest single-species fishery, with a catch of nearly 4×10^6 tonnes chiefly by the Japanese and Russians. Of this 1.8×10^6 tonnes came from the eastern Bering Sea, the remainder mostly from the north-west Pacific, closer to Japan. A modelling study by Laevastu and Favorite (1976) indicated that since older pollock are cannibals, and since the fishery takes older fish, the effect of the fishery is to decrease mortality of the faster growing juvenile fish, thus increasing the productivity of the stock. Larger pollock are predators on herring, so the model predicted that increased fishing pressure on pollock would lead to increases in herring stocks. The authors estimated that fur-seals and sea-lions removed at least as much pollock as the human fishery. Alton and Fredin (1974) drew attention to the decrease in catch per unit

effort in the early 1970's and suggested that there was a need for a reduction
in permissable catch. The concensus was that good management of the
Bering Sea stocks required that attention be paid not only to multispecies
fish interactions, but to the simultaneous management of marine bird and
mammal stocks.

9.8   MIGRANTS IN COASTAL WATERS:
THE CASE OF PACIFIC SALMON

All the countries bordering the North Pacific have substantial stocks of
salmon breeding in their rivers and lakes. Pacific salmon belong to the genus
Oncorhynchus and there are five species in the British Columbia fishery: pink
salmon *O.gorbuscha*; coho salmon *O.kisutch*; chinook salmon *O.tshawyt-
scha*; chum salmon *O.keta*, and sockeye salmon *O.nerka*. These differ in their
life history patterns. All migrate from the sea up rivers to breed, but pinks
and chums go to sea in their first year of life, while coho and sockeye require
a year of freshwater residence. Chinook are variable in this respect. The
species also differ in time spent at sea. Pink salmon normally return to the
parent river and breed at two years of age. Those populations hatched in odd
years have very little interaction with those born in even years, and in many
rivers there is a strong imbalance between the sizes of successive year classes.
The other species stay at sea longer, and their age at maturity is more
variable, but most fish return to the parent river to breed at age 3, 4 or 5.

Even the pink salmon, which spends little over a year on the high seas,
makes a major migration. Royce *et al.* (1968) showed that stocks originating
in British Columbia and south-east Alaska travel several thousand miles in
the Alaskan Gyre (Fig. 9.13) averaging more than 10 miles (16 km) per day.
The first part of the journey is northward, parallel with the coast, the remainder is in open ocean.

Roughly speaking, the catch of North Pacific salmon has dropped 50%
in the last 40 years, and much of the decline is attributed to human interference with the freshwater habitats in which the fish breed and grow during
early life. In an attempt to once more build up the stocks, action plans for
'salmon enhancement' have been developed in Oregon, Washington, British
Columbia, Alaska, the USSR and Japan (Peterman 1978).

Underlying these multi-million dollar enhancement programmes is the
assumption that increasing the production of juveniles from the rivers will
lead to an equivalent increase in the returning adults a few years later.
Peterman (1978) questioned this assumption and found that a considerable
number of stocks showed density-dependent marine survival. He used two
methods for testing for significant density dependence. One, attributable to
Morris (1959), considers the relationship between seaward migrating fish
(smolts) and returning adults (Fig. 9.14) and tests for significant departure

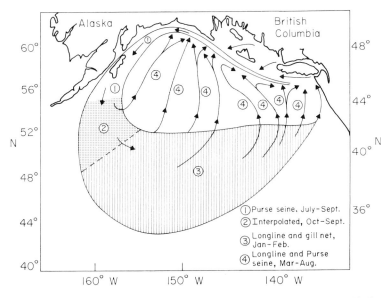

Fig. 9.13 Ocean migrations of pink salmon stocks originating in south-eastern Alaska and British Columbia. (From Royce *et al.* 1968.)

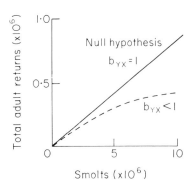

Fig. 9.14 Two possible types of relation between smolt abundance and total adult returns. Solid line represents the linear, null hypothesis of no density-dependent marine survival and dashed line indicates density dependence. The value of b is an estimate of k in the equation $y = c \cdot X^k \cdot \exp(v)$ where X = smolt abundance, y = adult returns, v = normally distributed random variate with mean zero and variance σ^2, and $\exp(v)$ = multiplicative, log-normal noise term. (For details, see Peterman 1978.)

from the null hypothesis of a linear relationship. The second method, devised by Varley and Gradwell (1963) is designed to overcome biases introduced by errors in population estimates, but is said by some to be too conservative, classing some situations as lacking density dependence when in fact it exists. The results of Peterman's study were to show that on the first test, 7 of the 12 stocks examined exhibited density-dependent marine survival within a cohort, whereas only one of those cases showed it according to the second test. Small numbers of cases of density dependence were exposed when interactions between cohorts in the same river, between stocks in the same river, and between stocks of distant rivers were examined. Peterman (1978) concluded that it would be particularly necessary to watch for the phenomenon when breeding stocks were further enhanced. There may well be an upper limit on the returning adults, no matter how many juveniles leave the river. Walters *et al.* (1978) concentrated attention on the capacity of the coastal zone to support the large numbers of juvenile salmon leaving the rivers and migrating northwards along the British Columbia coast between March and September each year. They built a model which incorporated four basic components of juvenile salmon production: (1) the space-time distribution of zooplankton production and availability; (2) rations and growth of young salmon; (3) timing of ocean arrival and migration of young salmon along the coast; (4) mortality of the young salmon due to predation or food limitation.

The data used to build the model were shown to be extremely inadequate, and for the mortality section there were no data at all for juvenile fish. Nevertheless, the interactions of the sections on zooplankton availability and food requirements of the young fish indicated that there appears to be enough food production to support several times the existing abundance of juvenile salmon without noticeable effects on growth and mortality. The authors concluded that 'we must look elsewhere for explanations of observed density dependence of marine survival rates in stocks like the Skeena sockeye'.

This interesting project on juvenile salmon, still in its infancy, shows well how management of commercially important fish species can be related to properties of large ecosystems. It is now recognized that the yield of fish stock cannot be predicted without a detailed understanding of the food web on which it is based, and that for this understanding we need to understand the physical setting and the biological interactions taking place there.

9.9 ECOSYSTEM INTERACTIONS INVOLVING A LOBSTER FISHERY

Studies by the author and his colleagues over the past decade have revealed a complex network of interactions involving primary producers, herbivores, detritivores and predators, all having a strong effect on the extremely valuable lobster fishery in Nova Scotia.

First let us review events observed in St. Margaret's Bay, Nova Scotia, between 1968 and 1976 and summarized in Mann (1977). The seaweed zone from high tide level, through the intertidal and down to a depth of about 30 m was surveyed in detail in 1968. It was found that the average population density of the sea-urchin *Strongylocentrotus droebachiensis* in the seaweed was 37 per m^2, but the distribution was uneven. There were dense aggregations of urchins, exceeding 100 per m^2, in areas where seaweeds had been cleared completely leaving almost bare rock and there were dense areas of kelp with less than 20 urchins per m^2. Over a period of about eight years the areas dominated by urchins grew larger and larger until they coalesced. This was achieved by the urchins forming dense feeding aggregations at the edges of kelp beds and progressively eating the plants or biting through the stipes so that they drifted away. A population of urchins remained on the rocks, preventing any permanent recolonization by macro-algae. Within eight years over 90 % of the subtidal seaweed beds in St. Margaret's Bay had been destroyed.

It was assumed that, after clearing the algae, the urchin populations would be reduced by starvation and the algae would return. This was not so. In the first year or two after algal clearance there was heavy recruitment of juvenile urchins. In succeeding years recruitment was less heavy, but the highly successful year classes could be identified as they moved through the population. Average population density first increased to a level close to that first seen in 1968. After 12 years, no case of permanent recolonization of a rocky surface by macro-algae had been discovered.

An obvious explanation for the population explosion of urchins was reduction of predator pressure. Potential predators include a variety of fish, crabs, starfish and lobsters. Of these, only lobsters had been the subject of heavy fishing, and it was shown that during the period 1961–71 the catch of lobsters in St. Margaret's Bay declined from 360 to <90 kg per man, a clear indication that the biomass of lobsters was declining. There was thought to be a positive feedback in the system, for although lobsters take shelter under rocks or in burrows during the day, they move about and forage for invertebrate food, especially at night. Young lobsters are vulnerable to predation by fish, crabs, seals, etc., and lobsters moving over a bare rock surface must inevitably suffer a heavier mortality than lobsters moving through a dense seaweed bed. Furthermore, the seaweed beds, with their greater productivity and habitat diversity have a much more abundant invertebrate fauna than the bare rock surfaces. Hence, it was predicted that areas where algal beds had been destroyed would support lower levels of lobster production than areas of healthy kelp.

Recently, the study has been expanded to cover a much larger geographical scale (Wharton 1980). It has been found that for nearly 600 km along the coastline of Nova Scotia, from the southern end at Pubnico to the Straits of Canso in the north, there can be found a spatial series of sea-urchin communities which corresponds closely with the time series observed in St. Margaret's Bay. At the southern end, the kelp cover is close to 100%, the urchin population is less than 0·1 m^{-2}, and those that are present live cryptically, as if hiding from predators. They feed on pieces of seaweed detritus which break off and drift under the rocks.

At Cape Sable, 20 km north-east of Pubnico there is a sudden change (Fig. 9.15). Within a few km urchin densities increase to over 40 m^{-2} and there is evidence of aggregation and kelp destruction. A few more km to the north-east, urchin densities are over 100 m^{-2}, dominated by new recruits, and kelp cover is less than 10%. Then, for 400 km of coast line, there is little to see but urchin-dominated barren grounds. The urchin density decreases slowly and the mean size increases as one moves north-east. Growth rates of urchins on the barren grounds are only about one third of the rate in dense kelp beds.

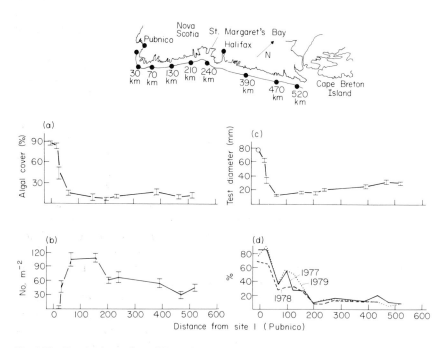

Fig. 9.15 Sketch of coastline of Nova Scotia and plots of various variables on an axis 'distance from Pubnico'. (a) Algal cover; (b) sea-urchin density; (c) sea-urchin mean size; (d) lobster catch, % 1947–56 mean catch. (From Wharton 1980.)

The inference from these observations is that there has been kelp-bed destruction all along the coast, except at the south-western tip of the province, and that the destruction took place many years ago in the north-east but quite recently towards the south-western end. In fact, the process is still going on in the vicinity of Cape Sable, and urchin populations are still encroaching on existing kelp beds around Pubnico.

A separate study was made of the records of lobster catches in various parts of the province. It was found that in many cases there had been a sharp drop in yield from which the fishery never recovered. The average of the catches in the ten year period 1947–56 was taken as 100%, and a drastic decline was defined as falling below 60% and never recovering. Fig. 9.15 shows that catches declined first in the north-east end of the study area, and showed a decline in progressively later years as one moved south-west. Hence, events in the lobster populations paralleled events in the sea-urchin–kelp community, but with a time lag, for there are two sites (70 km and 130 km from Pubnico) where kelp beds have been destroyed but the catches have not yet declined below 40%.

The sequence of events which we observed in St. Margaret's Bay and which we have every reason to believe occurred all along the coast of Nova Scotia is summarized in Fig. 9.16. Healthy, unperturbed kelp beds contain

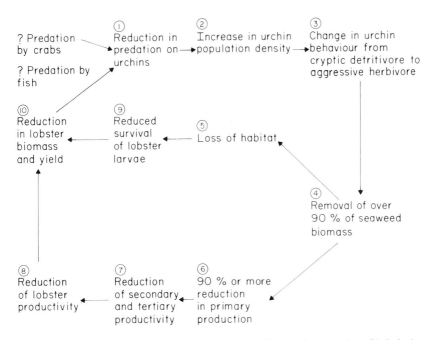

Fig. 9.16 Diagram summarizing events leading to the widespread destruction of kelp beds in Nova Scotia and consequent declines in the lobster stocks.

abundant predators, which keep urchin densities below $1\cdot0$ m^{-2}, and the urchins that survive spend most of their time under rocks making a living as detritivores. Reduction of predator pressure allows numbers to increase to around 40 m^{-2} and at this point a change in urchin behaviour occurs. They protect themselves from predators by forming dense aggregations at the edges of kelp beds and they eat their way into the beds. After a large area has been cleared, the predators disperse to find kelp beds that constitute their normal habitat, and the urchins can graze openly and singly on the tops of the rocks, effectively preventing kelp regeneration. As we have seen, barren grounds support very small lobster populations.

The main question that remains to be answered with good data is: What starts the whole process described above? There is a strong presumption that lobsters were the key predators in the natural system and that intense fishing, combined perhaps with adverse environmental conditions for recruitment, led to a decline in lobster stocks below a critical biomass. This question was explored by means of a computer model by Breen and Mann (1976a) and the model supported the presumption. However, one cannot rule out the possibility that some kinds of fish, crabs or even seals were partly responsible for controlling the urchin populations, and that some factor or factors led to their decline in numbers.

Whatever the facts of the case, it is clear that the lobster population is intricately enmeshed with a complex ecosystem, and that perturbation of the system can lead to marked changes in lobster abundance as a result of subtle, unexpected shifts in various parts of the system. It is the author's view that in all probability most fish stocks are related in equally complex and subtle ways with pelagic or benthic systems. It just happens that the kelp–urchin–lobster system is more accessible to detailed study than most. If this is the real state of affairs, it is abundantly clear that intelligent management of fish stocks requires a detailed knowledge of the ecosystems in which they are embedded.

9.10   CONCLUSIONS

This chapter has dealt with some recent developments in fisheries science, leaving on one side the large body of impressive and solid information on the population dynamics of single species stocks. Examples have been collected to show that stocks are subjected to forces arising at a different level in the ecological hierarchy, which we can no longer afford to ignore. In the North Sea, heavy cropping of pelagic stocks has led to increase in size of benthic stocks, and we now have a rough idea what trophic interactions produced this result. But even in the North Sea, which has a long history of intensive study by several nations, Steele (1974) was forced to admit that his diagram of trophic relations was very tentative indeed. In other areas, such as the Atlantic and Pacific coasts of North America, or the upwelling system off Peru, data are even more fragmentary than in the North Sea. Even so, people are finding that it is rewarding to look beyond the commercially important species to competitive or predatory interactions between species, and to interactions that may be felt at several stages removed in a food web. Some people argue that the broader view entails an unacceptable diversion of effort from close attention to the commercially important stocks, but sooner or later we have to recognize that nature cannot be confined to our mathematical representations of recruitment, growth and survival, but is infinitely more subtle than we have yet imagined.

CHAPTER 10
MODELS AND MANAGEMENT

10.1 INTRODUCTION

Of all the parts of the world ocean those adjacent to the land, which form the subject of this book, are the most vulnerable to disturbance by man. Historically, almost all major cities have grown up on a river or an estuary and the products or by-products of human excretion, industrialization and intensive agriculture have inevitably been channelled down the rivers to the coast. The coastal zone is the arena in which society battles over the competing demands of land-based industries for the right to discharge effluents, of fishing industries for the right to exploit the stocks, and of shipping industries for the right to dredge channels and construct harbour installations, while at the same time property owners and developers seek to preserve the natural amenities. Decisions are constantly being made about the probable effect of a human activity on a natural system, yet, as we have seen those effects are often devious and difficult to predict. It is in this context that I propose to discuss models.

The term model has been widely used in ecological literature only during the past twenty years or so, and its growth in popularity coincided with the development of computers. In Chapter 1 we traced the way in which process models, the mathematical concepts that have for long been at the heart of quantitative biological science, may be coupled together in a computer program to yield a dynamic simulation of several processes interacting. The techniques for doing this were borrowed from engineering, and when first recognized by biologists were avidly seized upon for the insights they gave into the complex workings of natural systems. As heuristic devices, computer simulations have undoubtedly been a great success. However, it was inevitable that when it appeared to be possible to make a computer simulation of a natural system, those charged with managing systems should eagerly seize upon models as techniques for making predictions. What could be more natural than to ask the man who runs a computer model of an estuary, 'Please double the input of phosphorus and nitrogen from upstream, and tell me how the ecosystem will respond' or 'Please raise the mean temperature by 5°C and tell me the effect upon the life of the estuary'. Similarly, it was hoped that complex simulations would be useful for the prediction of fishery yields, or for predicting the effects of dams, barrages and other major engineering works. In this chapter an attempt will be made to distinguish the two major objectives of modelling: gaining insights or making quantitative predictions. In general, the case is made that modelling has been of great value in deepening our understanding of the way ecosystems *may* work, but of limited value so far in enabling us to predict that this is the way a system *will* respond if perturbed in a particular way. Finally, we shall explore some alternatives in a tentative way.

10.2   INSIGHTS OBTAINED FROM DYNAMIC SIMULATION MODELS

10.2.1 Interactions between lobsters and sea-urchins

The distinction mentioned above can perhaps be made explicit by dealing with a small model of which I have first hand knowledge. In connection with the problems of the lobster fishery in eastern Canada discussed in the previous chapter, it was asked (Breen & Mann 1976a) whether it was likely that naturally occurring stocks of lobsters could be the key predators controlling the population density of sea-urchins in the area. Attempts to set up experiments in nature with differing densities of lobsters were unsuccessful because the lobsters would not remain in the areas to which they were introduced. As a substitute, the experiment was conducted by means of a simulation model. Process models that were built into the simulation included sea-urchin recruitment, growth and mortality, and size-selective predation by lobster populations of various population densities and size-class structures. The relative preferences of lobsters for various kinds of prey, and the effects of other predators, such as crabs and wolf-fish, were also taken into account. To run the model, urchin recruitment and lobster biomass were set at particular levels, and the model was run until lobster predation was in equilibrium with sea-urchin recruitment and growth. Hence, for each level of urchin recruitment and lobster biomass there was an equilibrium urchin biomass. The values are displayed in Fig. 10.1 where it is seen that for each recruitment rate there was indeed a lobster biomass that would keep the urchin biomass at a low value. This conclusion could only have been reached by the use of some model of this type, since the number of interactions involved made it impossible to arrive at the result by simple computation.

Nevertheless, it was not possible to predict, within any acceptable limits of confidence, what would be the result in any real-life situation. Urchins have techniques for defending themselves from predators, by hiding in crevices or by forming impenetrable aggregations. Crabs, when available, are the preferred prey of lobsters, and their abundance and availability vary from place to place. Hence, the model gave useful insights into *possible* relationships between lobsters and urchins, but could not be used for prediction. It could be argued that the model should be refined or extended to take account of the defence reactions of the urchins, or the distribution of the

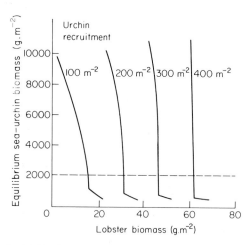

Fig. 10.1 Result of modelling the effect of lobsters as predators on populations of urchins with differing recruitment rates. The lines give values of equilibrium urchin biomass. The horizontal line shows the biomass below which urchins appear not to destroy kelp beds by overgrazing. (From Breen & Mann 1976a).

crabs, but in spite of more than a decade of study by an active group of research students, we have to admit that we still do not fully understand these topics. We have reached a point where our ability to make predictions is limited by our lack of basic biological knowledge. This point will recur several times in our discussion.

10.2.2 Simulation of a coastal ecosystem: Naragansett Bay

As a good recent example of a whole ecosystem simulation which provided valuable insights, but which the authors admit has limited predictive capability let us consider the Naragansett Bay model of Kremer and Nixon (1978). In a book devoted entirely to an account of the model, the authors give a useful summary of the history of ecosystem models, and explain the modelling process. Naragansett Bay, Rhode Island, USA, is an irregular basin with a length of 45 km, maximum width of 18 km, mean depth of 9 m, and semidiurnal tides with a mean range of 1·1 m at the mouth and 1·4 m at the head. The mean tidal prism is about 13% of the mean volume and over 250 times the mean total river flow during a tidal cycle. As a result the waters are well mixed from top to bottom, and salinities range from about 24 per thousand at the head of the bay to 32 per thousand at the mouth.

The ecosystem is phytoplankton-based, with the winter population dominated by diatoms and the summer population by flagellates. The major consumers of phytoplankton are the zooplankton species *Acartia clausi* and *A. tonsa*, and these in turn are preyed upon by the ctenophore *Mnemiopsis leidyi* and by fish, especially the menhaden *Brevoortia tyrannus*. Predators of the menhaden include striped bass (*Morone saxatilis*) and blue fish (*Pomatomus saltatrix*).

The benthos contains large numbers of the hard clam *Mercenaria mercenaria*, accompanied by the bivalves *Nucula proxima* and *Yoldia limatula* and the polychaete *Nephthys incisa*. Near the bottom are the benthic fish, especially flounder, with lobsters, crabs and shrimps. The simplified conceptual framework for the model is shown in Fig. 10.2. Only the phytoplankton, zooplankton and nutrient compartments were fully simulated with mechanistic detail. The bay was divided into eight geographic areas, and appropriate values and forcing functions were inserted to represent each one. All were assumed to be vertically and horizontally homogeneous, and were integrated into a numerical hydrodynamic model of Naragansett Bay driven by variations in tide height at the mouth. River flow was programmed to follow a seasonal cycle. The biological and chemical components were programmed to function on a daily basis, and the unit of solar input was total daily insolation. For further details of model construction, the original work should be consulted. We may now pass to the results obtained by running the model.

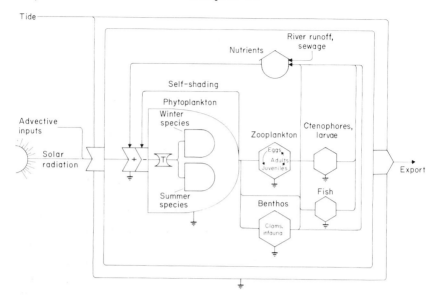

Fig. 10.2 Energy flow diagram used as a conceptual framework for the numerical simulation model of Naragansett Bay. (After Kremer & Nixon 1978.)

It was found that the timing and the magnitude of the winter–spring bloom of phytoplankton was well represented in the model, and it was interesting to note that the model consistently indicated that the pre-bloom winter phytoplankton biomass was insufficient to maintain even the low observed zooplankton stock. From this the authors concluded that the zooplankton were utilizing an alternative food source, perhaps detritus. This was an interesting finding, considering the debate that has taken place over the role of detritus in planktonic food chains.

The model did not represent well seasonal changes in dissolved inorganic nitrogen in the water, and the authors inferred from this that the model was missing some major source of nitrogen, possible dissolved organic nitrogen from the benthos, which was sustaining the phytoplankton during the summer–autumn period. They suggested that in the autumn, as algal growth diminished, the organic forms of nitrogen might be oxidized to provide for the yearly nutrient maximum which is observed to occur at this time, but which the model fails to reproduce. It was suggested that this failure 'is at the same time a disappointing shortcoming and a very useful result . . . it is precisely such indications for continued research that the model was designed to provide'.

When the model was run with all zooplankton grazing removed from the system, the phytoplankton biomass still followed a 'reasonable' pattern, and this led to the conclusion that nutrient limitation was the prime factor terminating the bloom, the actual removal of biomass being caused by flushing, plus some grazing by zooplankton and clams.

In constrast, when all carnivores were removed from the system dramatic changes occurred, in which phytoplankton and zooplankton populations became unstable and went into a series of oscillations that had no counterpart in the bay. It was therefore concluded that the zooplankton predators, mainly ctenophores and menhaden, exerted a strong stabilizing effect.

In the last chapter of this excellent book the authors discuss briefly some attempts to relate the performance of the model to some management questions. They simulated the effect of passing water through a nuclear-powered generating plant sited on the lower West Passage of Naragansett Bay, and found that even though they assumed 100% mortality of phytoplankton and zooplankton in water passing through the plant, the changes in standing crops, even in the general area around the plant would be almost undetectable, for the nutrients released by the mortality would be rapidly utilized in the synthesis of new biomass. When the model was run with nutrient input from sewage halved or doubled, the primary effect over most of the bay was a modest change in the intensity of the winter–spring bloom, with some consequences for later development of zooplankton stocks. In their assessment of limitations the authors pointed out that since many management decisons are tied to questions of large and/or long-term perturbations of the system, these questions cannot be solved by use of a deterministic, closed and non-evolving model. The interpretation of model results in management must be closely restricted to effects and relationships deliberately included in the model. It is most desirable that the management questions be posed at the outset and the model be designed to deal with them on the basis of the best information available.

This example, then, shows clearly that valuable insights into the functioning of ecosystems, and valuable ideas about topics for further research, can be obtained from simulation models, but that the results obtained are far from being the answer to the environmental manager's dream of an ideal predictive tool. One reason for the shortcomings is that the model was designed to work within the normal range of natural variations in key parameters. Management questions often involve extrapolation byond that range, and such extrapolation is only justified if the modeler is satisfied that the structure is right for all circumstances.

10.2.3 Simulation of a mangrove ecosystem

For a second example of a computer model which simulates the interactions of many processes within an ecosystem and provides insights that were not apparent without the aid of that model, let us take Lugo, Sell and Snedaker's (1976) model of a mangrove ecosystem in South Florida. The publication is noteworthy for the clarity with which the objectives of the simulation

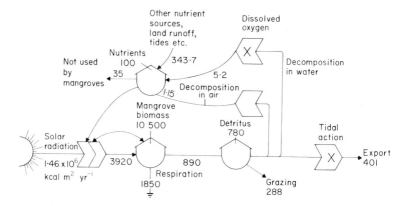

Fig. 10.3 Design of an analogue simulation of a mangrove forest, and values used in scaling. Biomasses are g C m^{-2} or g nutrients m^{-2}. Fluxes are g C or g nutrients m^{-2} yr^{-1}. (After Lugo *et al.* 1976.)

and the conclusions drawn from it were stated by the authors. The general biology of mangroves was discussed in Chapter 2 of this volume, but the authors explained that the area with which they were concerned is rather atypical, being a group of islands having an elevation of approximately 30 cm above mean sea level, which are inundated and overwashed on every tide. As a result, organic debris is carried away, instead of accumulating as it does in fringing communities.

The mangrove forests are dominated by red mangrove (*Rhizophora mangle*) and contain only occasional specimens of black mangrove (*Avicennia nitida*) or white mangrove (*Laguncularia racemosa*). The objectives of the simulation were: (1) to study the relative effects of terrestrial runoff and tides on nutrient cycling and productivity; (2) to study the effect of tidal flushing on accumulation and export of detritus; (3) to study the effect of mangroves on water quality; and (4) to assess the usefulness of modelling for research planning. The authors chose to use an analogue model. Its structure, together with the data used to scale it are shown in Fig. 10.3. Solar radiation interacts with nutrients and mangrove biomass to yield a gross production, some of which is respired by the forest, some is used to increase forest biomass, and the remainder is deposited as detritus. The losses from the detritus pool are (in order of importance) export by tidal flushing, grazing, decomposition when submerged and decomposition when exposed to air. The decomposition is a source of nutrient recycling, but is of minor importance compared with nutrients from terrestrial runoff and tidal flushing. The supply of nutrients to the mangrove forest determines the rate of photosynthesis and growth.

Starting with low mangrove biomass, the model forests appeared to reach equilibrium biomass in about 20 years. The frequency of destructive hurricanes in the area is about once every 20 years, so the authors concluded that the system is adapted to a slow return to maximum biomass after hurricane disturbance.

The mangrove biomass was shown to be extremely sensitive to runoff of nutrients from the land, and relatively insensitive to tidal amplitude. When terrestrial runoff was reduced, mangrove forests were unable to maintain themselves, and biomass decreased to low levels in 20–30 years. Thus, the mangrove community studied by the authors functioned by exporting its detritus to the adjacent waters and renewing its nutrient supply from terrestrail runoff instead of recycling. The authors pointed out that diversion of terrestrial runoff for human use would have the effect of subjecting the mangrove forests to nutrient stress, with resulting loss of vigour and selection for smaller stands. Such diversions are a common result of land development in Florida. Since the mangroves are important in protecting the coastline from erosion and since they export detritus which is a major contributor to fish and shellfish production in coastal waters (Chapter 2) the model demonstrated very clearly the possible consequences of human interference with patterns of land runoff.

10.2.4 Simulation of phytoplankton growth and nutrient distribution

For the third and last example of insights gained from simulation modelling I propose to discuss an example which is not strictly within the scope of this volume. It is the model of Jamart *et al.* (1977, 1979) of phytoplankton growth in the Pacific, in the offshore zone just beyond the continental shelf-break. The insights obtained seem to be particularly interesting, and almost certainly applicable, with modification, to the coastal zone. The first of the two papers described a two-dimensional (time and depth) numerical model of primary production in the phytoplankton. Equations were written to describe change in chlorophyll concentration in terms of vertical mixing, sinking, gross photosynthesis, respiration, and grazing. Vertical mixing was described by means of an eddy diffusion coefficient that was high and constant in the upper 10 m or so, decreased according to a Gaussian curve, and low and constant at depths approaching 100 m. Since sinking speed was thought to be a function of cell physiology it was set at 0.5 m day^{-1} in high inorganic nitrogen conditions, increasing to 2 m day^{-1} in the absence of inorganic nitrogen. The submodel for photosynthesis embodied adaptive responses to light and nutrient availability. Respiration was set at 10% of the maximum photosynthetic rate in the upper 10 m, and an exponential decrease below 10 m to give zero net production at the 10% light level.

Grazing pressure was allowed to change with season according to a pre-arranged pattern; it was found to be important and was the subject of fine scale adjustments during the numerical simulations. Fifty percent of the grazing pressure was assumed to be uniformly disturbed throughout the water column; the remainder was distributed with a vertical profile identical to that of the phytoplankton.

Nutrient uptake was arranged so that when ammonium nitrogen was above 0.5 μg atom 1^{-1} only ammonium was utilized; if ammonium was below this level but nitrate was above it, nitrate was used. If both were below it, they were used in proportion as they occurred. For further details of the model, the original should be consulted.

When the model was run, it soon settled to a quasi-stationary state with little temporal change in chlorophyll and total dissolved nitrogen. At day 96 rapid stabilization of the water column and increasing light flux led to a moderate algal bloom which soon reached 800 μg m^{-3} Chl a at a depth of 10 m, but over the next 30 days the inorganic nitrogen in the upper 20 m became severely depleted, and the chlorophyll maximum was found at 22 m on day 161. From then on, the chlorophyll maximum became progressively deeper, but also more pronounced, so that by day 245 there was a maximum of 1000 μg Chl a m^{-3} at a depth of 50 m. It was clear from the model that the deep chlorophyll maximum acts as a nutrient trap, intercepting nutrients tending to diffuse into the upper layers.

In summary, the model gave an adequate representation of the formation of the deep chlorophyll maximum using the interaction of conventional functions and parameters for physical and biological processes. The system was made to operate in a reasonable manner by specifying the seasonal light regime and a seasonal pattern of zooplankton biomass and distribution. In the second paper (Jamart *et al.* 1979) twenty 'experiments' were reported, in each of which a single parameter was varied. It was found that the dynamics of the formation of a deep chlorophyll maximum was independent of the exact values of most parameters, within reasonable limits. Hence, the authors concluded that they had identified the important processes governing phytoplankton and nutrient dynamics; the model was robust.

A further, tentative and very interesting conclusion was reached by what was called 'intuition gained from the modelling experience'. There was a close similarity between the temporal pattern of daily gross production and zooplankton ingestion rate which suggested that the system was controlled by the grazers. Yet, paradoxically, in experiments in which herbivore biomass, herbivore distribution or the grazing threshold were changed, primary production and zooplankton ingestion were little changed. The hypothesis put forward to explain what was going on was:

> The phytoplankton–nitrogen system, as it responds to zooplankton and light intensity, evolves in such a way that the amount of carbon

ingested by herbivores is determined mainly by the resources available to primary producers. Physical contraints affect the utilization of those resources. It appears that in a dynamical sense the chlorophyll distribution adjusts in time and depth so that the transfer of carbon to secondary producers is optimized.

The authors made it clear that they could not find a way to prove the hypothesis mathematically, but went on to show that the results of their experiments with the model were consistent with it. None of their perturbations led to sustained increases in the uptake of carbon by the grazers. It seems likely that this insight, if confirmed in nature, will have repercussions in studies of patchiness and in discussions of mechanisms controlling phytoplankton blooms (see Chapter 4). It will almost certainly make the historical discussion of whether nutrients or grazing are more important in controlling phytoplankton abundance seem irrelevant and redundant.

10.3 SIMULATION MODELS AS A BASIS FOR PREDICTION

Longhurst (1978) has drawn attention to a class of model in which considerable success has been achieved in making useful predictions. These are models of estuaries constructed for the purpose of predicting concentrations of dissolved oxygen and biological oxygen demand. An internationally known success story is the modelling and clean-up of the tidal portion of the River Thames below London. The story, as summarized by Potter (1973) is that a study was carried out with four objectives: (1) to identify sources of pollution in the River Thames; (2) to establish the significance and effects of individual pollutants; (3) to develop a mixing equation for the estuary; (4) to forecast the effect of changes in balance of the system and indicate management criteria for the stewardship of the river. It was demonstrated that the load of sewage effluent from London caused the oxygen content of the water to decline from a value close to saturation upstream of the effluent to under 10 % of saturation 10–40 km downstream. The effect of strong freshwater flows was to move the oxygen minimum further towards the sea. The effect of the rise and fall of the tide was to move the oxygen minimum up and down the river, causing wide semi-diurnal fluctuations in oxygen measurements made at a single station. Oxygenation of the water at the air–water interface was shown to be strongly influenced by wind strength. The physical oceanography of the estuary, as it pertained to the residence time of sewage effluent was summarized in the following over-simplified statement: 'A particle of matter introduced into the tidal water at London Bridge may flow 16 km downriver on the ebb-tide and return 15 km on the flood and oscillate in this manner for between 6 weeks and 3 months before reaching waters where there is a reasonable interflow with the North Sea'.

Using such general concepts, a model was built and was used to predict the circumstances under which the Thames would return to a well-oxygenated condition. A biological survey in 1957 showed that there were no fish in the tidal reaches for many km below London. Appropriate sewage treatment facilities were designed, constructed and brought into use in the early 1960's. By 1965 fish were beginning to return to the river, and by 1970 over 50 species had returned, mainly marine species in the lower half of the estuary and predominantly freshwater species close to London. Each year the smelt migrated further upstream, and by 1972 they were west of central London (Mann 1972). There is little doubt that the model served its purpose well, but in summarizing the story Potter (1973) issued a warning: 'If the changed state which the model is to anticipate differs very greatly from that of the condition in which the data are obtained, how relevant can we expect the results to be?'

Longhurst (1978), in discussing various estuarine dissolved oxygen models, said:

> To an ecologist, it is quite remarkable that simple models of the interaction between BOD and DO—even if based on a validated physical time-dependent model which integrates equations for conservation of volume and material—should have such success in predicting real conditions as has apparently often been the case. . . . Why, in fact, can success be obtained with any model which stops short of including all the known and apparently relevant ecological interactions? . . . I suggest that the answer to these questions may lie in the nature of the estuarine system, and perhaps especially of the simplified ecosystem which exists in highly polluted estuaries.

It seems, then, that there are situations requiring management in which a few relatively easily handled variables influence the important properties of the system, and in such situations a simulation model is an extremely valuable management tool. However, as the contents of this book clearly show, most coastal ecosystems are complex and subtle, and prediction of how they will respond to perturbation, in terms of yields of commercially important species, ability to absorb pollutants, or physical changes such as erosion or silting, requires consideration of a large number of interacting factors. This brings us to the question of how useful complex ecosystem simulation models have proved to be in making prediction for management purposes. In addition to searching the literature, the author has on numerous occasions invited active modellers to recommend ecosystem simulation models (other than the simplified estuarine models referred to earlier) which have been demonstrated as making valid predictions. The whole question is fraught with semantic difficulties. In traditional scientific activities it is normal to generate falsifiable hypotheses and judge the value of those hypotheses by the extent to which they survive attempts to prove them untrue (Popper 1963). If the hypothesis is quantitative, it is usual to state the confidence limits on the predicted values. To take a simple example, a person might put forward the hypothesis (or prediction) that the basal metabolism of a named fish of weight 100 g held at 20 C requires the consumption of 10 ± 2.2 mg O_2 h^{-1} where ± 2.2 is the 95% confidence interval on the prediction. The confidence interval is needed not so much to account for experimental error, as to recognize that the population from which the experimental fish were drawn has a genetic variability which gives rise to variation in metabolic rate and hence oxygen demand. If a second person produced data which were (statistically) significantly different from the prediction, the hypothesis would be considered falsified and in need of modification. However, in discussing the predictions of complex ecosystem simulation models it has proved impossible to use the terminology applicable to falsifiable hypotheses. Instead the term validation has been introduced, and a model is considered as validated when it can be seen to be behaving more or less in accordance with the behaviour of the natural system. Complex ecosystem simulation models have no unique output. In almost every case that I have discussed with modellers they have admitted that their model at first made nonsense predictions, and that adjustment of variables was required to get a 'reasonable' output. It is sometimes argued that having made the adjustments the modeller has found a combination of variables that fairly represents the situation in nature, but close enquiry often reveals that there are many ways of 'tuning' the model to get the desired effect. Some aspects of the problem outlined above were discussed by Caswell (1976).

It seems to me that there are two important reasons why reductionist compartmental simulation models of ecosystems are unlikely to be sound bases for prediction. The first reason is that organisms, which constitute the functional components of ecosystems, are inherently variable in their physiological properties. The variability of a species is genetically programmed and is an integral part of the evolutionary process. This variability in the properties of components makes an ecosystem basically different from an engineering system, and appears to make reductionist simulation modelling (which was devised for making predictions in engineering systems) an inappropriate technique for making predictions in ecology. This is not to say that engineering theory has nothing to offer ecology. Some innovate approaches based on physics and engineering are mentioned in section 10.5.1.

The second reason why reductionist simulation models are inappropriate for making ecological predictions derives from the hierarchical nature of ecosystems. One expression of hierarchical structure in a system is the appearance of different levels of organization. It is well known that there is a hierarchy within higher organisms in which we may recognize organs, tissues, cells, and molecules as levels of organization, each with well defined properties and associated with a particular field of knowledge. Similarly, in ecosystems, we may recognize communities, populations and individuals as differing levels of organization, each with distinctive properties. The important point in relation to predictive models is that it is virtually impossible to predict the behaviour of the integrated system from a study of lower levels of organization. It would not be feasible, for example, to predict the courtship behaviour of a fish by modelling the behaviour of all its cells and tissues. Similarly, it is not feasible to predict the behaviour of an ecosystem by modelling the properties of its organisms (or other functional groups). An outline of this argument was first published by Mann (1975), and there was further discussion in Platt *et al.* (1981). What follows is an elaboration of that point of view.

10.3.1 The problem of biological variability

Dynamic simulation has proved extremely useful in physical sciences and engineering, where the parameters of the models are often physical coefficients that are known with great precision. A large number of physical processes may be made to interact in a coupled process model, and reasonable confidence limits may be placed on the output. However, biological process models involving organisms almost all have much greater variance, due to the genetic variation between organisms. When a number of such biological processes are coupled, the variance on the output becomes extremely high. For example, Miller *et al.* (1971) modelled the production of benthic invertebrates in a sublittoral seaweed bed. Production was calculated from the relationship demonstrated by McNeill and Lawton (1970) between population respiration and population production. Population density was calculated from 165 quadrat samples. The relationship between body size, temperature and respiration was determined in the laboratory at two month intervals for a year. The confidence limits, taken as two standard errors of the mean, were accumulated through successive steps in the calculation and it was found that the upper limit of confidence in the production estimate was 446% above the mean. These data were probably as good or better than the data normally built into an ecosystem simulation, yet after only four steps of coupling the calculation had totally unacceptable confidence limits.

The above example was given in Mann (1975) but only recently has the problem been given further serious attention. O'Neill *et al.* (1980) showed that a 4% error in parameters led to a 12–40% variation in model output. Those accustomed to estimating population parameters in the field are aware that a 4% error is much smaller than that normally obtained, so that the error in the prediction of the model discussed by O'Neill *et al.* (1980) would be unacceptably large. In a subsequent paper from the same laboratory, Gardner *et al.* (1980) compared the error propagation properties in six models of a hypothetical predator-prey system, and concluded with the words:

> This study serves as a beginning, and we believe continued work on error analysis will be important in developing guidelines for model design which will help change ecological modelling from an art to a science.

Figure 10.4 is a humorous attempt to illustrate the contrasting properties of 'engineering-type' and 'biological' coupled process models. In practice, of course, ecosystem simulations do not have outputs with large amounts of uncontrolled and uncontrollable variability. This is because reasonable values are selected for each parameter, from within the range of variability that exists in nature. This value may be defended as being representative of some mean, but in almost all cases the justification for doing so, and for making the parameter invariate, is not given.

10.3.2 The hierarchical properties of ecosystems

The properties of hierarchies in biological systems have been discussed by Weiss (1969) and Pattee (1973), but in both cases they were concerned mainly with organization at and below the level of the organism. Nevertheless, Simon (in Pattee 1973) was prepared to recognize four intertwined hierarchic sequences: (1) from observable chemical substances, to molecules, to atoms, to nuclei and electrons, to elementary particles; (2) from living organisms, to tissues and organs, to cells, to macromolecules, to organic compounds; (3) from the statistics of inheritance, to genes and chromosomes, to 'DNA, and all that'; (4) from human societies, to organizations, to small groups, to individual human beings, to cognitive programs in the central nervous system, to elementary information processes.

Here is the clear recognition that hierarchies exist at levels above that of the organism. E. P. Odum (1971) in his introduction displayed a 'levels of organization spectrum' which proceeded continuously from genetic systems up to organic systems and on to ecosystems. Overton (1977) advocated an hierarchial approach to ecosystem modelling, and Webster (1979) examined the possibility that hierarchy theory might be applied to ecosystems. For a clear understanding of the last topic it is necessary to consider rather closely the properties of hierarchies.

The first generalization, that can readily be perceived as applying to the four hierarchies of Simon is that each level has a different behavioural frequency, and the lower one goes in the hierarchy, the shorter is the time scale of events. Since we ourselves exist on the organismal level, we need special tools to observe events on other time scales: chromatography enables us to observe the behaviour of compounds with different molecular

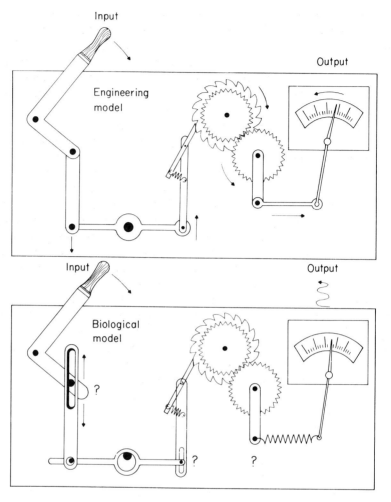

Fig. 10.4 The 'engineering-type' model and the 'biological model'. The former is constructed on the best engineering principles with well-fitting joints. A known input (movement of lever on left) leads to a unique output (movement of pointer on right). The biological model has a great deal of variability built into the connections between elements. A known input on the left may give rise to many possible outputs. Biological simulation models are like this, on account of the genetically programmed variability in the properties of the components.

velocities, and bubble chambers enable us to study sub-atomic particles. Looking in the other direction, satellite imagery enables us to perceive events on the scale of ecosystems. One result of differing time scales at different levels is that, viewed from a particular level, events at the level below are observed as statistical measures of a large number of rapid occurrences, while events at the level above occur at almost imperceptibly slow rates.

A second generalization about hierarchies is that they are constructed of nesting functional groups that have strong internal interactions but weaker external interactions. These units were named 'holons' by Koestler (1967). A group of holons with weak interactions nevertheless form a larger unit in the next level of the hierarchy. A holon conforms to the laws of behaviour of its constituent strongly interacting parts, but it is also constrained to conform with higher levels of organization. An example from a hierarchy in human society will be familiar to many scientists. We may think of a university department as a holon, with strong internal interactions between the students and the teachers. But the Department is usually part of a larger unit, the Faculty. Its interactions are less strong, but the behaviour of the students and teachers are none the less constrained by the rules for conduct of classes, examinations, etc., imposed by the Faculty. The Faculty itself constitutes a holon in the next level of organization, where Deans of Faculties meet to discuss allocation of resources, etc. One can also see in this example that the time scales are different in the various levels of organization. Departments deal with problems on the day-to-day level, while Faculties, notoriously ponderous in their deliberations, deal with problems on a year-by-year scale, and senior administration makes plans on the scale of decades.

The description of the same event in an hierarchical system is different at different levels of organization. For example, the behaviour of a gas may be described at one level by means of the gas laws, but at a lower level in terms of the motion of particles. Statistical mechanics provides a connection between the two, in terms of average particle behaviour (this example was given by Rosen 1969). Similarly, it may be possible to describe the behaviour of an organism in terms of its ethology, as an integrated functioning organism, or in terms of its neural and hormonal physiology.

There has been a long-standing debate about the relationship between properties at different levels in an hierarchy. The holistic philosophers have emphasized that behaviour at a higher level cannot be explained solely in terms of lower level properties, because each level has emergent properties that are more than the sum of their parts. On the other hand, reductionists maintain that higher level behaviour is explainable in terms of integrated lower level properties. It seems to the author that this is a false dichotomy, and that integration of all the properties and *interactions* of components of a lower level *results* in the emergence of properties not defined by the properties of the components of the lower level *considered in isolation*.

Webster (1979) considered the applicability of hierarchy theory to ecological problems. He suggested that an ecosystem, comprising the interacting organisms and physico-chemical processes of a suitably chosen unit of space, clearly meets the criterion of having strong internal interactions and weak external interactions. For example, there are usually stronger interactions within a lake ecosystem than there are across the land–water interface or the air–water interface, and such ecosystems fit the definition of a holon. From this Webster (1979) went on to explore the consequences of regarding ecosystems as extensions of the hierarchy that contains cells, organs, and organisms, and concluded that we should not expect to be able to model ecosystem behaviour from a set of organismic equations:

> Advances in ecosystem ecology must proceed first from an understanding of ecosystem-level behaviour and laws. Next comes specification of organism-level dynamics and finally identification of the statistical formalism connecting the two. . . . We now know so much about organism behaviour that we have difficulty finding the larger regularities. We must search for overriding simplicity in the large-scale complexity.

The writer agrees wholeheartedly with this point of view, and indeed this book is an attempt to point out some of the large-scale processes in coastal ecosystems. But, to return to the theme of this chapter, it does seem that almost all attempts at predictive modelling that have been made to date have been attempts to predict the properties of ecosystems entirely from the properties of their components. As such, they are doomed to failure. It is encouraging to note that in a volume entitled *Theoretical Systems Ecology* edited by Halfon (1979) there are, in addition to the chapter by Webster quoted above, several others concerned with the holistic properties of ecosystems, or with hierarchical structure. In one of them (Patten & Finn 1979) it is explicitly stated that the mechanistic approach to system ecology, that of building wholes from parts, has so far failed to develop 'realistic and practical ecosystem models'.

Silvert (1980) proposes a solution to the problem, which he calls 'top-down modelling'. He proposes that the first step in ecological modelling should be careful observation of the behaviour of the whole system. A conceptual framework of the complete model is made to be consistent with system behaviour, and detail is added as necessary during model development. In a paper which gives examples of the use of the technique (Silvert in press) it is shown that there may be a large set of models that generate output consistent with the experimental data. It is then necessary to select a smaller set through analysis of their structure and consideration of their consequences for the real world.

Summarizing to this point, we note that computer simulations of ecological systems have been a great success in giving insights into the ways in which ecosystems *may* work, under hypothetical conditions. Those responsible for making ecological management decisions make them with the aid of the best advice and the best models available. Often, their intent is to perturb a system beyond the range of its previously observed variation, and models which work well within that range often fail when extrapolated beyond it. Management decisions are also made in the context of socio-economic pressures, and although such considerations are beyond the range of this book, we should remember that the best management models seek to optimize both social and ecological benefits.

Up to now, the most common type of ecological model used for management purposes is the reductionist compartmental simulation model. We have seen that when the errors (or natural variance) of the parameters of such models are given due weight, the outputs of such models have unacceptably large variances in the outputs.

Natural systems have much smaller variations in their properties, and this is seen as attributable to the incredibly complex network of checks, balances and feedbacks which confer emergent properties at the ecosystem level. At the present state of the art, the best course seems to be to begin with detailed observation of system behaviour, and build the simplest models that are consistent with that behaviour and with the dynamics of the components.

No one can pretend that such techniques give fully satisfactory models. The remainder of this chapter is devoted to emphasizing the need to focus our attention on ecosystems and to explore new ways of developing ecosystem theory. Just as statistical mechanics provides a connection between the motion of particles and the behaviour of a gas, we need an ecological theory that will provide the connection between the dynamics of populations and the behaviour of ecosystems.

10.4 SOME PROBLEMS WITH THE CONCEPT OF ECOSYSTEM

10.4.1 Defining an ecosystem

For those accustomed to working at the level of organisms or populations, there are several difficulties that arise when it is advocated that serious attention be given to work at the ecosystem level. The first is a very fundamental problem of giving a precise definition of an ecosystem. If this is overcome, the question then arises, what is the structure of an ecosystem, what are its functional components, and what are its characteristic properties? E. P. Odum, long an advocate of the ecosystem approach to ecology, defines a population as a group of individuals of any one kind of organism, a community as all of the populations occupying a given area, and an ecosystem as the community and the non-living environment functioning together (Odum 1971). It is not difficult to see that all the organisms of an area do interact with each other and with their non-living environment. The question, for many people, is how to define the boundaries and the properties of this so-called ecosystem. The question of boundaries was touched upon in the discussion of hierarchies in the previous section. A unit in a hierarchy is characterized by having stronger interactions internally than it has externally. A lake with no inflowing or outflowing streams fits the definition perfectly, for almost all of its biological interactions are internal, and its exchanges with land and air are predominantly physical and chemical and relatively small. From this relatively closed system, there are all gradations to the system in which external interactions are of great importance, and the value of treating it as a distinct entity becomes questionable. Nevertheless, it seems to the author that the feature which distinguishes an ecosystem from any other ecological unit is that it is a level of organization in which all the biological interactions between organisms in an area and all the physical and chemical processes that impinge on those organisms are taken into account. *Ecosystems exist primarily as levels of organization.* In deciding what unit of area to investigate, it is expedient to choose as boundaries the surfaces of minimum interaction, but this can be done at various spatial scales of resolution. For some purposes a whole ocean basin may be the object of study at the ecosystem level, but it is equally valid to consider all the biotic and abiotic interactions in a single estuary, in a coral reef, or even in the sediment underlying 10 cm^2 of sea floor. In the latter case, there is every reason to suspect that horizontal interactions within the sediment are small compared with vertical interactions at the sediment–water interface, and with interactions between organisms remaining more or less stationary within the sediment, both of which can be measured.

10.4.2 Intermediate levels of organization

Odum (1971) in his discussion of levels of organization placed population systems as levels of organization intermediate between organisms and ecosystems, but Webster (1979) argued that neither populations nor communities necessarily have stronger interactions internally than externally. For populations, it is not clear that intraspecific interactions, such as competition, are necessarily stronger than interspecific interactions such as herbivore–plant or predator–prey interactions. For communities, he argued, interactions between species may be less strong than interactions with the abiotic environment. Lindeman (1942) emphasized trophic levels as the important components of ecosystems, and when these proved to have no concrete existence Cummins (1974) proposed 'functional groups' as alternatives. However, neither of these fit the criteria of a holon discussed earlier. Webster (1979) therefore argued that there were no universally acceptable levels of organization between organisms and ecosystems. On the other hand, aquatic systems could usefully be divided into benthic, planktonic and fringing subsystems, while forests could be divided into canopy, understorey, etc. In these units, interactions tend to be internally strong on account of physical proximity of the components. In general, there is agreement among workers of many persuasions that the word ecosystem denotes a level of organization that is clearly distinct and different from that of an organism, but there is little agreement about levels of organization intermediate between the two.

10.4.3 Cybernetic properties of ecosystems

Further problems arise in defining the properties of an ecosystem. Odum (1969) listed 24 properties. Many of them are readily defined once the boundaries of the system have been set: primary production, secondary production, community respiration, community biomass, mineral cycles, and so on. However, the last five on the list were in a group headed 'Overall homeostatisis', and the implication was that ecosystems tend to resist perturbation, and, like organisms, maintain an overall stability in many of their properties. Weiss (1969) referred to the same type of property when he said that in a living system the variance of properties of the total system is less than the sum of the variances of the component subsystems. It is not difficult to see that this is almost certainly true, although the hypothesis has seldom been tested in ecosystems. For example, in a body of water, the total primary productivity will usually be limited either by the supply of nutrients or by the penetration of light. This is a system constraint. Nevertheless, the productivity of individual species of phytoplankton is highly variable from year to year, depending on competitive relationships and chance events that favour one species at the expense of another. The net result is that total system primary production is much less variable from year to year than is the production of individual species.

Engelberg and Boyarsky (1979) argued that ecosystems do not possess the properties which other systems, such as organisms, human organizations and automated machines possess to enable them to regulate themselves. Specifically, they argued, ecosystems lack global information networks to integrate their parts, global informational feedback cycles to stabilize and regulate them, and they do not show the regulation of high-energy effects by low-energy causes. They pointed to the effectiveness of nerve impulses and hormones in regulating the activities of organisms and of information flow (in the conventional sense) in regulating the activities of human societies. This author believes that Engelberg and Boyarsky (1979) are greatly underestimating the information flow in ecosystems. A very major aspect of the functioning of ecosystems is the flow of energy and materials along trophic pathways. We still have a great deal to learn, but it seems highly probable that the magnitudes and directions of these flows are controlled by traces of substances that determine palatability, by low-energy signals such as pheromones and other visual and chemical cues that determine predator–prey interactions, and by feedbacks of trace elements from consumers to primary producers. Our ignorance of the details of the functioning of natural communities is so great that, at present, it is unlikely that the question will be settled to the satisfaction of all. Nevertheless, the whole of this book is concerned with presenting evidence that complex interactions occur in coastal ecosystems that cannot possibly be inferred from a consideration of the biology of each organism in isolation. Clearly, there is a class of phenomena that belongs to a different level of organization, the level that we call ecosystem.

10.5 SOME ALTERNATIVE APPROACHES TO UNDERSTANDING ECOSYSTEMS

10.5.1 New explorations of ecosystem properties

Platt *et al.* (1981) considered some of the possibilities for a radically fresh approach to understanding ecosystems. This is not the place to go over the same ground in detail, but it is useful to indicate the directions being considered. The first group of techniques to be considered were novel types of network analysis, as applied to food webs. Among these was input–output analysis, as developed in economics and later applied to ecology. The prime exponent of this technique is Finn (1976) who defined the total system throughput of energy as the sum of all the inputs (internal as well as external) to all the species. He showed that the average path length for a given network could be calculated from the total system throughput divided by the total external input, and suggested that this was a useful measure of the trophic complexity of the network. He also calculated an index of cycling within a system, from the ratio of cycled energy to once-through-energy. The two indices were used to make comparisons between ecosystems.

Input–output analysis requires a knowledge of the magnitude of the flows in a system. When only qualitative information is available about interactions, it is often possible to infer the result of compound interactions by loop analysis. Lane and Levins (1977) used the technique for studying the effect of nutrient enrichment on lakes.

A third technique worthy of note is Isaacs' (1973) attempt to deal with what he calls unstructured food webs. After discovering that the concentration of caesium in fish off the Gulf of California was approximately the same regardless of their trophic position, he abandoned all attempts to construct food webs according to Lindeman's (1942) trophic dynamic hypothesis, and substituted a matrix of all possible routes by which autotrophic material could be converted to living and non-living but retrievable matter. The approach was more fully developed by Lange and Hurley (1975). It was shown that the consequences of using this approach, involving no assumptions about the trophic position of an organism, are results that are reasonably in accordance with nature. The implications are not entirely clear, but should be a salutary lesson to those who attach undue importance to trophic structure. In some ways they remind us of the particle size spectrum approach used by Sheldon *et al.* (1977) and discussed in Chapter 9.

The second group of techniques discussed in Platt *et al.* (1981) were related to the thermodynamic or statistical mechanical properties of ecosystems. They reviewed what is known of the irreversible thermodynamics of ecosystems and concluded that there were at present no applications that could be foreseen. Ulanwicz (1972) discussed the application of information theory to ecosystem structure and concluded that it is possible to go a long way in describing community behaviour by discussing only the fluxes and not invoking forces. It is possible to argue that the way in which communities evolve is determined much more by the flow structure than by the traditional causative factors, the forces, and this causes us to question simulation models driven by forces.

In discussing the application of statistical mechanics to ecosystem theory, Fasham (in Platt *et al.* 1981) used an old quotation from Lotka (1925):

> ... what is needed is an analysis ... that shall envisage the units of a biological population as the established statistical mechanics envisages molecules, atoms and electrons; that shall deal with such average effects as population density, population pressure, and the like, after the manner thermodynamics deals with the average effects of gas concentration, gas pressure . . . .

If the idea is transposed to cover the units of an ecosystem, it comes very close to the ideas discussed in section 10.3.2 under hierarchies. Fasham reviewed attempts that have been made to analyse ecosystems in terms of statistical mechanics, and noted that the attempts have been severely criticized. Similar criticisms were levelled against certain models in many-body physics, but in the end the field benefited by those modelling efforts.

It is much too soon to say which, if any, of these new approaches will lead to improved understanding and predictive capability. One thing is clear, the older techniques of simulation modelling have not given us the predictive power we need, and new ideas are much needed.

10.5.2 Microcosms as simulations of ecosystems

One of the ideas that is currently being tried in several parts of the world is the use of microcosms as simulators of ecosystems. Microcosms may be defined as 'portions of ecosystems, or living models of ecosystems enclosed and maintained for observation and study' (Pilson & Nixon 1980). They range in size from small flasks to large containers of volume about 1300 m^3. Their great advantage over natural ecosystems is that they are more amenable to controlled experimentation. One of their advantages over numerical models is that they are liable to preserve intact many of the subtle feedbacks of natural systems, many of which we do not understand and therefore cannot build into our numerical models. There are many problems in using microcosms for prediction, and perhaps the greatest of these is the scaling problem. When the dimensions of an ecosystem are reduced, while the sizes of the organisms are not, it is difficult to reproduce the proper interactions between organisms of different sizes, and between the organisms and such physical factors as light and turbulence. The paper by Pilson and Nixon (1980) reviews 21 representative marine microcosms, so no attempt will be made to repeat that coverage. Instead, some remarks about the state of the art and prospects for the future appear to be appropriate.

The justification for funding several recent investigations involving large microcosms was that they could be used for studying the effect of pollutants on ecosystems. Good reviews of this aspect of the subject were given by Steele (1979) and Davies and Gamble (1979) in a symposium on *The Assessment of Sublethal Effects of Pollutants in the Sea*. Steele showed how the experimental approach may evolve from studies with a single species in the laboratory to those with a single food chain in large outdoor tanks, to those involving portions of ecosystems isolated in large plastic columns. Among the advantages of moving in this direction he listed increasing duration of exposure to pollutants and increasing sensitivity of the system to stress, but the disadvantages were decreasing cheapness, decreasing replication, decreasing operator control, and decreasing isolation of cause and effect. In the end, he concluded that the experiments conducted so far with large microcosms have probably taught us more about the general ecological interactions in such systems than about subtle long-term effects of pollutants. Since this book is more concerned with natural ecosystems than it is with pollutants, it is worth looking more closely at some of the results.

After discussions between marine ecologists in the UK, Canada and the USA, parallel experiments with 'captured water columns' were carried out in Saanich Inlet, near Vancouver, Canada, and in Loch Ewe, Scotland. In Saanich Inlet plastic bags were hauled up 'like an expanding concertina', to capture undisturbed, stratified water columns almost 20 m deep. In Loch Ewe a plastic bag 16 m deep was filled by pumping, so that the water column was initially well mixed. Steele (1979) compared two experiments carried out in 1974 at the two sites, involving the addition of copper at 10 $\mu g/1$ to the water columns. At Loch Ewe two containers were observed for 40 days before addition of the pollutant and there did not seem to be much stress resulting from enclosure. Chlorophyll and particulate carbon levels remained relatively constant, but the amount of herbivorous zooplankton in the two systems gradually diverged. This was thought to be due to differences in predator populations in the two bags.

At Saanich Inlet there was a sharp drop in phytoplankton biomass in the first three days, caused by a rapid sinking of large diatoms. This was in turn attributed to a reduction in turbulence, and hence in vertical mixing, within the bags. Steele (1979) concluded that at Saanich Inlet mixing and sinking was the major factor controlling phytoplankton populations, whereas at Loch Ewe grazing was the dominant controlling factor. Hence, enclosure of a water column has a much stronger effect on the phytoplankton in Saanich Inlet than at Loch Ewe. In the light of these differences, no simple statement about the effect of copper on a marine ecosystem was possible. Instead, it was seen that the mechanism of ecosystem function is itself a critical variable, and that pollutants have different effects in different systems.

Pilson and Nixon (1980) referred to their own work with 12 land-based tanks 5 m deep, and their attempts to replicate experiments and get consistent results. They wrestled with the difficult question of variability in nature and variability between replicates. From their own studies of Naragansett Bay (see section 10.2.2) it was clear to them that the timing of initiation and duration of phytoplankton blooms, and the species composition and succession in the blooms varied from place to place and from year to year. Some of this variability could be explained by variations in light, temperature, wind mixing, etc., but there was also a good deal of apparent randomness. This poses a dilemma regarding replicability of results in microcosms. For interpretation of experiments, low variation between replicates is desirable, but if this occurs one suspects that the microcosms are not faithfully reproducing the variations found in nature. As Pilson and Nixon put it, 'the better the microcosm the worse it replicates, and therefore the worse it is as an experimental tool'. Of course, this is an exaggeration of the dilemma. As they point out, we need to find ways of comparing the stochastic behaviour of nature with that of microcosms. Their current solution was to monitor several tanks weekly for a year, and compare them with Naragansett Bay. Although variation between tanks was considerable, and comparisons over short periods of time could be very discouraging, it was clear from a year's data that all the tanks tracked events in the bay remarkably well, but with their own random variations and slight differences in timing. Pilson and Nixon's view of all this is well summarized in the following quotation:

Variable behaviour of the natural ecosystem provides an envelope of uncertainty about our understanding of natural systems and about our quantitative knowledge of their average behaviour. This envelope of uncertainty is quite large, and sets a severe limit on the sensitivity with which we can hope to measure the impact of a change in the physical forcing functions or the impact of some chronic pollutant on the natural system. This same uncertainty also exists for microcosm work, and in some sense it can only be reduced by losing some essential elements in the behaviour of the system. We believe this problem may be inherent and inescapable.

10.5.3 Conclusions

In my view, the above statement is an excellent summary of the state of the art in our search for predictive capability in marine ecology. Natural systems are complex, subtle, and difficult to comprehend. Numerical simulation of these systems is possible only if we make strong, simplifying assumptions and ignore much of the variability but the consequence of doing so is to produce models which give considerable insight but little predictive power. Construction of living models in the form of microcosms enables us to preserve intact many of the intricacies of the natural system, but the inevitable changes in physical scale force us to alter turbulence, light regimes and other important physical factors. The consequences of these scale changes are poorly understood, and provide an exciting new field of investigation.

In parallel with continuing efforts in numerical simulation and microcosm experiments, we need to promote strong new initiatives in the study of the properties of natural ecosystems. We need far more basic data on the fluxes of energy and materials through the different kinds of marine ecosystems, and we need deeper insights into the theory of ecosystem function, to give us yet more guidance on how to best study natural systems. By comparison with our knowledge of the organismal level of nature's hierarchy, our knowledge of the ecosystem level is pitifully small and inadequate. Remedying this deficiency is one of the major challenges confronting our young scientists.

REFERENCES

Alldredge A. L. & King J. M. (1977) Distribution, abundance and substrate preferences of demersal reef zooplankton at Lizard Island Lagoon, Great Barrier Reef. *Mar. Biol.* **41**, 317–33.

Alton M. S. & Fredin R. A. (1974) Status of Alaska Pollock in the Eastern Bering Sea. *Int. North. Pac. Fish Comm. Doc.* **1725**.

Andrewartha H. G. & Birch L. C. (1954) *The Distribution and Abundance of Animals.* University of Chicago Press, Chicago.

Andrews P. & Williams P. J. le B. (1971) Heterotrophic utilization of dissolved organic compounds in the sea. III. Measurement of the oxidation rates and concentrations of glucose and amino acids in sea water. *J. mar. Biol. Ass. U.K.* **51**, 111–25.

Bainbridge R. (1957) The size, shape and density of marine plankton concentrations. *Biol. Rev.* **32**, 91–115.

Bakus G. J. (1966) Some relations of fishes to benthic organisms on coral reefs. *Nature* **210**, 280–4.

Banse K. (1974) On the role of bacterioplankton in the tropical ocean. *Mar. Biol.* **24**, 1–5.

Barber R. T., Dugdale R. C., MacIsaac J. J. & Smith R. L. (1971) Variations in phytoplankton growth associated with the source and condition of upwelling water. *Inv. Pesq.* **35**, 171–93.

Barber R. T. & Ryther J. H. (1969) Organic chelators: Factors affecting primary production in the Cromwell Current upwelling. *J. exp. mar. Biol. Ecol.* **3**, 191–9.

Barnes D. J. & Taylor D. L. (1973) *In Situ* studies of calcification and photosynthetic carbon fixation on the coral *Montastrea annularis. Helgol. wiss. Meeresunters.* **24**, 284–91.

Barsdate R. J., Prentki R. T. & Fenchel T. (1974).The phosphorus cycle of model ecosystems: significance for decomposer food chains and the effect of bacterial grazers. *Oikos* **25**, 239–51.

Barton E. D., Huyer A. & Smith R. L. (1977) Temporal variation observed in the hydrographic regime near Cabo Corviero in the north-west African upwelling region, February to April, 1974. *Deep-Sea Res.* **24**, 7–23.

Baylor E. R. & Sutcliffe W. H. (1963) Dissolved organic matter in sea water as a source of particulate food. *Limnol. Oceanogr.* **8**, 369–71.

Beeftink W. G. (1977) The coastal salt marshes of western and northern Europe: an ecological and phytosociological approach. In V. J. Chapman (ed.), *Wet Coastal Ecosystems*, pp. 109–55. Elsevier Scientific, Amsterdam.

Beers J. R. & Stewart G. L. (1971) Microzooplankters in the plankton communities of the upper waters of the eastern tropical Pacific. *Deep-Sea Res.* **18**, 861–83.

Bellamy J. D., John D. M. & Whittick A. (1968) The 'Kelp forest ecosystem' as a 'phytometer' in the study of pollution in the inshore environment. *Underwater Ass. Rep.* **1968**, 79–82.

Benson A. A. & Muscatine L. (1974) Wax in coral mucus: energy transfer from corals to reef fishes. *Limnol Oceanogr.* **19**, 810–4.

Berman T. & Holm-Hansen O. (1974) Release of photoassimilated carbon as dissolved organic matter by marine phytoplankton. *Mar. Biol.* **28**, 305–10.

Beverton R. J. H. & Holt S. J. (1957) On the dynamics of exploited fish populations. *Fishery Invest. (Lond.), Ser. 2* **19**, 1–533.

Billen G. (1978) A budget of nitrogen recycling in North Sea sediments off the Belgian coast. *Estuar. coast. mar. Sci.* **7**, 127–46.

Black R. (1976) The effect of grazing by the limpet *Acmaea insessa* on the kelp *Egregia laevigata* in the intertidal zone. *Ecology*, **57**, 265–77.

Blinks L. R. (1955) Photosynthesis and productivity of littoral marine algae. *J. mar. Res.* **14**, 363–73.

Boden B. P. & Kampa E. M. (1967) The influence of natural light on the vertical migrations of an animal community in the sea. *Symp. zool. Soc. (Lond.)* **19**, 15–26.

Boorman L. A. & Ranwell D. S. (1977) *Ecology of Maplin Sands and the Coastal Zones of Suffolk, Essex and North Kent.* Institute of Terrestrial Ecology, Cambridge.

Bowman M. J. (1978) Introduction and historical perspective. In M. J. Bowman & W. E. Esaias (eds), *Oceanic Fronts in Coastal Processes*, pp. 2–5. Springer-Verlag, Berlin.

Bowman M. J. & Esaias W. E. (eds) (1978) *Oceanic Fronts in Coastal Processes*. Springer-Verlag, Berlin.

Bowman M. J. & Iverson R. L. (1978) Estuarine and plume fronts. In M. J. Bowman & W. E. Esaias (eds), *Oceanic Fronts in Coastal Processes*, pp. 87–104. Springer-Verlag, Berlin.

Boyd C. M. (1976) Selection of particle sizes by filter-feeding copepods: a plea for reason. *Limnol. Oceanogr.* **21**, 175–80.

Breen P. A. & Mann K. H. (1976a) Changing lobster abundance and the destruction of kelp beds by sea-urchins. *Mar. Biol.* **34**, 137–42.

Breen P. A. & Mann K. H. (1976b) Destructive grazing of kelp by sea-urchins in Eastern Canada. *J. Fish. Res. Bd. Can.* **33**, 1278–83.

Brinkhuis B. H. (1976) The ecology of temperate salt-marsh fucoids. I. Occurrence and distribution of *Ascophyllum nodosum* ecads. *Mar. Biol.* **34**, 325–8.

Broome S. A., Woodhouse W. W. & Seneca E. D. (1975) The relationship of mineral nutrients to growth of *Spartina alterniflora* in North Carolina. (ii) The effects of N, P, and Fe fertilizers. *Soil Sci. Soc. Amer. Proc.* **39**, 327–34.

Brylinsky M. (1972) Steady-state sensitivity analysis of energy flow in a marine system. In B. C. Patten (ed.), *Systems Analysis and Simulation in Ecology*, pp. 81–101. Academic Press, New York.

Buchanan J. B. & Warwick R. M. (1974) An estimate of benthic macrofaunal production in the offshore mud of the Northumberland coast. *J. mar. Biol. Ass. U.K.* **54**, 197–222.

Cadée G. C. & Hegeman J. (1974) Primary production of the benthic microflora living on tidal flats in the Dutch Wadden Sea. *Neth. J. Sea Res.* **8**, 260–91.

Cameron W. M. & Pritchard D. W. (1963) Estuaries. In M. N. Hill (ed.), *The Sea*, Vol. 2, pp. 306–45. John Wiley Interscience, New York.

Caperon J., Cattell S. A. & Krasnick G. (1971) Phytoplankton kinetics in a subtropical estuary: Eutrophication. *Limnol. Oceanogr.* **16**, 599–607.

Cappenberg T. E. (1975) Relationship between sulphate-reducing and methane-producing bacteria. *Plant and Soil* **43**, 125–39.

Caswell H. (1976) The validation problem. In B. C. Patten (ed.), *Systems Analysis and Simulation in Ecology*, Vol. 4, pp. 313–25. Academic Press, New York.

Cederwall H. (1977) Annual macrofauna production of a soft bottom in the Northern Baltic proper. In B. F. Keegan, P. O. Ceidigh & P. J. S. Boaden (eds), *Biology of Benthic Organisms: Proc. 11th European Symp. Mar. Biol.*, pp. 155–64. Pergamon Press, Oxford.

Chapman A. R. O. & Craigie J. S. (1977) Seasonal growth in *Laminaria longicruris*: relations with dissolved inorganic nutrients and internal reserves of nitrogen. *Mar. Biol.* **40**, 197–205.

Chapman V. J. (1964) *Coastal Vegetation*. Pergamon Press, Oxford.

Chapman V. J. (1970) *Seaweeds and Their Uses*. 2nd edn. Methuen, London.

Chapman V. J. (1975) *Mangrove Vegetation*. Lehre, Cramer.

Chapman V. J. (1977) *Wet Coastal Ecosystems*. Elsevier Scientific Publishing Company, Amsterdam.

Chapman V. J. & Chapman D. J. (1973) *The Algae*. 2nd edn. Macmillan, London.

Chittleborough R. G. (1970) Studies on recruitment in the Western Australian rock lobster *Panulirus longipes cygnus* George: density and natural mortality of juveniles. *Aust. J. mar. freshwat. Res.* **21**, 131–48.

Choi C. I. (1972) Primary production and release of dissolved organic carbon from phytoplankton in the Western North Atlantic. *Deep-Sea Res.* **19**, 731–5.

Clark S. H. & B. E. Brown (1977) Changes in biomasses of fin fishes and squids from the Gulf of Maine to Cape Hatteras, 1963–74, as determined from research vessel survey data. *Fish. Bull. U.S.* **75**, 1–21.

Clendenning K. A. (1964) Photosynthesis and growth in *Macrocystis pyrifera*. *Proc. int. Seaweed Symp.* **4**, 55–65.

Connell J. H. (1978) Diversity in tropical rain forests and coral reefs. *Science*, **199**, 1302–10.

Conover R. J. (1974) Production in marine plankton communities. *Proceedings of the First International Congress of Ecology*, pp. 159–63. Centre for Agricultural Publishing and Documentation, Wageningen, Netherlands.

Conover R. J. (1978) Feeding interactions in the pelagic zone. *Rapp. P.-v. Réun. Cons. int. Explor. Mer.* **173**, 66–76.

Conover R. J. & Mayzaud P. (1975) Respiration and nitrogen excretion of neritic zooplankton in relation to potential food supply. *10th European Symposium on Marine Biology, Ostend, Belgium*, Vol. 2, pp. 151–63. Universa Press, Wettern, Belgium.

Conway H. L. (1977) Interactions of inorganic nitrogen in the uptake and assimilation by marine phytoplankton. *Mar. Biol.* **39**, 221–32.

Coote A. R. & Yeats P. A. (1979) Distribution of nutrients in the Gulf of St. Lawrence. *J. Fish. Res. Bd. Can.* **36**, 122–31.

Corner E. D. S. & Davies A. G. (1971) Plankton as a factor in the nitrogen and phosphorus cycles in the sea. *Adv. mar. Biol.* **9**, 101–204.

Correll D. L., Faust M. A. & Devern D. J. (1975) Phosphorus flux and cycling in estuaries. In L. E. Cronin (ed), *Estuarine Research*, Vol. 1, pp. 108–36. Academic Press, New York.

Coull B. C. (1973) Estuarine meiofauna: a review. In L. H. Stevenson & R. R. Colwell (eds), *Estuarine Microbial Ecology*, pp. 499–512. University of South Carolina, Columbia, South Carolina.

Crisp D. J. (1971) Energy flow measurements. In N. A. Holme & A. D. McIntyre (eds), *Methods for the Study of the Marine Benthos*, pp. 197–279. Blackwell Scientific Publications, Oxford.

Crossland C. J. & Barnes D. J. (1974) The role of metabolic nitrogen in coral calcification. *Mar. Biol.* **28**, 325–32.

Cummins K. W. (1974) Structure and function of stream ecosystems. *BioScience* **24**, 631–41.

Cushing D. H. (1959) The seasonal variation in oceanic production as a problem in population dynamics. *J. Cons. perm. int. Explor. Mer.* **24**, 455–64.

Cushing D. H. (1961) On the failure of the Plymouth herring fishery. *J. mar. Biol. Ass. U.K.* **41**, 899–916.

Cushing D. H. (1971a) Upwelling and the production of fish. *Adv. mar. Biol.* **9**, 255–334.

Cushing D. A. (1971b) A comparison of production in temperate seas and the upwelling areas. *Trans. roy. Soc. S. Africa.* **40**, 17–33.

Dale N. (1974) Bacteria in intertidal sediments: factors related to their distribution. *Limnol. Oceanogr.* **19**, 509–18.

Dame R. F. (1972) The ecological energetics of growth, respiration, and assimilation in the American oyster *Crassostrea virginica*. *Mar. Biol.* **17**, 243–50.

Dame R. F. (1976) Energy flow in an intertidal oyster population. *Estuar. mar. Sci.* **4**, 243–53.

Dana T. F., Newman W. A. & Fager E. W. (1972) *Acanthaster* aggregations: interpreted as primarily responses to natural phenomena. *Pacific Sci.* **26**, 355–72.

Darnell R. M. (1967) Organic detritus in relation to the estuarine ecosystem. In G. H. Lauff (ed.), *Estuaries*, pp. 376–82. American Association for the Advancement of Science, Washington D.C.

Dart J. K. G. (1972) Echinoids, algal lawn and coral recolonization. *Nature* **239**, 50–1.

Daubenmire R. F. (1947) *Plants and Environment.* Wiley and Son Inc., New York.

Davies J. M. & Gamble J. C. (1979) Experiments with large enclosed ecosystems. *Phil. Trans. roy. Soc. Lond. B.* **286**, 523–44.

Day J. A., Smith W. G., Wagner P. R. & Stowe W. C. (1973) *Community Structure and Carbon Budget of a Salt-marsh and Shallow Bay Estuarine System in Louisiana.* Centre for Wetland Resources, Louisiana State University.

Dayton P. K. (1971) Competition, disturbance and community organization: the provision and subsequent utilization of space in a rocky intertidal community. *Ecol. Monogr.* **41**, 351–89.

Dayton P. K. (1975) Experimental studies of algal canopy interactions in a sea otter-dominated kelp community at Amchitka Island, Alaska. *Fish. Bull.* **73**, 230–7.

Deason E. E. (1980) Potential effect of phytoplankton colony breakage on the calculation of zooplankton filtration rates. *Mar. Biol.* **57**, 279–86.

D'Elia C. F. & Webb K. L. (1977) The dissolved nitrogen flux of reef corals. In D. L. Taylor (ed.), *Proc. Third Internat. Coral Reef Sympos.*, pp. 325–30. Rosentiel School of Marine and Atmospheric Science, Miami.

den Hartog C. (1970) *The Seagrasses of the World.* North-Holland Publishing Company, London.

Denman K. (1976) Covariability of chlorophyll and temperature in the sea. *Deep-Sea Res.* **23**, 539–50.

Denman K. L. & Platt T. (1975) Coherence in the horizontal distributions of phytoplankton and temperature in the upper ocean. *Mém. Soc. Sci. Liège*, 6e sér. **7**, 19–30.

Denman K. L. & Platt T. (1976) The variance spectrum of phytoplankton in a turbulent ocean. *J. mar. Res.* **34**, 593–601.

Derenbach J. B. & Williams P. J. le B. (1974) Autotrophic and bacterial production: fractionation of plankton populations by differential filtration of samples from the English Channel. *Mar. Biol.* **25**, 263–9.

Dickie L. M. (1972) Food chains and fish production. *Spec. Publ. int. Comm. N.W. Atlantic Fish.* **8**, 201–21.

Digby P. S. B. (1953) Plankton production in Scoresby Sound, East Greenland. *J. anim. Ecol.* **22**, 289–322.

Donaghay P. L. & Small L. F. (1979) Food selection capabilities of the estuarine copepod *Acartia clausi. Mar. Biol.* **52**, 137–46.

Dugdale R. C. (1972) Chemical oceanography and primary productivity in upwelling regions. *Geoforum* **11**, 47–61.

Dugdale R. C. & Goering J. J. (1967) Uptake of new and regenerated forms of nitrogen in primary productivity. *Limnol. Oceanogr.* **12**, 196–206.

Duxbury A. C. (1979) Upwelling and estuary flushing. *Limnol. Oceanogr.* **24**, 627–33.

Edmondson W. T. (1970) Phosphorus, nitrogen and algae in Lake Washington after diversion of sewage. *Science* **169**, 690–1.

Edmondson W. T. & Winberg G. G. (1971) *A Manual on Methods for the Assessment of Secondary Productivity in Fresh Waters. IBP Handbook No. 17*, Blackwell Scientific Publications, Oxford.

Edwards R. L. (1976) Middle Atlantic fisheries: Recent changes in populations and outlook. In M. G. Gross (ed.), *Middle Atlantic Continental Shelf and the New York Bight*, pp. 302–11. The American Society of Limnology and Oceanography, Special Symposia Vol. 2.

El Sabh M. I. (1974) Transport and currents in the Gulf of St. Lawrence. PhD. Thesis, McGill University, Montreal.

Endean R. (1974) *Acanthaster planci* on the Great Barrier Reef. *Proc. 2nd. int. Symp. Coral Reefs*, **1**, 563–75.

Endean R. (1977) *Acanthaster planci* infestations of reefs of the Great Barrier Reef. *Proc. 3rd int. Symp. Coral Reefs*. **1**, 185–91.

Engleberg J. & Boyarsky L. L. (1979) The noncybernetic nature of ecosystems. *Am. Nat.* **114**, 317–24.

Enright J. T. (1977a) Copepods in a hurry: Sustained high-speed upward migration. *Limnol. Oceanogr.* **22**, 118–25.

Enright J. T. (1977b) Diurnal vertical migration. Adaptive significance and timing. Part 1. Selective advantage: A metabolic model. *Limnol. Oceanogr.* **22**, 856–72.

Enright J. T. & Honegger H. W. (1977) Diurnal vertical migration. Adaptive significance and timing. Part 2. Test of the model: Details of timing. *Limnol. Oceanogr.* **22**, 873–86.

Eppley R. W., Rogers J. N. & McCarthy J. J. (1969) Half-saturation constants for uptake of nitrate and ammonium by marine phytoplankton. *Limnol. Oceanogr.* **14**, 912–20.

Eriksson S., Sellei C. & Wallström K. (1977) The structure of the plankton community of the Öregrundsgrepen (South-west Bosnian Sea). *Helgol. wiss. Meeresunters.* **30**, 582–97.

Estes J. A. & Palmisano J. F. (1974) Sea otters: their role in structuring nearshore communities. *Science* **285**, 1058–60.

Evans P. D. & Mann K. H. (1977) Selection of prey by lobsters (*Homarus americanus*) when offered a choice between sea-urchins and crabs. *J. Fish. Res. Bd. Can.* **34**, 2203–7.

Fankboner P. V. & de Burgh M. E. (1977) Diurnal exudation of ^{14}C-labelled compounds by the large kelp *Macrocystis integrifolia* Bory. *J. exp. mar. Biol. Ecol.* **28**, 151–62.

Fasham M. J. & Pugh P. R. (1976) Observations on the horizontal coherence of chlorophyll *a* and temperature. *Deep-Sea Res.* **23**, 527–38.

Feller R. J. & Kaczynski V. W. (1975) Size selective predation by juvenile chum salmon (*Onchorhynchus chaeta*) on epibenthic prey in Puget Sound. *J. Fish. Res. Bd. Can.* **32**, 1419–29.

Fenchel T. (1969) The ecology of marine microbenthos IV. Structure and function of the benthic ecosystem, its chemical and physical factors and the microfauna communities with special reference to the ciliated protozoa. *Ophelia* **6**, 1–182.

Fenchel T. (1970) Studies on decomposition of organic detritus derived from the turtle grass *Thalassia testudinum*. *Limnol. Oceanogr.* **15**, 14–20.

Fenchel T. (1971) Aspects of decomposer food chains in marine benthos. *Deutsch. Zool. Gesell. Verh.* **65**, 14–23.

Fenchel T. (1972) Aspects of decomposer food chains in marine benthos. *Verh. deutsch. Zool. Gesell.* **65**. *Jahresversamml.* **14**, 14–22.

Fenchel T. (1974) Intrinsic rate of natural increase; the relationship with body size. *Oecologia (Berlin)* **14**, 317–26.

Fenchel T. (1977) Aspects of decomposition of seagrasses. In C. P. McRoy & C. Hellferich (eds.), *Seagrass Ecosystems: a Scientific Perspective*, pp. 123–45. Marcel Dekker, New York.

Fenchel T. M. (1978) The ecology of micro- and meiobenthos. *Ann. Rev. Ecol. Syst.* **9**, 99–121.

Fenchel T. & Harrison P. (1976) The significance of bacterial grazing and mineral cycling for the decomposition of particulate detritus. In J. M. Anderson & A. Macfadyen (eds), *The Role of Terrestrial and Aquatic Organisms in Decomposition Processes*, pp. 285–99. Blackwell Scientific Publications, Oxford.

Fenchel T. & Riedl R. (1971) The sulphide system. A new biotic community underneath the oxidized layer of marine sand-bottom. *Mar. Biol.* **7**, 255–68.

Ferguson R. L. & Rublee P. (1976) Contribution of bacteria to standing crop of coastal plankton. *Limnol. Oceanogr.* **21**, 141–5.

Fiebleman J. K. (1954) Theory of integrative levels. *Brit. J. Phil. Sci.* **5**, 59–66.

Field J. G. (1972) Some observations on the release of dissolved organic carbon by the sea-urchin *Strongylocentrotus droebachiensis*. *Limnol. Oceanogr.* **17**, 759–61.

Field J. G., Jarman N. G., Dieckman G. S., Griffiths C. L., Velimirov B. & Zoutendyk P. (1977) Sun, waves, seaweed and lobsters: The dynamics of a west coast kelp-bed. *South African J. Sci.* **73**, 7–10.

Finn J. T. (1976) Measurement of ecosystem structure and function derived from analysis of flows. *J. theor. Biol.* **41**, 535–46.

Flagg C. N. & Beardsley R. C. (1975) 1974 M.I.T. New England shelf dynamics experiment (March 1974) Part 1: hydrography. *M.I.T. Report* **75**, 1.

Fogg G. E. (1975) Primary productivity. In J. P. Riley & G. Skirrow (eds.), *Chemical Oceanography*, Vol. 2, 2nd edn., pp. 385–453. Academic Press, London.

Fogg G. E., Nalewajko C. & Watt W. D. (1965) Extracellular products of phytoplankton photosynthesis. *Proc. roy. Soc. Lond. B.* **162**, 517–34.

Fong W. C. & Mann K. H. (1980) Role of gut flora in the transfer of amino acids through a marine food chain. *Can. J. Fish. aquat. Sci.* **37**, 88–96.

Foreman R. E. (1977) Benthic community modification and recovery following intensive grazing by *Strongylocentrotus droebachiensis*. *Helgol. wiss. Meeresunters.* **30**, 468–84.

Foulds J. B. & Mann K. H. (1978) Cellulose digestion in *Mysis stenolepis* and its ecological implications. *Limnol. Oceanogr.* **23**, 760–6.

Fournier R. O., Marra J., Bohrer R. & van Det M. (1977) Phytoplankton dynamics and nutrient enrichment of the Scotian Shelf. *J. Fish. Res. Bd. Can.* **34**, 1004–18.

Fournier R. O., van Det M., Wilson J. S. & Hargreaves N. B. (1979) Influence of the shelf-break front off Nova Scotia on phytoplankton standing stock in winter. *J. Fish. Res. Bd. Can.* **36**, 1228–37.

Frankel E. (1977) Previous *Acanthaster* aggregations in the Great Barrier Reef. *Proc. 3rd. int. Coral Reef Symp.* **1**, 201–7.

Fredericks A. D. & Sackett W. M. (1970) Organic carbon in the Gulf of Mexico. *J. geophy. Res.* **75**, 2199–206.

Friedman M. M. & Strickler J. R. (1975) Chemoreceptors and feeding in calanoid copepods (*Arthropoda crustacea*), *Proc. nat. Acad. Sci. U.S.A.* **72**, 4185–8.

Frost B. W. (1975) A threshold feeding behaviour in *Calanus pacificus*. *Limnol. Oceanogr.* **20**, 263–6.

Gagné J. A. & Mann K. H. (1981). Comparison of growth strategy in *Laminaria* populations living under different seasonal patterns of nutrient availability. In T. Levring (ed.), *Proc. 10th int. Seaweed Symp.*, pp. 297–302. Walter de Gruyter, Berlin.

Gallagher J. L., Pfeiffer W. J. & Pomeroy L. R. (1976) Leaching and microbial utilization of disolved organic carbon from leaves of *Spartina alterniflora*. *Estuar. coast. mar. Sci.* **4**, 467–71.

Gardner R. H., O'Neill R. V., Mankin J. B. & Kumar D. (1980) Comparative error analysis of six predator-prey models. *Ecology* **61**, 323–32.

Garside C., Malone T. C., Roels O. A. & Scharfstein B. C. (1976) An evaluation of sewage-derived nutrients and their influences on the Hudson estuary and New York Bight. *Estuar. coast. mar. Sci.* **4**, 282–9.

Gerard V. A. & Mann K. H. (1979) Growth and production of *Laminaria longicruris* (Phaeophyta) populations exposed to different intensities of water movement. *J. Phycol.* **15**, 33–41.

Gerber R. P. & Marshall N. (1974) Ingestion of detritus by the lagoon pelagic community at Eniwetok Atoll. *Limnol. Oceanogr.* **19**, 815–24.

Gerking S. D. (1978) *The Ecology of Fish Production*. Blackwell Scientific Publications, Oxford.

Gerlach S. A. (1971) On the importance of marine meiofauna for benthos communities. *Oecologia (Berlin)* **6**, 176–90.

Gerlach S. A. (1978) Food-chain relationships in subtidal silty sand marine sediments and the role of meiofauna in stimulating bacterial productivity. *Oecologia (Berlin)* **33**, 55–69.

Gessner R. V., Goos R. D. & Sieburth J. McN. (1972) The fungal microcosm of the internodes of *Spartina alterniflora*. *Mar. Biol.* **16**, 269–73.

Gieskes W. W. C., Kraay G. W. & Baars M. A. (1979) Current ^{14}C methods for measuring primary production: gross underestimates in oceanic waters. *Neth. J. Sea Res.* **13**, 58–78.

Glynn P. W. (1973) Aspects of the ecology of coral reefs in the Western Atlantic region. In O. A. Jones & R. Endean (eds), *Biology and Geology of Coral Reefs*, pp. 271–324. Academic Press, New York and London.

Goldman B. & Talbot F. H. (1976) Aspects of ecology of coral reef fishes. In O. A. Jones & R. Endean (eds), *Biology and Geology of Coral Reefs*, Vol. 3, pp. 125–54. Academic Press, New York.

Golley F., Odum H. T. & Wilson R. F. (1962) The structure and metabolism of a Puerto Rican Red Mangrove forest in May. *Ecology* **43**, 9–19.

Gordon M. S. & Kelly H. M. (1962) Primary productivity of an Hawaiian coral reef: A critique of flow respirometry in turbulent waters. *Ecology*. **43**, 473–80.

Gordon D. C. (1970) Some studies on the distribution and composition of particulate organic carbon in the North Atlantic Ocean. *Deep-Sea Res.* **17**, 233–43.

Goreau T. F. (1959) The physiology of skeleton formation in corals. I. A method for measuring the rate of calcium decomposition by corals under different conditions. *Biol. Bull. mar. Biol. Lab. Woods Hole* **116**, 59–75.

Goreau T. F. (1961) On the relation of calcification to primary production in reef-building organisms. In H. M. Lenhoff & W. F. Loomis (eds), *The Biology of Hydra and some other Coelenterates*, pp. 269–85. University of Miami Press, Miami.

Goreau T. F. (1963) Calcium carbonate deposition by coralline algae and corals in relation to their roles as reef-builders. *Ann. N. Y. Acad. Sci.* **109**, 127–67.

Goreau T. F. & Goreau N. I. (1959) The physiology of skeleton formation in corals. II. Calcium deposition by hermatypic corals under various conditions in the reef. *Biol. Bull. mar. Biol. Lab. Woods Hole* **117**, 239–50.

Gosselink J. G. & Kirby C. J. (1974) Decomposition of salt marsh grass *Spartina alterniflora* Loisel. *Limnol. Oceanogr.* **19**, 825–32.

Grant D. A. & Rygh P. R. (1973) *Surveillance of Fishing Activities in the ICNAF areas of Canada's East Coast*. Canada Dept. of Nat. Defence, Commander Maritime Command, MC/ORB report 3/73.

Grassle J. F. (1973) Variety in coral reef communities. In O. A. Jones & P. Endean (eds), *Biology and Geology of Coral Reefs*, *Vol. 2*, pp. 247–70. Academic Press, New York.

Grindley J. R. (1964) Effect of low salinity water on vertical migration of estuarine plankton. *Nature* **203**, 781–2.

Guerinot M. L. (1979) The association of N_2-fixing bacteria with sea-urchins. PhD. Thesis, Dalhousie University, Halifax, Nova Scotia.

Guerinot M. L., Fong W. & Patriquin D. G. (1977) Nitrogen fixation (acetylene reduction) associated with sea-urchins (*Strongylocentrotus droebachiensis*) feeding on seaweeds and eelgrass. *J. Fish. Res. Bd. Can.* **34**, 416–20.

Gulland J. A. (1974) Fishery science and the problems of management. In F. R. Harden Jones (ed.), *Sea Fisheries Research*, pp. 413–29. Elek Science, London.

Gulland J. A. (1978) Fisheries management: new strategies for new conditions. *Trans. Amer. Fish. Soc.* **107**, 1–11.

Haines E. B. (1979) Interactions between Georgia salt-marshes and coastal waters: a changing paradigm. In R. J. Livingston (ed.), *Ecological Processes in Coastal and Marine Systems*, pp. 35–46. Plenum Press, New York.

Haines E., Chalmers A., Hanson R. & Sherr B. (1976) Nitrogen pools and fluxes in a Georgia salt marsh. In M. Wiley (ed.), *Estuarine Processes*, pp. 241–54. Academic Press, New York.

Halfon E. (ed.) (1979) *Theoretical Systems Ecology*. Academic Press, New York.

292 *References*

Hammer W. M. & Carleton J. H. (1979) Copepod swarms: Attributes and role in coral reef ecosystems. *Limnol. Oceanogr.* **24**, 1–14.

Hanson R. B. & Wiebe W. J. (1977) Heterotrophic activity associated with particulate size fractions in a *Spartina* salt-marsh estuary, Sapelo Island, Georgia, USA, and the continental shelf waters. *Mar. Biol.* **42**, 321–30.

Harbison G. R. & McAlister V. L. (1980) Fact and artifact in copepod feeding experiments. *Limnol. Oceanogr.* **25**, 971–81.

Hardy A. C. & Gunther E. R. (1935) The plankton of the South Georgia whaling grounds and adjacent waters, 1926–27. *Discovery Rep.* **11**, 1–456.

Hargrave B. T. (1973) Coupling carbon flow through some pelagic and benthic communities. *J. Fish. Res. Bd. Can.* **30**, 1317–26.

Hargrave B. T. (1975) The importance of total and mixed-layer depth in the supply of organic material to bottom communities. *Symp. Biol. Hung.* **15**, 157–65.

Hargrave B. T. (1976) The central role of invertebrate faeces in sediment decomposition. In J. M. Anderson & A. MacFadyen (eds), *The Role of Terrestrial and Aquatic Organisms in Decomposition Processes*, pp. 301–21. Blackwell Scientific Press, Oxford.

Hargrave B. T. (1980) Factors affecting the flux of organic matter to sediments in a marine bay. In K. R. Tenore & B. C. Coull (eds), *Marine Benthic Dynamics*, pp. 243–63, University of South Carolina Press, Columbia.

Harlin M. M. (1971) Translocation between marine hosts and their epiphytic algae. *Plant Physiol.* **47** (suppl.), 41 (abstract only).

Harris E. (1959) The nitrogen cycle in Long Island Sound. *Bull. Bingham. Oceanogr. Coll.* **15**, 315–23.

Harrison P. G. & Mann K. H. (1975a) Chemical changes during the seasonal cycle of growth and decay in eelgrass (*Zostera marina*) on the Atlantic Coast of Canada. *J. Fish. Res. Bd. Can.* **32**, 615–21.

Harrison P. G. & Mann K. H. (1975b) Detritus formation from eelgrass (*Zostera marina* L.): the relative effects of fragmentation, leaching and decay. *Limnol. Oceanogr.* **20**, 924–34.

Harrison W. G., Azam F., Renger E. H. & Eppley R. W. (1977) Some experiments on phosphate assimilation by coastal marine plankton. *Mar. Biol.* **40**, 9–18.

Hart T. J. & Currie R. I. (1960) The Benguela Current. *Discovery Rev.* **31**, 123–298.

Hartwig E. O. (1976) The impact of nitrogen and phosphorus release from a siliceous sediment on the overlying water. In M. Wiley (ed.), *Estuarine Processes*, pp. 103–17. Academic Press, New York.

Harvey H. W., Cooper L. H. N., Lebour M. V. & Russell F. S. (1935) Plankton production and its control. *J. mar. Biol. Ass. U.K.* **20**, 407–41.

Hatcher B. G. (1977) An apparatus for measuring photosynthesis and respiration of intact large marine algae and comparison of results with those from experiments with tissue segments. *Mar. Biol.* **43**, 381–5.

Hatcher B. G., Chapman A. R. O. & Mann K. H. (1977) An annual carbon budget for the kelp *Laminaria longicruris*. *Mar. Biol.* **44**, 85–96.

Hatcher B. G. & Mann K. H. (1975) Above-ground production of marsh cord grass (*Spartina alterniflora*) near the northern end of its range. *J. Fish. Res. Bd. Can.* **32**, 83–7.

Heald E. J. (1969) The production of organic detritus in a South Florida estuary. PhD. Thesis, University of Miami, Miami.

Heath R. A. (1973) Flushing of coastal embayments by changes in atmospheric conditions. *Limnol. Oceanogr.* **18**, 849–62.

Heinle D. R. & Flemer D. A. (1975) Carbon requirements of a population of the estuarine copepod *Eurytemora affinis*. *Mar. Biol.* **31**, 235–47.

Heinle D. R. & Flemer D. A. (1976) Flows of materials between poorly flooded tidal marshes and an estuary. *Mar. Biol.* **35**, 359–73.

Heinle D. R., Harris R. P., Ustach J. F. & Flemer D. A. (1977) Detritus as food for estuarine copepods. *Mar. Biol.* **40**, 341–53.

Heinsohn G. E., Wake J., Marsh H. & Spain A. V. (1977) The dugong (*Dugong dugong* Müller) in the seagrass system. *Aquaculture* **12**, 235–48.

Hjort J. (1914) Fluctuations in the great fisheries of northern Europe viewed in the light of biological research. *P.-v. Reun. perm. int. Explor. Mer.* **20**, 1–228.

Hobbie J. E. & Lee C. (1980) Microbial production of extracellular material: importance in benthic ecology. In K. R. Tenore & B. C. Coull (eds), *Marine Benthic Dynamics*, pp. 341–6. University of South Carolina Press, Columbia.

Hodgkin E. P. (1978) *Blackwood River Estuary Report No. 1.*, Dept. of Conservation and Environment, Perth, Western Australia.

Holme N. A. & McIntyre A. D. (1971) *Methods for the Study of the Marine Benthos.* Blackwell Scientific Publications, Oxford.

Hoppe H. G. (1978) Relations between active bacteria and heterotrophic potential in the sea. *Neth. J. Sea Res.* **12**, 78–98.

Horne E. P. W., Bowman M. J. & Okubo A. (1978) Crossfrontal mixing and cabbeling. In M. J. Bowman & W. E. Eaaias (eds), *Oceanic Fronts in Coastal Processes*, pp. 105–13. Springer-Verlag, Berlin.

Hughes R. N. (1970) An energy budget for a tidal flat population of the bivalve *Scrobicularia plana* (Da Costa). *J. Anim. Ecol.* **39**, 357–81.

Hughes R. N. (1971a) Ecological energetics of the keyhole limpet *Fissurella barbadensis* Gmelin *J. exp. mar. Biol. Ecol.* **6**, 167–78.

Hughes R. N. (1971b) Ecological energetics of *Nerita* populations on Barbados, West Indies. *Mar. Biol.* **11**, 12–22.

Huston M. (1979) A general hypothesis of species diversity. *Am. Nat.* **113**, 81–101.

Hutchinson G. E. (1961) The paradox of the plankton. *Am. Nat.* **95**, 137–46.

Idyll C. P. (1973) The Anchovy Crisis. *Sci. Am.* **228**. (6), 22–9.

Ikeda T. & Motoda S. (1978) Estimated zooplankton production and their ammonia excretion in the Kuroshio and adjacent seas. *Fishery Bull.* **76**, 357–67.

Ippen A. T. (1966) Sedimentation in estuaries. In A. T. Ippen (ed.), *Estuary and Coastline Hydrodynamics*, pp. 648–72. McGraw-Hill, New York.

Isaacs J. D. (1973) Potential trophic biomasses and trace concentrations in unstructured marine food webs. *Mar. Biol.* **22**, 97–104.

Iturriaga R. & Hoppe H. G. (1977) Observations of heterotrophic activity on photoassimilated organic matter. *Mar. Biol.* **40**, 101–8.

Jackson G. A. (1977) Nutrients and production of giant kelp *Macrocystis pyrifera* off Southern California. *Limnol. Oceanogr.* **22**, 979–95.

Jackson G. A. (1980) Phytoplankton growth and zooplankton grazing in oligotrophic oceans. *Nature* **284**, 439–41.

Jamart B. M., Winter D. F. & Banse K. (1979) Sensitivity analysis of a mathematical model of phytoplankton growth and nutrient distribution in the Pacific Ocean off the North-western US coast. *J. Plankt. Res.* **1**, 267–90.

Jamart B. M., Winter D. F., Banse K., Anderson G. C. & Liam R. K. (1977) A theoretical study of phytoplankton growth and nutrient distribution in the Pacific Ocean off north-western US coast. *Deep-sea Res.* **24**, 753–73.

Jefferies H. P. (1972) Fatty-acid ecology of a tidal marsh. *Limnol. Oceanogr.* **17**, 433–40.

Jefferies R. L. (1972) Aspects of salt-marsh ecology with particular reference to inorganic plant nutrition. In R. S. K. Barnes & J. Green (eds), *The Estuarine Environment*, pp. 61–85. Applied Science Publishers, London.

Johannes R. E. (1965) Influence of marine protozoa on nutrient regeneration. *Limnol. Oceanogr.* **10**, 434–42.

Johannes R. E. (1967) Ecology of organic aggregates in the vicinity of a coral reef. *Limnol. Oceanogr.* **12**, 189–95.

Johannes R. E. (1968) Nutrient regeneration in lakes and oceans. *Adv. Microbiol. Sea* **1**, 203–13.

Johannes R. E. & Tepley L. (1974) Examination of feeding of the reef coral *Porites lobata in situ*, using time lapse photography. *Proc. Second int. Coral Reef Symp.* **1**, 127–31.

Johannes R. E. *et al.* (1972) The metabolism of some coral reef communities: A team study of nutrient and energy flux at Eniwetok. *BioScience* **22**, 541–3.

Johnston C. S. (1969) The ecological distribution and primary production of macrophytic marine algae in the Eastern Canaries. *Int. Rev. ges. Hydrobiol.* **54**, 473–90.

Johnston C. S., Jones R. G. & Hunt R. D. (1977) A seasonal carbon budget for a laminarian population in a Scottish sea-loch. *Helgol. wiss. Meeresunters.* **30**, 527–45.

Joint I. R. (1978) Microbial production of an estuarine mudflat. *Estuar. coast mar. Sci.* **7**, 185–95.

Joiris C. (1977) On the role of heterotrophic bacteria in marine ecosystems: some problems. *Helgol. wiss. Meersunters.* **30**, 611–21.

Jones N. S. (1948) Observations and experiments on the biology of *Patella vulgata* at Port St. Mary, Isle of Man. *Proc. Liverpool Biol. Soc.* **56**, 60–77.

Jones J. A. (1968) Primary productivity of the tropical marine turtlegrass *Thallassia testatudinum* Konig and its epiphytes. PhD. Thesis, University of Miami, Coral Gables, Florida.

Jones K. (1974) Nitrogen fixation in a salt water marsh. *J. Ecol.* **62**, 553–65.

Jones K. & Stewart W. D. P. (1969) Nitrogen turnover in marine and brackish water habitats. 3. The production of extracellular nitrogen by *Calothrix scopulorum*. *J. mar. Biol. Ass. U.K.* **49**, 475–88.

Jones N. S. & Kain J. M. (1967) Subtidal algal colonization following the removal of *Echinus*. *Helgol. wiss. Meeresunters.* **15**, 460–6.

Jones R. (1976) An energy budget for North Sea fish species and its application for fisheries management. *ICES CM 1976, Demersal fish (Northern) Cttee. F.36 (Mimeo)*.

Jones R. & Richards J. (1976) Some observations on the inter-relationships between the major fish species in the North Sea. *ICES CM 1976, Demersal Fish (Northern) Cttee. F : 35 (Mimeo)*.

Jørgenson C. B. (1966) *Biology of Suspension Feeding*. Pergamon Press, Oxford.

Jørgensen B. B. (1977) The sulphur cycle of a coastal marine sediment (Limfjorden, Denmark). *Limnol. Oceanogr.* **22**, 814–32.

Jørgensen B. B. & Fenchel T. (1974) The sulphur cycle of a marine sediment model system. *Mar. Biol.* **24**, 189–201.

Kain J. M. (1966) The role of light in the ecology of *Laminaria hypoborea*. In R. Bainbridge, G. C. Evans & O. Rackman (eds), *Light as an Ecological Factor*, pp. 319–34. Blackwell Scientific Publications, Oxford.

Kamshilov M. M. (1958) Production of *Calanus finmarchicus* (Gunner) in the coastal zone of eastern Murman. *Trudy Murmansk. Biol. Sta.* **4**, 45–55 (in Russian).

Kanwisher J. W. (1966) Photosynthesis and respiration in some seaweeds. In H. Barnes (ed.), *Some Contemporary Studies in Marine Science*, pp. 407–20. Allen and Unwin, London.

Kanwisher J. W. & Wainwright S. A. (1967) Oxygen balance in some reef corals. *Biol. Bull. Woods Hole* **133**, 378–90.

Kay D. G. & Brafield A. E. (1973) The energy relations of the polychaete *Neanthes* (= *Nereis*) *virens* (sars). *J. Anim. Ecol.* **42**, 673–92.

Kerr S. R. (1974) The theory of size distribution in ecological communities. *J. Fish. Res. Bd. Can.* **31**, 1859–62.

Ketchum B. H. (1951) The exchanges of fresh and salt water in tidal estuaries. *J. mar. Res.* **10**, 19–38.

Ketchum B. H. (1967) Phytoplankton nutrients in estuaries. In G. H. Lauff (ed.), *Estuaries*, pp. 329–35. American Association for the Advancement of Science, Washington, D.C.

Khailov K. M. & Burklakova Z. P. (1969) Release of dissolved organic matter by marine seaweeds and distribution of their total organic production to inshore communities. *Limnol. Oceanogr.* **14**, 521–7.

Kierstead H. & Slobodkin L. B. (1953) The size of water masses containing plankton blooms. *J. mar. Res.* **12**, 141–7.

Kikuchi T. (1974) Japanese contributions on consumer ecology in eelgrass (*Zostera marina L.*) beds, with special reference to trophic relations and resources in inshore fisheries. *Aquaculture* **4**, 145–60.

Kikuchi T. & Pérè J. M. (1977) Consumer ecology of seagrass beds. In C. P. McRoy & C. Hellferich (eds), *Seagrass Ecosystems: a Scientific Perspective.* Marcel Dekker, New York.

Kinsey D. W. (1972) Preliminary observations on community metabolism and primary productivity of the pseudo-atoll reef at One Tree Island. In C. Mukedan and C. S. P. Pillai (eds), *Proc. of the Symp. on Corals and Coral Reefs*, pp. 13–32. Mar. Biol. Assoc. India, Cochin.

Kirby-Smith W. W. (1976) The detritus problem and the feeding and digestion of an estuarine organism. In M. Wiley (ed.), *Estuarine Processes*, Vol. 1, pp. 469–79. Academic Press, New York.

Kirkman H. & Reid D. D. (1979) A study of the role of a seagrass *Posidonia australis* in the carbon budget of an estuary. *Aquat. Bot.* **7**(2), 173–83.

Koblentz-Mishke O. J., Volkovinsky V. V. & Kabanova J. G. (1970) Plankton primary production in the world ocean. In W. S. Wooster (ed.), *Scientific Exploration of the South Pacific*, pp. 183–93. Nat. Acad. Sciences, Washington.

Koestler A. (1967) *The Ghost in the Machine.* MacMillan, New York.

Kohn A. J. & Helfrich P. (1957) Primary organic productivity of an Hawaiian coral reef. *Limnol. Oceanogr.* **2**, 241–51.

Kolmogorov A. N. (1941) The local structure of turbulence in an incompressible viscous fluid for very large Reynolds number. *Dokl. Acad. Nauk, U.S.S.R.* **30**, 299–303 (in Russian).

'Korringa P. (1973) The edge of the North Sea as a nursery ground and shellfish area. In E. D. Goldberg (ed.), *North Sea Science*, pp. 361–81. M. I.T. Press, Cambridge, Mass.

Kosiur D. R. & Warford A. L. (1979) Methane production and oxidation in Santa Barbara basin sediments. *Estuar. coast. mar. Sci.* **8**, 379–85.

Kranck K. (1979) Dynamics and distribution of suspended particulate matter in the St. Lawrence estuary. *Naturaliste Can.* **106**, 163–73.

Kremer J. N. & Nixon S. W. (1978) *A Coastal Marine Ecosystem: Simulation and Analysis.* Springer-Verlag, Berlin.

Kristensen J. H. (1972) Carbohydrates of some marine invertebrates with notes on their food and on the natural occurrence of the carbohydrates studied. *Mar. Biol.* **14**, 130–42.

Kuenzler E. J. (1961) Structure and energy flow of a mussel population in a Georgia salt-marsh. *Limnol. Oceanogr.* **6**, 191–204.

Kuenzler E. J. (1974) Mangrove swamp systems. In H. T. Odum, B. J. Copeland & E. A. McMahon (eds), *Coastal Ecological Systems of the United States*, Vol. 1, pp. 346–71. The Conservation Foundation, Washington D.C.

Ladd H. S. (1977) Types of coral reefs, and their distribution. In O. A. Jones & R. Endean (eds), *Biology and Geology of Coral Reefs*, Vol. 4, pp. 1–19. Academic Press, New York.

Laevastu T. & Favorite F. (1976) Dynamics of pollock and herring biomasses in the eastern Bering Sea. *Natl. Mar. Fish. Serv. North-west and Alaska Fish. Center Proc. Rep.* (MS.).

Laevastu T & Favorite F. (1978) The control of pelagic fishery resources in the eastern Bering Sea. *Natl. Mar. Fish. Serv., Northwest and Alaska Fish. Center, Proc. Rep.* (MS.).

Land K. S., Lang J. C. & Smith B. N. (1975) Preliminary observations on the carbon isotopic composition of some reef coral tissues and symbiotic zooxanthellae. *Limnol. Oceanogr.* **20**, 283–7.

Landry M. R. (1976) The structure of marine ecosystems: an alternative. *Mar. Biol.* **35**, 1–7.

Lane P. A. & Levins R. (1977) The dynamics of aquatic systems, II. The effect of nutrient enrichment on model plankton communities. *Limnol. Oceanogr.* **22**, 454–71.

Lange G. D. & Hurley A. C. (1975) A theoretical treatment of unstructured food webs. *Fish. Bull.* **73**, 373–81.

Langmuir I. (1938) Surface motion of water induced by wind. *Science* **87**, 119–23.

Lasker R. (1975) Field criteria for survival of anchovy larvae: The relation between inshore chlorophyll maximum layers and successful first feeding. *Fish. Bull.* **73**, 453–62.

Lasker R. (1978) The relation between oceanographic conditions and larval anchovy food in the California current: Identification of factors contributing to recruitment failure. *Rapp. P, -v Reun. Cons. int. Explor. Mer.* **173**, 212–30.

Lawrence J. M. (1975) On the relationship between marine plants and sea-urchins. *Oceanogr. mar. Biol. Rev.*, **13**, 213–86.

Laycock, R. A. (1974) The detrital food chain on seaweeds. I. Bacteria associated with the surface of *Laminaria* fronds. *Mar. Biol.* **25**, 223–31.

Leach J. H. (1970) Epibenthic production on an intertidal mud flat. *Limnol. Oceanogr.* **4**, 386–97.

Leadbetter M. (1979) Langmuir circulations and plankton patchiness. *Ecol. Modelling* **7**, 289–310.

Leighton D. L. (1971) Grazing activities of benthic invertebrates in Southern California kelp beds. In W. J. North (ed.), *The Biology of Giant Kelp Beds (Macrocystis) in California*, pp. 421–53. *Nova Hedwigia* Suppl. **32**.

Leighton D. L., Jones L. G. & North W. J. (1966) Ecological relationships between giant kelp and sea-urchins in southern California. In E. G. Young & J. L. McLachlan (eds), *Proc. 5th Int. Seaweed Symp.*, pp. 141–53. Pergamon Press, Oxford.

Lehman J. T. (1980) Release and cycling of nutrients between planktonic algae and herbivores. *Limnol. Oceanogr.* **25**, 620–32.

Lett P. F. (1980) The interactions of the recruitment mechanisms of cod and mackerel, and its implications for dual stock management. *Rapp. P.-v. Reun. Cons. int. Explor. Mer.* **177**, 314 (abstr. only).

Lett P. F. & Kohler A. C. (1976) Recruitment: A problem of multispecies interaction and environmental perturbations, with special reference to Gulf of St. Lawrence Atlantic Herring (*Clupea harengus harengus*). *J. Fish. Res. Bd. Can.* **33**, 1353–71.

Lewis J. B. (1977) Processes of organic production on coral reefs. *Biol. Rev.* **52**, 305–47.

LIMER Expedition Team. (1975) Metabolic processes of coral reef communities at Lizard Island, Queensland. *Search* **7**, 463–8.

Lindeman R. L. (1942) The trophic-dynamic aspect of ecology. *Ecology* **23**, 399–418.

Littler M. M. & Murray S. N. (1974) The primary productivity of marine macrophytes from a rocky intertidal community. *Mar. Biol.* **27**, 131–5.

Lock A. R. & McLaren I. A. (1970) The effect of varying and constant temperatures on size of a marine copepod. *Limnol. Oceanogr.* **15**, 638–40.

Longbotton M. R. (1970) The distribution of *Arenicola marina* (L.) with particular reference to the effects of particle size and organic matter of the sediments. *J. exp. Mar. Biol. Ecol.* **5**, 138–57.

Longhurst A. R. (1976) Vertical migration. In D. H. Cushing & J. J. Walsh (eds), *The Ecology of the Seas*, pp. 116–40. Blackwell Scientific Publications, Oxford.

Longhurst A. R. (1978) Ecological models in estuarine management. *Ocean Management* **4**, 287–302.

Longstreth D. J. & Strain B. R. (1977) Effects of salinity and illumination on photosynthesis and water balance of *Spartina alterniflora* Loisel. *Oecologia (Berlin)* **31**, 191–9.

Lopez G. R. & Levinton J. S. (1978) The availability of micro-organisms attached to sediment particles as food for *Hydrobia ventrosa* Montagu (Gastropoda: Prosobranchia). *Oecologia (Berlin)*, **32**, 263–75.

Lorenzen C. J. (1966) A method for the continuous measurement of *in vivo* chlorophyll concentration. *Deep-Sea Res.* **13**, 223–7.

Lorenzen C. J. (1971) Continuity in the distribution of surface chlorophyll. *J. Cons. int. Explor. Mer.* **34**, 18–23.

Lotka A. J. (1925) *Elements of Physical Biology*. Williams and Wilkins, Baltimore.

Lowry L. F. & Pearse J. S. (1973) Abalones and sea-urchins in an area inhabited by sea otters. *Mar. Biol.* **23**, 213–9.

Lugo A. E. & Snedaker S. C. (1974) The ecology of mangroves. *Ann. Rev. Ecol. Syst.* **5**, 39–64.

Lugo A. E., Sell M. & Snedaker S. C. (1976) Mangrove ecosystem analysis. In B. C. Pattern (ed.), *Systems Analysis and Simulation in Ecology*, Vol. 4, pp. 114–45. Academic Press, New York.

Lüning K. (1969) Growth of amputated and dark-exposed individuals of the brown alga *Laminaria hypoborea*. *Mar. Biol.* **2**, 218–23.

Lüning K. (1971) Seasonal growth of *Laminaria hypoborea* under recorded underwater light conditions near Helgoland. In D. J. Crisp (ed.), *Proc. 4th Europ. mar. Biol. Symp.*, pp. 347–61. Cambridge University Press, Cambridge.

McAllister C. D. (1969) Aspects of estimating zooplankton production from phytoplankton production. *J. Fish. Res. Bd. Can.* **26**, 199–220.

McAllister C. D. (1970) Zooplankton rations, phytoplankton mortality, and the estimation of marine production. In J. H. Steele (ed.), *Marine Food Chains*, pp. 419–57. Oliver and Boyd, Edinburgh.

McAllister C. D. (1971) Some aspects of nocturnal and continuous grazing by planktonic herbivores in relation to production studies. *Tech. Rep. Fish. Res. Bd. Can.* **248**, 1–281.

McCarthy J. J. & Goldman J. C. (1979) Nitrogenous nutrition of marine phytoplankton in nutrient-depleted waters. *Science* **203**, 670–2.

McCarthy J. J., Taylor W. R. & Loftus M. E. (1974) Significance of nanoplankton in the Cheaspeake Bay estuary and problems associated with measurement of nanoplankton productivity. *Mar. Biol.* **24**, 7–16.

McHugh J. L. (1976) Estuarine fisheries: are they doomed? In M. Wiley (ed.), *Estuarine Processes*, Vol. 1, pp. 15–27. Academic Press, New York.

McIntyre A. D. (1969) Ecology of marine meiobenthos. *Biol. Rev.* **44**, 245–90.

MacIsaac J. J. & Dugdale R. C. (1969) The kinetics of nitrate and ammonium uptake by natural population of marine phytoplankton. *Deep-Sea Res.* **16**, 47–57.

McLaren I. A. (1963) Effects of temperature on growth of zooplankton, and the adaptive value of vertical migration. *J. Fish. Res. Bd. Can.* **26**, 199–220.

McLaren I. A. (1974) Demographic strategy of vertical migration by a marine copepod. *Am. Nat.* **108**, 91–102.

MacNae W. (1968) A general account of the fauna and flora of mangrove swamps and forests in the Indo-West-Pacific Region. *Adv. mar. Biol.* **6**, 73–270.

McNeill S. & Lawton J. H. (1970) Annual production and respiration in animal populations. *Nature (London)* **225**, 472–4.

McRoy C. P. & Barsdate R. J. (1970) Phosphate absorption in eelgrass. *Limnol. Oceanogr.* **15**, 6–13.

McRoy C. P., Barsdate R. J. & Nebert M. (1972) Phosphorus cycling in eelgrass (*Zostera marina* L.) ecosystem. *Limnol. Oceanogr.* **17**, 58–67.

McRoy C. P. & Goering J. J. (1974) Nutrient transfer between the seagrass *Zostera marina* and its epiphytes. *Nature* **248**, 173–4.

McRoy C. P., Goering J. J. & Chaney B. (1973) Nitrogen fixation associated with seagrasses. *Limnol. Oceanogr.* **18**, 998–1002.

298 *References*

McRoy C. P. & Helfferich C. (1977) *Seagrass Ecosystems: a Scientific Perspective.* Marcel Dekker, New York.

Malone T. C. (1971) The relative importance of nannoplankton and net-plankton as primary producers in tropical oceanic and neritic plankton communities. *Limnol. Oceanogr.* **16**, 633–9.

Malone T. C. (1976) Phytoplankton productivity in the apex of the New York Bight: Environmental regulation of productivity/chlorophyll *a. Am. Soc. Limnol. Oceanogr. Spec. Symp.* **2**, 260–72.

Mann K. H. (1969) The dynamics of aquatic ecosystems. *Adv. ecol. Res.* **6**, 1–81.

Mann K. H. (1972) Case history: River Thames. In R. T. Oglesby, C. A. Carson & J. A. McCann (eds), *River Ecology and Man*, pp. 215–32. Academic Press, New York.

Mann K. H. (1972a) Ecological energetics of the seaweed zone in a marine bay on the Atlantic Coast of Canada. I. Zonation and biomass of seaweeds. *Mar. Biol.* **12**, 1–10.

Mann K. H. (1972b) Ecological energetics of the seaweed zone in a marine bay on the Atlantic coast of Canada. II. Productivity of the seaweeds. *Mar. Biol.* **14**, 199–209.

Mann K. H. (1975) Relationship between morphometry and biological functioning in three coastal inlets of Nova Scotia. In L. E. Cronin (ed.), *Estuarine Research*, Vol. 1, pp. 634–44. Academic Press, New York.

Mann K. H. (1976) Production on the bottom of the sea. In D. H. Cushing & J. J. Walsh, *The Ecology of the Seas*, pp. 225–50. Blackwell Scientific Publications, Oxford.

Mann K. H. (1977) Destruction of kelp beds by sea-urchins: Cyclic phenomenon or irreversible degradation? *Helgol. wiss. Meeresunders.* **30**, 455–67.

Mann K. H. (1978) Predicting the food consumption of fish. In S. D. Gerking (ed.), *The Ecology of Freshwater Fish Production*, pp. 250–73. Blackwell Scientific Publications, Oxford.

Mann K. H. (1979) Nitrogen limitations on the productivity of *Spartina* marshes, *Laminaria* kelp beds and higher trophic levels. In R. L. Jefferies & A. J. Davy (eds), *Ecological Processes on Coastal Environments*, pp. 363–70. Blackwell Scientific Publications, Oxford.

Mann K. H., Jarman N. & Dieckman G. (1979) Development of a method for measuring the productivity of the kelp *Ecklonia maxima* (Osbeck) Papenf. *Trans. roy. Soc. S. Afr.* **44**, 27–41.

Mann K. H. & Kirkman H. (1981) Biomass method for measuring productivity of *Ecklonia radiata* with the potential for adaptation to other large brown algae. *Aust. J. mar. freshwat. Res.* **32**, 279–304.

Margalel R. (1967) El ecosistema. In *Ecologia marina.* **14**, 377–453. Foundation la salle de ciencias naturales, Caracas.

Margalef R. (1968) *Perspectives in Ecological Theory.* University of Chicago Press, Chicago.

Marr J. C. (1960) The causes of major variations in the catch of the Pacific sardine (*Sardinops caerulea*) Dirard. In H. Rosa & G. Murphy (eds), *Proc. World Scientific Meeting on the Biol. Sardines and Related Species*, Vol. 3, pp. 667–791. FAO, Rome.

Marsh J. A. (1970) Primary productivity of reef-building calcareous red algae. *Ecology* **51**, 255-63.

Marsh J. A. (1974) Preliminary observations on the productivity of a Guam reef flat community. In A. M. Cameron, B. M. Campbell, A. B. Cribb, R. Endean, J. S. Jell, O. A. Jones, P. Mather & F. H. Talbot (eds), *Proc. 2nd int. Symp. on Coral Reefs*, Vol. 1, pp. 139–45. The Great Barrier Reef Committee, Brisbane.

Marshall N., Durbin A. G., Gerber R. & Telek G. (1975) Observations on particulate and dissolved organic matter in coral reef areas. *Int. Rev. ges. Hydrobiol.* **60**, 335–45.

Marshall N., Oviatt C. A. & Skauen D. M. (1971) Productivity of the benthic microflora of shoal estuarine environments of Southern New England. *Int. Rev. ges. Hydrobiol. Hydrogr.* **56**, 947–56.

Martin J. H. (1968) Phytoplankton–zooplankton relations in Naragansett Bay. III. Seasonal changes in zooplankton excretion rates in relation to phytoplankton abundance. *Limnol. Oceanogr.* **13**, 63–71.

Massalski A. & Leppard G. G. (1979) Morphological examination of fibrillar colloids associated with algae and bacteria in lakes. *J. Fish. Res. Bd. Can.* **36**, 922–38.

Mattison J. E., Trent J. D., Shanks A. L. & Pearse J. S. (1977) Movement and feeding activity of red sea-urchins. (*Strongylocentrotus franciscianus*) adjacent to a kelp forest. *Mar. Biol.* **39**, 25–30.

Menge B. A. & Sutherland J. P. (1976) Species diversity gradients: synthesis of the roles of predation, competition and temporal heterogeneity. *Am. Nat.* **110**, 351–69.

Methot R. D. & Kramer D. (1979) Growth of Northern Anchovy, *Engraulis mordax*, larvae in the sea. *Fish. Bull.* **77**, 413–23.

Meyers S. P. (1974) Contribution of fungi to biodegradation of *Spartina* and other brackish marshland vegetation. *Veröff. Inst. Meeresforsch. Bremerh.* Suppl. **5**, 357–75.

Michanek G. (1975) *Seaweed Resources of the Ocean.* FAO, Rome.

Miller P. C. (1972) Bioclimate, leaf temperature, and primary production in red mangrove canopies in South Florida. *Ecology* **53**, 22–45.

Miller R. J. & Mann K. H. (1973) Ecological energetics of the seaweed zone in a marine bay on the Atlantic coast of Canada III. Energy transformations by sea-urchins. *Mar. Biol.* **18**, 99–114.

Miller R. J., Mann K. H. & Scarratt D. J. (1971) Production potential of a seaweed–lobster community in Eastern Canada. *J. Fish. Res. Bd. Can.* **28**, 1733–8.

Milliman J. D. (1974) *Marine Carbonates.* Springer-Verlag, New York.

Mills E. L. (1969) The community concept in marine zoology, with comments on continua and instability in some marine communities: A review. *J. Fish. Res. Bd. Can.* **26**, 1415–28.

Mills E. L. (1975) Benthic organisms and the structure of marine ecosystems. *J. Fish. Res. Bd. Can.* **32**, 1657–63.

Mills E. L. (1980) *The Structure and Dynamics of Shelf and Slope Ecosystems off the North-east Coast of North America.* Belle W. Baruch Library Mar. Sci., Univ. S. Carolina Press.

Mills E. L. & Fournier R. O. (1979) Fish production and the marine ecosystems of the Scotian Shelf, Eastern Canada. *Mar. Biol.* **54**, 101–8.

Moebus K. & Johnson K. H. (1974) Exudation of dissolved organic carbon by brown algae. *Mar. Biol.* **26**, 117–25.

Moiseev P. A. (1971) *The Living Resources of the World Ocean.* (Transl. from Russian by Israel Programme for Scientific Translations.) National Science Foundation, Washington D.C.

Mooers C. N. K., Flagg C. N. & Boicourt W. C. (1978) Prograde and retrograde fronts. In M. J. Bowman & W. E. Esaias (eds), *Oceanic Fronts in Coastal Processes*, pp. 43–58. Springer-Verlag, Berlin.

Mooring M. T., Cooper A. W. & Seneca E. D. (1971) Seed germination response and evidence for height ecophenes in *Spartina alterniflora* from North Carolina. *Amer. J. Bot.* **58**, 48–55.

Morantz D. (1976) Productivity and export from a marsh with a 15 m tidal range, and the effect of impoundment of selected areas. M. Sc. Thesis, Dalhousie University, Halifax, Canada.

Moriarty D. J. W. (1976) Quantitative studies on bacteria and algae in the food of the mullet *Mugil cephalus* L. and the prawn *Matapenaeus bennettae* (Racek and Dall). *J. exp. mar. Biol. Ecol.* **22**, 131–43.

Moriarty D. J. W. (1977) Quantification of carbon, nitrogen, and bacterial biomass in the food of some penaeid prawns. *Aust. J. mar. freshwat. Res.* **28**, 113–18.

Moriarty D. J. W. (1979) Biomass of suspended bacteria over coral reefs. *Mar. Biol.* **53**, 193–200.

Morita R. Y. (1977) The role of microorganisms in the environment. In N. R. Anderson & B. J. Zahuranec (eds), *Oceanic Sound Scattering Prediction*, pp. 445–55. Plenum Press, New York.

Morris R. F. (1959) Single-factor analysis in population dynamics. *Ecology* **40**, 580–8.

Muir L. (1979) Internal tides in the middle estuary of the St. Lawrence. *Naturaliste Can.* **106**, 27–36.

Mulholland R. J. & Simms G. S. (1976) Control theory and the regulation of ecosystems. In B. C. Patten (ed.), *Systems Analysis and Simulation in Ecology*, pp. 373–89. Academic Press, New York.

Mullin M. M. & Brooks E. R. (1970) Production of the planktonic copepod *Calanus helgolandicus. Bull. Scripps. Inst. Oceanogr.* **17**, 89–103.

Mullin M. M. & Brooks E. R. (1976) Some consequences of distributional heterogeneity of phytoplankton and zooplankton. *Limnol. Oceanogr.* **21**, 784–96.

Mullin M. M., Stewart E. F. & Fuglister F. J. (1975) Ingestion by planktonic grazers as a function of concentration of food. *Limnol. Oceanogr.* **20**, 259–62.

Murphy G. I. (1966) Population biology of the Pacific sardine (*Sardinops caerulea*). *Proc. calif. Acad. Sci.* **34**, 1–84.

Muscatine L. (1973) Nutrition of corals. In O.A. Jones & R. Endean (eds), *Biology and Geology of Coral Reefs*, Vol. 2, pp. 77–115. Academic Press, New York.

Muscatine L. & Cernichiara E. (1969) Assimilation of photosynthetic products of zooxanthellae by a reef coral. *Biol. Bull.* **137**, 506–23.

Muscatine L. & Porter J. W. (1977) Reef Corals: Mutualistic symbioses adapted to nutrient-poor environments. *BioScience* **27**, 454–60.

Naiman R. J. & Sibert J. R. (1979) Detritus and juvenile salmon production in the Nanaimo estuary. III. Importance of detrital carbon to the estuarine ecosystem. *J. Fish. Res. Bd. Can.* **36**, 504–20.

Nestler J. (1977) Interstitial salinity as a cause of ecophenic variation in *Spartina alterniflora. Estuar. coast. mar. Sci.* **5**, 707–14.

Neushul M. (1972) Functional interpretation of benthic marine algal morphology. In I. A. Abbott & M. Kurogi (eds), *Contributions to the Systematics of Benthic Algae in the North Pacific*, pp. 47–72. Japanese Society of Phycology, Tokyo.

Newell R. C. (1965) The role of detritus in the nutrition of two marine deposit feeders, the prosobranch *Hydrobia ulvae* and the bivalve *Macoma balthica. Proc. zool. Soc. Lond.* **144**, 25–45.

Niemeck R. A. & Mathieson A. C. (1976) An ecological study of *Fucus spiralis* L. *J. exp. mar. Biol. Ecol.* **24**, 33–48.

Nihoul J. C. L., Ronday F. C., Smitz J. & Billen G. (1979) Hydrodynamic and water quality model of the Scheldt Estuary. In R. F. Dame (ed.), *Marsh–Estuarine Systems Simulation*, pp. 71–82. Univ. of South Carolina Press, Columbia, South Carolina.

Nixon S. W. & Oviatt C. A. (1973) Ecology of a New England salt-marsh. *Ecol. Monogr.* **43**, 463–98.

Nixon S. W., Oviatt C. A. & Hale S. S. (1976) Nitrogen regeneration and the metabolism of coastal marine bottom communities. In J. M. Anderson & A. MacFadyen (eds), *The Role of Terrestrial and Aquatic Organisms in Decomposition Processes*, pp. 269–83. Blackwell Scientific Publications, Oxford.

Odum E. P. (1969) The strategy of ecosystem development. *Science* **164**, 262–76.

Odum E. P. (1971) *Fundamentals of Ecology*, 3rd edn. W. B. Saunders, Philadelphia.

Odum E. P. (1974) Halophytes, energetics and ecosystems. In R. J. Reinold & W. H. Queen (eds), *Ecology of Halophytes*, pp. 599–602. Academic Press, New York.

Odum E. P. & de la Cruz A. A. (1967) Particulate organic detritus in a Georgia salt-marsh-estuarine ecosystem. In G. H. Lauff (ed.), *Estuaries*, pp. 383–8. Amer. Assoc. for the Adv. of Sci., Washington.

Odum E. P. & Fanning M. E. (1973) Comparisons of the productivity of *Sparting alterniflora* and *S. cynosuroides* in Georgia coastal marshes. *Bull. Georgia Acad. Sci.* **31**, 1–12.

Odum E. P. & Smalley A. E. (1959) Comparison of population energy flow of a herbivorous and deposit-feeding invertebrate in a salt-marsh ecosystem. *Proc. Nat. Acad. Sci. USA.* **45**, 617–22.

Odum H. T. (1957) Primary production measurements in eleven Florida springs and a marine turtle grass community. *Limnol. Oceanogr.* **3**, 85–97.

Odum H. T., Burkholder P. R. & Rivero J. (1959) Measurements of productivity of turtle grass flats, reefs and the Bahia Fosforescente of Southern Puerto Rico. *Publications of the Inst. of Mar. Sci. Univ. of Texas* **6**, 159–70.

Odum H. T. & Hoskin C. M. (1958) Comparitive studies on the metabolism of marine waters. *Publications of the Inst. of Mar. Sci. Univ. of Texas* **5**, 16–46.

Odum H. T. & Odum E. P. (1955) Trophic structure and productivity of a windward reef coral community on Eniwetok Atoll. *Ecol. Monogr.* **25**, 291–320.

Odum W. E. & Heald E. J. (1975) The detritus-based food web of an estuarine mangrove community. In L. E. Cronin (ed.), *Estuarine Research*, Vol. 1, pp. 265–86. Academic Press, New York.

Ogden J. C., Brown R. A. & Salesky N. (1973) Grazing by the echinoid *Diadema antillarum* Philippi: Formation of halos round West Indian patch reefs. *Science (New York)* **182**, 715–17.

Ogden J. C. & Lobel P. S. (1978) The role of herbivorous fishes and urchins in coral reef communities. *Env. Biol. Fish.* **3**, 49–63.

O'Neill R. V., Gardner R. H. & Mankin J. B. (1980) Analysis of parameter error in a nonlinear model. *Ecological Modelling*, **8**, 297–311.

Orme G. R. (1977) Aspects of sedimentation in the coral reef environment. In O. A. Jones & R. Endean (eds), *Biology and Geology of Coral Reefs*, Vol. 4, pp. 129–82. Academic Press, New York.

Overton W. S. (1977) A strategy of model construction. In C.A.S. Hall & J. W. Day (eds), *Ecosystem Modelling in Theory and Practice*, pp. 49–73. John Wiley, New York.

Paerl H. W. (1974) Bacterial uptake of dissolved organic matter in relation to detrital aggregation in marine and freshwater systems. *Limnol. Oceanogr.* **19**, 966–72.

Paerl H. W. (1978) Microbial organic carbon recovery in aquatic ecosystems. *Limnol. Oceanogr.* **23**, 927–35.

Paine R. T. (1971) Energy flow in a natural population of the herbivorous gastropod *Tegula funebralis. Limnol. Oceanogr.* **16**, 86–98.

Paine R. T. (1974) Intertidal community structure: experimental studies on the relationship between a dominant competitor and its principal predator. *Oecologia (Berlin)* **15**, 93–120.

Paine R. T. (1977) Controlled manipulations in the marine intertidal zone, and their contributions to ecological theory. In C. E. Goulden (ed.), *The Changing Scenes in Natural Sciences, 1776–1976*, pp. 245–70. Acad. of Nat. Sci. Spec. Publ. 12, Philadelphia.

Paine R. T. & Vadas R. L. (1969) The effects of grazing by sea-urchins *Strongylocentrotus* spp. on benthic algal populations. *Limnol. Oceanogr.* **14**, 710–9.

Palumbo A. V. & Ferguson R. L. (1978) Distribution of suspended bacteria in the Newport River Estuary, North Carolina. *Estuar. coast. mar. Sci.* **7**, 521–9.

Pamatmat M. M. (1971) Oxygen consumption by the sea bed. VI. Seasonal cycle of chemical oxidation and respiration in Puget Sound. *Int. Rev. ges. Hydrobiol.* **56**, 769–93.

Parke M. (1948) Studies on British Laminariaceae. I. Growth in *Laminaria saccharina* (L.) Lamour. *J. mar. Biol. Ass. U.K.* **27**, 651–709.

Parker R. R., Sibert J. & Brown T. J. (1975) Inhibition of primary productivity through heterotrophic competition for nitrate in a stratified estuary. *J. Fish. Res. Bd. Can.* **32**, 72–7.

Parsons T. R. (1975) Particulate organic carbon in the sea. In J. P. Riley & G. Skirrow (eds), *Chemical Oceanography*, Vol. 2, 2nd edn., pp. 365–83. Academic Press, London.

Parsons T. R., Le Brasseur R. J. & Barraclough W. E. (1970) Levels of production in the pelagic environment of the Straits of Georgia, British Columbia: a review. *J. Fish. Res. Bd. Can.* **27**, 1251–64.

Parsons T. R. & Takahashi M. (1973) Environmental control of phytoplankton cell size. *Limnol. Oceanogr.* **18**, 511–25.

Parsons T. R., Takahashi M. & Hargrave B. T. (1977) *Biological Oceanographic Processes.* 2nd edn. Pergamon Press, Oxford.

Patriquin D. G. (1972) The origin of nitrogen and phosphorus for growth of the marine angiosperm *Thalassia testudinum. Mar. Biol.* **15**, 35–46.

Patriquin D. G. (1978) Nitrogen fixation (acetylene reduction) associated with cord grass *Spartina alterniflora* Loisel. *Ecol. Bull. (Stockholm)* **26**, 20–7.

Patriquin D. G. & Knowles R. (1972) Nitrogen fixation in the rhizosphere of marine angiosperms. *Mar. Biol.* **16**, 49–58.

Patriquin D. G. & McLung C. R. (1978) Nitrogen accretion, and the nature and possible significance of N_2 fixation (Acetylene reduction) in a Nova Scotian *Spartina alterniflora* stand. *Mar. Biol.* **47**, 227–42.

Patte H. H. (ed.) (1973) *Hierarchy Theory.* George Braziller, New York.

Patten B. C. & Finn J. T. (1979) Systems approach to continental shelf ecosystems. In E. Halfon (ed.), *Theoretical Systems Ecology,* pp. 184–212. Academic Press, New York.

Paulik G. K. (1971) Anchovies, birds and fisherman in the Peru current. In W. W. Murdoch (ed.), *Environment,* pp. 156–85. Conn. Sinauer Associates, Stamford.

Pearse J. S., Clark M. E., Leighton D. L., Mitchell C. T. & North W. J. (1970) *Kelp Habitat Improvement Project, 1969–1970.* California Inst. of Technology, Los Angeles.

Pearse V. B. & Muscatine L. (1971) Role of symbiotic algae (Zooxanthallae) on coral calcification. *Biol. Bull. mar. Biol. Woods Hole* **141**, 350–63.

Pearson T. H. & Rosenberg R. (1978) Macrobenthic succession in relation to organic enrichment and pollution of the marine environment. *Oceanogr. mar. Biol. Ann. Rev.* **16**, 229–311.

Penhale P. A. (1977) Macrophyte–epiphyte biomass and productivity in an eelgrass (*Zostera marine* L) community. *J. exp. mar. Biol. Ecol.* **26**, 211–24.

Peterman R. M. (1978) Testing for density-dependent marine survival in Pacific salmonids. *J. Fish. Res. Bd. Can.* **35**, 1434–50.

Peterson C. H. (1979) Predation, competitive exclusion, and diversity in the soft-sediment benthic communities of estuaries and lagoons. In R. J. Livingston (ed.), *Ecological Processes in Coastal and Marine Systems,* pp. 233–64. Plenum Press, New York.

Phillips R. C. (1974) Temperate grass flats. In H. T. Odum, B. J. Copeland & E. A. McMahan (eds), *Coastal Ecological Systems of the United States,* Vol. 2, pp. 244–99. Conservation Foundation, Washington, DC.

Phleger C. F. (1971) Effect of salinity on growth of a salt marsh grass. *Ecology* **52**, 908–11.

Pigott C. D. (1968) Influence of mineral nutrition on the zonation of flowering plants in coastal marshes. In I. H. Rorison (ed.), *Ecological Aspects of Mineral Nutrition of Plants,* pp. 25–35. Blackwell Scientific Publications, Oxford.

Pilson M. E. Q. & Betzer S. B. (1973) Phosphorus flux across a coral reef. *Ecology* **54**, 581–8.

Pilson M. E. Q. & Nixon S. W. (1980) Marine microcosms in ecological research. In J. P. Geisy (ed.), *Microcosms in Ecological Research,* pp. 724–40. Technical Information Center, U.S. Dept. of Energy, Washington, DC.

Pingree R. D., Bowman M. J. & Esaias W. E. (1978) Headland fronts. In M. J. Bowman & W. E. Esaias (eds), *Oceanic Fronts in Coastal Processes,* pp. 78–86. Springer-Verlag, Berlin.

Platt T. (1972) Local phytoplankton abundance and turbulence. *Deep-Sea Res.,* **19**, 183–7.

Platt T. & Denman K. L. (1975) A general equation for the mesoscale distribution of phytoplankton in the sea. *Mem. Soc. R. Sci. Liège* 6e Ser **7**, 31–42.

Platt T. & Denman K. (1977) Organization in the pelagic ecosystem. *Helgo. wiss. Meeresunters.* **30**, 575–81.

Platt T. & Denman K. (1980) Patchiness in phytoplankton distribution. In I. Morris (ed.) *The Ecology of Phytoplankton,* pp. 413–31. Blackwell Scientific Publications, Oxford.

Platt T. & Irwin B. (1971) Primary productivity measurements in St. Margaret's Bay, 1968–70. *Fish. Res. Bd. Can. Tech. Rep.*, **203**.

Platt T. & Jassby A. D. (1976) The relationship between photosynthesis and light for natural assemblages of coastal marine phytoplankton. *J. Phycol.* **12**, 421–30.

Platt T. Mann, K. H. & Ulanowicz R. E. (eds), (1981) *Mathematical Models in Biological Oceanography.* UNESCO, Paris.

Platt T., Prakash A. & Irwin B. (1972) Phytoplankton nutrients and flushing of inlet on the coast of Nova Scotia. *Naturaliste Can.* **99**, 253–61.

Platt T. & Subba Rao D. V. (1970) Primary production measurements on a natural plankton bloom. *J. Fish. Res. Bd. Can.* **27**, 887–99.

Platt T. & Subba Rao D. V. (1975) Primary production of marine microphytes. In Cooper J. P. (ed.), *Photosynthesis and Productivity in Different Environments*, International Biological Programme, Vol. 3, pp. 249–80. Cambridge University Press, Cambridge.

Platt T., Subba Rao D. V. & Denman K. L. (1977) Quantitative stimulation of phytoplankton productivity by deep water admixture in a coastal inlet. *Estuar. coast. mar. Sci.* **5**, 567–73.

Pomeroy L. R. (1959) Algal productivity in salt-marshes of Georgia. *Limnol. Oceanogr.* **4**, 386–97.

Pomeroy L. R. (1974) The ocean's food web, a changing paradigm. *BioScience* **24**, 499–504.

Pomeroy L. R. (1979) Secondary production mechanisms of continental shelf communities. In P. J. Livingston (ed.), *Ecological Processes in Coastal and Marine Systems*, pp. 163–86. Plenum Press, New York.

Pomeroy L. R. & Deibel D. (1980) Aggregation of organic matter by pelagic tunicates. *Limnol. Oceanogr.* **25**, 645–54.

Pomeroy L. R. & Johannes R. E. (1966) Total plankton respiration. *Deep-Sea Res.* **13**, 971–3.

Pomeroy L. R. & Johannes R. E. (1968) Occurrence and respiration of ultraplankton in the upper 500 meters of the ocean. *Deep-Sea Res.* **15**, 381–91.

Popper K. (1963) *Conjectures and Refutations: The Growth of Scientific Knowledge.* Harper and Row, New York.

Porter J. W. (1974) Zooplankton feeding by the Caribbean reef-building coral *Montastrea cavernosa. Proc. 2nd int. Coral Reef Sympos.* **1**, 111–25.

Porter J. W. (1976) Autotrophy heterotrophy and resource partitioning in Caribbean reef-building corals. *Am. Nat.* **110**, 731–42.

Postgate J. R. (1971) Relevant aspects of the physiological chemistry of nitrogen fixation. In D. E. Hughes & A. H. Rose (eds), *Microbes and Biological Productivity*, Vol. 21, pp. 287–307. Cambridge University Press, London.

Potter J. H. (1973) Management of the tidal Thames. In A. L. H. Gameson (ed.), *Mathematical and Hydraulic Modelling of Estuarine Pollution.* HMSO, London.

Poulet S. A. (1978) Comparison between five coexisting species of marine copepods feeding on naturally occurring particulate matter. *Limnol. Oceanogr.* **23**, 1126–43.

Prinslow T. E., Valiela I. & Teal J. M. (1974) The effect of detritus and ration size on the growth of *Fundulus heteroclitus* (L). *J. exp. mar. Biol.* **16**, 1–10.

Pritchard D. W. (1967) What is an estuary: Physical viewpoint. In G. H. Lauff (ed.), *Estuaries*, pp. 3–5. *Amer. Assoc. for the Adv. of Sci.*, Washington, D.C.

Pritchard D. W. & Carter H. H. (1971) Estuaries and Estuarine Sedimentation. In Schubel J. R. (ed.), *The Estuarine Environment*, pp. IV-1 to IV-17. Amer. Geol. Inst. *Short Course Lect. Notes*, Washington, DC.

Qasim S. Z. & Bhattathiri P. M. A. (1971) Primary production of a seagrass bed on Kavaratti Atoll (Laccadives). *Hydrobiologia* **38**, 29–38.

Qasim S. Z. & Sankaranarayanan V. N. (1970) Production of particulate organic matter by the reef on Kavaratti Atoll (Laccadives). *Limnol. Oceanogr.* **15**, 574–8.

Qasim S. Z. & Sankaranarayanan V. N. (1972) Organic detritus of a tropical estuary. *Mar. Biol.* **15**, 193–9.

Ramus J., Beale A. I., Mauzerall D. & Howard K. L. (1976a) Changes in photosynthetic pigment concentration in seaweeds as a function of water depth. *Mar. Biol.* **37**, 223–9.

Ramus J., Beale S. I. & Mauzerall D. (1976b) Correlation of changes in pigment content with photosynthetic capacity of seaweeds as a function of water depth. *Mar. Biol.* **37**, 231–8.

Ranwell D. S. (1961) *Spartina* marshes in Southern England. 1. The effects of sheep grazing at the upper limits of *Spartina* marsh in Bridgwater Bay. *J. Ecol.* **49**, 325–40.

Ranwell D. S. & Downing B. M. (1959) Brent goose (*Branta bernicula* (L)) winter feeding pattern and *Zostera* resources at Scolt Head Island, Norfolk. *Anim. Behav.* **7**, 42–56.

Resmussen E. (1977) The wasting disease of eelgrass (*Zostera marina*) and its effects on environmental factors and fauna. In C. P. McRoy & C. Helfferich (eds), *Seagrass Ecosystems*, pp. 1–51. Marcel Dekker, New York.

Raymont J. E. G. (1963) *Plankton and Productivity in the Oceans.* Pergamon Press, Oxford.

Redfield A. C. (1972) Development of a New England salt-marsh. *Ecol. Monogr.* **42**, 201–37.

Redfield A. C., Ketchum B. H. & Richards F. A. (1963) The influence of organisms on the composition of seawater. In M. N. Hill (ed.), *The Sea*, Vol. 2, pp. 26–77. Wiley-Interscience, New York.

Reiswig H. M. (1971) Particle feeding in natural populations of three marine demosponges. *Biol. Bull.* **141**, 568–91.

Rhoads D. C. (1973) The influence of deposit-feeding benthos on water turbidity and nutrient cycling. *Am. J. Sci.* **273**, 1–22.

Rhoads D. C. (1974) Organism–sediment relations on the muddy sea floor. *Oceanogr. mar. Biol. Ann. Rev.* **12**, 263–300.

Rhoads D. C. & Young D. K. (1970) The influence of deposit-feeding organisms on sediment stability and community trophic structure. *J. mar. Res.* **28**, 150–78.

Rhoads D. C. & Young D. K. (1971) Animal–sediment relationships in Cape Cod Bay, Massachusetts. II. Reworking by *Molpadia oolitica* (Holothuroidea). *Mar. Biol.* **11**, 255–61.

Ribelin B. W. & Collier A. W. (1979) Ecological considerations of detrital aggregates in the salt-marsh. In R. J. Livingston (ed.), *Ecological Processes in Coastal and Marine Systems*, pp. 47–68. Plenum Press, New York.

Richardson P., Armstrong R. & Goldman C. R. (1970) Contemporaneous disequilibrium, a new hypothesis to explain 'The Paradox of the Plankton'. *Proc. Nat. Acad. Sci. U.S.A.* **67**, 1710–14.

Richman S., Heinle D. R. & Huff R. (1977) Grazing by adult estuarine copepods of the Chesapeake Bay. *Mar. Biol.* **42**, 69–84.

Richman S., Loya Y. & Slobodkin L. B. (1975) The rate of mucus production by corals and its assimilation by the coral reef copepod *Acartia hegligens*, *Limnol. Oceanogr.* **20**, 918–23.

Ricker W. E. (1971) *Methods for Assessment of Fish Production in Fresh Waters*, 2nd edn. Blackwell Scientific Publications, Oxford.

Riley G. A. (1941) Plankton studies III. *Bull. Bingh. Oceanogr. Coll.* **7**, 1–93.

Riley G. A. (1956) Oceanography of Long Island Sound, 1952–54. IX. Production and utilization of organic matter. *Bull. Bingham Oceanogr. Coll.* **15**, 324–53.

Riley G. A. (1963a) Theory of food-chain relations in the ocean. In M. N. Hill (ed.), *The Sea*, Vol. 2, pp. 438–63. John Wiley Interscience, New York.

Riley G. A. (1963b) Organic aggregates in sea water and the dynamics of their formation and utilization. *Limnol. Oceanogr.* **8**, 372–81.

Riley G. A. (1970) Particulate and organic matter in sea water. *Adv. mar. Biol.* **8**, 1–118.

Riley G. A. (1976) A model of plankton patchiness. *Limnol. Oceanogr.* **21**, 873–80.

Riley G. A. & Bumpus D. F. (1946) Phytoplankton–zooplankton relationships on George's Bank. *J. mar. Res.* **6**, 33–47.

Robertson A. I. (1977) Ecology of juvenile King George Whiting, *Sillaginodes punctatus* (Cuvier and Valenciennes) (Pisces: Perciformes) in Western Port, Victoria. *Aust. J. mar. freshwater Res.* **28**, 35–43.

Robertson A. I. (1979) The relationship between annual production: biomass ratios and life-spans for marine macrobenthos. *Oecologia (Berlin)* **38**, 193–202.

Robertson A. I. & Howard R. K. (1978) Diel trophic interactions between vertically migrating zooplankton and their fish predators in an eelgrass community. *Mar. Biol.* **48**, 207–13.

Robinson J. D. (1980) The conversion of *Lminaria* detritus to bacterial biomass. M.Sc. Thesis, Dalhousie University, Halifax, Canada.

Rosen R. (1969) Hierarchial organization in automata: theoretic models of biological systems. In L. L. Whyte, A. G. Wilson & D. Wilson (eds), *Hierarchical Structures.* pp. 179–99. Elsevier, New York.

Rosenthal R. J., Clarke W. D. & Dayton P. K. (1974) Ecology and natural history of a stand of giant kelp, *Macrocystis pyrifera* off Del Mar, California. *Fish. Bull.* **72**, 670–84.

Rowe G. T., Clifford C. H., Smith K. L. & Hamilton P. L. (1975) Benthic nutrient regeneration and its coupling to primary productivity in coastal waters. *Nature* **255**, 215–7.

Rowe G. T. & Smith K. L. (1977) Benthic-pelagic coupling in the mid-Atlantic Bight. In B. C. Coull (ed.), *Ecology of Marine Benthos*, pp. 55–65. University of South Carolina Press, Columbia.

Royce W. F., Smith L. S. & Hartt A. C. (1968) Models of oceanic migration of Pacific salmon and comments on guidance mechanisms. *Fish. Bull.* **66**, 441–62.

Russell-Hunter W. D. (1970) *Aquatic Productivity.* Macmillan, New York.

Ryther J. H. (1963) Geographical variations in productivity. In M. N. Hill (ed.), *The Sea*, pp. 347–80. John Wiley Interscience, New York.

Ryther, J. H. (1969) Photosynthesis and fish production in the sea. *Science* **166**, 72–6.

Ryther J. H. & Dunstan W. M. (1971) Nitrogen, phosphorus and eutrophication in the coastal marine environment. *Science* **171**, 1008–12.

Sale P. F., McWilliam P. S. & Anderson D. T. (1976) Composition of the near-reef zooplankton at Heron Reef, Great Barrier Reef. *Mar. Biol.* **34**, 59–66.

Sale P. F., McWilliam P. S. & Anderson D. T. (1978) Faunal relationships among the near-reef zooplankton at three locations on Heron Reef, Great Barrier Reef, and seasonal changes in this fauna. *Mar. Biol.* **49**, 133–45.

Sammarco P. W., Levinton S. J. & Ogden J. C. (1974) Grazing and control of coral reef community structure by *Diadema antillarum* Phillippi (Echinodermata: Echinoida): A preliminary study. *J. mar. Res.* **32**, 47–53.

Sanders H. L. (1956) The biology of marine bottom communities. *Bull. Bingh. Oceanogr. Coll.* **15**, 344–414.

Sanders H. L. (1958) Benthic studies in Buzzards Bay. I. Animal–sediment relationships. *Limnol. Oceanogr.* **3**, 245–58.

Sanders H. L. (1968) Marine benthic diversity: a comparative study. *Am. Nat.* **102**, 243–82.

Sargent M. C. & Austin T. S. (1954) Biologic economy of coral reefs. *U.S. Geological Survey Professional Papers* **260-E**, 293–300.

Schaeffer M. B. (1970) Men, birds and achovies in the Peru current—dynamic interactions. *Trans. am. Fish Soc.* **99**, 461–7.

Schaeffer M. B. & Beverton R. J. H. (1963) Fishery dynamics—their analysis and interpretation. In M. N. Hill (ed.), *The Sea*, Vol. 2, pp. 464–83. Wiley Interscience, New York.

Scholander P. F. (1968) How mangroves desalinate seawater. *Physiol. Plant.* **21**, 251–61.

Scholander P. F., van Dam L. & Scholander S. I. (1955) Gas exchange in the roots of mangroves. *Am. J. Bot.* **42**, 92–8.

Scholander P. F., Hemmingsen E. & Garey W. (1962) Salt balance in mangroves. *Plant Physiol.* **37**, 722–9.

Scott B. D. & Jitts H. R. (1977) Photosynthesis of phytoplankton and zooxanthellae on a coral reef. *Mar. Biol.* **41**, 307–15.

Semens K. P. & De Riemer K. (1977) Diel cycles of expansion and contraction in coral reef anthozoans. *Mar. Biol.* **43**, 247–56.

Sevigny J.-M., Sinclair M., El-Sabh M. I. & Coote A. (1979) Summer plankton distributions associated with the physical and nutrient properties of the North-western Gulf of St. Lawrence. *J. Fish. Res. Bd. Can.* **36**, 187–203.

Sheldon R. W. (1969) A universal grade scale for particulate materials. *Proc. Geol. Soc. Lond.* **1659**, 293–5.

Sheldon R. W. & Parsons T. R. (1967) A continuous size spectrum for particulate matter in the sea. *J. Fish. Res. Bd. Can.* **24**, 909–15.

Sheldon R. W., Prakash A. & Sutcliffe W. H. (1972) The size distribution of particles in the ocean. *Limnol. Oceanogr.* 327–40.

Sheldon R. W. & Sutcliffe W. H. Jr. (1978) Generation times of 3h for Sargasso Sea micro-plankton determined by ATP analysis. *Limnol. Oceanogr.* **23**, 1051–5.

Sheldon R. W., Sutcliffe W. H. Jr. & Paranjape M. A. (1977) Structure of pelagic food chain and relationship between plankton and fish production. *J. Fish. Res. Bd. Can.* **34**, 2344–53.

Sheldon R. W., Sutcliffe W. H. Jr. & Prakash A. (1973) The production of particles in the surface waters of the ocean with particular reference to the Sargasso Sea. *Limnol. Oceanogr.* **18**, 719–33.

Shepherd S. A. & Womersley H. B. S. (1970) The sublittoral ecology of West Island, Southern Australia. 1. Environmental features and algal ecology. *Trans. roy. Soc. S. Aust.* **94**, 105–38.

Shepherd S. A. & Womersley H. B. S. (1976) The subtidal algal and seagrass ecology of St. Francis Island, South Australia. *Trans. roy. Soc. S. Aust.* **100**, 177–91.

Sherman K., Cohen E., Sissenwine M., Grosslein M., Langton R. & Green J. (1978) Food requirements of fish stocks of the Gulf of Maine, George's Bank and adjacent waters. I.C.E.S. Biological Oceanogr. Comm. CM 1978/Gen: 8. (symp.)

Sibert J., Brown T. J., Healey M. C., Kask B. A. & Naiman R. J. (1977) Detritus-based food webs: Exploitation by juvenile Chum Salmon. (*Oncorhynchus keta*). *Science* **196**, 649–50.

Sieburth J. McN. (1969) Studies on algal substances in the sea. III. The production of extra-cellular organic matter by littoral marine algae. *J. exp. Biol. Ecol.* **3**, 290–309.

Sieburth J. McN. (1976) Bacterial substrates and productivity in marine ecosystems. *Ann. Rev. Ecol. Syst.* **7**, 259–85.

Sieburth J. McN. (1977) International Helgoland Symposium: Convener's report on the infor-mal session on biomass and productivity of microorganisms in planktonic ecosystems. *Helgol. wiss. Meeresunters.* **30**, 697–704.

Silvert W. (1980) Principles of ecosystem modelling. In A. R. Longhurst (ed.), *Analysis of Marine Ecosystems*, pp. 651–76. Academic Press, New York.

Silvert W. (in press) Top-down modelling in marine ecology. *Proceedings of 2nd int. Conf. on State-of-the-Art in Ecological Modelling.*

Simpson J. H. & Hunter J. R. (1974) Fronts in the Irish Sea. *Nature* **350**, 404–6.

Simpson J. H. & Pingree R. D. (1978) Shallow sea fronts produced by tidal stirring. In M. J. Bowman & W. E. Esaias (eds), *Oceanic Fronts in Coastal Processes*, pp. 29–42. Springer-Verlag, Berlin.

Slobodkin L. B. (1959) Energetics in *Daphnia pulex* populations. *Ecology* **40**, 232–43.

Smayda T. J. (1970) The suspension and sinking of phytoplankton in the sea. *Oceanogr. mar. Biol. Ann. Rev.* **8**, 353–414.

Smith P. E. (1972) The increase on spawning biomass of northern anchovy. *Engraulis mordax.* *Fish. Bull. U.S.* **70**, 849–74.

Smith S. V. (1974) Coral reef carbon dioxide flux. In A. M. Cameron, B. M. Campbell, A. B. Cribb, R. Endean, J. S. Jell, O. A. Jones, P. Mather & F. H. Talbot (eds), *Proc. 2nd int. Symp. on Coral Reefs*, Vol. 1, pp. 77–85. The Great Barrier Reef Committee, Brisbane.

Smith K. L., Burns K. A. & Teal J. M. (1972) *In situ* respiration of benthic communities in Castle Harbour, Bermuda. *Mar. Biol.* **12**, 196–9.

Smith S. V. & Marsh J. A. (1973) Organic carbon production and consumption on the windward reef flat at Eniwetok Atoll. *Limnol. Oceanogr.* **18**, 953–61.

Smith S. L. & Whitledge T. E. (1977) The role of zooplankton in the regeneration of nitrogen in a coastal upwelling system off North-west Africa. *Deep-Sea Res.* **24**, 49–56.

Smith S. V. & Kinsey D. W. (1978) Calcification and organic carbon metabolism as indicated by carbon dioxide. In D. R. Stoddart & R. E. Johannes (eds), *Coral Reefs: Research Methods*, pp. 469–84. UNESCO, Paris.

Smith D. F., Bulleid N. C., Campbell R., Higgins H. W., Rowe F., Tranter D. J. & Tranter H. (1979) Marine food web analysis. An experimental study of demersal zooplankton using isotopically labelled prey species. *Mar. Biol.* **54**, 49–59.

Sorokin Y. I. (1965) On the trophic role of chemosynthesis and bacterial biosynthesis in water bodies. *Mem. Ist. Ital. Idrobiol.* **18** (suppl.), 187–205.

Sorokin Y. I. (1971a) On the role of bacteria in the productivity of tropical oceanic waters. *Int. Rev. ges. Hydrobiol.* **56**, 1–48.

Sorokin Y. I. (1971b) Population, activity and production of bacteria in bottom sediments of the Central Pacific. *Oceanology* **10**, 853–63.

Sorokin Y. I. (1973) Trophical role of bacteria in the ecosystem of the coral reef. *Nature* **242**, 415–7.

Sorokin Y. I. (1974) Bacteria as a component of the coral reef community. In A. M. Cameron, B. M. Campbell, A. B. Cribb, R. Endean, J. S. Jell, O. A. Jones, P. Mather & F. H. Talbot (eds), *Proceedings of the 2nd int. Symp. on Coral Reefs*, Vol. 1, pp. 3–10. The Great Barrier Reef Committee, Brisbane.

Sournia A. (1976) Primary production of sands in the lagoon of an atoll, and the role of foraminiferan symbionts. *Mar. Biol.* **37**, 29–32.

Sournia A. (1977) Analyse et bilan de la production primaire les récifs coralliens. *Ann. Inst. Oceanogr. Paris.* **53**, 47–74.

Southward A. J. (1953) The ecology of some rocky shores in the south of the Isle of Man. *Proc. Liverpool biol. Soc.* **59**, 1–50.

Southward A. J. (1960) On changes of sea temperature in the English Channel. *J. mar. Biol. Ass. U.K.* **39**, 449–58.

Stavn R. H. (1971) The horizontal–vertical distribution hypothesis: Langmuir circulation and *Daphnia* distribution. *Limnol. Oceanogr.* **16**, 543–66.

Steele J. H. (1974) *The Structure of Marine Ecosystems*. Harvard Univ. Press, Cambridge, Mass.

Steele J. H. (1976) Patchiness. In D. H. Cushing & J. J. Walsh (eds), *The Ecology of the Seas*, pp. 98–115. Blackwell Scientific Publications, Oxford.

Steele J. H. (ed.) (1978) *Spatial Pattern in Plankton Communities*. Plenum Press, New York and London.

Steele J. H. (1979) Some problems in the management of marine resources. *Appl. Biol.* **4**, 103–40.

Steele J. H. (1979a) The uses of experimental ecosystems. *Phil. Trans. roy. Soc. Lond. B.* **286**, 583–95.

Steele J. H. & Baird I. E. (1972) Sedimentation of organic matter in a Scottish Sea Loch. *Mem. Ist. Ital. Idrobiol.* **20** (suppl.), 73–88.

Steeman-Nielsen E. (1954) On organic production in the ocean. *J. Cons. Perm. int. Explor. Mer.* **49**, 309–28.

Steever Z. E., Warren R. S. & Niering W. A. (1976) Tidal energy subsidy and standing crop production of *Spartina alterniflora*. *Estuar. coast. mar. Sci.* **4**, 473–8.

Stephens K. R., Sheldon R. H. & Parsons T. R. (1967) Seasonal variations in the availability of food for benthos in a coastal environment. *Ecology* **48**, 852–5.

Steven D. M. (1974) *Primary and Secondary Production in the Gulf of St. Lawrence*, MS Report. No. 26. McGill Univ. Mar. Sciences Centre, Montreal.

Stewart G. R., Lee G. A. & Orebamjo T. O. (1972) Nitrate reluctase activity in *Sueda maritima*. *New Phyt.* **71**, 263–7.

Stoddart D. R. (1969) Ecology and morphology of recent coral reefs, *Biol. Rev.* **44**, 433–98.

Strickland J. D. H. (1972) Research on the marine planktonic food web at the Inst. of Mar. Resources: A review of the past seven years of work. *Oceanogr. mar. Biol. Ann. Rev.* **10**, 349–414.

Sutcliffe W. H. Jr. (1972) Some relations of land drainage, nutrients, particulate material and fish catch in two eastern Canadian bays. *J. Fish. Res. Bd. Can.* **29**, 357–62.

Sutcliffe W. H. Jr. (1973) Correlations between seasonal discharge and local landings of American lobster (*Homarus americanus*) and Atlantic halibut (*Hippoglossus hippoglossus*) in the Gulf of St. Lawrence. *J. Fish. Res. Bd. Can.* **30**, 856–9.

Sutcliffe W. H. Jr., Drinkwater K. & Muir B. S. (1977) Correlation of fish catch and environmental factors in the Gulf of Maine. *J. Fish. Res. Bd. Can.* **34**, 19–30.

Sutcliffe W. H. Jr., Loucks R. H. & Drinkwater K. F. (1976) Coastal circulation and physical oceanography of the Scotian Shelf and the Gulf of Maine. *J. Fish. Res. Bd. Can.* **33**, 98–115.

Taguchi S. & Platt T. (1977) Assimilation of $^{14}CO_2$ in the dark compared to phytoplankton production in a small coastal inlet. *Estuar. coast. mar. Sci.* **5**, 679–84.

Takahashi M., Fujii K. & Parsons T. R. (1973) Simulation study of phytoplankton photosynthesis and growth in the Fraser River Estuary. *Mar. Biol.* **19**, 102–16.

Teal J. M. (1957) Community metabolism in a temperate cold spring. *Ecol. Monogr.* **27**, 283–302.

Teal J. M. (1962) Energy flow in the salt marsh ecosystem of Georgia. *Ecology* **43**, 614–24.

Teal J. M. & Kanwisher J. W. (1966) Gas transport in the marsh grass. *Spartina alterniflora. J. exp. Bot.* **17**, 353–61.

Teal J. M., Valiela I. & Berlo D. (1979) Nitrogen fixation by rhizosphere and free-living bacteria in salt marsh sediments. *Limnol. Oceanogr.* **24**, 126–32.

Tenore K. R. (1977a) Growth of *Capitella capitata* cultured on various levels of detritus derived from different sources. *Limnol. Oceanogr.* **22**, 936–41.

Tenore K. R. (1977b) Utilization of aged detritus from different sources by the polychaete *Capitella capitata. Mar. Biol.* **44**, 51–5.

Tenore K. R., Tietjen J. H. & Lee J. J. (1977) Effect of meiofauna on incorporation of aged eelgrass detritus by the polychaete *Nephtys incisa. J. Fish. Res. Bd. Can.* **34**, 563–7.

Thayer G. W. (1974) Identity and regulation of nutrients limiting phytoplankton production in the shallow estuaries near Beaufort, N.C. *Oecologia (Berlin)* **14**, 75–92.

Thayer G. W., Adams S. M. & La Croix M. W. (1975) Structural and functional aspects of a recently established *Zostera marina* community. In L. E. Cronin (ed.), *Estuarine Research*, Vol. 1, pp. 518–40. Academic Press, New York.

Thayer G. A., Wolfe D. A. & Williams R. B. (1975) The impact of man on seagrass systems. *Amer. Sci.* **63**, 288–96.

Therriault J. C. & Lacroix G. (1976) Nutrients, chlorophyll and internal tides in the St. Lawrence Estuary. *J. Fish. Res. Bd. Can.* **33**, 2747–57.

Therriault J. C., Lawrence D. J. & Platt T. (1978) Spatial variability of phytoplankton turnover in relation to physical processes in a coastal environment. *Linmol. Oceanogr.* **23**, 900–11.

Therriault J. C. & Platt T. (1978) Spatial heterogeneity of phytoplankton biomass and related factors in the near-surface waters of an exposed coastal embayment. *Limnol. Oceanogr.* **23**, 888–99.

Thomas J. P. (1971) Release of dissolved organic matter from natural populations of marine phytoplankton. *Mar. Biol.* **11**, 311–23.

Thomas W. H. (1970) A nitrogen deficiency in tropical Pacific oceanic phytoplankton: Photosynthetic parameters in poor and rich water. *Limnol. Oceanogr.* **15**, 380–5.

Topinka J. A. (1975) An investigation of nitrogen uptake and nitrogen status in *Fucus spiralis* L. Ph.D. Thesis, University of Massachusetts, Amherst, Mass.

Topinka J. A. & Robbins J. V. (1976) Effects of nitrate and ammonium enrichment on growth and nitrogen physiology in *Fucus spiralis. Limnol. Oceanogr.* **21**, 659–64.

Towle D. W. & Pearse J. S. (1973) Production of the giant kelp *Macrocystis*, estimated by *in situ* incorporation of ^{14}C in polythene bags. *Limnol. Oceanogr.* **18**, 155–8.

Tranter D. J. (1976) Herbivore production. In D. H. Cushing and J. J. Walsh (eds), *The Ecology of the Seas*, pp. 186–224. Blackwell Scientific Publications, Oxford.

Trites R. W. (1972) The Gulf of St. Lawrence from a pollution viewpoint. In *Marine Pollution and Sea Life*, pp. 59–72. F.A.O., Rome.

Turner R. E. (1976) Geographic variations in salt marsh macrophyte production: a review. *Contr. Mar. Sci. Univ. Tex.* **20**, 47–68.

Ubben M. S. & Hanson R. B. (1980) Tidally induced regulation of nitrogen fixation activity (C_2H_4 production) in a Georgia salt-marsh. *Estuar. coast. mar. Sci.* **10**, 445–53.

Ulanowicz R. E. (1972) Mass and energy flow in closed ecosystems. *J. theor. Biol.* **34**, 239–53.

Valiela I., Koumjian L., Swain T., Teal J. M. & Hobbie J. E. (1979) Cinnamic acid inhibition of detritus feeding. *Nature* **180**, 55–7.

Valiela I. & Teal J. M. (1974) Nutrient limitation in salt-marsh vegetation. In R. J. Reimold & W. H. Queen (eds), *Ecology of Halophytes*, pp. 547–63. Academic Press, New York.

Valiela I., Teal J. M., Volkman S., Schafer D. & Carpenter E. J. (1978) Nutrient and particulate fluxes in a salt-marsh ecosystem: Tidal exchanges and inputs by precipitation and ground-water. *Limnol. Oceanogr.* **23**, 798–812.

Vandermeulen J. H., Davis N. D. & Muscatine L. (1972) The effect of inhibitors of photo-synthesis on zooxanthellae in corals and other invertebrates. *Mar. Biol.* **16**, 185–91.

Varley G. C. & Gradwell G. R. (1963) Predatory insects as density dependent mortality factors. In J. A. Moore (ed.), *Proc. XVI int. Congress Zool.*, Vol. 1, p. 240.

Van Raalte C. D., Valiela I., Carpenter E. J. & Teal J. M. (1974) Inhibition of nitrogen fixation in salt-marshes measured by acetylene reduction. *Estuar. coast. mar. Sci.* **2**, 301–5.

Vaughan T. W. (1919) Corals and the formation of coral reefs. *Ann. Rep. Smithsonian Inst.* **1917** 189–238.

Velimirov B., Field J. G., Griffiths C. L. & Zoutendyck P. (1977) The ecology of kelp bed communities in the Benguela upwelling system. *Helgol. wiss. Meeresunters.* **30**, 495–518.

Verhulst P. F. (1838) Notice sur la loi que la suit dans son accroissement. *Math. et Phys.* **10**, 113–21.

Vernberg W. B. & Coull B. C. (1974) Respiration of an interstitial ciliate and benthic energy relationships. *Oecologia (Berlin)* **16**, 259–64.

Vine P. J. (1974) Effects of algal grazing and aggressive behaviour of the fishes *Pomacentrus lividus* and *Acanthurus sohal* on coral-reef ecology. *Mar. Biol.* **24**, 131–6.

Vlymen W. J. (1970) Energy expenditure of swimming copepods. *Limnol. Oceanogr.* **15**, 348–56.

Vollenweider R. A. (ed.) (1969) *A Manual on Methods for Measuring Primary Production in Aquatic Environments*. Blackwell Scientific Publications, Oxford.

Vollenweider R. A. (1974) *A Manual on Methods for Measuring Primary Production in Aquatic Environments*, I.B.P. Handbook 12, 2nd edn. Blackwell Scientific Publications, Oxford.

Volterra Vito. (1926) Variations and fluctuations of the number of individuals in animal species living together. In R. N. Chapman (ed.), *Animal Ecology*, pp. 409–48. McGraw-Hill, New York.

Vosjan J. H. & Olanczuk-Neyman K. M. (1977) Vertical distribution of mineralization processes in a tidal sediment. *Neth. J. Sea Res.* **11**, 14–23.

Vozzhinskaya V. B. (1972) Vegetation of the coastal zone. *Priroda* **2**, 38–45. (Nat. Research Council of Canada, technical translation).

Vrooman A. M. & Smith P. E. (1970) Biomass of the subpopulations of northern anchovy *Engraulis mordax* Girard. *Calif. Coop. Ocean. Fish. Invest. Rept.* **15**, 49–51.

Wainwright P. & Mann K. H. (in press). Effect of antimicrobial substances on the ability of the mysid shrimp *Mysis stenolepis* to digest cellulose. *Marine Biology Progress Series*.

Walsh J. J. (1972) Implications of a systems approach to oceanography. *Science* **176**, 969–75.

Walsh J. J. (1976) Models of the sea. In D. H. Cushing & J. J. Walsh (eds), *The Ecology of the Seas*, pp. 388–446. Blackwell Scientific Publications, Oxford.

Walsh J. J., Kelley J. C., Whiteledge T. E. & MacIsaac J. J. (1974) Spin-up of the Baja California upwelling ecosystem. *Limnol. Oceanogr.* **19**, 553–72.

Walters C. J., Hilborn R., Peterman R. M. & Staley M. J. (1978) Model for examining early ocean limitation of Pacific salmon production. *J. Fish. Res. Bd. Can.* **35**, 1301–15.

Wanders J. B. W. (1976a) The role of benthic algae in the shallow reef of Curacao (Netherlands Antilles). I. Primary productivity in the coral reef. *Aquatic Botany* **2**, 235–70.

Wanders J. B. W. (1976b) The role of benthic algae in the shallow reef of Curacao (Netherlands Antilles) II. Primary productivity of the *Sargassum* beds on the north-east coast submarine plateau. *Aquatic Botany* **2**, 327–35.

Wanders J. B. W. (1977) The role of benthic algae in the shallow reef of Curacao (Netherlands Antilles) III: The significance of grazing. *Aquatic Botany* **3**, 357–90.

Wangersky P. J. (1977) The role of particulate matter in the productivity of surface waters. *Helgol. wiss. Meeresunters.* **30**, 546–64.

Warwick R. M., George C. L. & Davies J. R. (1978) Annual macrofauna production in a *Venus* community. *Estuar. coast. mar. Sci.* **7**, 215–41.

Warwick R. M., Joint I. R. & Radford P. J. (1979) Secondary production of the benthos in an estuarine environment. In R. L. Jefferies & A. J. Davy (eds), *Ecological Processes in Coastal Environments*, pp. 429–50. Blackwell Scientific Publications, Oxford.

Warwick R. M. & Price R. (1975) Macrofauna production on an estuarine mudflat. *J. mar. Biol. Ass. U.K.* **55**, 1–18.

Wassman R. & Ramus J. (1973) Seaweed invasion. *Nat. Hist. N.Y.* **82**, 24–36.

Watson J. G. (1928) Mangrove forests of the Malay Peninsula. *Malay Forest Rec.* **6**, 1–275.

Webb K. L., DuPaul W., Wiebe W. J., Sottile II W. S. & Johannes R. E. (1975) Aspects of the nitrogen cycle on a coral reef. *Limnol. Oceanogr.* **20**, 198–210.

Webster J. R. (1979) Hierarchical organization of ecosystems. In E. Halfon (ed.), *Theoretical Systems Ecology*, pp. 119–29. Academic Press, New York.

Webster T. J. M., Paranjape M. & Mann K. H. (1975) Sedimentation of organic matter in St. Margaret's Bay, Nova Scotia. *J. Fish. Res. Bd. Can.* **32**, 1399–407.

Weiss P. (1969) The living system: determination stratified. In A. Koestler & J. R. Smythies (eds), *Beyond Reductionism*, pp. 3–55. Hutchinson, London.

Welsh B. L. (1975) The role of the grass shrimp *Palaemonetes pugia* in a tidal marsh ecosystem. *Ecology* **56**, 513–30.

Westlake D. F. (1963) Comparisons of plant productivity. *Biol. Rev.* **38**, 385–429.

Wetzel R. L. (1976) Carbon resources of a benthic salt-marsh invertebrate *Nassarius obsoletus* Say (Mollusca: Nassariidae). In M. Wiley (ed.), *Estuarine Processes*, Vol. 2, pp. 293–308. Academic Press, New York.

Wharton G. (1980) The relationship between destructive grazing by the sea-urchin *Strongylocentrotus droebachiensis* and the abundance of American Lobster *Homarus americanus* on the Atlantic Coast of Nova Scotia. M.Sc. Thesis, Dalhousie University, Halifax, Canada.

Wharton W. G. & Mann K. H. (1981) Relationships between destructive grazing by sea-urchin *Strongylocentrobus droebachiensis* and the abundance of the American lobster *Homarus americanus* on the Atlantic coast of Nova Scotia. *Can. J. Fish. aquat. Sci.* **38**, (in press).

Wheeler W. N. (1978) Ecophysiological studies on the Giant Kelp, *Macrocystis*. Ph.D. Thesis, University of California, Santa Barbara.

Whitney D. E., Woodwell G. M. & Howarth R. W. (1975) Nitrogen fixation in Flax Pond: A Long Island salt-marsh. *Limnol. Oceanogr.* **20**, 640–3.

Whittle K. J. (1977) Marine organisms and their contribution to organic matter in the oceans. *Mar. Chem.* **5**, 381–411.

Wiebe W. J. (1979) Anaerobic benthic microbial processes: Changes from the estuary to the continental shelf. In P. J. Livingston (ed.), *Ecological Processes in Coastal and Marine Systems*, pp. 469–85. Plenum Press, New York.

Wiebe W. J., Johannes R. E. & Webb K. L. (1975) Nitrogen fixation on a coral reef. *Science* **188**, 257–9.

Wiebe W. J. & Smith D. F. (1977) Direct measurement of dissolved organic carbon release by phytoplankton and incorporation by microheterotrophs. *Mar. Biol.* **42**, 213–23.

Wildish D. J. (1977) Factors controlling marine and estuarine sublittoral macrofauna. *Helgol. wiss. Meeresunters.* **30**, 445–54.

Wildish D. J. & Kristmanson D. D. (1979) Tidal energy and sublittoral benthic animals in estuarines. *J. Fish. Res. Bd. Can.* **36**, 1197–206.

Williams P. J. le B. (1970) Heterotrophic utilization of dissolved organic compounds in the sea. I. Size distribution of population and relationship between respiration and incorporation of growth substrates. *J. mar. Biol. Ass. U.K.* **50**, 859–70.

Williams P. J. le B. (1975) Biological and chemical aspects of dissolved organic material in sea water. In J. P. Riley & G. Skirrow (eds), *Chemical Oceanography*, Vol. 2, 2nd edn., pp. 301–63. Academic Press, London.

Williams P. J. le B. & Yentsch C. S. (1976) An examination of photosynthetic production, excretion of photosynthetic products, and heterotrophic utilization of dissolved organic compounds with reference to results from a coastal subtropical sea. *Mar. Biol.* **35**, 31–40.

Winberg G. G. (1956) *Rate of metabolism and food requirement of fishes*. Nauchn, Tr. Belorussovo Gos. Univ. imeni. V.I., Lenina, Minsk. (Fish. Res. Bd. Can. Transl. Ser. 194).

Winters G. H. (1976) Recruitment mechanisms of southern Gulf of St. Lawrence Atlantic herring (*Clupea harengus harengus*). *J. Fish. Res. Bd. Can.* **33**, 1751–63.

Wolff W. J. & de Wolff L. (1977) Biomass and production of zoobenthos in the Gravelingen Estuary, The Netherlands. *Estuar. coast mar. Sci.* **5**, 1–24.

Wood E. J. F., Odum W. E. & Zieman J. C. (1967) Influence of seagrasses on the productivity of coastal lagoons. In *Lagunas Costeras, un Symposia Mem. Simp. Intern. Lagunas Costeras*, pp. 495–502. UNAM-UNESCO, Mexico, D.F.

Woodin A. S. (1978) Refuges, disturbance and community structure: a marine soft-bottom example. *Ecology* **59**, 274–84.

Woodwell G. M., Whitney D. R., Hall C. A. S. & Houghton R. A. (1977) The Flax Pond ecosystem study: exchanges of carbon in water between a salt-marsh and Long Island Sound. *Limnol. Oceanogr.* **22**, 833–8.

Yentsch C. S. & Ryther J. H. (1959) Relative significance of the net phytoplankton and nannoplankton in the waters of Vineyard Sound. *J. Cons. Perm int. Explor. Mer.* **24**, 231–8.

Yentsch C. M., Yentsch C. S. & Strube L. R. (1977) Variations in ammonium enhancement, an indication of nitrogen deficiency in New England coastal phytoplankton populations. *J. mar. Res.* **35**, 537–55.

Yetka J. E. & Wiebe W. J. (1974) Ecological applications of antibiotics as respiratory inhibitors of bacterial populations. *Appl. Microbiol.* **28**, 1033–9.

Yonge C. M. (1930) Studies on the physiology of corals 1. Feeding mechanisms and food. *Sci. Rept. Great Barrier Reef Exped. 1928–29* **1**, 15–27.

Yonge C. M. (1940) The biology of reef-building corals. *Sci. Rept. Great Barrier Reef Exped.* **1**, 353–91.

Yonge C. M. (1972) Aspects of productivity in coral reefs. In C. Mukundan & C. S. Gopinadha Pillai (eds), *Proceedings of the Symposium on Coral Reefs*, pp. 1–12. Mar. Biol. Assoc. of India, Cochin.

Young E. L. (1938) *Labyrinthula* on Pacific coast eelgrass. *Can. J. Res.* **16**, 115–17.

Young P. C. (1978) Moreton Bay, Queensland: a nursery area for juvenile penaeid prawns. *Aust. J. mar. freshwat. Res.* **29**, 55–75.

Zaret T. M. & Suffern J. S. (1976) Vertical migration in zooplankton as a predator avoidance mechanism. *Limnol. Oceanogr.* **21**, 804–13.

Zhukova A. I. & Fedosov M. V. (1963) Significance of microorganisms of upper sediment layer of shallow water basin in transformation of organic matter. In C. H. Oppenheimer (ed.), *Marine Microbiology*, pp. 711–19. Charles C. Thomas, Springfield, Illinois.

Zieman J. C. Jr. (1968) A study of the growth and decomposition of the sea-grass *Thallassia testudinum*. MS Thesis, University of Miami.

Zieman J. C. Jr. (1970) The effect of a thermal effluent stress on the seagrasses and macroalgae in the vicinity of Turkey Point, Biscayne Bay, Florida. Ph.D. Thesis, University of Miami.

INDEX

313

Index